30 DAYS TO THE LSAT*

2ND EDITION

TEACHER-TESTED STRATEGIES AND TECHNIQUES FOR SCORING HIGH

MARK ALAN STEWART
FREDERICK J. O'TOOLE

ARCO ™

THOMSON LEARNING

Australia • Canada • Mexico • Singapore • Spain • United Kingdom • United States

An ARCO Book

About Peterson's

Founded in 1966, Peterson's, a division of Thomson Learning, is the nation's largest and most respected provider of lifelong learning online resources, software, reference guides, and books. The Education Supersite[SM] at petersons.com—the Web's most heavily traveled education resource—has searchable databases and interactive tools for contacting U.S.-accredited institutions and programs. CollegeQuest[®] (CollegeQuest.com) offers a complete solution for every step of the college decision-making process. GradAdvantage[TM] (GradAdvantage.org), developed with Educational Testing Service, is the only electronic admissions service capable of sending official graduate test score reports with a candidate's online application. Peterson's serves more than 55 million education consumers annually.

Thomson Learning is among the world's leading providers of lifelong learning, serving the needs of individuals, learning institutions, and corporations with products and services for both traditional classrooms and for online learning. For more information about the products and services offered by Thomson Learning, please visit www.thomsonlearning.com. Headquartered in Stamford, Connecticut, with offices worldwide, Thomson Learning is part of The Thomson Corporation (www.thomson.com), a leading e-information and solutions company in the business, professional, and education marketplaces. The Corporation's common shares are listed on the Toronto and London stock exchanges.

For more information, contact Peterson's, 2000 Lenox Drive, Lawrenceville, NJ 08648; 800-338-3282; or find us on the World Wide Web at: www.petersons.com/about

ISBN: 0-7689-0634-2

Printed in Canada

10 9 8 7 6 5 4 3 2   03 02

About the Authors

Mark Alan Stewart (B.A., Economics, J.D., University of California at Los Angeles) is an attorney and one of today's preeminent authorities and top-selling authors on the subject of graduate-level entrance exams. For more than a decade Mr. Stewart served as consultant to schools in the University of California and California State University systems in graduate-level entrance-exam programs. His books on LSAT, GRE and GMAT preparation continue to be top sellers among aspiring law, business, and graduate students. His other book-length publications for graduate-level admissions include the following (all are published by Peterson's except as indicated):

- *GRE-LSAT Logic Workbook*
- *GRE-LSAT-GMAT-MCAT Reading Comprehension Workbook*
- *Teach Yourself the GMAT CAT in 24 Hours (IDG Books)*
- *Teach Yourself the GRE in 24 Hours (IDG Books)*
- *GRE—Answers to the Real Essay Questions*
- *GMAT CAT—Answers to the Real Essay Questions*
- *30 Days to the GMAT CAT*
- *Words for Smart Test Takers*
- *Math for Smart Test Takers*
- *Perfect Personal Statements—Law, Business, Medical, Graduate School*

Frederick J. O'Toole (Ph.D. Philosophy, University of California) is a Professor of Philosophy at California State Polytechnic University, San Luis Obispo. His areas of specialization include critical thinking, symbolic logic, and history and philosophy of science. He brings to this publication over two decades of experience teaching students critical thinking concepts and skills. His other publications include the following:

- *GMAT CAT—Answers to the Real Essay Questions (Peterson's)*
- *30 Days to the GMAT CAT (Peterson's)*
- *Teach Yourself the GMAT CAT in 24 Hours (IDG Books)*
- *Teach Yourself the GRE in 24 Hours (IDG Books)*
- *Critical Thinking Interactive Exercises (Philosophical Documentation Center)*
- *The Fundamentals of Modern Logic (Blake Publishing)*

Online Updates for *30 Days to the LSAT*

At the lead author's LSAT website you'll find updates and supplements to this book, as well as useful information about other resources for law-school candidates. Point your Web browser to: **www.west.net/~stewart/lsat**

THE 30-DAY PROGRAM

Authors' Acknowledgments

The authors wish to thank Linda Bernbach at ARCO for her editorial assistance. Mark Stewart also wishes to thank Patrick Cunningham for his contribution and Annette Davis for her support and encouragement. Fred O'Toole would like to thank his beautiful ladies, Joyce Connelly and Oona O'Toole, for their patience and support.

CREDITS

Day 1

Getting to Know the LSAT

Today you will familiarize yourself with the format of the LSAT, learn how the LSAT is scored, and learn some basic success strategies.

Today's Topics

1. The LSAT at a glance
2. The exam sections at a glance
3. The evolution of the LSAT
4. How the LSAT is scored
5. Evaluating your LSAT score
6. Is the LSAT required for law school admission?
7. How law schools evaluate LSAT scores
8. When should you take the LSAT?
9. Registering for the LSAT
10. Registering for the LSDAS
11. Scoring your best on the LSAT

THE LSAT AT A GLANCE

Total number of scored questions: 101–103
Total number of test sections: 6
Total testing time: 3 hours, 25 minutes

Format

Section	Time	Questions
Logical Reasoning	35 min.	25–26
Logical Reasoning	35 min.	25–26
Analytical Reasoning	35 min.	23–24
Reading Comprehension	35 min.	28
Trial Section	35 min.	23–28
Writing Sample	30 min.	1 topic

Exam sections—order of appearance:

- The Writing Sample is always administered last (after other sections)
- Other sections may appear in *any* order

Ground rules:

- Scratch paper is permitted only for the Writing Sample section
- Pencils and highlighters only (no pens), except for the Writing Sample section
- No penalty assessed for incorrect responses
- Silent timing devices permitted
- Working ahead or going back to other test sections is prohibited

THE EXAM SECTIONS AT A GLANCE

Logical Reasoning

These questions are designed to evaluate your ability to understand, criticize, and draw reasonable conclusions from *arguments*. Each argument is presented in a brief one-paragraph passage. The LSAT includes *two* scored Logical Reasoning sections; thus, Logical Reasoning questions account for approximately 50% of all LSAT scored questions! The two scored Logical Reasoning sections are similar to each other in format, style, and difficulty level.

Analytical Reasoning

These questions are designed to measure your ability to understand a system of relationships and to draw appropriate *deductive* conclusions about those relationships. The questions are presented as a series of four distinct question *sets*—or *logic games*. Each "game" is accompanied by five to eight questions. For each game, you will need to draw *diagrams* in your test booklet in order to organize the information (premise and rules) and to analyze the questions. Each game will be presented on *two facing pages* of your test booklet. Thus, you respond to all

questions for a game without turning pages.

Reading Comprehension

These questions are designed to measure your ability to read carefully and accurately, to determine the relationships among the various parts of the passage, and to draw reasonable inferences from the material in the passage. The questions are presented as a series of four distinct question sets. All questions in one set pertain to one particular passage. Each passage is 400–500 words in length. Passages are drawn from a variety of subjects—including the humanities, the social sciences, the physical sciences, ethics, philosophy, and law. Each question set will be presented on *two facing pages* of your test booklet.

The Trial Section

The 35-minute Trial section will look just like one of the scored sections (Logical Reasoning, Analytical Reasoning, or Reading Comprehension); however, the Trial section itself is not scored. The testing service includes this section in order to assess the integrity and difficulty level of new questions and, in turn, to determine whether to include them as scored questions on future exams. Trial questions are *not* interspersed among scored questions within one exam section.

The Trial section may appear at any point during the exam, and you will not be able to tell which section it is. However, by the conclusion of the exam, you will know which *type* of section was included as a Trial section. For example, if two Analytical Reasoning sections appeared on your exam, you know that one of those two sections was the Trial section.

The Writing Sample

The 30-minute Writing Sample topic is designed to evaluate (1) your ability to formulate persuasive and cogent arguments, (2) your ability to write an organized, coherent essay in a short time period, and (3) your command of the language and the conventions of Standard Written English. The Writing Sample topic will present *two alternatives* and call for you to argue in favor of one alternative over the other. The writing sample section is always administered after all other sections of the LSAT. You must respond in the writing space provided in the test booklet. Scratch paper will be provided for taking notes and constructing outlines. The Writing Sample is *not* scored or evaluated by the testing service. Instead, the service provides a photocopy to the law schools to which you direct your LSAT score for their own evaluation.

THE EVOLUTION OF THE LSAT

The basic design and makeup of the LSAT has not changed since 1982, with one exception. In 1988, one of five different sections was removed from the exam, leaving the four different sections—Logical Reasoning, Analytical Reasoning, Reading Comprehension, and the Writing Sample Topic—that make up the current LSAT. In 1989, a second Logical Reasoning section was added to replace the section that was removed, and the difficulty level of the Logical Reasoning questions was increased somewhat. Until 1992, the testing service administered the Writing Sample section *before* all other exam sections. Since 1992, the Writing Sample section has been administered at the end of the exam.

Are any changes in store for the LSAT in the future? The most likely change in the near future will be procedural, not substantive. The Graduate Record Exam (GRE) and Graduate Management Admission Test (GMAT) are now administered by computer, and the LSAT will no doubt follow suit at some time in the near future.

HOW THE LSAT IS SCORED

First, the total number of correct responses (out of 101–103 *scored* questions) is determined. This is your *raw score*. Remember: There is no deduction from your raw score for incorrect responses. Next, your raw score is converted to a *scaled score*, which ranges from 120 to 180. The purpose of converting raw scores to scaled scores is to account for slight variations in overall difficulty level and in total number of questions among the different exams administered over the years.

EVALUATING YOUR LSAT SCORE

Your LSAT score (which the testing service will send to you approximately five weeks after the test) will indicate your raw score, your scaled score, and your *percentile ranking* (0% to 99%). The percentile ranking shows how you performed relative to all others taking the LSAT over a recent multi-year period. A percentile ranking of 60%, for example, indicates that you scored higher than 60% of all test takers (and lower than 39% of all test takers). (The percentile ranking is not reported to the law schools.)

The following score-conversion table, based on a 101-question exam, will help you evaluate your performance on practice exams. The figures in this table are average (mean) conversion figures for several previously administered exams. Keep in mind that scaled scores and percentile rankings vary slightly from exam to exam.

Here are a few revealing observations about the figures in the score conversion table:

- You don't need to respond correctly to every question to attain a "perfect" score of 180.

- If you respond correctly to 3 out of 4 questions (on average), you will score higher than 90% of all test takers.

- If you respond correctly to 2 out of 3 questions (on average), you will score higher than 75% of all test takers.

- If you respond correctly to every 1 out of 2 questions (on average), you will score higher than 40% of all test takers.

- One additional correct response makes the biggest percentile difference near the *middle* of the performance "curve," where one additional correct response can boost your percentile ranking by almost 5%!

IS THE LSAT REQUIRED FOR LAW SCHOOL ADMISSION?

All of the nearly 200 American law schools accred-

raw score	scaled score	percent below	raw score	scaled score	percent below
98–101	180	99.9	51–52	149	41.4
97	179	99.9	50	148	37.9
96	178	99.9	48–49	147	33.6
94–95	177	99.8	46–47	146	29.4
93	176	99.8	45	145	26.5
92	175	99.7	43–44	144	23.8
91	174	99.6	42	143	20.4
90	173	99.4	40–41	142	17.4
88–89	172	99.1	38–39	141	15.4
87	171	98.8	37	140	13.2
86	170	98.4	35–36	139	10.7
84–85	169	97.8	34	138	9.7
83	168	97.2	33	137	7.7
81–82	167	96.4	31–32	136	6.9
80	166	95.2	30	135	5.4
78–79	165	94.1	29	134	4.5
77	164	92.5	28	133	3.9
75–76	163	91.1	27	132	3.0
73–74	162	88.9	26	131	2.5
72	161	86.5	25	130	2.0
70–71	160	83.9	24	129	1.6
68–69	159	81.3	23	128	1.3
67	158	78.3	22	127	1.0
65–66	157	74.5	21	126	0.9
63–64	156	70.4	20	125	0.8
61–62	155	66.5	19	124	0.6
60	154	63.3	18	123	0.5
58–59	153	58.7	17	122	0.4
56–57	152	54.8	16	121	0.4
55	151	50.5	0–15	120	0.0
53–54	150	45.9			

ited by the ABA (American Bar Association) require the LSAT for admission. Most nonaccredited and state-accredited schools, on the other hand, do not require the LSAT.

How Law Schools Evaluate LSAT Scores

Each law school develops and implements its own policies for evaluating LSAT scores. Some schools place equal weight on LSAT scores and GPA, others weigh LSAT scores more heavily, while others weigh GPA more heavily. Your three most recent LSAT scores are reported by the LSDAS (see "Registering for the LSDAS") to each law school receiving your scores and transcripts. Most law schools *average* reported scores; a minority of schools consider only your *highest* reported score. A few schools have adopted a *hybrid* approach by which reported scores are averaged unless there is a sufficiently large discrepancy between scores, in which case the scores are not averaged.

When Should You Take the LSAT?

The LSAT is offered four times each year—in February, June, October, and December. Most law schools admit new students for the fall term only. Although application deadlines vary among the schools, if you plan to take the LSAT no later than December prior to matriculation, you are certain to meet application deadlines at all but a few schools. Ideally, you should take the LSAT for the first time no later than October of the year prior to matriculation, so that you can take the exam a second time if necessary and still meet application deadlines.

You can take the LSAT at any time—even during your freshman or sophomore year. However, because the intellectual abilities that the LSAT evaluates are developed to a large extent during your four years of college, postponing the test may allow for further intellectual development—and higher LSAT scores. Most college students take the LSAT for the first time either late in their junior year or early in their senior year.

Registering for the LSAT

You must register in advance for the LSAT by submitting a registration form included in the *LSAT/ LSDAS Registration and Information Book*. This book is published annually in April (for the subsequent June, October, December, and February exams). The *Registration Book* is available free-of-charge directly from the LSAC (Law School Admission Council):

Telephone: (215) 968-1001
World Wide Web: http://www.lsac.org

Copies of the *Registration Book* are also available through career-planning offices at most four-year colleges and universities.

Registering for the LSDAS

The Law School Data Assembly Service (LSDAS) is operated by the Law School Admission Council (LSAC)—the organization that designs and administers the LSAT. The function of the LSDAS is to collect your undergraduate transcripts and LSAT reports and to assemble a report or summary, which is sent to the law schools that you specify. You will need to register for this service during the year you are applying for admission. Registration is for one year only; if you register during one year but postpone law school entrance, you will need to register for the service again later. Detailed information about the LSDAS and a registration form are included in the *LSAT/LSDAS Registration and Information Book*.

Scoring Your Best on the LSAT

Find Your Optimal Pace and Stay on That Pace

Time is most definitely a factor on the LSAT. Almost every test taker runs out of time before finishing at least one section of the exam. In fact, if you don't work constantly at a somewhat quicker pace than what is comfortable for you, you're not likely to finish any section! Why does the testing service impose such great time pressure? Well, given enough time, most test takers can respond correctly to perhaps eighty percent or more of the questions. Imposing a short time limit is necessary to achieve a wide distribution of test scores. Develop a sense for your optimal pace—one that results in the greatest number of correct responses. As you take the mini-tests and the full-length practice test in this book, learn to get comfortable with a quick pace by adhering strictly to the time limits imposed.

Don't Try to Be a Perfectionist

You can miss quite a few questions and still get a very high score on the LSAT. Resist the temptation to stick with a "tough" question until you're sure your response is correct. Stubborn, perfectionist tendencies will only defeat you on the LSAT! All questions—difficult ones and easy ones alike—are worth one point each.

Don't Over-Analyze

LSAT questions are not designed to trick you in any way. The testing service takes every precaution to ensure that all questions are clear and unambiguous and that there is one best response to every question. As long as you believe your thinking is fairly clear as you read and consider a question, do not second guess your own judgment as to which response is the correct one. You'll only waste valuable time by over-analyzing a question.

Maintain a "Dialogue" with the Exam

While taking the LSAT, it's remarkably easy to fall into a *passive* mode—one in which you allow your eyes to simply pass over the words while you hope that the correct response will jump out at you as you scan the answer choices. This tendency is understandable, given the dry nature of the material on the LSAT. But you can fight it by interacting with the test as you read. For example, as you work through the Reading Comprehension and Logical Reasoning sections, frequently ask yourself questions such as:

- What's the point here?

- How is the test maker trying to trip me up here?

- Why does the author make this point?

- Is there some portion of this paragraph that relates most directly to the specific question?

Use your pencil to help keep you in an active mode. Circle and underline key words and phrases; make brief notes in the margins; draw flow charts and other diagrams to help you understand what you are reading.

Don't Obsess About Your Practice-Test Scores

As you take the mini-tests and practice test in this book, chances are that you will not perform as well as you would ideally like to perform. You may have a particular law school in mind as your first choice, and you may think you need a particular LSAT score to gain admission to that school. It is understandable, therefore, to establish a particular LSAT score as your goal. Nevertheless, try not to concern yourself as much with your scores as with what you can constructively do between now and exam day to improve your performance.

Avoid "Cramming" and "Burnout"

Preparing for the LSAT is a bit like training for an athletic event. You need to familiarize yourself with the event, learn to be comfortable with it, and build up your endurance. At some point—hopefully, around exam day—your motivation, interest, and performance will *peak*. Because the LSAT does not measure substantive knowledge, "cramming" for the test makes no sense. Devoting one month of your attention, energy, and concern to the LSAT is plenty of time. Don't drag the process out by starting several months in advance or by postponing the exam to allow yourself more time than you really need for preparation.

Will Particular College Courses Help You on the LSAT?

The LSAT is *not* a test of substantive knowledge. Thus, no one *specific* academic course will provide you with a distinct advantage for the exam. Some academic fields, however, do bear more directly than others on the LSAT in the kinds of intellectual abilities involved. Those areas that correlate most closely with the LSAT in this respect include:

- philosophy and ethics
- English and literature
- political science
- history

Historically, test takers with substantial philosophy coursework perform better than any other group on the LSAT. That doesn't means that you should rush over to the Registrar's office and change your major just for the LSAT. Remember that, to a large extent, the LSAT is designed to evaluate the kinds of intellectual abilities that are developed over a lifetime.

Be Realistic in Your Expectations

Be realistic about the benefits you should expect from this or any other LSAT preparation book. There is only so much you can do in a month—or even a year—to boost your LSAT score. Although anybody is theoretically capable of attaining a perfect score on the LSAT, in reality each individual is constrained by his or her innate abilities and talents. Accept your limitations. With regular study and practice, you will perform as well as *you* can reasonably expect to perform.

Other Resources for LSAT Preparation

How much should you "invest" in your LSAT education—in terms of both time and money? The conventional wisdom is that since the LSAT is one of the most important tests you'll ever take, you should invest as much time and money in it as possible. I disagree; the law of diminishing returns applies to LSAT preparation. This book, along with a few other thoughtfully selected books and online resources, can provide virtually all of the potential benefits of a full-blown LSAT prep course.

LSAT prep books

Visit any major brick-and-mortar or online book-

store, and prepare to be overwhelmed by the number of available books for LSAT prep. Here are some suggestions to help you cut through the glut:

- Peruse a book carefully before committing to it. Yes, this means visiting your local brick-and-mortar bookstore.

- Look for a book that emphasizes skill development, not just practice questions.

- Rule out any book that does not include a complete analysis of *all five* answer choices for each Logical Reasoning and Reading Comprehension question. (You gain just as much from learning why wrong answer choices are wrong as why best answer choices are best.)

- Rule out any book that emphasizes so-called "secrets" and "shortcuts," or makes the test out to be easier than it appears. Do you really think the Law School Admission Council would devise a test that can be "cracked" like a cheap safe? If so, think again.

- Limit the number of comprehensive LSAT books you use to two or three altogether. Any more and you'll find yourself reading the same strategies and test-taking tips again.

- Identify your weakest skill area, and supplement this book with a workbook targeted for that area.

- If you must shop for LSAT books at an online bookstore, ignore customer comments and ratings, especially if they are few in number.

The bottom line: You don't need to spend more than 40 or 50 dollars, on three or four books altogether, to be fully prepared for the LSAT.

Online LSAT resources

The Web is now littered with LSAT advice and practice questions—freely available for public consumption. To separate the wheat from the chaff, limit your LSAT web-surfing to the official LSAC site (www.lsac.org) and the sites of test-prep publishers with a time-tested reputation for producing high-quality content, such as Peterson's (www.petersons.com).

You'll find links to these and other useful LSAT sites at the online supplement for this book (www.west.net/~stewart/lsat).

LSAT preparation courses

Would it be worthwhile to enroll in an LSAT prep course? Well, here are their advantages:

1. The dynamics of a live classroom setting can help you learn difficult concepts by affording different perspectives. But why not start your own study group? You're just as likely to gain useful insights from your peers as from an LSAT instructor.

2. Having made a substantial financial investment, you'll probably be motivated to "get your money's worth" out of that investment. But this is an expensive head game, isn't it? And if you can't afford the course, it doesn't matter anyway.

3. You're less likely to procrastinate with a set class schedule. But if you're disciplined enough, this is no advantage.

4. All the materials are provided, so you don't need to decide which books and/or software to buy.

5. You can commiserate and compare notes with your classmates. In fact, LSAT prep classes typically morph into de facto pre-law support groups. But why not start your own LSAT study/support group?

Here are some drawbacks and caveats to keep in mind if you're thinking about taking an LSAT prep course:

1. They're expensive; you can easily spend $1000. (If you're near a university, you might find a course sponsored by the university for a fraction of the cost of a private course.)

2. Despite their claims, private test-prep companies pass along no "secrets" to you—nothing at all that you can't find for yourself in test-prep books.

3. The popular test-prep services require each of their LSAT instructors to have taken the real LSAT and attained a high score (typically above the 90th percentile). But this screen hardly ensures that your instructor will be an effective teacher.

4. During peak times of the year, you might have difficulty scheduling out-of-class time in the computer lab, at least during reasonable hours.

5. If you're not located in a major urban area or near a large college or university, the class location might be too remote for you.

If you decide to enroll in an LSAT prep course, keep in mind the following points of advice:

1. Ask about the policy for repeating the course. Insist on an option to repeat the course at least once without charge at any time (not just within the next year).

2. Ask about merit-based or financial-based "scholarships" (fee reductions).

3. If you repeat the course, be sure to arrange for a different instructor; just as with LSAT books, each LSAT instructor has his or her own pedagogical and communication style.

4. The most significant benefit of an LSAT course is the live classroom; so be sure to attend as many classes as you can.

5. Take full advantage of the chance to meet other students and set up out-of-class study sessions. As I've already noted, you can learn just as much from your peers as from an instructor.

Day 2

Analytical Reasoning Lesson 1: Basic Strategies

Today you will familiarize yourself with the format of the Analytical Reasoning section and learn strategies for handling the questions.

Today's Topics

1. Analytical reasoning at a glance
2. Anatomy of a "logic game"
3. Strategies for handling a logic game
4. Analysis of sample game
5. Pacing and time allocation (questions and answers)
6. Formal logic—everything you need to know for logic games

ANALYTICAL REASONING AT A GLANCE

Number questions: 24
Time allowed: 35 minutes
Number of sections:

- 1 scored section
- possibly 1 Trial section

Basic format:

- the questions are divided into 4 *sets*
- each set involves a different *logic game*
- each logic game includes 4–8 questions

Ground rules:

- no scratch paper is permitted (make notes in the test booklet)
- only pencils and highlighters are allowed (no pens)

- no penalties are assessed for incorrect responses
- each question is considered independently of all others

Directions printed in test booklet:
"Each group of questions in this section is based on a set of conditions. In answering some of the questions, it may be useful to draw a rough diagram. Choose the response that most accurately and completely answers each question and blacken the corresponding space on your answer sheet."

This section tests your ability to:

- understand a system of relationships
- draw deductive conclusions about those relationships
- assimilate and organize information quickly and accurately
- visualize spatial relationships

ANATOMY OF A "LOGIC GAME"

On the LSAT, Analytical Reasoning questions appear in *sets*. Each set presents a distinct puzzle or *logic game*, which includes three elements:

1. The *premise* is a brief introductory paragraph establishing the setting for the game, identifying the subjects involved, and describing generally how the subjects are related to one another. The number of subjects in a game generally ranges from four to ten (five to eight is typical).

2. A series of conditions or *rules* impose specific restrictions upon the relationships among the subjects. A logic game may include as few as two or as many as ten conditions, although the number of conditions typically ranges from four to six.

3. The *questions* involve the relationships defined by the rules. The questions call for *deductive* analysis by which one and only one response can be proven beyond any doubt to be the correct one. The number of questions per game ranges from four to eight, although six or seven questions is most common.

Example: The "Roller-Coaster" Game

An amusement park roller coaster includes five cars, numbered 1 through 5 from front to back. Each car accommodates up to two riders, seated side by side. Six people—Tom, Gwen, Laurie, Mark, Paul, and Jack—are riding the coaster at the same time.

Laurie is sharing a car.

Mark is not sharing a car and is seated immediately behind an empty car.

Tom is not sharing a car with either Gwen or Paul.

Gwen is riding in either the third or fourth car.

1. Which of the following groups of riders could occupy the second car?

   (A) Laurie only
   (B) Tom and Gwen
   (C) Laurie and Mark
   (D) Jack and Tom
   (E) Jack, Gwen, and Paul

2. If Gwen is riding immediately behind Laurie's car and immediately ahead of Tom's car, all of the following must be true EXCEPT:

   (A) Gwen is riding in the fourth car.
   (B) Paul is riding in the third car.
   (C) Tom is riding in the fifth car.
   (D) Laurie is riding in the third car.
   (E) The first car is empty.

3. Which one of the following statements CANNOT be true?

   (A) Neither Tom nor Gwen is sharing a car with another rider.
   (B) Neither Mark nor Jack is sharing a car with another rider.
   (C) Tom is sharing a car, and Jack is sharing a car.
   (D) Gwen is sharing a car, and Paul is sharing a car.
   (E) Tom is sharing a car, and Gwen is sharing a car.

4. If Paul is riding in the second car, how many different combinations of riders are possible for the third car?

   (A) 1
   (B) 2
   (C) 3
   (D) 4
   (E) 5

5. Assume that Roger, a seventh rider, is riding with Jack in the first car, but that all other conditions remain unchanged. Which of the following is a complete and accurate list of the riders who might be riding in the fifth car?

   (A) Mark
   (B) Tom, Paul
   (C) Tom, Laurie, Paul
   (D) Tom, Laurie, Mark
   (E) Mark, Paul, Tom, Laurie

STRATEGIES FOR HANDLING
A LOGIC GAME

In this section you'll learn various strategies for handling any logic game—including the roller-coaster game in the preceding section—as efficiently as possible. Here you'll learn how to (1) quickly "size up" a logic game, (2) organize a game's information using a "master diagram," and (3) respond appropriately to the questions. Answers and explanations for questions 1–5 of the roller-coaster game begin on page 14 ("Analysis of Sample Game").

Sizing Up the Game

Survey the game for key information. Take a quick glance around the page to see what words and phrases appear frequently among the questions and answer choices. Then read the premise and conditions quickly. Try to determine:

- what type of game you're dealing with

- how many subjects are included in the game

- the game's difficulty level and whether you should skip it

- how you might organize the information in a diagram

Don't let the "length" of the game fool you. There is no automatic correlation between the length of a game—either the number of questions or the number of conditions—and the difficulty level of the game. Do not bypass a game merely because it either (1) fills up more space on the page than the other games in the section or (2) includes more (or fewer) questions than the other games.

Assimilating the Rules

Jot down a list or "roster" of the subjects. It is remarkably easy to forget how many subjects (people, events, etc.) a particular game involves and their identities unless you list them near your diagram. Use first letters as symbols, and use uppercase and lowercase letters to distinguish males and females (or any other binary distinction for which letter size

is a clear indicator). Put a box around the list to identify it clearly.

Don't let the wording of the rules trip you up. Read the rules with great precision and care. The single most common mistake made by test takers in logic games is to misread a rule or condition. Such a mistake can be costly; it taints your analysis of the entire game and may cause you to respond incorrectly to several, if not all, of the questions.

Accept the rules at face value. The rules are designed to be as clear as possible, not to trick you; do not read into the rules what does not appear on their face.

Example: The "roller-coaster" game (page 10)
Perhaps one person could ride in two cars at one time by straddling them in some fashion. If you insist on finding such subtle ambiguities or double-meanings in the rules, you will only defeat your purpose.

Creating a Template or "Master Diagram"

Avoid listing all possible combinations. In attempting the sample game on page 10, did you try to jot down all the possible seat assignments for the riders, considering all rules simultaneously? If so, was the result a confusing mess? Probably. Stop this "strategy" now before it becomes a bad habit. Instead, use one (or perhaps two) master diagrams that encompass all of the various possibilities (see the following page).

Depict the relationships spatially as pictures. Try to construct a picture that allows you to visualize the relationships among the subjects of the game at a glance. An effective picture, or diagram, can transform a seemingly impossible game into a piece of cake. For many games, a single basic diagram or picture can be used as a "template" for all questions.

Look for a "key" rule to begin diagramming. Look for a rule that allows you to organize the game into *two* basic alternative scenarios. A rule that includes an "either/or" statement, for example, suggests two alternative situations and thus two alternative pictures. This technique will greatly simplify the game. NOTE: Not every game includes a "key" rule that allows you to organize the game in this manner. Always look for it, however.

Example: The "roller-coaster" game (page 10)
All of the possibilities fall into one of two alternative scenarios based upon the last condition ("Gwen is riding in either the third or fourth car."). Accordingly, you can draw two distinct diagrams to represent these two scenarios:

<u>SCENARIO #1</u>   <u>SCENARIO #2</u>

1	1
2	2
3 G	3
4	4 G
5	5

Account for every rule, either in or around your diagram. Use your pencil to display each and every rule in your workspace. Try to represent the rules as pictures that indicate visually how they fit into your diagram. If a rule cannot be expressed as a picture, restate the rule near your diagram, using *symbols* or *shorthand*. Otherwise, you may forget about it. Remember that every rule will come into play at some point in the game.

Example: The "roller-coaster" game (page 10)
After creating two alternative diagrams based upon Gwen's position, consider the remaining rules. If we try to incorporate any of these rules directly in our diagram, we would have to add several scenarios to account for all of the additional possibilities. What if we overlook a possibility? Run out of space on our paper? Run out of time? Instead of complicating our diagram, let's simply indicate the remaining rules either as pictures or symbols near our master diagrams (the inequality symbol is used to signify that two riders are not sharing a car):

<u>SCENARIO #1</u>   <u>SCENARIO #2</u>

1	1
2	2
3 Ⓖ	3
4	4 Ⓖ
5	5

[L_]   ⊠/M   T ≠ G/P

TGLMPJ

Based on the rules, draw useful conclusions. Once you have displayed all of the rules in your workspace, ask yourself, "What conclusions can I draw from the rules?" This step is crucial. If additional information can be deduced, you will probably need to know this information to analyze most, if not all, of the questions. In looking for these hidden pieces to the puzzle, bear in mind the following:

- *Some conclusions are less helpful than others.* Conclusions about what *cannot* be true (in the roller-coaster game, for example, which cars a particular rider *cannot* occupy) are generally not very useful. Focus instead on the affirmative.

- *Not all games contain clues to additional information.* With practice, you will develop an instinct for knowing when you can or cannot draw additional conclusions from the rules.

- *Limit your time looking for additional information.* In most cases, you will not be 100% certain that you have deduced all that you can from the rules. With enough practice, you will develop a sense for what type of additional information to look for, as well as a sense for when to move on to the questions.

Example: The "roller-coaster" game (page 10)
What else can you deduce from the premise and conditions? Can you "fit" any other riders into the diagram? Not without adding restrictions. However, you can draw certain conclusions about the *number* of riders in each car. The game's premise states that each car can accommodate up to two riders, but one of the conditions states that Mark is seated alone behind an empty car. That leaves three other cars to accommodate the other five riders. Thus, accommodating all six riders requires this distribution:

- one and only one car (the car immediately ahead of Mark's car) is empty

- of the other four cars, two (including Mark's car) are occupied by one rider each

- two riders share each of the remaining two cars

This additional information is important in analyzing the questions. In fact, by drawing these conclusions prior to answering the questions, you've already done much of the work required to answer the questions.

Keep your diagrams neat. Remember: Scratch paper is not permitted for this section of the exam. Use the margins and the bottom portion of each page (usually about one-fourth the area of the page) for diagrams and notes. Given this limited workspace, it is crucial that you keep your diagrams neat and compact.

Responding to the Questions

The first few questions will tell you if you're on track. The first one or two questions in a game are usually somewhat simpler than the others. Earlier questions generally involve the more basic and obvious relationships established by the rules of the game. Some might require no analysis other than recognizing rule violations among the answer choices. Others might focus on just one or two of the rules, without requiring more than one or two deductive steps. In fact, you might be able to respond to the first one or two questions without using a diagram. If you are "stumped" by the first few questions, then you've:

- misread or misinterpreted a rule

- neglected to include a rule in or around your diagram, or

- overlooked a conclusion inferable from the rules

Before you invest more time in the remaining questions, go back and find out where you got off track.
Example: The "roller-coaster" game (page 10)
Question 1 is a typical first question. It does not require any analysis other than recognizing that particular answer choices violate particular rules. A diagram is not needed for this question.

Don't confuse the question with its "inverse." It is remarkably easy to become confused as to what a question asks. To avoid this common error: (1) review the question repeatedly as you analyze the answer choices, and (2) underline the operative phrase in the question.
Example: The "roller-coaster" game (page 10)
Question 3 asks you to identify the *one* statement that "CANNOT be true." Be careful not to turn the question on its head by looking for a statement that *must* be true.

Predict the answer, if possible. If the question stem provides additional information, begin to draw additional conclusions before reviewing the answer choices. Then scan the answer choices, looking for your predetermined answer.
Example: The "roller-coaster" game (page 10)
In Question 2, you can determine the positions of Mark, Laurie, Gwen, and Tom from the information in the question stem. Accordingly, the correct response to the question ("All of the following must be true EXCEPT") will probably involve either Paul or Jack. The correct response (B) jumps out at you as you quickly scan the choices.

Shortcut potentially time-consuming questions by looking to the answer choices for clues. Questions such as "Which of the following must be true?" can be time consuming, since you must analyze each answer choice in turn. If the correct answer turns out to be choice (E), you could spend an inordinate amount of time getting to it. The nature of the answer choices often provides a clue as to what rule or rules you should focus on. You may be able to identify the correct answer without analyzing the other choices.

Example: The "roller-coaster" game (page 10)
Question 3 is potentially time-consuming since the question stem provides no clue as to what issues the question will focus on. However, by glancing quickly at the answer choices, you might *intuit* that the correct response will focus on *single* riders, and so you should first analyze answer choices (A) and (B).

Don't do more work than is necessary to determine the answer. Most questions can be answered without considering every rule and without determining all that you can from the additional information supplied by the question stem. Avoid doing more work than necessary to determine the answer.

Example: The "roller-coaster" game (page 10)
Question 5 asks who might occupy the fifth car. In considering Scenario #1 in the diagram on page 12 (Gwen occupies the third car), you only need to go as far as determining that Mark occupies the fifth car alone, even though the positions of all other riders can also be determined.

Beware of "sleeper" rules. A game might include a rule that comes into play only in one or two of the later questions. Make sure to account for every rule as you diagram a game so that you don't forget about sleepers.

Example: The "roller-coaster" game (page 10)
The third rule—"Tom is not sharing a car with either Gwen or Paul"—is a sleeper. It does not come into play in drawing your initial conclusions; in fact, it is not needed until question 5.

The last question may be easier than it looks. While the final question is typically a bit more complex than the others, you'll probably be ready for it simply because you have already played the game for a while and have become familiar and comfortable with it. In fact, you may actually find it easier than some of the earlier questions.

Example: The "roller-coaster" game (page 10)
Question 5 is a typical *last* question; every original rule comes into play, and the additional

information does not permit you to eliminate either of the two basic scenarios. However, if you've successfully handled the other questions, question 5 isn't all that tough.

Use a highlighter or other method to preserve your master diagram from question to question. Avoid the time and risk of error involved in redrawing your diagram for each question. Use your master diagram for as many questions as possible. Insert variable information, then erase that information before proceeding to the next question. In doing so, be careful not to erase part of your master diagram. No pens are permitted, so earmark "fixed" information with a highlighter or by circling those subjects in your master diagram that remain fixed in position for all questions.

Example: The "roller-coaster" game (page 10)
In our final master diagram on page 12, notice that "G" (Gwen) is circled in both alternative diagrams. This technique ensures that those "G"s won't be erased as you fill in the diagrams with variable information from question to question. (Remember: You can use a highlighter as an alternative to circling fixed information.)

ANALYSIS OF SAMPLE GAME

Question 1

The correct answer is (D). Each of the other choices violates the premise or one of the conditions. (A) violates the rule that Laurie is sharing a car. (B) violates the rule that Gwen is riding in either the third or fourth car; (B) also violates the rule that Tom is not sharing a car with Gwen (although either rule violation suffices to eliminate this answer choice). (C) violates the rule that Mark is not sharing a car. (E) violates the premise that states that each car can accommodate *up to two* riders.

Question 2

The correct answer is (B). Consider the information in the question stem in light of the two alternative scenarios in our final master diagram (see page 12). Scenario #1 may be eliminated from consideration.

Why? In Scenario #1, Laurie, Gwen, and Tom would occupy the second, third, and fourth cars, respectively. This arrangement, however, would not accommodate Mark seated alone immediately behind an empty car (as required by one of the game's conditions). Scenario #2 is the only one that applies to this question. Given the additional information in the question stem, Laurie must occupy the third car while Tom occupies the fifth car. Accordingly, Mark must occupy the second car, and the first car must be empty:

SCENARIO #1   SCENARIO #2

```
1                1 ⊠
2 [L_]           2 ⊡M
3 Ⓖ             3 [L_]
4 T              4 Ⓖ
5                5 T
```

However, Paul may occupy either the third or fourth car. Thus, Statement (B) is not necessarily true.

Question 3

The correct answer is (A). Mark and only one other rider are each seated alone; otherwise, the coaster could not accommodate all six riders. (Remember, each car can accommodate no more than two riders.) Thus, Tom and Gwen cannot both be seated alone.

Question 4

The correct answer to Question 4 is (C). Question 4, like Question 2, provides additional information that allows you to eliminate one of the two alternative scenarios. In Question 4, however, Scenario #2 in our final master diagram (see page 12) is the one that may be entirely eliminated. If Paul and Gwen occupy the second and fourth cars, respectively, Mark cannot sit alone immediately behind an empty car (as required by one of the game's conditions). Focusing, then, on Scenario #1 (Gwen occupies the third car), given that Paul occupies the second car, Mark must occupy the fifth car, and the fourth car must be empty:

SCENARIO #1   SCENARIO #2

```
1                1
2 P              2 P
3 Ⓖ             3
4 ⊠             4 Ⓖ
5 ⊡M            5
```

Considering the four remaining riders, the rules expressly prohibit Tom from riding with Gwen (in the third car). Accordingly, Gwen may occupy the third car, either alone or with Laurie or Jack. Thus, one of exactly three combinations of riders could be riding in the third car: Gwen only, Gwen and Laurie, or Gwen and Jack.

Question 5

The correct answer is (D). Consider the two alternative scenarios in our final master diagram (see page 12). In Scenario #1 (Gwen in the third car), given that Jack and Roger occupy the first car, Mark must occupy the fifth car alone. Next, consider Scenario #2 (Gwen in the fourth car). Given that Jack and Roger occupy the first car, Mark must occupy the third car (while the second car is empty). Since Tom cannot share a car with Gwen, Tom must occupy the fifth car. Since Tom cannot share a car with Paul, Paul must share the fourth car with Gwen. Accordingly, Laurie must share the fifth car with Tom.

SCENARIO #1   SCENARIO #2

```
1 J R            1 J R
2                2 ⊠
3 Ⓖ             3 ⊡M
4 ⊠             4 Ⓖ P
5 ⊡M            5 T L
```

Thus, either Mark alone (under Scenario #1) or both Tom and Laurie (under Scenario #2) must occupy the fifth car.

PACING AND TIME ALLOCATION (QUESTIONS AND ANSWERS)

How much time should I allot for any one logic game? Some games are more complex than others and thus are inherently more time consuming. Most test takers require at least 7 or 8 minutes for even the simplest of games. Complex games may realistically take as much as 10 minutes of your time. Do not devote more than 10 minutes to any one logic game, unless you have decided to attempt fewer than all of the games in the section.

Is there any pattern in difficulty level among games within an exam section? If so, should I skip the tough ones? Logic games vary considerably in their complexity and difficulty level. It is safe to say that the first game will not be the most difficult one. Beyond this, there really is no discernible pattern, so be ready for anything. Logic games are easier for some test takers than for others. You may find that you will achieve your best score by skipping one of the games in a section and devoting the entire time to the remaining three games. In any event, do not skip more than one game; allocating your entire time to only two of four games results in a pace that is far too slow and is not justifiable for even the most challenging games.

How do you know when to "give up" on a game and move on? Once you commit yourself to a game, it can be difficult to force yourself to "throw in the towel" and move on to the next game. The tendency is to be stubborn and insist on figuring out every question before moving on. Do not succumb to this self-defeating mentality. Answer the easier questions; if you have time at the end (you probably won't), return to the game and try again.

What if I have only one or two minutes to attempt a game? Perhaps your pace has been too slow and only a few minutes remain for your final game. In this event, you need to decide quickly which two or three questions of the final game to attempt. Bear in mind that some of the questions (most likely the earlier ones) might be answerable without reading the premise or all of the rules. A quick glance at the question stem, along with a quick reading of the rule(s) relating to the question, may suffice to respond to that question.

FORMAL LOGIC—EVERYTHING YOU NEED TO KNOW FOR LOGIC GAMES

You do not need a formal college-level logic course to perform well on the Analytical Reasoning section of the LSAT. Much of what you would learn in such a course—particularly the terminology and symbols used in formal logic—is of little practical use in handling LSAT logic games. Nevertheless, there is one particular concept in formal deductive logic that is so crucial for success in handling logic games that we must examine it.

Conditional Statements and the "Contrapositive" Rule

A *conditional* statement is one in which an event occurs (or does not occur) if some other event occurs (or does not occur). Consider the following four statements:

1. If a shirt is red, then it must have long sleeves.
2. All red shirts have long sleeves.
3. Only long-sleeved shirts are red.
4. A shirt is red only if it has long sleeves.

All of the statements above are essentially the same in meaning—a shirt's being red is *conditioned upon* the shirt's having long sleeves. Given this premise, consider whether each of the following statements may be logically deduced:

1. If a shirt does not have long sleeves, then it cannot be red.
2. If a shirt has long sleeves, then it is red.
3. If a shirt is not red, then it does not have long sleeves.

The first of the three statements immediately above is referred to in formal logic as the *contrapositive of the conditional*—it reverses the "if" clause and the "then" clause, and negates both. The conclusion of a conditional statement is such that the "then" clause is always inferable from the "if" clause.

Neither Statement 2 nor 3, however, is inferable—long-sleeved shirts may also be any other color. To restate all of this more generally:

Premise:

>   If A, then B
>   (or)   All A are B
>   (or)   Only B are A
>   (or)   A only if B

Conclusion:

>   1. If not B, then not A. (contrapositive—valid)
>   2. If B, then A. (not inferable)
>   3. If not A, then not B. (not inferable)

Conditional rules make a logic game more complex and more confusing because you must:

- remember that the rule applies only under certain circumstances

- be alert to the contrapositive inference as you work through the questions

- be careful to avoid the two fallacious inferences identified above

Be ready for conditional statements! You can be sure that at least one game will include this feature.

Day 3

Analytical Reasoning Lesson 2: Linear Sequence Games

Today you will examine "linear sequence" games, the most common logic games on the LSAT.

Today's Topics

1. What are linear sequence games?
2. Sequencing terminology
3. The simple sequence game
4. The double-decker sequence game
5. The sequence/attributes game
6. The cluster sequence game
7. The dual sequence game
8. The sequence formula game

WHAT ARE LINEAR SEQUENCE GAMES?

Among LSAT logic games, *linear sequence* games are the most common. Linear sequencing involves placing the game's subjects in order *in a row*—or sequence—from left to right (or perhaps from top to bottom). The nature of the order might be spatial, chronological, or quantifiable (e.g., size, weight). In any case, your task is the same—line them up in order! Several variations of sequencing appear on the LSAT. Today you will explore the six most common variations, looking at one example of each type.

NOTE: Each example in today's lesson includes only one illustrative question; keep in mind, however, that on the LSAT every logic game includes 4–8 questions. Also, each example involves exactly five positions or "slots" in a sequence; keep in mind, however, that the number of slots in a sequence game can vary.

SEQUENCING TERMINOLOGY

The rules in sequencing games include certain terminology that you must be sure to interpret accurately. Consider a game in which several people, including A, B, and C, are seated in a row of chairs from left to right. In this scenario,

All of these rules carry the same meaning:

"A is seated *next* to B."

"A is seated *adjacent* to B."

"A is seated *immediately next* to B."

"A is seated *directly next* to B."

Both of these rules carry the same meaning:

"A is seated *immediately* to the left of B."

"A is seated *directly* to the left of B."

Both of these rules carry the same meaning:

"A is seated *exactly* two chairs from B."

"A is seated *two chairs from* B."

Both of these rules carry the same meaning:

"A is seated *to the left of* B."

"A is seated *farther left than* B."

All of these rules carry the same meaning:

"C is seated *immediately between* A and B."

"C is seated *next to both* A and B."

"*Only* C is seated *between* A and B."

Both of these rules carry the same meaning:

"*Two chairs separate* A from B."

"A is seated *three chairs from* B."

All of these rules carry the same meaning:

"A and B are seated *two chairs apart*."

"*One chair separates* A from B."

"A is seated *two chairs from* B."

THE SIMPLE SEQUENCE GAME

A *simple sequence* game involves nothing more than arranging the subjects linearly in a string of blank spaces, using a fill-in-the-blank approach. Make sure that you keep straight which end of the sequence is which, and you should not have much trouble with this type of game.

Example 3-1

Five students—Joe, Kim, Linda, Mark, and Nicole—are enrolled in grades ranging from first to fifth. Each is in a different grade.

Mark is in a lower grade than Kim.

Nicole and Linda are in the first and fifth grades, although not necessarily in that order.

Which of the following statements provides sufficient information to determine that Kim is in the fourth grade?

(A) Linda is in a higher grade than Kim.

(B) Nicole is in a higher grade than Joe.

(C) Joe is in a lower grade than Mark.

(D) Linda is in a lower grade than Mark.

(E) Nicole is in a lower grade than Mark.

This is a straightforward linear sequence game in which two alternative diagrams based upon the last rule may be constructed:

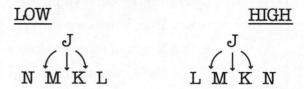

The only major concern in the game is to keep straight in your mind that "lower" refers to the left of your diagram and that "higher" refers to the right.

The correct response to the question is (C). Before examining any of the answer choices, determine what must be true in order for Kim to be in the fourth grade. The diagrams above make clear that Joe must be to the left of (in a lower grade than) Kim to achieve this result. The correct answer is now easy to spot—if Joe is to the left of (in a lower grade than) Mark, then Joe is also to the left of (in a lower grade than) Kim.

THE DOUBLE-DECKER SEQUENCE GAME

Your task in a *double-decker sequence* game is to pair each subject with another subject *and* sequence the pairs. This type of game typically involves teams (of two subjects) competing in a race or other contest.

Example 3-2

In a two-man bobsled race, ten athletes—A, B, C, D, E, F, G, H, I, and J—each finished in one of five places in the standings. There were no ties.

H and I were teamed together.

C and F were not teamed together.

E and G were teamed together and did not place last in the standings.

B placed immediately ahead of F in the standings.

If H and B placed second and third, respectively, which of the following must be true?

(A) C placed fourth.

(B) G placed first.

(C) F placed fifth.

(D) A placed fourth.

(E) D placed third.

Use a diagram such as the one below to assign each subject (athlete) to one of five positions:

$$
\begin{array}{l}
1 \\
2 \\
3 \\
4 \\
5
\end{array}
\Big\}[E\ G]
\qquad
\begin{array}{l}
[H\ I] \\[1em]
\left[\begin{array}{l} B \\ F\cancel{\ } \end{array}\right]
\end{array}
$$

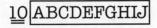

Notice that the [EG] and [HI] teams are indicated to the right of the master diagram, ready to be pasted into the diagram as needed to respond to the question. The relationship between B and F is also indicated in picture form. Also notice the use of the elimination or "strikethrough" symbol (/) to indicate that a team including C and F is not permitted. In working with this diagram, keep in mind that left-right orientation between team members is irrelevant.

The correct response to the question is (B). Since B placed third, F must place fourth. According to one of the conditions, E and G did not place last; therefore, the only place in which E and G could finish is first.

$$
\begin{array}{ll}
1 & [E\ G] \\
2 & [H\ I] \\
3 & B \\
4 & F \\
5 &
\end{array}
\Big\}[E\ G]
$$

THE SEQUENCE/ATTRIBUTES GAME

In this type of game your task is twofold: (1) line up (sequence) the subjects, and (2) assign one or two characteristics or *attributes* to each subject.

Example 3-3

Five horses—A, B, C, D, and E—are kept in five adjacent stalls. Three of the horses are male, and two of the horses are female.

B is a male.

The females are not kept in adjacent stalls.

C is separated from E by one stall.

A is kept in one of the three middle stalls.

If all three males are kept in adjacent stalls, which of the following is a complete and accurate list of the horses whose gender (male or female) can be determined?

(A) A and B

(B) B and D

(C) A, B, and D

(D) A, B, C, and E

(E) B, C, D, and E

Your initial diagram for this game might include a sequence along with a shorthand restatement of the rules:

(M) (F) ≠ (F)

— — — — —   B

⎵⎵⎵⎵

A   [C _E]

Now considering the question, three males must be in stalls 2, 3, and 4 in order to satisfy the rule that the two females must be separated. Thus, although you have not constructed a sequence for the five horses, you do know the gender of the horse in each stall. B is a male and thus must be in one of the three middle stalls. A is in one of the three middle stalls and thus must be a male. That leaves D, C, and E. C and E cannot be in stalls 2 and 4 (in either order), because either A or B must occupy one of those stalls. (In the diagram below, A and B could be reversed.) C and E must therefore be either in stalls 1 and 3 (in either order) or in stalls 3 and 5 (in either order):

(F) (M) (M) (M) (F)

_ A C/E B _

⎵⎵⎵

A

In either event, you cannot determine the gender of either C or E (although they are not of the same gender). Finally, D must be in either stall 1 or 5, and thus must be female. The correct response is (C).

THE CLUSTER SEQUENCE GAME

As with any sequence game, your task here is to assign each subject to one position in a sequence. In a *cluster sequence* game, however, any number of subjects (perhaps none, perhaps all) might occupy a given position.

Example 3-4

Each of five detectives—Arkin, Billings, Cobart, Dansen, and Eckles—has been assigned to search one floor of the house of a murder victim for clues. The house includes five floors—the basement, the first floor, the second floor, the third floor, and the attic.

> Cobart has been assigned to a higher floor than any other detective.

> Billings has been assigned to a lower floor than Dansen.

> At least two detectives have been assigned to the second floor.

> Exactly one detective has been assigned to the first floor, and exactly one detective has been assigned to the third floor.

If exactly one floor separates the floor to which Eckles is assigned from the floor to which Arkin is assigned, which of the following must be false?

(A) Arkin is assigned to the basement.

(B) Billings is assigned to the first floor.

(C) Dansen is assigned to the second floor.

(D) Cobart is assigned to the third floor.

(E) Eckles is assigned to the third floor.

The key to working through this game quickly is to determine alternative scenarios based upon the number of detectives assigned to each floor. Given that exactly one detective is assigned to the first floor and one to the third floor, the three others must be allocated among the second floor, the basement, and the attic. Since at least two detectives are assigned to the second floor, three basic possibilities emerge. Because Cobart is assigned to a higher floor than any other detective, and because Dansen is assigned to a higher floor than Billings, the three alternative diagrams may be partially completed as follows ("X" indicates a floor to which no detective is assigned):

Floor

Be careful in this game not to confuse the *first* floor with the *bottom* floor, which is the basement.

The correct response to the question is (E). The second alternative diagram above may be eliminated from consideration since Eckles and Arkin would be assigned to the first and third floors (in either order), restricting both Dansen and Billings to the second floor, thereby violating the rule that Billings is assigned to a lower floor than Dansen. The third alternative diagram may be eliminated from consideration since it requires that Arkin and Eckles be assigned to the same floor. In the first diagram, Dansen and Billings must be assigned to the second and first floors, respectively, while Arkin and Eckles are assigned to the second floor and to the basement (in either order):

Floor

A	X
3	C
2	DA
1	B
B	E

In neither scenario can Eckles be assigned to the third floor; thus, statement (E) must be false.

THE DUAL SEQUENCE GAME

Dual sequence games involve two separate and distinct sequences. Be careful in constructing your diagrams not to confuse the two sequences. Also clearly identify which end is which in both sequences. In more complex dual sequence games (such as Example 3-5 below), the two sequences might be interrelated, requiring you to work back and forth between them.

Example 3-5

Each of five museum tours—A, B, C, D, and E—is conducted once a day. All tours begin and end in the lobby of the museum. The five tours depart in ten-minute intervals of one another and arrive in ten-minute intervals of one another. Each tour is at least ten minutes long.

> Tour A departs before any other tour, and Tour A arrives before any other tour.
>
> Tour B departs either ten minutes before Tour C or ten minutes after Tour C.
>
> Tour C is the last tour to arrive, but Tour C is not the last tour to depart.
>
> Tour D arrives after Tour B, and Tour D departs at least ten minutes before at least two other tours, one of which is Tour E.

If the last of the five tours arrives exactly one hour after the first of the five tours departs, which of the following CANNOT be true?

(A) Tour A arrives before Tour C departs.

(B) Tour E arrives before Tour C departs.

(C) Tour B arrives before Tour E departs.

(D) Tour E arrives before Tour B departs.

(E) Tour A arrives before Tour B departs.

To handle this game, consider the possible departure sequences separately from the possible arrival sequences. You can deduce from the rules that Tour A and Tour D must depart first and second, respectively, while Tour E departs either immediately before or after both Tour B and Tour C. The result is exactly three possible departure sequences (Tour C cannot depart last). As for tour arrivals, Tour A and Tour C must arrive first and last, respectively, while Tour B must arrive before Tour D. The result is exactly three arrival sequences:

<u>Depart</u>   <u>Arrive</u>

A D B C E   E

A D E C B   A B D C

A D C B E

The correct response to the question is (B). Since the tours must depart and arrive in ten-minute intervals, the departure and arrival sequences overlap as follows:

Elapsed Time: 0 10 20 30 40 50 60

Departure: A D _ _ _

Arrival: A _ _ _ C

If Tour C departs fourth, Tour A will arrive before Tour C departs; thus, (A) might be true. Tour E arrives no earlier than at the same time the fourth tour departs; since Tour C departs no later than fourth, Tour E cannot arrive before Tour C departs, and (B) must be false. Tour E may be the last to depart, in which event Tour B may arrive before Tour E departs; thus, (C) might be true. Tour E could arrive second while Tour B departs last (10 minutes after Tour E arrives); thus, (D) might be true. Finally, since Tour A arrives at the same time that the third tour departs, Tour B might depart after Tour A arrives; thus, (E) might be true.

THE SEQUENCE FORMULA GAME

Sequence formula games, more than any other type of LSAT logic game, resemble the kind of games we have all played at the kitchen table with a special board, some dice, and different colored tokens. The "players" in a sequence formula game begin in a certain sequence and are then manipulated according to a designated set of simple rules.

Example 3-6

A chess tournament among five boys involves one match at a time in which each player in turn elects to challenge the player either immediately above him or below him in the current rankings. At the outset of the tournament, Rodney, Kyle, Gary, Vladimir, and Peter are ranked first through fifth, in that order. The players must take turns making challenges in the order of their initial rankings.

> If the challenger wins the match, his opponent is demoted to fifth in the rankings.
>
> If the challenger loses the match, the challenger is demoted to fifth in the rankings.
>
> If the match results in a stalemate, the challenger is demoted one position in the rankings.

Each time a player is demoted, the rankings of the other four players in relation to one another remain unchanged.

If the first two matches both result in stalemates, any of the following might represent the players' rankings, from first to fifth, after the first three matches EXCEPT:

(A) Rodney, Gary, Vladimir, Peter, Kyle

(B) Rodney, Kyle, Gary, Peter, Vladimir

(C) Rodney, Kyle, Vladimir, Peter, Gary

(D) Rodney, Gary, Kyle, Vladimir, Peter

(E) Rodney, Kyle, Vladimir, Gary, Peter

In sequence formula games such as this one, take the extra time to internalize the rules and visualize the game as it is played. The only written diagram you're likely to find useful for every question is a list of the subjects in their initial order or ranking.

The correct response to the question is (D). Since Rodney is initially ranked first, he makes the first challenge and must challenge Kyle (because a player may challenge another player only if they are positioned consecutively in the current rankings). Given that the first match results in a stalemate, Rodney is demoted one position, and the rankings after the first match are as follows:

R challenges K: K, R, G, V, P

The next match involves a challenge by Kyle since he was initially ranked second. Kyle must challenge Rodney, and a stalemate would return the players to their initial rankings:

K challenges R: R, K, G, V, P

The third match involves a challenge by Gary since he was initially ranked third. Gary may challenge either Kyle or Vladimir. In each case, one of three different rankings would result:

G challenges K:

G wins	R, G, V, P, K
G loses	R, K, V, P, G
stalemate	R, K, V, G, P

G challenges V:

G wins	R, K, G, P, V
G loses	R, K, V, P, G
stalemate	R, K, V, G, P

Only answer choice (D) is not among the possible rankings listed above.

Analytical Reasoning Lesson 3: Mini-Test and Review

Today you will apply what you learned on Days 2 and 3 to three logic games. Take this mini-test under timed conditions; then review the explanations that follow. For each question, the game type and difficulty level are identified.

ANALYTICAL REASONING MINI-TEST

Number of questions: 17
Suggested time: 26 minutes

Directions (as printed in test booklet): Each group of questions in this section is based on a set of conditions. In answering some of the questions, it may be useful to draw a rough diagram. Choose the response that most accurately and completely answers each question and blacken the corresponding space on your answer sheet.

Questions 1–6

A law firm occupies five of the six floors in a new office building. The remaining floor is still vacant. The law firm consists of four departments—civil litigation, tax, antitrust, and securities. Each of the four departments occupies a separate floor, and the antitrust department occupies two adjacent floors.

   The securities department occupies the floor either immediately above or immediately below the tax department.

   At least two floors separate the floor occupied by the tax department from each floor occupied by the antitrust department.

1. Which of the following lists, in order from the first floor to the sixth floor, is acceptable?
   (A) securities, tax, vacant floor, antitrust, antitrust, civil litigation
   (B) vacant floor, antitrust, civil litigation, antitrust, securities, tax
   (C) vacant floor, tax, civil litigation, securities, antitrust, antitrust
   (D) antitrust, antitrust, civil litigation, tax, securities, vacant floor
   (E) civil litigation, antitrust, antitrust, vacant floor, securities, tax

2. Which of the following is a complete and accurate list of the floors that may be vacant?
   (A) first, third, fifth
   (B) third, fourth, sixth
   (C) second, third, fourth, sixth
   (D) first, third, fourth, sixth
   (E) first, third, fifth, sixth

3. The antitrust department CANNOT occupy which two floors?
   (A) first and second
   (B) second and third
   (C) third and fourth
   (D) fourth and fifth
   (E) fifth and sixth

4. Which of the following is a complete and accurate list of the departments that may occupy the fifth floor?

(A) antitrust, tax

(B) securities, antitrust, civil litigation

(C) civil litigation, securities, tax

(D) antitrust, tax, securities

(E) securities, antitrust

5. If the antitrust department occupies the third floor, how many different floor arrangements are possible?

(A) 1

(B) 2

(C) 3

(D) 4

(E) 5

6. If the civil litigation department occupies the sixth floor, which of the following must be true?

(A) The third floor is vacant.

(B) The securities department occupies the second floor.

(C) The tax department occupies the fifth floor.

(D) The antitrust department occupies the first floor.

(E) The securities department occupies the fourth floor.

Questions 7–11

There are nine sponsors—A, B, C, D, E, F, G, H, and I—of a particular television program, each with its own commercial. The program is interrupted by five commercial breaks. Two commercials appear at each break, except for the fifth break, at which only one commercial appears. Each of the nine different commercials appears exactly once during the program.

E's commercial appears at an earlier break than C's commercial.

D's commercial appears at a later break than both F's commercial and B's commercial.

A's commercial appears at the same break as C's commercial.

B's commercial does not appear at the same break as E's commercial.

G's commercial appears during the same break as H's commercial.

7. Which of the following must be false?

(A) C's commercial appears at the second break.

(B) E's commercial appears at the fifth break.

(C) D's commercial appears at the second break.

(D) F's commercial appears at the third break.

(E) G's commercial appears at the fourth break.

8. Each of the following pairs of commercials may appear at the same break together EXCEPT:

(A) I's commercial and F's commercial

(B) B's commercial and I's commercial

(C) F's commercial and B's commercial

(D) E's commercial and D's commercial

(E) I's commercial and E's commercial

9. If two complete commercial breaks separate B's commercial from F's commercial, for how many commercials is it possible to determine the break during which the commercial appears?

(A) 1

(B) 2

(C) 3

(D) 4

(E) 5

10. If C's commercial appears at the second break, how many different pairs of commercials could appear at the first break?

(A) 1

(B) 2

(C) 3

(D) 4

(E) 5

11. If G's commercial appears at the third break, which of the following statements is sufficient to determine the break at which each and every commercial appears?

(A) A's commercial appears at the fourth break.

(B) B's commercial appears at the first break.

(C) C's commercial appears at the second break.

(D) E's commercial appears at the first break.

(E) F's commercial appears at the fourth break.

Questions 12–17

The students in a music class must take turns changing a melody by making one and only one of the following alterations to the melody created by the previous student:

Each student may add one note at the end of the melody.

Each student may delete one note from the melody.

Each student may replace one note of the melody with a different note.

Each student may exchange one note with another in the melody, but the two exchanged notes must be different.

The initial melody consists of four notes. In order from first to last, the notes are: C, D, E, and F. In changing a melody, each student must also comply with the following restrictions:

Note D must neither immediately precede nor immediately follow note F.

Note E may be exchanged with note C only if neither note occurs as the first or last note of the melody.

Each of the four notes—C, D, E, and F—must occur in the melody at least once, and the melody must not include any notes of the musical scale other than these four.

12. The number of different five-note melodies that can be created by the first student is:

(A) 0

(B) 1

(C) 2

(D) 3

(E) 4

13. Which of the following melodies can be created by the first student?

(A) C F D E

(B) E D C F

(C) C F E D

(D) E D E F C

(E) C D E F D

14. The fewest number of students that must take a turn in order to create a melody consisting of notes E, D, C, F, C, and D, in sequence, is:

(A) 2

(B) 3

(C) 4

(D) 5

(E) 6

15. If a student wishes to exchange one note with another, which of the following melodies offers the greatest number of possible changes of this kind?

(A) D C E F

(B) C F E D

(C) E D C F C

(D) C D D E F

(E) E F F C D

16. Which of the following could not be the second and third notes, respectively, of the melody created by the first student?

(A) D and E

(B) F and E

(C) D and C

(D) E and E

(E) E and D

17. Any of the following melodies might have been created by the second student EXCEPT:

(A) D E F C

(B) C D F E

(C) E D C F

(D) F C E D

(E) D E C F

Quick Answer Guide

Analytical Reasoning Mini-Test

1. E	6. A	11. E	16. E
2. D	7. B	12. D	17. C
3. C	8. A	13. C	
4. D	9. E	14. C	
5. B	10. B	15. A	

EXPLANATIONS

Questions 1–6: Simple linear sequence game (easier).

You *could* construct alternate diagrams—for example, representing all possible positions of the antitrust department (eliminating those that are inconsistent with the rules). A simpler and more elegant approach, however, is to draw one master diagram, depicting the rules near the diagram for reference:

$$\boxed{\text{T S A A C X}}$$

$$\overline{1} \; \overline{2} \; \overline{3} \; \overline{4} \; \overline{5} \; \overline{6}$$

$$[\text{A A}] \neq [\overset{\frown}{\text{T S}}]$$

* ≥ 2 Floors Between A & T

In the explanations below, letters are used to signify departments (e.g., "A" for antitrust department).

1. Answer: E.

Consider one rule at a time, eliminating answer choices that violate the rule. (A) and (D) violate the rule that T must be separated from A by at least two floors. (B) violates the rule that A must occupy adjacent floors. (C) violates the rule that T and S are adjacent to each other.

2. Answer: D.

If either floor 2 or floor 5 were vacant, then A and T could not be separated by at least two floors. However, any one of the remaining floors might be vacant.

3. Answer: C.

A cannot occupy floors 3 and 4; otherwise, A and T would be separated by no more than one floor (floor 2 or floor 5), resulting in a rule violation.

4. Answer: D.

Try positioning each department on floor 5 to see whether a rule violation results. C cannot occupy floor 5 without violating the rule that A and T must be separated by at least two floors.

5. Answer: B.

If A occupies floor 3, then it must also occupy floor 2. Otherwise, A and T could not be separated by at least two floors. Accordingly, T must occupy floor 6, and S must occupy floor 5. C must occupy either floor 1 or floor 4; the remaining floor—either 1 or 4—is vacant. Thus, two possible sequences result:

$$\underset{1\ \ \ 2\ \ \ 3\ \ \ 4\ \ \ 5\ \ \ 6}{C\ [A\ A]\ X\ [S\ T]}$$
$$\underset{}{X\ [A\ A]\ C\ [S\ T]}$$

6. Answer: A.

If C occupies floor 6, only two arrangements will ensure that A and T are separated by at least two floors:

$$\underset{1\ \ \ 2\ \ \ 3\ \ \ 4\ \ \ 5\ \ \ 6}{[A\ A]\ \ \ \ [S\ T]\ C}$$
$$[T\ S]\ \ \_\ \ [A\ A]\ C$$

In either case, the third floor must be vacant.

Questions 7–11: Double-decker sequence game (moderate).

As the diagram below suggests, each commercial break in the sequence includes two commercials. After displaying the information provided in the rules near your master diagram, you can deduce that either D or I must appear at the fifth break. Why? Only one commercial appears at the fifth break. C and A appear together, as do H and G. Thus, none of these four may appear at the fifth break. Also, since F and B both appear at an earlier break than D, neither F nor B may appear at the fifth break:

7. Answer: B.

Either D's commercial or I's commercial must appear at the fifth break (see general comments above); thus, statement (B) must be false.

8. Answer: A.

If I's commercial were paired with F's commercial, then B's commercial would have to be paired with E's commercial. This would result, however, in a rule violation. Thus, I's commercial cannot be paired with F's commercial.

9. Answer: E.

The condition in the question restricts the positions of B's commercial and F's commercial to the first and fourth breaks. Thus, the [GH] and [CA] pairs must appear at the second and third breaks, but in either order. Since E's commercial must precede C's commercial, E's commercial must appear at the first break. Since B's commercial and E's commercial cannot appear at the same break together, B's commercial must appear at the fourth break (and F's commercial must appear at the first break). Since D's commercial must appear at a later break than B's commercial, D's commercial must appear at the fifth break. Accordingly, I's commercial must appear with B's commercial at the fourth break.

10. Answer: B.

If C's commercial (together with A's commercial) appears at the second break, E's commercial must appear at the first break. B's commercial cannot appear with E's commercial, and so B's commercial cannot appear at the first break. D's commercial must follow both B's and F's commercials, and so D's commercial cannot appear during the first break. Only F's commercial and I's commercial remain, either of which could appear at the first break with E's commercial.

11. Answer: E.

Given that G's commercial appears at the third break, H's commercial must also appear at that break. Now consider Statement (E). If F's commercial appears at the fourth break, D's commercial must appear at the fifth break, since the rules stipulate that D's commercial appears at a later break than the break at which F's commercial appears. The [AC] pair must therefore precede the [GH] pair. Because E's commercial appears at an earlier break than C's commercial, E's commercial must appear at the first break, and the [AC] pair must appear at the second break. B's commercial cannot appear at the first break with E's commercial, and so B's commercial must appear at the fourth break with F's commercial, while I's commercial appears with E's commercial at the first break:

```
    1 2 3 4 5
   ┌─┬─┬─┬─┬─┐
   │E│C│G│F│D│
   ├─┼─┼─┼─┼─┤
   │I│A│H│B│ │
   └─┴─┴─┴─┴─┘
```

Questions 12–17: Sequence formula game (challenging).

This sequence-formula game may appear intimidating at first due to its lengthy premise. Once you have internalized the rules of the game, analyzing the questions involves applying the same formula repeatedly to the initial sequence. No initial diagram other than the original sequence or "melody" (C D E F) is necessary. Questions 14 and 17 are more difficult than the others. Question 14 requires you to work backwards from a predetermined end result through unknown interim steps, and a bit of intuition is needed to answer Question 17.

12. Answer: D.

In order to create a five-note melody, the first student must add one note to the end of the initial four-note melody. The last note of the initial melody is F. Thus, D cannot be added to this melody because F and D cannot occur in succession. However, any of the other three notes may be added. Thus, the first student may create any one of three different five-note melodies:

C D E F C

C D E F E

C D E F F

13. Answer: C.

The first student can create melody (C) by exchanging D and F in the initial sequence. Melody (A) violates the rule that F and D cannot occur in immediate succession; also, the first student cannot create (A) without also making another change. Melody (B) can be created by the first student only by exchanging C and E in the initial melody; however, this exchange would violate the rule that C and E can be exchanged only if neither occurs as the first or last note of the melody. Melody (D) can be created only by adding a note to the end of the initial melody as well as making some other change to the initial melody; the first student, however, is permitted to make one and only one change to the initial melody. Melody (E) violates the rule that F and D cannot occur in immediate succession.

14. Answer: C.

Notes D and F remain in their initial positions. Notes C and D have been added to the end of the melody by different students, and notes C and E (the first and third notes in the initial melody) have been exchanged. However, one student could not have effected an exchange between C and E since C initially occurred as the first note of the melody. Thus, a third student changed the C to an E while a fourth student changed the E to a C. For example:

original	C D E F
student 1	C D E F C
student 2	C D E F C D
student 3	E D E F C D
student 4	E D C F C D

(Note: These four changes need not occur in the precise order indicated above.)

15. Answer: A.

In melody (A), a student may make four different exchanges—D and C, C and E, E and F, or D and F.

In melody (B), a student may make one of two different exchanges—C and F or F and D. In melody (C), a student may make one of three different exchanges—E and D, D and F, or F and the second C. In melody (D), a student may make one of two different exchanges—C and the first D or C and the second D. In melody (E), a student may make one of two different exchanges—E and the first F or E and the second F.

16. Answer: E.

The second and third notes (D and E) could remain unchanged by adding a note to the end of the melody; thus, (A) is a possibility. (B), (C), and (D) each require that a note be replaced; doing so, however, would result in a four-note melody with only three different notes (a rule violation). (E) requires that D and E be exchanged; the result, however, is that D would immediately precede F (a rule violation).

17. Answer: C.

Each answer choice includes four notes, suggesting one of two scenarios: (1) both students exchanged two notes (rather than adding, deleting, or altering notes) or (2) the first student added a note, then the second student deleted one of the two occurrences of that note (remember: the melody must include all four notes). Under the first scenario, the first student may exchange either D and F or C and D. The second student may then either reverse the exchange, restoring the initial melody, or create one of four new four-note melodies without violating a rule:

F C E D

D E C F

D C F E

F C E D

Under the second scenario, the first student could add either a C, E, or F to the end of the original melody. The second student could then either restore the initial melody or create one of two new four-note melodies without violating a rule:

D E F C

C D F E

Answer choice (C) is not among the possible four-note melodies listed above.

Logical Reasoning Lesson 1:
Basic Concepts and Strategies

Today you will familiarize yourself with the format of the Logical Reasoning sections, learn strategies for handling the questions, and review the basic logical concepts presupposed on the LSAT.

Today's Topics

1. Logical reasoning at a glance

2. Anatomy of a logical reasoning section

3. Anatomy of a logical reasoning problem

4. Strategies for dealing with logical reasoning problems

5. Managing your time

6. Applying the strategies

7. Review of the logical concepts presupposed on the test

LOGICAL REASONING AT A GLANCE

Number of questions: 24–26 (usually 25)
Time allowed: 35 minutes
Average time per question: 81–88 seconds
Number of scored sections: 2

Basic format:

- brief passage containing an argument followed by a question and five answer choices

Ground rules:

- no scratch paper is permitted (make notes in the test booklet)

- pencils and highlighters (no pens)

- each question is considered independently of all others

- no penalty (deduction) assessed for incorrect responses

Directions printed in test booklet:
"The questions in this section are based on the reasoning contained in brief statements or passages. For some questions, more than one of the choices could conceivably answer the question. However, you are to choose the *best* answer; that is, the response that most accurately and completely answers the question. You should not make assumptions that are by commonsense standards implausible, superfluous, or incompatible with the passage. After you have chosen the best answer, blacken the corresponding space on your answer sheet."

Terminology of formal logic presupposed: none.

Logical concepts presupposed:

- argument
- issue
- premise
- conclusion
- assumption

Primary logical reasoning skills tested:

- identifying the main point or conclusion of an argument
- making inferences or drawing conclusions from given premises
- identifying assumptions employed in specific arguments
- assessing the effect of additional information on an argument
- identifying principles that underlie or justify the reasoning employed in an argument
- identifying the method of reasoning employed in an argument
- detecting reasoning errors
- recognizing arguments that have similar structure or employ a similar method

ANATOMY OF A LOGICAL REASONING SECTION

There are two Logical Reasoning sections on the LSAT, each containing 25–26 questions. Logical Reasoning questions make up 50% of the multiple-choice portion of the test and are designed to evaluate your ability to understand, criticize, and analyze arguments. At least eight basic logical reasoning skills are tested.

Here is a breakdown of a typical Logical Reasoning section on the LSAT by question type.

Question Type	% of Questions	# of Questions
Identifying Conclusions	5–8%	1–2
Finding Assumptions	12%	3
Making Inferences	16%	4
Assessing Additional Evidence	24%	6
Identifying Argument Structure	12%	3
Identifying Method of Argument	5–8%	1–2
Detecting Reasoning Errors	8%	2
Identifying Principles	5–8%	1–2
Miscellaneous	4–13%	1–3

ANATOMY OF A LOGICAL REASONING PROBLEM

On the LSAT, Logical Reasoning problems have three elements:

1. A brief passage that contains an argument or a set of facts. The writing style and format of the passages varies considerably from problem to problem. In addition, the content of the passages covers a broad spectrum of topics.

2. A question dealing with the argument or the information stated in the passage. There are only eight basic question types, but there is extensive variation in the way in which each type is phrased.

3. Five answer choices, from which you are to choose the *best*.

Here are two typical examples:

Example 5-1

Eighty percent of the homeless people interviewed in a recent survey said that they prefer to eat and sleep on the streets rather than go to shelters. Surprisingly, this survey proves that contrary to popular opinion, homeless people prefer the discomfort and uncertainty of life on the streets to the comfort and security afforded by shelters.

Which of the following, if true, would cast most doubt on the conclusion of the above argument?

(A) Some of the persons interviewed in the survey possessed warm clothing and adequate sleeping bags.

(B) The survey was conducted in several small rural communities.

(C) The only question asked in the survey was: "Which do you prefer more, eating and sleeping on the streets or eating and sleeping in shelters?"

(D) The survey was conducted by a person who was also homeless.

(E) The survey was conducted concurrently in several different metropolitan communities during the winter.

Example 5-2

Politician: In opposition to the proposed reforms in welfare assistance, my esteemed colleague argues that children of welfare mothers ought to be sent to orphanages rather than remain a source of income for their work-dodging, lazy parents. My reply to him is that this is exactly the kind of argument we should expect from someone who abandoned his own children and left his wife penniless to fend for herself.

Which of the following argumentative techniques is employed by the politician in his reply to his esteemed colleague's argument?

(A) Drawing attention away from the real issue of the argument and focusing attention on a side issue

(B) Misrepresenting a person's argument for the purpose of making it easier to attack

(C) Questioning the motives of the person advancing the argument

(D) Attacking the character of the person advancing the argument rather than attacking the argument itself

(E) Attacking an argument on the grounds that the person making it is guilty of the very thing he or she is arguing against

STRATEGIES FOR DEALING WITH LOGICAL REASONING PROBLEMS

It's important to have a plan in mind before you begin any complex task. This is especially true when dealing with the Logical Reasoning questions on the LSAT. Knowing in advance how you will approach each problem is just as important as having the requisite knowledge to solve the problem. The following four-step approach will help you work through the test methodically and answer the questions with the greatest possible speed and accuracy.

Step One: Read the Question Stem Carefully

Identify the problem type. When reading the question stem (i.e., the question itself, apart from the passage and answer choices), try to determine which logical reasoning skill is being tested in the problem and decide what task needs to be performed to reach the answer. If you cannot quickly decide which skill is being tested, don't even bother reading the passage; just move on to the next problem. Since each problem is independent of any other, there is no need to proceed sequentially through the test. In fact, there are potential disadvantages to proceeding in this manner; the most significant being a loss of valuable time and a loss of confidence in your abilities. The best way to gain confidence and use your time effectively is to skip the problems you find to be difficult and focus initially on those you find to be easy. Also, since some tasks require more time to perform than others, consider doing those that take less time first, even if you feel confident in your ability to handle the problem.

Follow directions carefully. Pay close attention to any special directions mentioned in the question. For example, if the question directs you to assume that the information stated in the passage is true, do so even if some or all of it appears to you to be false. Or, if the question directs you to assume that each of the answers is true, do so even if they state something that you believe is false.

Step Two: Read the Passage Carefully

Identify the premise(s) and the conclusion. With the task firmly in mind, read the passage very carefully. What you look for when reading the passage depends entirely upon what task is to be performed. In most cases, however, it is important to begin by determining which statements in the passage are *premises* of the argument and which is the *conclusion*. Once you do this, it's a good idea to underline the key words in the premises and conclusion, leaving out as much of the unnecessary verbiage as possible.

Pay attention to key words. You must pay careful attention to detail when reading the passage, and you must confine your understanding of the topic under discussion to the information stated in the passage unless specifically directed otherwise. In other words, pay very close attention to facts, numbers, percentages, and the stated relationships between them, and do not make superfluous assumptions or draw unwarranted conclusions. Pay particular attention to words and phrases that have logical meanings. Words like "all," "some," "none," "most," and phrases like "only if" and "given that" signify logical relationships that are crucial to understanding the reasoning in an argument.

Put your knowledge of the topic aside. If you are knowledgeable about the topic of the passage, don't quarrel with the stated information. Put your knowledge of the topic aside and treat the topic as though you knew nothing whatsoever about it other than what is stated in the passage. It is extremely important that you focus on the *logic* of the argument rather than on the *content* of the argument. Never choose an answer simply because you happen to believe that it is true or because you agree with it, and conversely, never reject an answer simply because you believe that it is false or because you disagree with it. Keep this in mind: Logical Reasoning questions test your ability to recognize correct and incorrect reasoning; they do *not* test your knowledge of the topic under discussion. Remember this too: An argument can employ correct reasoning even if all of the statements in the argument are *false*, and conversely, an argument can employ incorrect reasoning even if all of the statements in the argument are *true*.

Step Three: Read the Answers Carefully

When choosing your answer, it is important to keep in mind the directions stated at the beginning of the test. Remember, unless otherwise instructed, "you are to choose the *best* answer; that is, the response that most accurately and completely answers the question." If you don't know the answer or none appears to you to be the best, then narrow down the alternatives by eliminating those that appear to be the *worst* answers and make a guess. Never leave a problem on which you have spent time without selecting an answer. If you have time at the end of the test, you can always come back and change your answer if you find a better one.

Step Four: Go Back to Skipped Problems

Once you have worked your way through the entire section, return to the problems you skipped and spend the remaining time working on them. Check the time and divide it evenly among the skipped problems. Make sure that you answer every problem, even if you have to guess. Remember, there is no penalty for wrong answers. When making guesses, always eliminate the worst answers first, then choose from the ones remaining. Doing this will greatly enhance your odds of getting the right answer. It's a good idea to flag skipped problems so that you can return to them quickly. An easy way to do this is just to write a big "S" next to the problem number in the test booklet.

MANAGING YOUR TIME

The advice in the strategies discussed above can be summed up in two simple maxims:

- Know what you're looking for before you go looking.

and,

- If you're unsure of how to find what you're looking for, don't waste time looking.

This is important advice in light of the fact that you have an average of only eighty-five seconds to come up with the correct answer for a problem. Of course, this does not mean that you can or should spend only eighty-five seconds on each problem, but it does serve to highlight the importance of wise time management.

The first maxim points out the importance of being methodical in your approach to each problem. One obvious reason for this is that it saves time. The second maxim points out the importance of making the best use of your time in handling a problem. More specifically, the importance of not letting yourself get bogged down. The fact is some questions on the test are much harder than others. Moreover, there is no pattern in the difficulty level of the problems; the first problem on the test might be difficult and the last one easy or the other way around. This means that you may have to skip a few questions in order to finish in time. It also means that you are going to have to develop a strict schedule and keep close track of time. Basically your pacing should be 6–7 problems every 9 minutes in order to finish the test. Given this, it's a good idea to check the clock every 9 minutes to see how you are doing. If you're ahead of schedule, don't slack off; if you're behind schedule, don't panic. In other words, try to keep as even a pace as possible.

APPLYING THE STRATEGIES

Let's try applying these strategies to Example 5-1 on page 36.

First, read the question. Ask yourself, "Which logical reasoning skill is being tested in this problem?" Once you have decided, ask yourself, "What is the task?"

Which of the following, if true, would cast most doubt on the conclusion of the above argument?

This problem tests your ability to assess the effect of additional information on an argument. The task in this case is to find a statement that weakens the argument; that is, one that makes it less likely that the conclusion is true. Notice that the question directs you to assume that the statements in the answers are true.

Second, read the passage. To solve this particular problem you are going to have to figure out which of the statements in the passage is the

conclusion and which is the premise. This isn't hard to do in this case. List the premise first, followed by the conclusion.

> **Premise:** Eighty percent of the homeless people interviewed in a recent survey said that they prefer to eat and sleep on the streets rather than go to shelters.
>
> **Conclusion:** Homeless people prefer the discomfort and uncertainty of life on the streets to the comfort and security afforded by shelters.

Notice that the unnecessary verbiage in the passage has been eliminated in the above restatement of the argument.

In this argument, data gathered from a survey are offered in support of a general claim. Notice that the conclusion refers to *all* homeless people, not merely some of them. Notice also that only eighty percent of the homeless people interviewed agree with the conclusion. It's pretty clear from these two observations that the data gathered by the survey are going to have to be drawn from a sample that is sufficiently large and representative to support the inference in the argument. Any answer suggesting that the data are drawn from a sample that is *not* representative of the entire homeless community will cast doubt on the conclusion.

You may have noticed that this argument is flawed in that it draws a conclusion that is more general than is warranted by the premise. That is, to put it simply, the conclusion is too strong, given the evidence. A more appropriate conclusion, given the evidence, would be that *most* homeless people would rather eat and sleep on the streets than to go to a shelter. The fact that this argument is flawed in this way, however, is irrelevant to the question that is being asked in this case. The question does not ask you to criticize the argument; it asks you to assess the effect additional information would have on the argument.

Third, read the answers. Remember, you are looking for an answer which suggests that the data gathered in the survey are drawn from a sample that is *not* representative of the entire homeless community. Remember also, that you are looking for the *best* answer which does this.

(A) Some of the persons interviewed in the survey possessed warm clothing and adequate sleeping bags.

Response (A) does not suggest that the data are drawn from a sample that is not representative of the entire homeless community. In fact, (A) states something that we should expect to be the case if the sample is in fact representative of the entire homeless community. Had (A) stated that all or most or none of those interviewed possessed warm clothing and adequate sleeping bags, this would suggest that the sample was not representative, but this is not what (A) asserts. Eliminate answer (A).

(B) The survey was conducted in several small rural communities.

Response (B) suggests that the data are drawn from a sample that is not representative of the entire homeless community. After all, small rural communities are significantly different from large metropolitan communities, and these differences could bias the sample considerably. Keep answer (B), but look to see whether there is a better answer.

(C) The only question asked in the survey was: "Which do you prefer more, eating and sleeping on the streets or eating and sleeping in shelters?"

Response (C) does not suggest that the data are drawn from a sample that is not representative of the entire homeless community. (C) suggests that the survey may be unreliable because of the way in which the question was phrased, but it does not undermine the representativeness of the sample. Eliminate answer (C).

(D) The survey was conducted by a person who was also homeless.

Response (D) does not suggest that the data are drawn from a sample that is not representative of the entire homeless community. Clearly, the fact that the person conducting the survey was homeless does not, by itself, call the representativeness of the sample into question. Eliminate answer (D).

(E) The survey was conducted concurrently in several different metropolitan communities during the winter.

Response (E) suggests that the data are drawn from a sample that is representative of the entire homeless community. Moreover, the fact that the survey was conducted during the winter gives even greater credence to the results. Rather than weaken the argument, (E) would strengthen it considerably. Eliminate answer (E).

Mark response (B) on your answer sheet. It is the *best* answer of the given choices.

Notice that many of the answer choices were "sucker bait"; in this example answers (A), (C), and (D). Had you not first identified the task, then focused clearly on the task when reading the passage, chances are you would have selected one of these as the correct answer. The moral is: Know what you are looking for before you go looking—it pays.

REVIEW OF THE LOGICAL CONCEPTS PRESUPPOSED ON THE TEST

The LSAT Logical Reasoning questions do not presuppose knowledge of the terminology of formal logic. Specialized terms such as "syllogism," "valid," and "*modus ponens*" will not be used in asking questions. There are, however, some basic concepts that you will be expected to understand. The primary expectation is that you will be able to understand and critique the reasoning contained in arguments. To do this requires, at a minimum, that you understand basic concepts such as argument, issue, premise, conclusion, main point, and assumption. Following is a brief discussion of each of these fundamental concepts.

The Concept of Argument

The word "argument" can be used in two quite different ways. When we say that two or more people are "having an argument" or "are arguing," we mean merely that there is a discussion going on in which the participants disagree about some topic. This is not the sense of "argument" intended in LSAT Logical Reasoning questions. In this context, to argue is to offer reasons in support of the truth of some claim or the correctness of some action. Since these reasons and the claim they are intended to support are expressed in statements, an *argument* can be characterized as a set of statements; the statements that express the reasons are called *premises*; those that express claims that are supported by reasons are called *conclusions*.

The *topic* or subject of an argument is simply what the argument is about (e.g., censorship). The *issue* of an argument is the question that is being addressed on the topic (e.g., Does national security justify censorship?). The *main point* of an argument is the particular claim or position on the issue that the author argues for (e.g., National security does not justify censorship). The main point is typically expressed in the conclusion of the argument.

Unstated Premises

An argument may have any number of premises, but it must have at least one. Some of the premises of an argument might be unstated. Unstated premises in arguments are referred to as *assumptions*. Assumptions are statements that fill logical gaps in the stated argument. They are left unstated in most cases because the author believes that they are obvious or that they express claims that the audience already accepts as true or correct. Consider the following example:

Example 5-3

Abortion is morally wrong for the simple reason that murder is morally wrong.

The argument in Example 5-3 can be rewritten as follows:

Premise: Murder is morally wrong.

Conclusion: Abortion is morally wrong.

The unstated premise that fills the logical gap in this argument is the statement: "Abortion is murder." This statement is an assumption in the argument.

Intermediate vs. Final Conclusions

An argument may have any number of conclusions, but it must have at least one. In complex arguments that have more than one conclusion, some will be *intermediate* conclusions and one will be the *final conclusion*. Intermediate conclusions function as reasons

in support of the final conclusion. That is, they are claims that are supported by reasons that in turn become reasons to support the final claim in the argument. Consider the following example:

Example 5-4

Sexual harassment against women is often fostered by economic motives, since women generally have greater difficulty in finding jobs, and hence can be intimidated more easily.

The argument in Example 5-4 has two conclusions. The claim "[Women] can be intimidated more easily," is an intermediate conclusion supported by the statement "Women generally have greater difficulty in finding jobs." In the argument above, this intermediate conclusion in turn becomes a reason for the final conclusion that is stated in the first part of the sentence.

Example 5-4 can be rewritten to explicitly reveal its structure as follows:

Premise: Women generally have greater difficulty in finding jobs.

Intermediate Conclusion: Women can be intimidated more easily than men.

Final Conclusion: Sexual harassment against women is often fostered by economic motives.

Unstated Conclusions

The final conclusion or main point of an argument isn't always explicitly stated. Since it is a powerful rhetorical ploy to let readers reach the conclusion on their own, writers often leave it unstated. In these cases, however, the author usually presents the reasons in such a way that there is really only one obvious conclusion that can be drawn from them. This implicit conclusion, even though unstated in the argument, is the main point or final conclusion of the argument. Consider the following example:

Example 5-5

Sexual preference is not something over which persons have control. To hold a person accountable for something over which he or she has no control is irrational.

In Example 5-5, the implicit conclusion to be drawn is that it is irrational to hold a person accountable for his or her sexual preference. This conclusion, while unstated, is clearly implied by the passage. Example 5-5 can be rewritten to explicitly reveal its structure as follows:

Premise: Sexual preference is not something over which persons have control.

Premise: Holding a person accountable for something over which he or she has no control is irrational.

Unstated Conclusion: It is irrational to hold a person accountable for his or her sexual preference.

WHAT'S NEXT?

You'll learn more about Logical Reasoning in Days 6, 16, and 17. Each of these lessons focuses on the Logical Reasoning skills tested on the LSAT. Each one will teach you how to recognize which skill is being tested in any given problem and how to perform the task associated with that skill as quickly and easily as possible.

Logical Reasoning Lesson 2: Basic Logical Reasoning Skills

Today you will learn the first four of the eight basic Logical Reasoning skills listed in Day 5.

Today's Topics

1. Identifying the main point or conclusion of an argument
2. Making inferences from given premises
3. Detecting assumptions involved in an argument
4. Assessing the effect of additional information on an argument

IDENTIFYING THE MAIN POINT OR CONCLUSION OF AN ARGUMENT

The ability to identify premises and conclusions of arguments correctly is essential to answering almost all of the Logical Reasoning questions on the LSAT. Because of this, it is a skill that warrants close attention and complete mastery, even though only a small percentage (5–8 percent) of all Logical Reasoning questions test this skill directly.

Conclusion questions are typically worded as follows:

- Which of the following best expresses the main point of the passage?

- The conclusion of the argument is best expressed by which of the following?

The main point of an argument is typically expressed by the final conclusion of the argument. In arguments that contain more than one conclusion, the final conclusion is the statement that is supported by other statements but does not itself support any other statement; intermediate conclusions are statements that are supported by other statements and that, in turn, support further statements.

Look for Indicator Words and Phrases

In most cases, the conclusion of an argument can be quickly identified simply by paying close attention to key words and phrases in the passage. Here are some words and phrases commonly used to indicate that the sentence that follows is a conclusion:

therefore	entails that	allows us to infer that
shows that	as a result	hence
consequently	it follows that	proves that
implies that	so	it is likely that
thus	suggests that	demonstrates that

In cases where the above words and phrases are absent, it is possible to identify the conclusion by first identifying the premises and then looking for the sentence they are intended to support. Here are some words and phrases commonly used to indicate that the sentence that follows is a premise:

since	for	because
inasmuch as	follows from	given that
is suggested by	is proved by	for the reason that
is entailed by	assuming that	is substantiated by
is shown by	as a result	on the supposition that

Let's look at a few examples to see how these words and phrases can help you identify the conclusion of an argument.

Example 6-1

Einstein is as great a cult figure as Madonna, *so* T-shirts with Einstein's picture on them will sell as well as shirts with Madonna's picture.

Example 6-2

Since Einstein is as great a cult figure as Madonna, T-shirts with Einstein's picture on them will sell as well as shirts with Madonna's picture.

In Example 6-1 the word "so" indicates the conclusion; in Example 6-2 the word "since" indicates the premise. The argument in each of these examples is identical and can be rewritten as follows:

Premise: Einstein is as great a cult figure as Madonna.

Conclusion: T-shirts with Einstein's picture on them will sell as well as shirts with Madonna's picture.

Here's a more complicated example:

Example 6-3

Inasmuch as Einstein is as great a cult figure as Madonna, *it is likely that* T-shirts with Einstein's picture on them will sell as well as shirts with Madonna's picture, *so* we should add them to our inventory.

Each of the three italicized expressions in Example 6-3 is an indicator. The first indicates a premise, the other two indicate conclusions. The final conclusion is indicated by the word "so." The intermediate conclusion is indicated by the phrase

"it is likely that." This argument can be rewritten to reveal its structure as follows:

Premise: Einstein is as great a cult figure as Madonna.

Intermediate conclusion: T-shirts with Einstein's picture on them will sell as well as shirts with Madonna's picture.

Final conclusion: We should add T-shirts with Einstein's picture on them to our inventory.

Look for Rhetorical Questions

In addition to the indicator expressions listed above, another common way of signaling the conclusion of an argument is to express it as a rhetorical question or as an answer to a rhetorical question. The purpose of such questions is not to solicit information, but rather to emphatically express a particular point or to raise a particular issue. Rhetorical questions typically (but not always) appear at the very beginning of the passage. The remaining sentences in the passage are typically premises that support a position on the issue encompassed by the rhetorical question. Consider the following example:

Example 6-4

Can anyone really deny that abortion is morally wrong? After all, killing humans is wrong, and abortion is just another way of killing a human.

The rhetorical question in Example 6-4 leaves little doubt about the author's position on this issue. The way in which the question is posed clearly indicates that, at least for the author, this is not an open question. Generally speaking, the more sarcastic the tone of the question the more obvious the author's position on the issue encompassed by the question. The converse of this is generally the case as well. The conclusion of the argument in Example 6-4 is simply a restatement of the rhetorical question expressed in the first sentence, specifically, abortion is morally wrong. The remaining sentences in Example 6-4 are premises that support this conclusion. The argument in Example 6-4 can be rewritten as follows:

Premise: Killing humans is wrong.

Premise: Abortion is just another way of killing a human.

Conclusion: Abortion is morally wrong.

Here's another example:

Example 6-5

Is abortion morally wrong or not? I would answer "no!" because while killing humans is morally wrong, abortion kills a fetus, and a fetus is not a human being.

The first sentence in Example 6-5 is a rhetorical question that raises the issue the author wishes to address. Next, the author indicates which side of this issue will be argued for—specifically, that abortion is not morally wrong. This is the conclusion of the argument. The remaining statements in Example 6-5 are intended as reasons in support of this claim. In this example, it is not obvious from the question itself which side of the issue the author will argue for. The way in which the question is posed indicates that this is an open question at least initially. In cases like this, you will have to read on to find out which side of the issue the author will argue for. The argument in Example 6-5 can be rewritten as follows:

Premise: Killing humans is morally wrong.

Premise: A fetus is not a human being.

Premise: Abortion kills a fetus.

Conclusion: Abortion is not morally wrong.

Passages That Contain No Indicator Expressions and No Rhetorical Questions

In passages that contain no indicator expressions and no rhetorical questions, it is much more difficult to figure out which sentence is the conclusion. One way to proceed is to add indicator words to the passage and determine whether the result makes sense to you. Consider the following example:

Example 6-6

There is a lot more to being an actress than having a pretty face. One has to learn how to move correctly. One has to learn how to project one's voice. One must learn how to speak clearly.

A plausible interpretation of the passage is that the author is giving reasons for the claim expressed in the first sentence. This interpretation is arrived at simply by adding the word "since" to the beginning of the second sentence. According to this interpretation, the argument goes as follows:

There is a lot more to being an actress than having a pretty face, *since*: (1) one has to learn how to move correctly, (2) one has to learn how to project one's voice, and (3) one must learn how to speak clearly.

When dealing with passages in which the conclusion is unstated, the best way to proceed is to ask yourself what the author is trying to establish in the passage. Consider the following example:

Example 6-7

When we regard a person to be morally responsible for her actions, we regard her as being the object of praise or blame with respect to those actions. But it seems evident that a person cannot be the object of praise or blame for her actions unless she performed them of her own free will.

What is the author working toward or trying to establish? Asking this question while reading the passage will lead you to the conclusion of the passage. In this case, the unstated conclusion is that people are only morally responsible for actions that they perform of their own free will.

Checklist for Identifying a Main Point or Conclusion

Here's a brief summary of the procedure for identifying the main point or conclusion of an argument.

1. Scan the passage looking for conclusion and/or premise indicator words or phrases. These words and phrases provide important clues to the author's organizational scheme. Typically you are looking for the final conclusion of the argument, so in arguments with more than one conclusion, determine which sentences lead to or support other sentences in the passage. The final conclusion will be the one that is supported by others but does not itself support any others.

2. Alternatively, look for a rhetorical question in the passage—typically it will appear at the very beginning. The main point will be either a restatement of this question or a direct answer to this question. If the author's position on the issue addressed in the question is not obvious from the way in which the question is asked, a quick scan of the passage will usually tell you which side of the issue the author is supporting.

3. If there are no indicator expressions and no rhetorical questions in the passage, the best way to proceed is to ask yourself: "What is the author trying to establish in the passage?"

MAKING INFERENCES FROM GIVEN PREMISES

Inference questions test your ability to draw conclusions from the information stated in the passage; that is, your ability to determine what else *must* be true or *is likely* to be true, given that the statements in the passage are true. In problems of this type, the information in the passage functions as the premises of the argument, and the conclusions are found among the answer choices. In answering these questions keep in mind the admonition against making implausible, superfluous, or incompatible assumptions. You are, however, to assume that the information stated in the passage is true, even if you do not agree with it or believe that it is false.

Types of Inference Questions

Inference questions are typically worded as follows:

- If all of the statements in the passage are true, which one of the following must also be true?

- Which one of the following conclusions is most strongly supported by the statements in the passage?

- Which of the following statements can be properly inferred from the passage?

Notice that there are three basic types of questions: (1) those that ask for the conclusion that *must be true* given the information in the passage, (2) those that ask for the conclusion that is *most strongly supported* given the information in the passage, and (3) those that ask for the conclusion that can be *properly drawn or inferred* from the passage.

The difference between the first two types of questions is significant. The conclusion that must be true given the information stated in the passage is the one that cannot conceivably be false, given this information. The conclusion that is most strongly supported by the information stated in the passage is the one that is most unlikely to be false (i.e., most likely to be true), given this information.

Questions that ask for what can be "properly inferred" or "properly drawn" from the passage are somewhat tricky. Strictly speaking, for an inference to be "proper" it must be made in accordance with acceptable inference rules or meet certain standards of acceptable inference. In the case of *deductive* reasoning, these rules and standards are designed to ensure that the truth of the premises *guarantees* the truth of the conclusion, whereas in the case of *inductive* reasoning they are designed to ensure that the truth of the premises makes it *highly likely* that the conclusion is true. Without getting bogged down with too many details here, the upshot is that questions that ask for what can "properly" be inferred or drawn from the statements in a passage can be understood in two ways. They can be understood as asking either for the conclusion that must be true, or for the conclusion that is most strongly supported.

Without training in formal logic you pretty much have to "fly by the seat of your pants" when dealing with these problems. Saying this, however, doesn't mean that you should just guess on these problems. There are some definite guidelines or procedures that you will want to follow.

Dealing with "Must Be True" Inference Questions

Here's the procedure for dealing with questions that ask you to find the statement that *must be true* given the information stated in the passage.

1. Read the passage very carefully. If necessary, underline the premises (or list them on separate lines) leaving out any unnecessary verbiage.

2. Read each of the answers, and ask yourself whether it can conceivably be false given that the sentences in the passage are true.

3. The correct answer is the one that cannot conceivably be false given the information stated in the passage.

To illustrate this procedure let's look at a simple example:

Example 6-8

Cheating on your taxes is lying, and lying, as we all know, is morally wrong.

If the statements in the passage are true, which one of the following must also be true?

(A) Cheating on your taxes is illegal.

(B) Cheating is morally wrong.

(C) Cheating on your taxes is morally wrong.

(D) Lying is cheating.

(E) Cheating is immoral.

First, read the passage very carefully. Underline the premises leaving out the unnecessary verbiage as follows:

Cheating on your taxes is lying, and lying, as we all know, is morally wrong.

Second, read each answer in turn and determine whether it can conceivably be false, given the information stated in the premises. The correct answer is the one that cannot conceivably be false, given this information.

Could (A) conceivably be false given the stated information? The answer is "yes" because the given information does not explicitly mention anything about what is legal or illegal. Remember, don't make *any* assumptions beyond what is explicitly stated in the passage.

Could (B) conceivably be false given the stated information? Again, the answer is "yes" because the given information does not tell us that *all kinds* of cheating are lying. It tells us only that a particular kind of cheating is lying (i.e., cheating on your taxes).

Could (C) conceivably be false given the stated information? In this case the answer is "no" because if all tax cheating is lying and all lying is morally

wrong, then all tax cheating *must* be morally wrong. Response (C) is the correct answer.

Once you have found an answer that must be true given the information there is no need to go on and look at the rest. It is the correct answer. Simply record it and go on to the next problem.

Here's a slightly more complicated example:

Example 6-9

All professors are outgoing and all outgoing people are popular, but even so some introverts are professors.

If the above statements are true, which one of the following must also be true?

(A) All popular people are outgoing.

(B) All outgoing people are professors.

(C) Some introverts are popular.

(D) No introverts are professors.

(E) No introverts are popular.

First, read the passage very carefully. Underline the premises leaving out the unnecessary verbiage as follows:

All professors are outgoing and all outgoing people are popular, but even so some introverts are professors.

Next, read each of the answers, and ask yourself whether it can conceivably be false, given that the underlined sentences are true.

Could (A) conceivably be false, given the information stated in the premises? The answer is "yes" because the passage states that all outgoing people are popular, and it is consistent with this that not all popular people are outgoing.

Could (B) conceivably be false, given the information stated in the premises? The answer is "yes" because the passage states that all professors are outgoing people, and it is consistent with this that not all outgoing people are professors.

Could (C) conceivably be false, given the information stated in the premises? The answer is "no" because if all professors are outgoing and all outgoing people are popular, then it must be true that all professors are popular. Moreover, if all professors are popular and some introverts are professors, then it must be true that some introverts are popular. Response (C) is the correct answer.

A variation of this type of question asks not for the single statement that must be true, but rather for the answer that is the exception (i.e., the statement that need not be true given the stated information). In this case, the question is worded as follows:

If the above statements are true, all of the following statements must also be true EXCEPT:

In this version of the question, four of the five answer choices must be true and only one need not be true. Your job is to find the one that need not be true given the information in the passage. The procedure for dealing with this type of question is the same as above. The only difference is the correct answer will be the one that could conceivably be false given the stated information.

Dealing with "Most Strongly Supported" Inference Questions

Here's the procedure for dealing with questions that ask you to find the statement that is *most strongly supported* given the information stated in the passage.

1. Read the passage very carefully. If necessary, underline the premises (or list them on separate lines) leaving out any unnecessary verbiage.

2. Read each of the answers, and determine how likely it is to be true given the information stated in the passage. Use a simple 4-point scale to score each of the answers (e.g., 1 = very unlikely, 2 = not very likely, 3 = somewhat likely, 4 = very likely).

3. The correct answer is the one that gets the highest score.

To illustrate this procedure, consider the following example:

Example 6-10

Dogs taken to humane shelters are routinely checked for rabies. The dog that bit the little boy was obtained from the humane shelter just a day before it bit the boy.

If the statements in the passage are true, which of the following is most strongly supported?

(A) The humane shelter technicians never make mistakes when testing dogs for rabies.

(B) The dog contracted rabies after it was released from the shelter but before it bit the boy.

(C) The dog does not have rabies.

(D) The little boy has rabies.

(E) The humane shelter technicians are incompetent.

With the information stated in the passage in mind, rank each answer using the 4-point scale.

The score for (A) is 2. Response (A) is not very likely because the information in the passage really doesn't address itself to the issue of whether or not the testing procedures are reliable.

The score for (B) is 2. While it is possible that the dog contracted rabies during this brief period, without additional information it is difficult to assess the likelihood that this is the case.

The score for (C) is 4. The fact that the dog was tested for rabies just a short time before the incident makes it very likely that the dog was not rabid at the time of the incident.

The score for (D) is 1. The likelihood that (D) is true is a function of the likelihood that (C) is true, so if it is very likely that the dog does not have rabies, then it is very unlikely that the little boy has rabies.

The score for (E) is 2. While it is possible that the technicians are incompetent, the stated information does not support that claim.

Looking back over the scores, response (C) is most strongly supported; thus (C) is the correct answer.

Dealing with "Properly Inferred" Inference Questions

The procedure above can also be used for dealing with questions that ask you to find the statement that is *properly inferred* from the information in the passage by simply expanding the 4-point scale to a 5-point scale, letting 5 equal "must be true."

DETECTING ASSUMPTIONS INVOLVED IN AN ARGUMENT

An *assumption of an argument* is a statement that is not expressed in the argument but that must be true if the conclusion is to be true. Put simply, it's a missing piece of information that is required to support the conclusion.

In looking for the assumptions in an argument, you can use the author's stated information as a guide to the author's hidden assumptions. Typically, hidden assumptions in arguments serve to connect key ideas in the author's reasoning. Authors fail to state these ideas explicitly because they believe that their audience already accepts them or that they are too obvious to state.

Problems of this type make up roughly 12 percent of the Logical Reasoning questions on the LSAT, so you can expect to see at least three assumption questions on each of the two Logical Reasoning sections in the exam.

Assumption questions are typically worded as follows:

- The conclusion of the argument is properly drawn if which one of the following is assumed?

- For the argument to be logically correct, it must make which of the following assumptions?

- Which one of the following is an assumption upon which the argument in the passage depends?

- Which of the following is a presupposition in the argument?

The exact conditions that must be satisfied for an argument to be "logically correct," or for the conclusion to be "properly drawn," will be different, depending upon the argument type. As a general rule, however, the more unlikely it is for the conclusion to be false given that the premises are true, the more "logically correct" the argument. Since this is the case, when looking for an assumption that will make the argument logically correct, you are looking for a statement that, when taken with the stated premises, will significantly increase the likelihood that the conclusion is true. Moreover, given a selection of possible assumptions, the one that increases this likelihood the most will be the best candidate.

Consider the following brief argument:

Example 6-11

All humans have inherent worth; this is why they have an inalienable right to privacy.

This argument can be rewritten as follows:

Premise: All people have inherent worth.

Conclusion: All people have an inalienable right to privacy.

As it stands, the above argument is not compelling; that is, the stated premise does not, by itself, ensure that the conclusion is true or even that it is highly likely to be true. The assumption required to make this argument logically correct must fill this logical gap. Moreover, to fill the logical gap the assumption must connect the key ideas in the argument in such a way that it is either impossible, or (if this cannot be achieved) highly unlikely for the conclusion to be false, given the stated premise. In Example 6-11, the logical gap in the argument can be filled with the following statement: Anything that has inherent worth has an inalienable right to privacy. Adding this statement to the argument ensures that the conclusion is true, given that the premises are true—as is clearly demonstrated in the following reconstruction of the argument.

Assumption: Anything that has inherent worth has an inalienable right to privacy.

Premise: All people have inherent worth.

Conclusion: All people have an inalienable right to privacy.

Consider another brief argument:

Example 6-12

John stays at home whenever he is sick, so, he's probably at home.

This argument can be rewritten as follows:

Premise: If John is sick, then he'll stay at home.

Conclusion: John is probably at home.

For the conclusion to be properly drawn in Example 6-12, additional information is needed. The information required to increase the likelihood that the conclusion is true is that John is probably sick. As is evident in the following reconstruction of the argument, adding this statement to the argument increases the likelihood that the conclusion is true given that the premises are true:

Assumption: John is probably sick.

Premise: If John is sick, then he'll stay at home.

Conclusion: John is probably at home.

Here's the procedure for finding assumptions:

1. Identify the premises and the conclusion of the argument. To help keep things straight, it's a good idea to underline the premises and the conclusion (marking premises with a "P," and the conclusion with a "C") or list them on separate lines, placing the premises above the conclusion.

2. Locate the logical gap in the argument. It will usually be obvious that something is missing because the argument just won't "make sense." That is, it will seem to you that the stated reasons, by themselves, just don't completely support the conclusion. Once you have located the logical gap between the premises and the conclusion, all you have to do is figure out what additional information would be required to fill it. Ask yourself the following question:

What additional information would be required to ensure the truth of the conclusion?

To illustrate this procedure, let's look at an example in the style of an LSAT problem.

Example 6-13

Captive animals exhibit a wider range of physical and behavioral traits than animals in the wild, and this is why researchers who study them are able to study a wider range of genetic possibilities than researchers who study wild animals.

For this argument to be logically correct, it must make which one of the following assumptions?

(A) Animals that are captive exhibit a wider range of physical and behavioral traits than animals that are wild.

(B) Animals that permit researchers to study a wide range of genetic possibilities are better research subjects than animals that do not.

(C) The wider the range of the physical and behavioral traits in a population of animals, the greater the range of their genetic possibilities.

(D) Captive animals are studied more than wild animals.

(E) Animals in the wild exhibit a narrow range of physical and behavioral traits.

The argument in the passage can be rewritten as follows:

Premise: Captive animals exhibit a wider range of physical and behavioral traits than animals in the wild.

Conclusion: Researchers who study captive animals are able to study a wider range of genetic possibilities than researchers who study wild animals.

In this argument, there is an obvious logical gap between the premise and the conclusion. The assumption required to fill this gap can be determined simply by asking what information in addition to the stated premise would be required to ensure that the conclusion is true. In this instance, a little thought reveals that the required information must link the range of physical and behavioral traits with the range of genetic possibilities. Moreover, they must be linked such that the wider the range of physical and behavioral traits, the wider the range of genetic possibilities. Turning to the answer choices with this in mind, it is obvious that (C) is the best choice.

To sum up: To find an assumption that will make the argument logically correct, look for a statement that connects key ideas in the argument in such a way that when this statement is added to the stated premises of the argument the conclusion of the argument either cannot be false or the likelihood of its being false is greatly diminished.

ASSESSING THE EFFECT OF ADDITIONAL INFORMATION ON AN ARGUMENT

Questions of this type begin with a passage that contains an argument. Your job is to assess the effect additional information has on the argument. There are basically just two types of problems: (1) those which ask you to select the answer that will *strengthen* the argument and (2) those that ask you to select the answer that will *weaken* the argument. Of the 25 problems in a typical Logical Reasoning section of the LSAT exam, roughly 20 percent will test your ability to assess the effect of additional information on an argument, so you can expect to see at least five of these problems on each of the two Logical Reasoning sections in the exam.

Additional-information-assessment (AIA) questions are worded in a large variety of ways. To avoid confusion it is important to remember that there are just two types of problems: strengthen problems and weaken problems. The following lists of questions illustrate the various ways these two types can be expressed.

Questions that ask you to select the choice that *weakens* the argument may be worded as follows:

- Which of the following, if true, would refute the argument in the passage?

- Which one of the following, if true, casts the most doubt on the argument?

- Which one of the following, if accepted by the author, would require him to reconsider his conclusion?

- Which of the following, if true, most seriously calls the conclusion above into question?

- The argument is most vulnerable to which of the following criticisms?

- Which of the following, if true, most seriously undermines the author's contention?

- Which of the following, if true, most substantially weakens the argument?

Questions that ask you to select the choice that *strengthens* the argument may be worded as follows:

- Which of the following, if true, most strengthens the argument?

- Which of the following would provide the most support for the conclusion above?

- Which of the following supports the conclusion in the above passage?

- The conclusion in the above argument would be more reasonable if which one of the following were true?

- Which of the following, if true, would confirm the author's conclusion?

- Which one of the following, if true, provides the most support for the argument?

Weakening an Argument

There are basically three ways to weaken an argument: (1) undermine a major assumption of the argument, (2) attack one of the premises of the argument, or (3) suggest an alternative conclusion that can be inferred from the given premises. In problems that ask you to choose a statement that will weaken an argument, the correct answer will do one of these three things. For this reason, it is important at the outset when working these problems to identify the premises, the conclusion, and the major assumption of the argument in the passage.

Here's the procedure to find the statement that will *weaken* an argument.

1. Identify the premises and the conclusion of the argument.

2. Identify the major assumption of the argument.

3. Look for an answer choice that:
   - undermines the major assumption, or
   - attacks a stated premise, or
   - suggests an alternative conclusion that could be inferred from the stated premises.

4. The correct answer is one that does any one of the above.

To illustrate this procedure, let's look at an example.

Example 6-14

Mountain lion sightings in outlying areas of Los Angeles have increased dramatically over the past two years. Hence, the population of mountain lions must be increasing.

Which of the following, if true, most effectively weakens the above argument?

(A) People have become more active in outdoor activities during the past two years.

(B) Mountain lion habitat has dramatically diminished over the past two years.

(C) Human population in the outlying areas of Los Angeles has dramatically increased over the past two years.

(D) There has been a dramatic increase in the number of television programs about mountain lions during the past two years.

(E) Reports of people and animals being killed by mountain lions have increased dramatically over the past two years.

The premise and conclusion of Example 6-14 are easy to identify; the premise is the first statement, and the conclusion is the statement that follows the word "hence." The major assumption in Example 6-14 is that the population of humans in the outlying areas of Los Angeles has remained relatively constant over the two year period. Given this assumption, an increase in sightings would strongly indicate an increase in the population of mountain lions. Without this assumption, however, the argument is weakened considerably. The answer choice that most directly challenges this assumption is (C); thus (C) is the correct answer.

Strengthening an Argument

There are two ways to strengthen an argument: (1) offer support for the major assumption of the argument, or (2) provide additional evidence for the conclusion (i.e., beyond what is stated in the given premises). In a problem that asks you to choose a statement that will strengthen an argument, the correct response will do one of these two things.

Here's the procedure to find the statement that will *strengthen* an argument.

1. Identify the premises and the conclusion of the argument.

2. Identify the major assumption of the argument.

3. Look for an answer choice that:

   • offers support for the major assumption, or

   • provides additional evidence for the conclusion.

4. The correct answer is one that does either of the above.

To illustrate this procedure, let's look at an example.

Example 6-15

The portrayal of violence on television and in movies has increased dramatically over the past ten years. It is primarily for this reason that we have seen a dramatic increase in the rate of violent crime during the last decade.

Which one of the following, if true, provides the most support for the argument?

(A) Liberal sentencing policies over the past ten years have resulted in reduced sentences for perpetrators of violent acts.

(B) Persons who commit violent acts are less prone to being influenced by portrayals of violence.

(C) Recent studies have shown that repeated exposure to portrayals of violence significantly increases the tendency to commit violent acts.

(D) There has been a dramatic increase in the number of homeless people during the last decade.

(E) Due to severe overcrowding during the past decade, prisons have been forced to release violent criminals before their full sentences were served.

The premise and conclusion in Example 6-15 are relatively easy to identify. The phrase "It is primarily for this reason that" indicates that the first sentence in the passage is the premise; the conclusion follows this phrase. The major assumption of the argument is that exposure to portrayals of violence results in violent acts. Answer choices (A), (D), and (E) state plausible alternative reasons for the increase in violence and, as such, might be considered as providing additional support for the conclusion. However, neither (A), (D), nor (E) directly support the argument's main contention that increased portrayal of violence is the "primary" reason for the increase in violent acts. Answer choice (B) weakens the argument since it undermines the major assumption of the argument, so it can be eliminated. Answer choice (C) supports the major assumption of the argument; thus (C) is the correct answer.

Day 7

Logical Reasoning Lesson 3: Mini-Test and Review

Today you will apply what you learned on Days 5 and 6 to a series of Logical Reasoning passages. Take the mini-test under timed conditions; then review the explanations that follow.

LOGICAL REASONING MINI-TEST

Number of questions: 14
Suggested time: 18 minutes

Directions (as printed in test booklet): The questions in this section are based on the reasoning contained in brief statements or passages. For some questions, more than one of the choices could conceivably answer the question. However, you are to choose the best answer; that is, the response that most accurately and completely answers the question. You should not make assumptions that are by commonsense standards implausible, superfluous, or incompatible with the passage.

1. Because animal liberationists place a higher value on protecting animals from harm than on protecting their autonomy, they cannot possibly be environmentalists. By insisting that we have a moral obligation to efficiently relieve animal suffering, animal liberationists are thereby committed to any plan that attains this goal. But this goal can be achieved most efficiently by converting our national parks and wilderness areas into humanely managed farms. The reasons for this are fairly obvious. The suffering of animals in the wild is unimaginable. Animal populations are violently managed by nature in a drama in which few individuals are spared injury or death. In comparison, animals live much longer and much less painful lives on the farm than in the wild. Any such plan, however, would be totally unacceptable to environmentalists since it would violate their guiding tenet that we have a moral obligation to preserve as much of the environment and its inhabitants in a natural state as is humanly possible.

The main point of the argument is best expressed by which of the following?

(A) The most efficient way to relieve the suffering of animals would be to convert our national parks and wilderness areas into humanely managed farms.

(B) Animal liberationists are committed to any plan that relieves animal suffering.

(C) Animal liberationism and environmentalism are incompatible.

(D) Animal liberationists place a higher value on protecting animals from harm than on protecting their autonomy.

(E) The plan of converting our national parks and wilderness areas into humanely managed farms would be totally unacceptable to environmentalists.

2. Is it wrong for doctors to lie about their patients' illnesses? Aren't doctors just like any other people we hire to do a job for us? Surely, we would not tolerate not being told the truth about the condition of our automobile from the mechanic we hired to fix it, or the condition of our roof from the carpenter we employed to repair it. Just as these workers would be guilty of violating their good faith contracts with us if they were to do this, doctors who lie to their patients about their illnesses violate these contracts as well, and this is clearly wrong.

The conclusion of the argument is best expressed by which of the following?

(A) Doctors who lie to their patients about their illnesses violate their good faith contracts with their patients.

(B) Doctors often lie to their patients about their illnesses.

(C) Doctors are just hired workers like mechanics and carpenters.

(D) It is wrong for doctors to lie about their patients' illnesses.

(E) Doctors, like mechanics and carpenters, enter into good faith contracts with us when we hire them.

3. Testifying before the Senate committee investigating charges that cigarette manufacturers had manipulated nicotine levels in cigarettes in order to addict consumers to their products, tobacco executives argued that cigarette smoking is not addictive. The primary reason they gave in support of this claim was that cigarette smoking was not regulated by the Federal Drug Administration.

For the tobacco executives' argument to be logically correct, which of the following must be assumed?

(A) Substances that are not addictive are not regulated by the Federal Drug Administration.

(B) Substances that are not regulated by the Federal Drug Administration are not addictive.

(C) Some addictive substances are not regulated by the Federal Drug Administration.

(D) There is no scientific proof that cigarette smoking is addictive.

(E) The tobacco executives lied when they claimed that cigarette smoking was not addictive.

4. *Sean:* I think the university orchestra's performance of Beethoven's symphony was terrible.

   Kelly: Why do you say that?

   Sean: Because the way they played it was not the way Beethoven intended it to be played.

What must be assumed for Sean's argument to be logically correct?

(A) Beethoven intended the symphony to be performed in a way different from the way the university orchestra performed it.

(B) Only the composer of a musical work knows how it should be performed.

(C) In general, university orchestras cannot perform Beethoven's symphony in the way it was intended to be performed.

(D) No performance of a composer's work that is not in keeping with the composer's original intention is a good performance.

(E) University orchestras lack the musical sophistication to do justice to Beethoven's symphony.

5. Nonhuman primates are excellent animal models for the study of human disease because of their close genetic relationship to humans. Indeed, comparisons of the chromosomes and DNA of nonhuman primates and humans reveals a startling similarity in their structure and primitive origin, and testifies to the commonality of the genetic material between these phylogenetically related species.

Which one of the following is an assumption upon which the argument depends?

(A) Animals that are related to humans make good models for studying human disease.

(B) The more commonality of the genetic material between two species the better one is as a model for studying the other.

(C) The more similar in structure and primitive origin of the chromosomes and DNA of species, the more commonalities in their genetic material.

(D) Phylogenetically related species make good models for studying one another.

(E) Nonhuman primates are closely related to humans.

6. A study of native-born residents in Oonaland found that two-thirds of the children developed considerable levels of nearsightedness after starting school, while their illiterate parents and grandparents, who had no opportunity for formal schooling, showed no signs of this disability.

If the above statements are true, which of the following conclusions is most strongly supported by them?

(A) The nearsightedness in the children is caused by the visual stress required by reading and other class work.

(B) People who are illiterate do not suffer from nearsightedness.

(C) Only people who have the opportunity for formal schooling develop nearsightedness.

(D) Only literate people are nearsighted.

(E) One-third of the children are illiterate.

7. Some of the most beautiful cars in the world are manufactured by Contempo Motors. Unfortunately however, Contempo cars are notoriously unreliable, and as everyone knows, unreliable cars are exasperating.

If the statements above are true, each of the following must also be true EXCEPT:

(A) Some of the world's most beautiful cars are exasperating.

(B) Contempo cars are exasperating.

(C) No Contempo cars are reliable.

(D) No reliable cars are exasperating.

(E) Some of the most beautiful cars in the world are unreliable.

8. The budget deficit will continue to grow unless taxes are raised soon. However, that's not going to happen in the foreseeable future. The upshot is that if the budget deficit continues to grow, the next generation of taxpayers will be burdened by an almost unbearable debt.

If the above statements are true, which of the following must be true?

(A) Taxes will be raised soon.

(B) The budget deficit will not continue to grow.

(C) The political climate will not change in the foreseeable future.

(D) The budget deficit will continue to grow but the next generation of taxpayers will not be burdened with an almost unbearable debt.

(E) The next generation of taxpayers will be burdened with an almost unbearable debt.

9. Compare the human fetus at any stage of pregnancy with a newborn lamb. While it is evident that there are obvious differences between them resulting from the fact that they belong to different animal species, they are similar in their capacities for pleasure and pain and in their levels of awareness and rationality. Yet, the value placed on the newborn lamb's life is quite low; so low in fact, that taking its life is a routine occurrence that happens everyday without protest.

Which one of the following is a conclusion that the statements above, if true, most strongly support?

(A) It is wrong to take the lives of newborn lambs.

(B) We should protest the practice of killing newborn lambs.

(C) The differences between newborn lambs and human fetuses far outweigh the similarities between them.

(D) We should not place a high value on the life of a human fetus.

(E) Placing a higher value on the life of a human fetus than on the life of a newborn lamb is completely justified.

10. There is clear evidence that the mandated use of safety seats by children under age four has resulted in fewer child fatalities over the past five years. Compared to the five-year period prior to the passage of laws requiring the use of safety seats, fatalities of children under age four have decreased by 30 percent.

Which one of the following, if true, most substantially strengthens the argument above?

(A) The number of serious automobile accidents involving children under age four has remained steady over the past five years.

(B) Automobile accidents involving children have decreased sharply over the past five years.

(C) The use of air bags in automobiles has increased by 30 percent over the past five years.

(D) Most fatal automobile accidents involving children under age four occur in the driveway of their home.

(E) The number of teenage drivers has increased by 30 percent over the past five years.

11. Nonpurebred horses are a better choice than purebred horses for potential horse owners who want to avoid costly medical bills. The main reason is that purebred horses are extremely susceptible to genetic abnormalities that can only be corrected by expensive surgery. Since nonpurebred horses rarely suffer from these problems, they are obviously the better choice.

Which of the following, if true, most seriously undermines the author's contention?

(A) All horses are prone to the same environmentally determined diseases.

(B) Purebred horses are, for the most part, more attractive than nonpurebred horses.

(C) Nonpurebred horses have significantly longer life spans than purebred horses.

(D) Most genetically caused abnormalities in horses are cosmetic and do not impair the horse's general health.

(E) The initial cost of a purebred horse is much greater than that of a nonpurebred horse.

12. Ten years ago the death rate from Neural Synapse Deficiency (NSD) related causes was 5 percent of all persons infected with the dreaded anti-synapse virus (ASV) that causes it. Today, the corresponding figure has risen to over 15 percent. This is clear evidence that over the past ten years the rate of propagation and the malignancy of the virus has increased substantially.

Which of the following, if true, most substantially strengthens the argument in the above passage?

(A) ASV screening and detection methods have been dramatically improved over the past decade.

(B) The number of ASV infected persons has increased tenfold over the past ten years.

(C) The number of persons who are willing to submit to ASV screening has increased significantly over the past ten years.

(D) The number of recognized NSD related causes of death has remained relatively constant over the past ten years.

(E) New drugs have been developed over the past ten years that significantly abate the debilitating effects of the NSD virus.

13. Lycopene, glutathione, and glutamine are powerful antioxidants that neutralize the free radicals that are produced in the body as a result of routine bodily processes. An excess of these free radicals in your system causes rapid aging because they accelerate the rate of cellular damage. Aging is simply the result of this damage. Thus, to slow down aging it is necessary to supplement your diet with these antioxidants on a daily basis.

Which of the following, if true, most seriously undermines the author's contention?

(A) Most persons aren't concerned with the effects of aging until it is too late to do anything about it.

(B) Exercise associated with normal daily activities effectively neutralizes and dissipates the free radicals that are produced as a result of routine bodily processes.

(C) The cost of antioxidants is exorbitantly high and well beyond the budget of most consumers.

(D) Only overweight people who do not exercise on a daily basis are likely to have an excess of free radicals in their systems.

(E) Smoking cigarettes is one of the main causes of cellular damage in humans.

14. Does having a large amount of money guarantee happiness? Results of a recent survey overwhelmingly confirm that having a sizable quantity of money is the key to happiness. In the survey, 78 percent of those who responded who also claimed that they possessed a large amount of money said that they were happy.

Which of the following, if true, most seriously calls the survey finding into doubt?

(A) No clear quantitative definition of "large amount of money" was provided to the respondents.

(B) No clear qualitative definition of "happiness" was provided to the respondents.

(C) Most of the respondents who claimed to have a large amount of money in fact did not.

(D) Many people are happy even though they do not possess a great deal of money.

(E) Many people who have a great deal of money are not happy.

Quick Answer Guide

Logical Reasoning Mini-Test

1. C	5. B	9. D	13. B
2. D	6. A	10. A	14. C
3. B	7. D	11. D	
4. D	8. E	12. D	

EXPLANATIONS

1. Conclusion (challenging). Answer: C.

The main point of the argument is expressed in the first sentence where it is concluded that animal liberationists "cannot possibly be environmentalists." This conclusion is based on the premise that "animal liberationists place a higher value on protecting animals from harm than on protecting their autonomy." The remainder of the passage is devoted to demonstrating that these two values are incompatible and that environmentalists are committed to the latter value. (A), (B), (D), and (E) are all premises of the argument.

2. Conclusion (moderate). Answer: D.

The rhetorical question at the beginning of the passage introduces the issue to be discussed in the argument which is whether it is wrong for doctors to lie about their patients' illness. In the final sentence it is concluded that this practice is wrong because it would be a violation of the good faith contract we enter into when we hire the doctor.

(A) is a premise of the argument.

(B) is unsupported by the passage. The passage does not state that doctors often lie to their patients about their illnesses, nor is this the main focus of the

passage. The main focus of the passage is to determine not whether they *do*, but whether they *should* engage in this practice.

(C) is a premise of the argument.

(E) is implied by the passage.

3. Assumption (moderate). Answer: B.

The tobacco executives' argument can be represented as follows:

Premise: Cigarette smoking is not regulated by the Federal Drug Administration.

Conclusion: Cigarette smoking is not addictive.

The logical gap in the argument that needs to be filled is the link between substances that are regulated by the Federal Drug Administration and substances that are addictive. Moreover, to make the argument logically correct, the link between them must be such that the fact that something is not regulated entails that it is not addictive. Response (B) is equivalent in meaning to the claim that all substances that are not regulated by the Federal Drug Administration are not addictive. This is exactly the assumption required to fill the gap in the tobacco executives' argument.

(A) does not fill the logical gap in the tobacco executives' argument. Response (A) is equivalent in meaning to the claim that all substances that are not addictive are not regulated by the Federal Drug Administration. The assumption required to fill the gap in the tobacco executives' argument is that all substances that are not regulated by the Federal Drug Administration are not addictive.

(C) does not fill the logical gap in the tobacco executives' argument. The fact that some of the substances that are regulated by the Federal Drug Administration are not addictive is irrelevant to the tobacco executives' argument. Their conclusion is based on the premise that cigarette smoking is *not* regulated—not that it *is* regulated.

(D) brings in information not mentioned in the passage. The claim asserted in response (D), if true, could serve as an additional premise in support of the conclusion.

(E) brings in information not mentioned in the passage. The issue of whether or not the tobacco executives lied when they claimed that cigarette smoking is not addictive is irrelevant to the logic of their argument.

4. Assumption (moderate). Answer: D.

Sean's argument can be restated as follows:

> **Premise:** The university orchestra's performance of Beethoven's symphony was not in accordance with the way Beethoven intended it to be performed.
>
> **Conclusion:** The university orchestra's performance of Beethoven's symphony was not a good performance.

The logical gap in Sean's argument that needs to be filled is the link between good performances and performances that are in accordance with the way in which the composer intended the music to be performed. Moreover, to make the argument logically correct, the link between them must be such that the fact that a performance is not in accordance with the composer's intentions regarding the way it should be played implies that it is not a good performance. Response (D) is equivalent in meaning to the claim that any performance that is not in keeping with the composer's intentions regarding how it be played is not a good performance. This is exactly the assumption required to fill the gap in Sean's argument.

(A) is not an assumption of Sean's argument. Response (A) is a restatement of the major premise of Sean's argument.

(B) does not fill the logical gap in Sean's argument. Response (B) is equivalent in meaning to the claim that all performances that are performed in the way in which the composer intended are good performances. This, in turn, is equivalent to the claim that all performances that are not good are not performed in a way in which the composer intended. This latter claim, however, does not entail that performances that are not in accordance with the way the composer intended are not good performances.

(C) and (D) provide plausible explanations of why the university orchestra's performance of Beethoven's symphony was not in accordance with the way Beethoven intended it to be performed; as such, (C) and (D) provide support for the major premise—they do not state assumptions of Sean's argument.

5. Assumption (moderate). Answer: B.

The argument in the passage can be restated as follows:

> **Premise:** Nonhuman primates are closely related genetically to humans.
>
> **Conclusion:** Nonhuman primates are excellent animal models for the study of human disease.

The logical gap in the argument that needs to be filled is the link between being closely related genetically to humans and being an excellent animal model for the study of human disease. Moreover, this link between them must be such that the fact that something is closely related genetically to humans implies that, or increases the likelihood that, it will be an excellent model for the study of human disease. Response (B) states the general principle that the more closely related two species are genetically the better one is as a model for studying the other. The assumption required to fill the gap in the argument is an instance of this general principle.

(A) is too broad. Response (A) does not specify the type of relationship required viz., a close *genetic* relationship.

(C) is implied by the passage. The passage states that "comparisons of the chromosomes and DNA of nonhuman primates and humans reveals a startling similarity in their structure and primitive origin, and testifies to the commonality of the genetic material between these phylogenetically related species." From this information it can be reasonably inferred that the more similar in structure and primitive origin of the chromosomes and DNA of species, the more commonalities in their genetic material.

(D) is too broad. It is not the mere fact that the species are related phylogenetically to another that makes one a good model for studying the other; what is required is that they have a *close* genetic relationship to one another.

(E) is a paraphrase of the major premise of the argument.

6. Inference (easier). Answer: A.

The task in this problem is to find the answer choice that is most strongly supported, that is, the one that is most likely to be true, given that the information stated in the passage is true.

(A) is the best response. The only difference cited in the passage between the children who developed nearsightedness and the parents and grandparents who did not have this disability is the fact that the children went to school whereas the parents and grandparents did not. The inference to be drawn from this information is that school activities such as reading that require the use of vision are somehow causally related to the nearsightedness. Admittedly, the information stated in the passage would not, by itself, prove that these activities are the cause of the children's nearsightedness but it would provide strong support for this claim.

(B) is not strongly supported by the passage. From the information in the passage it can be inferred that there are some people who are illiterate and who also do not suffer from nearsightedness viz., the parents and grandparents of the children. However, it does not follow from this that *all* people who are illiterate do not suffer from nearsightedness

nor is this latter claim strongly supported by this inference.

(C) is unsupported by the passage. Response (C) is equivalent in meaning to the claim that all nearsighted people have had the opportunity for formal schooling. Admittedly, formal schooling is implicated with nearsightedness in the passage, but the implication is that formal schooling is, in some instances, a significant difference between persons who are nearsighted and persons who are not.

(D) is unsupported by the passage. Response (D) is equivalent in meaning to the claim that all nearsighted people are literate. While it is implied in the passage that *some* illiterate people are not nearsighted viz., the parents and grandparents of the nearsighted children, it does not follow from this that *all* illiterate people are not nearsighted, nor is this claim strongly supported by this.

(E) is unsupported by the passage. The passage states only that "two-thirds of the children developed considerable levels of nearsightedness after starting school." No inference regarding the remaining one-third of the students is warranted.

7. Inference (moderate). Answer: D.

The task in this problem is to find the answer choice that need not be true given that the information in the passage is true. The best way to proceed is to find all of those answers that *must* be true, and by a process of elimination select the correct answer. The premises in the passage can be represented as follows:

Premise 1: Some of the most beautiful cars in the world are manufactured by Contempo Motors.

Premise 2: All cars manufactured by Contempo Motors are unreliable.

Premise 3: All unreliable cars are exasperating.

(D) is the best response. From premise 2 and premise 3 above it follows necessarily that:

Conclusion 1: All cars manufactured by Contempo Motors are exasperating.

Conclusion 1 eliminates response (B).

Premise 3 is equivalent in meaning to the claim that no cars that are manufactured by Contempo Motors are reliable. Since we are assuming that the statements in the passage are true it must also be true that:

Conclusion 2: No Contempo cars are reliable.

Conclusion 2 eliminates response (C).

From premise 1 and conclusion 1 it follows necessarily that:

Conclusion 3: Some of the most beautiful cars in the world are exasperating.

Conclusion 3 eliminates response (A).

From premise 1 and premise 2 it follows *necessarily* that:

Conclusion 4: Some of the most beautiful cars in the world are unreliable.

Conclusion 4 eliminates response (E).

Since responses (A), (B), (C), and (E) *necessarily follow* from the information stated in the passage, they each *must* be true given that this information is true, so the remaining answer choice viz., (D) is the correct answer.

(A) must be true if the statements in the passage are true. From premise 2 and premise 3 on page 62 it follows necessarily that:

Conclusion 1: All cars manufactured by Contempo Motors are exasperating.

From premise 1 and conclusion 1 it follows necessarily that:

Conclusion 3: Some of the most beautiful cars in the world are exasperating.

(B) must be true if the statements in the passage are true. From premise 2 and premise 3 above it follows necessarily that all cars manufactured by Contempo Motors are exasperating.

(C) must be true if the statements in the passage are true. Premise 3 is equivalent in meaning to the claim that no cars that are manufactured by Contempo Motors are reliable. Since we are assuming

that the statements in the passage are true it must also be true that no Contempo cars are reliable.

(E) must be true if the statements in the passage are true. From premise 1 and premise 2 above it follows necessarily that some of the most beautiful cars in the world are unreliable.

8. Inference (moderate). Answer: E.

The task in this problem is to find the answer that must be true, that is, the one that cannot conceivably be false, given that the information stated in the passage is true. The premises in the passage can be represented as follows:

Premise 1: Either the budget deficit will continue to grow or taxes will be raised soon.

Premise 2: Taxes will not be raised soon.

Premise 3: If the budget deficit continues to grow, then the next generation of taxpayers will be burdened with an almost unbearable debt.

(E) is the best response. From premise 1 and premise 2 above it necessarily follows that:

Conclusion 1: The budget deficit will continue to grow.

From conclusion 1 and premise 3 it necessarily follows that:

Conclusion 2: The next generation of taxpayers will be burdened with an almost unbearable debt.

Since conclusion 2 necessarily follows from the information stated in the passage it cannot conceivably be false if this information is true.

(A) is contradicted by the passage. The passage states that "given the current political climate that's not going to happen in the foreseeable future." In this sentence the pronoun "that" refers to the phrase "taxes are raised soon" in the previous sentence.

(B) is implicitly contradicted by the passage. From premise 1 and premise 2 above, it necessarily follows that the statement "The budget deficit will continue to grow" is true.

(C) is unsupported by the passage. No information in the passage supports a prediction about what the political climate will be in the foreseeable future.

(D) is contradicted by the passage. From premise 1 and premise 2 above it necessarily follows that:

Conclusion 1: The budget deficit will continue to grow.

From conclusion 1 and premise 3 it necessarily follows that:

Conclusion 2: The next generation of taxpayers will be burdened with an almost unbearable debt.

Since (D) states a conjunction of two sentences, one of which must be false, (D) must be false.

9. Inference (moderate). Answer: D.

The task in this problem is to find the answer choice that is most strongly supported, that is, the one that is most likely to be true, given that the information stated in the passage is true. The major premises of the argument in the passage can be represented as follows:

Premise 1: The human fetus and the newborn lamb are similar in their capacities for pleasure and pain and in their levels of awareness and rationality.

Premise 2: The value placed on the newborn lamb's life is quite low.

(D) is the best response. The analogy between the human fetus and the newborn lamb points to significant and relevant similarities between them that suggest that the value that is placed on their lives should also be similar. Since the value placed on the lamb's life is quite low, it can be inferred that the value placed on the human fetus should be quite low as well. Another way to look at this is to consider how we could justify placing a higher value on the life of the unborn fetus than the life of the newborn lamb in light of the similarities stated in the passage.

(A) brings in information not mentioned in the passage. The rightness or wrongness of taking the lives of newborn lambs is not discussed.

(B) is unsupported by the passage. While it is stated that "taking <the newborn lamb's> life is a routine occurrence that happens everyday without

protest," it is not suggested that this practice should be protested.

(C) is unsupported by the passage. Given the information in the passage the relative number of differences and similarities cannot be ascertained.

(E) is unsupported by the passage. Given the information in the passage it would be difficult to justify placing a higher value on the life of a human fetus than on the life of a newborn lamb. To do so would require pointing out some relevant difference between the two that would outweigh the similarities cited in the passage.

10. Assessing the effect of additional information (easier). Answer: A.

The task in this problem is to find an answer that strengthens the argument; that is, one that offers support for the major assumption of the argument or that provides additional evidence for the conclusion. The argument in the passage can be represented as follows:

Premise: Compared to the five-year period prior to the passage of laws requiring the use of safety seats by children, fatalities of children under age four have decreased by 30 percent.

Conclusion: The passage of laws requiring the use of safety seats by children under age four has resulted in fewer child fatalities over the past five years.

(A) is the best response. The major assumption of the argument is that there are no significant differences between the five-year period preceding the passage of the laws and the five-year period since their passage that could account for the decrease in fatalities. Response (A) supports this assumption.

(B) weakens the argument. The major assumption of the argument is that there are no significant differences between the five-year period preceding the passage of the laws and the five-year period since their passage that could account for the decrease in fatalities. Response (B) undermines this assumption.

(C), (D), and (E) do not offer support for the major assumption of the argument nor do they provide additional evidence for the conclusion of the argument.

11. Assessing the effect of additional information (moderate). Answer: D.

The task in this problem is to find an answer that weakens the argument; that is, one that undermines the major assumption of the argument, attacks a stated premise, or that suggests an alternative conclusion that could be inferred from the premises. The argument in the passage can be represented as follows:

> **Premise:** Purebred horses are extremely susceptible to genetic abnormalities that can only be corrected by expensive surgery.
>
> **Premise:** Nonpurebred horses rarely suffer from genetic abnormalities that can only be corrected by expensive surgery.
>
> **Conclusion:** Nonpurebred horses are a better choice than purebred horses for potential horse owners who want to avoid costly medical bills.

(D) is the best response. The major assumption of the argument is that it is necessary to correct the genetic abnormalities to protect the horse's health, and that consequently, costly medical bills will necessarily be incurred. Response (D) undermines this assumption.

(A) brings in information not mentioned in the passage. The passage deals only with genetic abnormalities; environmentally determined diseases are not discussed in the passage.

(B) brings in information not mentioned in the passage. The relative attractiveness of purebred and nonpurebred horses is not discussed in the passage.

(C) strengthens the argument. Response (C) provides additional evidence for the conclusion by providing another reason for preferring nonpurebred horses over purebred horses.

(E) brings in information not mentioned in the passage. The relative difference in initial costs of purebred and nonpurebred horses is not discussed in the passage.

12. Assessing the effect of additional information (moderate). Answer: D.

The task in this problem is to find an answer that strengthens the argument; that is, one that offers support for the major assumption of the argument or that provides additional evidence for the conclusion. The argument in the passage can be represented as follows:

> **Premise:** Ten years ago the death rate from Neural Synapse Deficiency (NSD) related causes was 5 percent of all persons infected with the anti-synapse virus (ASV) that causes it.
>
> **Premise:** Today, the death rate from Neural Synapse Deficiency (NSD) related causes is 15 percent of all persons infected with the anti-synapse virus (ASV) that causes it.
>
> **Conclusion:** The rate of propagation and the malignancy of the anti-synapse virus has increased substantially over the past ten years.

(D) is the best response. The major assumption of the argument is that no additional NSD related causes of death have been discovered in the interim that could account for the increase in the death rate. In other words, the number of recognized NSD related causes of death has remained relatively constant over the past ten years.

(B) is the second best response. Response (B) provides additional evidence for the claim that the rate of propagation of the anti-synapse virus has increased over the past ten years; however, it does not provide additional evidence for the claim that the malignancy of the virus has increased over this period. The conclusion of the argument states that *both* the rate of propagation and the malignancy of the virus have increased.

(A), (C), and (E) do not offer support for the major assumption of the argument nor do they provide additional evidence for the conclusion of the argument.

13. Assessing the effect of additional information (moderate). Answer: B.

The task in this problem is to find an answer that weakens the argument; that is, one that undermines the major assumption of the argument, attacks a stated premise, or that suggests an alternative conclusion that could be inferred from the premises. The argument in the passage can be represented as follows:

Premise: Lycopene, glutathione, and glutamine are powerful antioxidants that neutralize the free radicals that are produced in the body as a result of routine bodily processes.

Premise: An excess in your system of the free radicals that are produced in the body as a result of routine bodily processes causes rapid aging.

Conclusion: To slow down aging, it is necessary to supplement your diet with these antioxidants on a daily basis.

(B) is the best response. The major assumption in the argument is that daily ingestion of the antioxidants mentioned in the passage is the only way to rid your system of the free radicals produced as a result of routine bodily processes. Response (B) undermines this assumption.

(A) brings in information not mentioned in the passage. Whether or not persons are concerned with the problem of aging and the time at which that concern is realized are not discussed in the passage.

(C) brings in information not mentioned in the passage. Admittedly, the high cost may prevent some people from using these antioxidants on a daily basis, but the fact that they are beyond the budget of most consumers does not attack a premise of the argument nor does it subvert the major assumption of the argument or suggest an alternative conclusion.

(D) does not undermine the major assumption of the argument, attack a stated premise, or suggest an alternative conclusion that could be inferred from the premises.

(E) brings in information not mentioned in the passage. Additional causes of cellular damage such as smoking are not discussed in the passage.

14. Assessing the effect of additional information (easier). Answer: C.

The task in this problem is to find an answer that weakens the argument; that is, one that undermines the major assumption of the argument, attacks a stated premise, or that suggests an alternative conclusion that could be inferred from the premises. The argument in the passage can be represented as follows:

Premise: 78 percent of the respondents said that they were happy.

Premise: The same 78 percent of the respondents claimed that they possessed a large amount of money.

Conclusion: Having a sizable quantity of money is the key to happiness.

(C) is the best response. Response (C) directly attacks the second premise listed above thereby seriously calling survey finding into doubt. If (C) is true, the second premise listed above is false. As a consequence, the argument falls apart because the connection between having money and being happy in the argument is completely severed.

(A) and (B) state possible problems that could have an adverse effect on the reliability of the survey, but neither of these responses directly attacks the truth of a stated premise, nor do they undermine the major assumption or suggest an alternative conclusion that could be inferred from the premises.

(D) is consistent with the conclusion of the argument. The conclusion does not state that everyone who is happy has a large amount of money; it states that persons who have a large amount of money are happy. Response (D) does not suggest an alternative conclusion that could be inferred from the premises nor does it undermine the major assumption of the argument or attack a stated premise.

(E) contradicts the conclusion of the argument. The conclusion states that persons who have a large amount of money are happy; response (E) states the opposite of this claim. Response (D) does not weaken the argument because it does not undermine the major assumption of the argument, attack a stated premise, or suggest an alternative conclusion that could be inferred from the premises.

Day 8

Reading Comprehension Lesson 1: Strategies and Techniques

Today you will familiarize yourself with the format of the Reading Comprehension section and learn basic reading strategies.

Today's Topics

1. Reading Comprehension at a glance
2. Questions and answers about reading comprehension
3. Anatomy of a reading comprehension set
4. Techniques to help you read more actively
5. Techniques to help you follow the author's train of thought
6. Questions and answers about pacing and time allocation

READING COMPREHENSION AT A GLANCE

Number questions: 28
Time allowed: 35 minutes

Number of sections:

- 1 scored section
- possibly 1 Trial section

Basic format:

- the questions are divided into 4 *sets*
- each set involves a different reading *passage*
- each passage is accompanied by 5–8 questions

Directions printed in test booklet:

"Each passage in this section is followed by a group of questions to be answered on the basis of what is *stated* or *implied* in the passage. For some of the questions, more than one of the choices could conceivably answer the question. You are to choose the *best* answer; that is, the response that most accurately and completely answers the question, and blacken the appropriate space on your answer sheet."

Ground rules:

- no scratch paper is permitted (make notes in the test booklet)
- no pens are allowed (pencils and highlighters only)
- no penalty (deduction) assessed for incorrect responses

- each question is considered independently of all others

This section tests your ability to:

- read carefully and accurately

- determine the relationships among the various parts of the passage

- draw reasonable inferences from the material in the passage

QUESTIONS AND ANSWERS ABOUT READING COMPREHENSION

Can I really improve my reading skills in a few weeks? A few weeks, although probably not sufficient time to drastically alter your reading habits, is enough time to train yourself to read more actively and efficiently and to learn how to better choose between "best" and "second-best" responses to LSAT Reading Comprehension questions.

Would it be worthwhile to increase my vocabulary by learning as many new words as possible before exam day? No. Reading Comprehension questions are not designed to test your vocabulary. Where a technical term is introduced in a passage but not defined, the passage will supply all that you need to know about the term to respond to the questions.

From what sources are the Reading Comprehension passages taken? Passages are drawn from a variety of subjects—including the humanities, social sciences, the physical sciences, ethics, philosophy, and law. Specific sources include professional journals and periodicals, dissertations, as well as periodicals and books that deal with sophisticated subjects of intellectual interest. Most passages are written within the last 10 or 20 years and have been edited to increase their "density."

Am I at an advantage if a passage involves a topic that is familiar to me? Probably not. The testing service is careful to ensure that all questions are answerable based solely upon the information provided in the passage. Also, the exam will include passages from a variety of disciplines, so it is

unlikely that any particular test taker will be knowledgeable enough about two or more of the areas included on the test to hold a significant advantage over other test takers. You may nevertheless be at a slight advantage if you have some familiarity with the general area treated in a passage. You may find it easier to concentrate because the passage is more interesting and the terminology is familiar.

ANATOMY OF A READING COMPREHENSION SET

The Passage

Each of the four question "sets" in an LSAT Reading Comprehension section includes a passage and 5–8 questions. The average passage length is 450 words. Passages vary somewhat in difficulty and complexity. Most test takers would consider the following passage to be more complex than average, although it is a bit shorter than average (430 words). Read this passage, limiting your time to 4 minutes.

Sample Passage

A "radiative forcing" is any change imposed on the Earth that affects the planetary energy balance. Radiative forcings include changes in greenhouse gases (such as carbon dioxide and
(5) ozone), aerosols in the atmosphere, solar irradiance, and surface reflectivity. A forcing may result from either a natural or an anthropogenic cause, or from both, as in the case of atmospheric aerosol concentrations, which can be altered ei-
(10) ther by volcanic action or the burning of fossil fuels. Radiative forcings are typically specified for the purpose of theoretical global climate simulations. In contrast, radiative "feedbacks" are environmental changes resulting from climate
(15) changes and are calculated from scientific observation. Radiative feedbacks include changes in such phenomena as clouds, atmospheric water vapor, sea-ice cover, and snow cover.

The interplay between forcings and feedbacks
(20) can be quite complex. For example, an increase in the concentration of atmospheric water vapor increases solar irradiance, thereby warming the

atmosphere and, in turn, increasing evaporation and the concentration of atmospheric water va-
(25) por. A related example of this complex interplay also shows the uncertainty of future climatic changes associated with forcings and feedbacks. Scientists are unsure how the depletion of ozone will ultimately affect clouds and, in turn, the
(30) Earth's temperature. Clouds trap outgoing, cooling radiation, thereby providing a warming influence. However, they also reflect incoming solar radiation and thus provide a cooling influence. Current measurements indicate that the net
(35) effect of clouds is to cool the Earth. However, scientists do not know how the balance might shift in the future as cloud formation and dissipation are affected by ozone depletion.

Contributing to this uncertainty is the com-
(40) plexity of the mechanisms at work in the process of ozone depletion. The amount of radiation reaching the earth's surface and the amount of reradiated radiation that is trapped by the greenhouse effect influence the Earth's temperature in
(45) opposite directions. Both mechanisms are affected by the vertical distribution of ozone. Also, the relative importance of these two competing mechanisms depends on the altitude at which ozone changes occur. In a recent NASA-
(50) sponsored aircraft study of the Antarctic ozone hole, chlorine monoxide was measured at varying altitudes. The measurements suggest that chlorine plays a greater role, and oxides of nitrogen a lesser role, than previously thought in the
(55) destruction of ozone in the lower atmosphere. The study concluded that simultaneous high-resolution measurements at many different altitudes (on the scale of 0.1 kilometer in vertical extent) are necessary to diagnose the operative
(60) mechanisms. These findings have called into question conventional explanations for ozone depletion, which fail to adequately account for the new evidence.

The Questions

Reading Comprehension questions are not designed simply to measure your ability to remember what you read. Rather, they are designed to gauge your ability to assimilate and understand the ideas presented. For example, consider the seven question "stems" below, all of which relate to the foregoing passage and all of which require you to go beyond merely memorizing or recalling what you have read:

1. Which of the following best expresses the author's primary purpose in the passage?

2. It can be inferred from the information in the passage that "burning of fossil fuels" (lines 10–11)

3. Based upon the information in the passage, it is reasonable to infer that decreased evaporation is most likely to result in which of the following?

4. According to the passage, radiative forcings can be distinguished from radiative feedbacks in which of the following ways?

5. The author discusses the effect of clouds on atmospheric temperature most likely in order to show that

6. Based upon the information in the passage, the author would probably agree that scientists could more accurately predict the extent and direction of the greenhouse effect if they were to

7. The information in the last paragraph does NOT:

These seven question stems illustrate the following general observations about Reading Comprehension question sets:

- Some of the questions will be "memory" questions, requiring only that you *recall* specific information in the passage (e.g., Question 4). However, most of the questions will require that you *understand* the ideas conveyed in the passage.

- One of the questions will ask about the passage as a whole, and that question will probably be either the first or last question in the set (e.g., Question 1).

- With most questions, you will find all of the information needed to answer the question in one particular paragraph.

- Questions focusing on information in the first paragraph (e.g., Question 2) typically appear early among the questions, while those focusing solely on information in the last paragraph (e.g.,

Question 7) typically appear as the last question. Otherwise, there are no predictable patterns in question sequence.

- Questions vary somewhat in difficulty. Some require close judgment calls, while with others the "best" response is far better than any of the others. Questions requiring you to simply recall one or two specific bits of information are generally easier than those requiring you to assimilate and assess an entire paragraph or the entire passage.

The Answer Choices

Now consider Question 1 along with five answer choices (we will examine answer choices for the other six questions in Day 9):

1. Which of the following best expresses the author's primary purpose in the passage?

    (A) To examine the environmental effects of radiative forcings and feedbacks

    (B) To challenge conventional theories about the impact of radiative changes on ozone depletion and the greenhouse effect

    (C) To illustrate the complexity and uncertainty of some radiative changes

    (D) To evaluate current methods of determining radiative changes

    (E) To identify the factors that contribute to ozone changes and to the greenhouse effect

In handling Reading Comprehension questions, your job is to determine the "best" response among the five choices. In doing so, you must make qualitative distinctions among the answer choices. The two or three "worst" choices may jump out at you as obviously incorrect responses. However, the qualitative distinctions among the remaining choices can be subtle. Determining the "best" answer generally requires comparing the quality of the two (or three) "best" choices.

The worst responses (A and B). In Question 1 above, (A) and (B) should have struck you as the worst choices. (A) is far *too broad* a statement of the

author's primary purpose. The author is primarily concerned with how radiative changes relate more specifically to ozone depletion and to the resulting greenhouse effect, not to the environment in general. (B) is entirely *off-focus* and far *too narrow* to serve as a viable "best" response. The author makes no attempt in the passage to discuss the "conventional explanations" to which the last sentence of the passage refers. Moreover, the recent scientific study discussed in the final paragraph (which calls into question those "conventional explanations" about ozone depletion) illustrates the author's *primary* point that predicting radiative changes is difficult due to their complex and uncertain interaction.

Responses that have merit but are nevertheless incorrect (D and E). (D) and (E) both have merit, and either one might be considered the "best" response but for (C). With respect to (D), the author does point out the insufficiency of certain types of data in predicting climate changes (second paragraph), and the accuracy of previous explanations for Antarctic ozone depletion (final paragraph). These points are secondary, however, to the broader and primary point that predicting radiative changes is difficult due to their complexity and uncertainty. Thus, (D) is *too narrow* in its scope. (E) is also too narrow in one sense, yet too broad in another sense. Although the author does indeed identify various factors contributing to ozone depletion, the author's concern is not merely with identifying these factors but also with pointing out problems in isolating and measuring these factors and the resulting problem of making accurate predictions about the greenhouse effect. In this sense, then, (E) is *too narrow*. In addition, there may be other factors that contribute to ozone depletion not discussed in the passage; the author does not necessarily intend to identify all such factors; in this sense, then, (E) is *too broad*.

The best response. (C) is the best response. While the first paragraph is introductory in nature, the author stresses in the second paragraph that the effects of radiative changes can be complex and uncertain; in fact, the author devotes the second and third paragraphs (the bulk of the passage) to demonstrating this point.

TECHNIQUES TO HELP YOU READ MORE ACTIVELY

Most Reading Comprehension questions are designed to measure your ability to understand the ideas presented in the passage rather than to simply recall the information stated. In order to understand a passage, you must be able to (1) identify the thesis (or main idea) and the author's primary purpose and (2) follow the author's line of reasoning from paragraph to paragraph. Both of these tasks require an *active* frame of mind in which you are constantly interacting with the material as you read.

Poor scores on LSAT Reading Comprehension questions generally result from one of the following:

- poor concentration

- slow reading speed (inability to complete the section in time)

- need to search the passage again and again for the information needed to respond to each question

- difficulty narrowing down the answer choices to one clear best answer

All of these problems come from the same bad habit: *passive* reading. You can add points to your LSAT score by becoming a more active reader. Begin right now by adopting this operating principle: *Understand each paragraph well enough to be able to briefly explain the main point and line of reasoning to someone who has not read the passage.*

Avoid the Passive Reading Mode

Most test takers take a rather passive approach toward the Reading Comprehension passages. They give equal time and attention to every sentence in a passage, reading the passage from beginning to end without interruption and with very little thought as to what particular information is most important in order to respond to the specific questions. This strategy is actually better characterized as a *non*-strategy. What is the probable result of this approach? The reader may remember some scattered factual information and ideas, thereby enabling him or her to respond correctly to some easier questions. However, the reader is not likely to respond effectively to most questions, which require some insight into and assessment of the passage's information.

Pause After Reading Each Paragraph to Sum Up and Anticipate

After you read each paragraph, pause for a moment to evaluate the paragraph as a whole. Try to recapitulate or summarize the paragraph as two or three basic ideas. After each paragraph, answer the following questions for yourself:

- How would I sum up the discussion to this point?

- At what point is the discussion now?

- What basic points is the author trying to get across in this paragraph? Do these ideas continue a line of thought, or do they begin a new one?

- Where is the discussion likely to go from here?

Example: In the passage on pages 68 and 69, after reading the first paragraph, you might engage yourself in the following mental dialogue:

"This paragraph doesn't express a thesis or main idea; it seems introductory in nature. The paragraph defines forcings and feedbacks, distinguishes them, and gives examples of each. I don't understand these concepts, but the general idea is that forcings and feedbacks are environmental changes that affect the Earth's climate. The passage might continue by focusing on one specific type of radiative change; or perhaps the passage will continue by discussing a theory or theories about radiative changes. I'm not sure."

Respond Tentatively to Certain Questions as You Read the Passage

After reading the first paragraph, scan the question stems for questions that you might respond to at this point, at least tentatively. The first paragraph will most certainly provide enough information for you to respond (tentatively) to any question that asks about the overall thesis, topic, or author's purpose. Additionally, the first paragraph might contain more detailed information that is being tested in one of the questions.

Example: The first paragraph of the passage on pages 68 and 69 probably provides sufficient information to respond to Questions 2 and 4. In addition, you might be able to respond tentatively to Question 1. (E) appears to be too broad in scope, based upon the subject matter of the first paragraph. It's too early to tell about the other responses, though. They each look viable without knowing how the passage will continue. Tentatively eliminate (E) and keep the other responses in mind as you read on.

Return to the passage and read the next paragraph. Scan the question stems for any additional questions that you can respond to at this time. Then take a few seconds to reconsider any thesis or primary-purpose questions that you responded to after reading the first paragraph. Have you changed your mind about your tentative response after reading the second paragraph? Or has the second paragraph confirmed that your initial response was correct?

Example: After reading the second paragraph, briefly reconsider Question 1. Response (A) looks a bit broad now, and (B) appears to be narrow, considering you have read most of the passage and have yet to encounter any theories about ozone depletion. Eliminate (A) and (E). Keep in mind (C) and (D) as you read the rest of the passage.

Summarize the Passage After Reading It in Its Entirety

After reading the entire passage, take a few seconds to recap the passage in your mind. What was the author's main point and what were the major supporting points? Just remind yourself at this point about the flow of the discussion; don't be concerned with remembering all of the detailed factual information.

Example: After reading the entire passage on pages 68 and 69, you might recap the discussion and formulate a thesis as follows:

"Let's recap! The first paragraph defines forcings and feedbacks. The second paragraph gives an example (water vapor) of their complex interaction, then an example (clouds and ozone/greenhouse) of how this complex interaction makes it difficult to predict some forcings and feedbacks. The

third paragraph goes into more detail about the second example (ozone/greenhouse), citing a recent ozone study showing that the relative importance of forcings having opposite effects varies with altitude."

"What was this passage about as a whole? It is difficult to predict certain forcings and feedbacks because their interaction is complex and uncertain. Case in point: ozone depletion and the greenhouse effect."

Should You Preview Before Reading the Passage?

Test-preparation publications typically recommend that, before reading a passage straight through (from beginning to end), you should perform one or both of the following "pre-reading" steps:

- *Read all of the question "stems"* (the questions but not the answer choices) for hints about the subject of the passage and possible thesis

- *Preview the passage* by reading the first (and perhaps last) sentence of each paragraph

The first technique supposedly helps you to anticipate the particular information in the passage that is tested. The second technique supposedly provides clues about the scope of the passage, the author's thesis or major conclusions, and the structure and flow of the discussion. Although these techniques make sense *in theory*, there are several reasons why *in practice* they are rarely helpful on the LSAT:

1. Once immersed in the passage itself, you will quickly forget most if not all of what you learned from previewing.

2. These techniques call for you to read the same material twice. Does that sound efficient to you?

3. Previewing takes time (perhaps 30 seconds to a minute)—time that you probably cannot afford under timed conditions.

4. While reading the beginning and end of each paragraph may be helpful for some passages, for others this technique will be of little or no help. (The passage on pages 68 and 69 is a good example of the latter type!)

There is one exceptional situation where previewing is appropriate—if you are running out of time (more on that later).

TECHNIQUES TO HELP YOU FOLLOW THE AUTHOR'S TRAIN OF THOUGHT

Look for Common Organization Patterns

How a passage is organized reveals the flow of the author's argument. Focusing on structure will help you to:

- understand the author's main idea and primary purpose

- identify supporting evidence

- understand the author's purpose in mentioning various details

- distinguish between main points and minor details

You can probably respond correctly to all of the more "general" questions (e.g., "main idea" and "primary purpose" questions) just by determining the basic structure of the passage and organization of the materials.

No two passages will reflect identical patterns of organization; however, three general organizational patterns appear most often among the passages: (1) theory and critique, (2) historical influence, and (3) classification.

Familiarizing yourself with these patterns will help you to anticipate the flow of the discussion in a passage. As you examine these patterns, bear in mind that not all passages fall neatly into one of these common patterns. A particular passage might, for example, (1) reflect two patterns, (2) present a variation of one of the three common patterns, or (3) reflect a less common pattern not discussed below. (While the passage on pages 68 and 69 involves classifying various radiative changes as forcings or feedbacks, it really isn't a classification passage *per se*. Instead, it exemplifies a less common and simpler organizational pattern—point and example—in

which a main point is asserted and examples are discussed to illustrate/explain that point.)

Pattern #1: Theory and Critique

Introductory Sentences/First Paragraph. The author identifies the conventional (older, established, traditional) view, theory, or explanation of a phenomenon. The introduction also either implies or states that the conventional view is flawed. (If the conventional view could not be criticized, the author probably would not be interested in writing about the topic in the first place.)

Body. Look for one of the following patterns:

- The author focuses on one (or perhaps two) newer, more enlightened views. The author may attribute the new view either to a particular individual (e.g., a scientist, author, sociologist) or to a school of thought in general (e.g., the leaders of the feminist movement of the 1970s).

- The author points to specific examples, observations, data, or other evidence that support a different theory. The author may also point out that the evidence is conflicting (and so no firm conclusions can be reached).

Final Sentences. Look for one of the following typical patterns:

- The author admits that both views have their merits and shortcomings.

- The author suggests that all views are incomplete in their understanding and insight and that we need to study the subject further.

- The author introduces (but does not describe in detail) a new piece of evidence that suggests yet another view, an explanation for conflicting views, or a synthesis of numerous views.

In any case, the author will almost always have an opinion on the subject.

Pattern #2: Historical Influence

Introductory Sentences/First Paragraph. The author describes the state of affairs either currently or at a relatively recent time in history; the author asserts that this state of affairs can be attributed to (i.e.—has directly or indirectly resulted from) certain previous historical phenomena.

Body. Look for one of the following typical patterns:

- The author discusses alternative theories regarding historical cause and effect (e.g., some historians believe X was the primary contributing cause of Y, while other historians disagree and believe instead that Z . . .). However, if this discussion turns out to be the author's primary concern, you are really dealing with a "theory and explanation" pattern rather than a "historical influence" pattern.

- The author traces in chronological order the events leading up to and contributing to a phenomenon.

Final Sentences. Look for one of the following typical patterns:

- The author recaps by concluding that the current phenomenon is rooted in one or more particular ideology, movement, school of thought, event, etc.

- The author concludes that no single influence adequately explains the course of events; instead, we should recognize all contributing factors.

Pattern #3: Classification
Introductory Sentences/First Paragraph. The author identifies two or three basic types, categories, or classes of a phenomenon.

Body. Look for the author to accomplish all of the following:

- describe each class in some detail

- compare and contrast characteristics of members of the different classes

- further divide one or more classes into subclasses

Final Sentences. Look for one of the following patterns (the first pattern is by far the most common):

- The discussion concludes simply by finishing the description of the classes and subclasses (in other words, the author comes to no conclusions and asserts no arguments).

- The author points out new evidence that suggests an additional class or subclass.

- The author explains briefly how the classification system is used by practitioners to observe and test theories.

- The author points out a problem with the current classification system and suggests that some modification may be appropriate.

Look for Structural Clues or "Triggers"

"Triggers" are key words and phrases that provide clues as to the structure and organization of the passage and the direction in which the discussion is flowing. The lists below contain many common trigger words and phrases. Underline or circle trigger words as you read the passage. By reviewing your annotations, you can effectively recap structure and organization of the passage.

These words precede an item in a list (e.g., examples, classes, reasons, or characteristics):

first, second (etc.)
in addition
also
another

These words signal that the author is contrasting two phenomena:

alternatively
by contrast
however
on the other hand
rather than
while
yet

These words signal a logical conclusion based upon preceding material:

consequently
in conclusion
then
thus

therefore

as a result

accordingly

These words signal that the author is comparing (identifying similarities between) two phenomena:

similarly

in the same way

analogous

parallel

likewise

just as

to

also

as

These words signal evidence (factual information) used to support the author's argument:

because

since

in light of

These words signal that the author is providing an example of a phenomenon:

for instance

e.g.

such as

. . . is an illustration of

Don't Be Overly Concerned with the Details as You Read

LSAT Reading Comprehension passages are packed with details. In trying to absorb all of the details as you read, you will not only lose sight of the main points but also lose reading speed. Don't get bogged down in the details; gloss over them. In the left-hand margin, note where particular *examples*, *lists*, and other details are located. Then, if a particular question involving those details is included, you can quickly and easily locate them and read them in more detail.

Example: In the passage on pages 68 and 69, three examples are provided in the second paragraph to make the author's point that the effect of radiative changes on climate are complex and uncertain: (1) water vapor, (2) clouds, and (3) ozone depletion and the greenhouse effect. As you read the passage, as long as you briefly noted what each example dealt with and understood the author's broader purpose in discussing them, you would be able to handle the questions quite easily. However, if you were overly concerned with understanding the complex interactions described in any of these technical examples, you probably lost sight of the author's purpose and forgot what one or more of the examples dealt with.

Annotate the Passage

Selective annotating (e.g., circling and underlining key words and phrases) serves three important purposes:

1. Annotating the passage helps you to maintain an active frame of mind since you are shopping for ideas and information that are sufficiently important to earmark.

2. Annotating the passage provides an outline of sorts. After you read (and annotate) the entire passage, reviewing the annotated words and phrases can be an effective way to recap the passage for yourself.

3. If you need to refer to the passage as you answer the questions, effective annotating will help you to locate the relevant discussion quickly.

What sort of information should you annotate? If you under-annotate, you will not be able to effectively recap the passage by reviewing your annotations. On the other hand, if you over-annotate, your annotations lose their meaning, and you might as well not have annotated at all. Consider the following suggestions for annotating the passage:

1. Mark areas of discussion that you may need to locate again to answer one or more questions.

2. Let your annotations provide an outline so that you can recap the passage by reviewing only the annotated words and phrases.

3. Refrain from underlining complete sentences. Instead, select key words (or phrases) that "trigger" for you the idea or point that is made in this sentence or this part of the paragraph. (Remember: Avoid over-annotating.)

4. Mark structural connectors—key words that connect the logical building blocks of the passage.

5. In chronological passages, annotate historical benchmarks and divisions—centuries, years, decades, or historical periods—that help to form the structure of the author's discussion.

6. Use arrows to physically connect particular words whose connection is actually a logical, chronological, or conceptual one; for example:

   - to clarify cause and effect in the natural sciences or in the context of historical events

   - to indicate who was influenced by whom in literature, music, psychology, etc.

   - to connect names (philosophers, scientists, authors, etc.) with dates, events, other names, theories, or schools of thought, works, etc.

   - to indicate the chronological order in which historical events occurred

8. Create your own visual cues to earmark
   - possible thesis statements

   - major supporting points

   - points of author disagreement

Margin Notes and Outlines

In the left-hand margin, make shorthand notes to summarize paragraphs, earmark areas of discussion, and otherwise provide signals for yourself so that you can locate details more quickly and recap the passage more effectively. Keep your notes as brief as possible; two or three words should provide a sufficient cue.

There is no need and not enough time to construct an outline of the passage *per se*. Instead, rely on your margin notes and other annotations to indicate the flow of the discussion. For certain high-density passages, however, some organized notes—a "mini-outline"—may be necessary. Some shorthand notes at the bottom of the page may help to keep particular details straight in your mind. The following scenarios typically call for the mini-outline:

- If the passage categorizes or classifies various phenomenon, notes may help clarify which phenomena belong in which categories.

- If the passage mentions numerous individual names (e.g., of authors, artists, political figures, etc.), use notes to link them according to influence, agreement or disagreement, and so forth.

QUESTIONS AND ANSWERS ABOUT PACING AND TIME ALLOCATION

One of the most common complaints about the LSAT Reading Comprehension section is that there is not enough time to finish. Reading *speed*, however, is not the key to success here. You are not being tested on how *fast* you read, but rather on how *effectively*—or how "smart"—you read. Your effectiveness on the Reading Comprehension section(s) depends in part on how you pace yourself and how you manage your time, as explored by way of the following questions and answers.

Should I skip one entire question set so that I have more time for each question set that I attempt? By slowing down your pace and examining fewer passages in the allotted time (and random guessing for the remainder), you might actually improve your overall score. Most test takers discover, however, that this approach actually results in lower scores. By slowing down, their overall comprehension actually suffers. Why? Most likely, because in reading too slowly and too carefully, you tend to focus on details and lose sight of the larger picture—i.e., the flow of the argument and the author's main points. Also, if you have extra time to think about the answer choices, you begin to over-analyze them, read too much into them, and ignore your intuition. Nevertheless, you should try this approach as you practice; a minority of test takers find that when they slow down and examine fewer than all question sets, some of the anxiety caused by the time pressure disappears, and their overall performance improves as a result.

Should I move on to the next question set after a certain number of minutes, even if I haven't finished a question set? Not necessarily. You have invested a certain amount of time in reading and assimilating the materials in each passage. Having made this investment, you should by all means take the time to consider every question in the set. However, if you have already responded to (made at least an educated guess for) all of the questions, it is probably not the best use of your time to go back and re-examine those questions that you are least certain about. Even if you are ahead of your predetermined pace, move forward to the next question set. Once you begin losing momentum, you are in trouble; you will either become obsessed with a particular question or find yourself hunting through the passage again just to eliminate one answer choice for one question—both results are highly unproductive uses of your time.

Should I reserve some time at the end of the timed section to go back and re-examine questions about which I was uncertain? Not as a hard-and-fast rule. By all means, earmark those questions for which you think another 30 seconds of consideration would help. However, do not assume that you will have extra time, and by all means do not hurry through the test or skip questions or passages to ensure that you have extra time left over.

Should I read the passages in the order in which they appear? Not necessarily. Begin with a passage that looks comfortable to you. Take a few seconds to size up the first passage. Consider starting with another passage if: (1) the topic is intimidating or unfamiliar, (2) the passage appears to be extremely dense in details, or (3) the passage is longer than average in length.

Do the passages appear in ascending order of difficulty? If not, is there any pattern at all? The passages do not necessarily appear either in ascending or descending order of difficulty. However, the first passage in a section is rarely the most challenging one. Accordingly, you should probably not skip the first question set.

Should I skip a passage if it is not accompanied by as many questions as the other passages? No. This may seem like a good strategy, since the return on your investment of time would seem to be greater for passages that are accompanied by more questions. However, the number of questions from passage to passage is not likely to vary by more than one or two. Your comfort level with the subject of the passage should be the determining factor when deciding whether to skip a passage.

Are some types of questions inherently more difficult than others? If so, should I skip them? Well, yes and no. Questions that require you merely to recall or locate factual information ("explicit detail" questions) do not require any insight or understanding on your part, and so these questions would seem to be inherently easier. However, if the passage is extremely dense in details, it may be so difficult to recall or locate the specific information that you need to respond to one of these "easy" questions that in actuality the question is rather difficult.

Also, certain question types may seem more difficult than others to you, depending upon your own strengths and weaknesses. For example, if you have a great memory for details but often have trouble understanding broader concepts, you will probably find that the detail-oriented questions are easier than the more general questions. Even so, this fact would probably not justify your skipping the more general questions, except perhaps if you are very short on time.

What if I'm running out of time? If you do find yourself in a time "crunch," try the following techniques to maximize what time you have remaining:

- Find a question that includes a specific line reference (e.g., "in lines 20–22") and that requires specific factual information explicitly provided in the passage. Then, with that question in mind, read those lines as well as one or two lines immediately preceding and following those lines.

- Make an educated guess at the "main idea" and "primary purpose" questions. Quickly read the first paragraph and the last sentence of the passage for clues.

- Scan the passage for specific names, dates, events, titles, and proper (capitalized) nouns. These items are likely to be the focus of specific questions. Then scan the question stems to see if you can respond to any questions merely by reading one or two sentences around the particular noun in the passage.

Sometimes these techniques work, and sometimes they don't. A passage that is more technical in subject and/or that includes a great number of facts and raw data is an ideal candidate since in these passages most questions are likely to focus on detailed information rather than general concepts.

Day 9

Reading Comprehension Lesson 2: Question Types and Wrong-Answer Ploys

Today you will examine the various Reading Comprehension question types, focusing particularly on common wrong-answer "ploys."

Today's Topics

1. Question types and wrong-answer ploys

2. Question type #1: Recognizing the main idea or primary purpose

3. Question type #2: Recalling explicit information

4. Question type #3: Inferring from or interpreting specific information

5. Question type #4: Recognizing the function of specific information

6. Question type #5: Extrapolating from or applying passage ideas

7. The LSAT's favorite wrong-answer ploys

8. Tips for responding to LSAT reading questions

QUESTION TYPES AND WRONG-ANSWER PLOYS

Yesterday's question set (about radiative forcings and feedbacks) includes examples of each of the five types of questions you will encounter in LSAT Reading Comprehension sets, distinguished by the skill that is being tested:

1. Recognizing the *main idea* or *primary purpose* of the passage

2. Recalling *explicit information*

3. *Inferring* from or *interpreting* specific information

4. Recognizing the *function of specific information*

5. *Extrapolating* from or *applying* passage ideas (this type appears less frequently than the others)

The wrong-answer choices in yesterday's question set illustrate many of the LSAT's favorite wrong-answer types, which include answer choices that:

- distort, understate, or overstate the ideas presented in the passage

- are mentioned in the passage but do not respond to the question at hand

- call for speculation or unsupported inference

- are contrary to or contradicted by the passage or are stated "backwards" (for example, reversing cause and effect)

- confuse one opinion or position with another

- are too narrow or too specific

- are too broad, too general, or too vague

- bring in extrinsic information (information not included in the passage)

Let's take a closer look at each of the 5 question types, focusing on the proper approach and wrong-answer ploys commonly used with each type. The questions we will be examining are all based on the passage in yesterday's lesson (pages 68–69).

QUESTION TYPE #1: RECOGNIZING THE MAIN IDEA OR PRIMARY PURPOSE

Some questions test whether you recognize the author's main point or overall concern/purpose. These questions require you *to discern between the forest and the trees*—that is, to distinguish broader ideas and points from supporting evidence and details. At least one such question accompanies every passage. Here's how to approach these questions:

- After reading the entire passage, formulate your own thesis statement and statement of author's purpose—*before* considering the answer choices. If you know what sort of response to look for, you will be far less tempted by the other (wrong) responses. Ask yourself these two questions:

  - Toward what point is the author's effort primarily directed?

  - What does the author spend most of his or her time discussing? (This may sound simplistic,

but it helps to keep your thinking straight for this type of question.)

- Every passage has a "main idea" (thesis) and a primary purpose. You may find a particular sentence or two, usually in the first paragraph or at the very end of the passage, that sums up the passage. Don't insist on finding it, however; not all passages include *explicit* thesis statements or statements of purpose.

- There should be a consistency between the main idea of the passage and the author's primary purpose. If both question types appear in the question set, be sure your answers to these two questions are consistent with each other.

- As you read the passage, pay particular attention to all words and phrases that indicate or suggest the *author's attitude* (tone, opinion, perspective). It's a good idea to circle all such words and phrases as you read the passage. The best response must reflect or at least show consistency with the author's attitude.

Look for These Wrong-Answer Ploys

- **The response that is *too narrow* in scope.** The response focuses on one element of the passage, ignoring other important elements. If a particular topic is discussed in only one of three or four paragraphs, you can pretty safely conclude that the author's primary concern is not with that specific topic. Be particularly suspicious of a response that refers to a *single specific person, event, idea, or work* (book, composition, etc.). For example:

  - If the passage is concerned with comparing two phenomena, a response that ignores this concern and focuses on only one of the two phenomena is too narrow to be a viable best response.

  - If the author uses specific examples to support an argument, a response that ignores the author's larger point and focuses on one of the examples is too narrow to be a viable best response.

- If the author describes two existing theories and goes on to propose and describe a new and better theory, the author's primary purpose is not to examine, describe, or criticize current theories; the best response would go further and include the author's concern with proposing a new theory.

- **The response that is *too broad* in scope.** The response encompasses the author's main concern or idea but extends that concern or idea beyond the author's intended scope—for example, in terms of topic, geographic region, or time frame.

- **The response that *distorts* the author's position.** For example, if the author's ultimate concern is to argue for a particular position or to propose a new and better explanation for some phenomenon, any response that ignores the author's opinion and instead implies objectivity on the author's part is not a viable best response.

Example from Yesterday's Question Set

1. Which of the following best expresses the author's primary purpose in the passage?

    (A) To examine the environmental effects of radiative forcings and feedbacks *(too broad)*

    (B) To challenge conventional theories about the impact of radiative changes on ozone depletion and the greenhouse effect *(too narrow/distortion)*

    (C) To illustrate the complexity and uncertainty of some radiative changes *(correct response)*

    (D) To evaluate current methods of determining radiative changes *(too narrow)*

    (E) To identify the factors that contribute to ozone changes and to the greenhouse effect *(too broad)*

(For a detailed analysis of this question, see Day 8, page 70.)

QUESTION TYPE #2: RECALLING EXPLICIT INFORMATION

Some questions are designed to measure your ability to assimilate detailed information accurately as well as your efficiency in "looking up" information. The question may either ask which choice (among the five) *is* mentioned or which choice (among the five) is *not* mentioned. Here's how to approach these questions:

- Effective margin notes and annotations will help you locate the relevant information quickly. Wherever some sort of list is included in the passage—a list of characteristics, a list of examples, or some other list—earmark it. You can be sure that there will be an "explicit information" question that focuses on that list.

- Do not insist on finding a best response that repeats word-for-word what is stated in the passage. The best answer is usually not expressed exactly as it is in the passage, but rather paraphrases the language used in the passage.

- Do not rely on your memory to answer these questions. Always go to the relevant portion of the passage at the time you are considering the question, and read around the particular excerpt (from the preceding sentence to the following sentence) referred to in the question stem.

- Most "explicit information" questions focus on information contained in one particular paragraph. Some questions may explicitly refer to a specific line or paragraph in the passage. Even without a line reference, you can often locate the relevant portion of the passage within five or ten seconds based solely on the information in the question stem (quite helpful if you are in a time "crunch").

Look for These Wrong-Answer Ploys

- **The response that *confuses the information* in the passage by referring to *unrelated details*.**

- **The response that is *not mentioned* in the passage.** One or more answer choices might provide information completely unsupported by or not mentioned anywhere in the passage. These wrong answers can be quite tempting; your natural reaction is that the information appeared somewhere in the passage, but you missed it. Well, probably not! Don't fall for this ploy.

- **The response that *contradicts* the information in the passage.** The response may appear viable at first glance, but it actually contradicts what is stated in the passage. This ploy will trap you if you fail to read each answer choice carefully.

Example from Yesterday's Question Set

4. According to the passage, radiative forcings can be distinguished from radiative feedbacks in which of the following ways?
   (A) Whether the radiative change is global or more localized *(unsupported)*
   (B) The precision with which the amounts of radiative change can be determined *(unsupported)*
   (C) The altitude at which the radiative change occurs *(confuses passage information)*
   (D) Whether the amount of radiative change is specified or calculated *(correct response)*
   (E) Whether the radiative change is directed toward or away from the earth *(confuses passage information)*

(D) is the best response. According to the passage, radiative forcings are normally specified in global climate simulations, while feedbacks are calculated changes based on observation (lines 11–16). (A) is wholly *unsupported* by the passage. The author never discusses the geographic extent of radiative changes in any context. (B) is also unsupported by the passage. The fact that feedbacks are "calculated" while forcings are "specified" does not in itself suggest that one can be more precisely deter-

mined than the other. (C) and (E) *confuse the information* in the passage in a similar way. The subject of altitude is discussed in the third paragraph as a factor influencing the relative effects upon ozone changes (a radiative forcing) of radiation directed toward the earth and radiation directed away from the earth. This discussion does not, however, serve to distinguish forcings and feedbacks.

QUESTION TYPE #3: INFERRING FROM OR INTERPRETING SPECIFIC INFORMATION

Some questions require you to draw simple inferences or to recognize somewhat broader points by interpreting specific passage information. Here's how to approach these questions:

- Don't overlook the obvious! This question type calls for you to make only very "tight" inferences—in other words, the inference will be so strongly suggested in the passage that there really is no other reasonable interpretation. Do not fight the passage by looking for a more subtle or a deeper interpretation.

- An author inference usually requires that you piece together (logically speaking) no more than two *consecutive* sentences. To analyze the question, locate the relevant line or lines in the passage, read around those lines—the sentence preceding and the sentence following—and the inference should be clear enough to you.

- The question stem might refer to specific lines or a specific paragraph in the passage. In any event, based upon the information in the question stem, you will probably be able to locate the relevant portion of the passage within five to ten seconds (very helpful if you are in a time "crunch").

Look for These Wrong-Answer Ploys

- **The unwarranted or unsupported inference/ interpretation.** This response will leap to a conclusion that is not supported by the area of the passage where the inference occurs. It might bring in material that is outside the scope of the passage or exaggerate or distort the author's relatively narrow inference.

- **The response that is either backwards or runs contrary to the passage.** You might be surprised how easy it is to turn around certain facts or to confuse author agreement with author disagreement. The testing service knows this and will typically include an answer choice that is contradicted by, runs contrary to, or states certain information in the passage "backwards" (for example, reversing cause and effect).

- **The response that *confuses one thing with another*.** The response may mention details that are mentioned somewhere else in the passage but don't respond to the question at hand.

- **The response that *distorts* the meaning of the information in the passage.** This response may either twist or exaggerate the author's intended meaning.

Examples from Yesterday's Question Set

2. It can be inferred from the information in the passage that "burning of fossil fuels" (lines 10–11)

   (A) is an anthropogenic cause of radiative forcings *(correct response)*

   (B) results in both radiative forcings and radiative feedbacks *(partly unsupported)*

   (C) does not affect atmospheric forcings or feedbacks *(contradicted)*

   (D) is a significant type of radiative forcing *(backwards)*

   (E) is an anthropogenic cause of radiative feedback *(confuses information)*

   (A) is the best response. The author states in the first paragraph that forcings can arise from natural or anthropogenic causes. In the following sentence, the author describes two specific causes of forcings, presumably to illustrate the point of the previous sentence. It can be reasonably inferred by considering both sentences together that the first example (volcanic activity) is a natural cause, while the second (the burning of fossil fuels) is an anthropo-

genic cause. (B) is *only partly supported* by the passage. Although it can be inferred that the burning of fossil fuels causes radiative forcings, the author neither states nor suggests that this activity also causes radiative feedback. (C) *contradicts the information* presented in this part of the passage, which states explicitly that the concentration of sulfate aerosols is affected ("can be altered") by burning of fossil fuels. Thus, although burning of fossil fuels may not affect radiative feedback, it can be inferred that such activity does affect radiative forcings. (D) gets the passage information *backwards*. The burning of fossil fuels is a cause, not a type, of radiative forcing. (E) *confuses* forcings with feedbacks.

3. Based upon the information in the passage, it is reasonable to infer that decreased evaporation is most likely to result in which of the following?

   (A) An increase in water vapor concentration *(contrary)*

   (B) A decrease in solar irradiance *(correct response)*

   (C) A decrease in other radiative forcings *(confuses passage information)*

   (D) An increase in atmospheric temperatures *(contrary)*

   (E) A decrease in surface reflectivity *(confuses passage information)*

   (B) is the best response. According to the passage, increased evaporation leads to increased water vapor concentration (lines 23–25), which leads to an increase solar irradiance (lines 20–22). Accordingly, it is likely that a decrease in evaporation would lead to a decrease in the other two amounts. (A) *runs contrary* (although not explicitly) to the information in the passage, which states that increased (not decreased) evaporation leads to increased water vapor concentration (see lines 23–25). (C) *confuses the information* in the passage. The pertinent part of the passage (lines 13–18) deals solely with feedbacks and not forcings. (D) *runs contrary* (although not explicitly) to the information in the passage, which states that increased (not decreased) evaporation leads to a warming of the atmosphere. (E) *confuses the information* in the passage. The pertinent part of the passage (lines 13–18) deals solely with feedbacks. However, surface reflectivity is a type of forcing (line 6).

7. The information in the last paragraph does NOT:

(A) provide evidence of the variability of ozone amounts at different altitudes *(inferable)*

(B) underscore the complexity in measuring radiative changes *(inferable)*

(C) call into question current methods of determining radiative changes *(correct response—contrary to passage information)*

(D) support the author's position that predicting future ozone changes is problematic *(inferable)*

(E) explain a discrepancy between an earlier theory and more recent scientific evidence *(inferable)*

(C) is the best response. Response (C) actually *runs contrary* (although not explicitly) to the information in the final paragraph. The author seems to accept the findings of the recent aircraft studies and certainly does not call into question the methods used in those studies. (A) is incorrect based upon the last sentence of the passage. Since high (vertical) resolution observations are required to detect concentrations of greenhouse gases, it can be inferred that changes in such concentrations vary quickly with altitude. Moreover, the author suggests in the previous paragraph that this is the case [referring to the "vertical distribution of ozone" (line 46) and to the dependence of climate forcings upon the altitude of ozone changes (lines 46–49)]. (B) is incorrect since the studies discussed in the last paragraph suggest that determining the amounts of forcings is more complex than previously thought; specifically, that relative amounts vary quickly and significantly with altitude. (D) is incorrect for essentially the same reason as (B). The newfound variability of chemical concentration among different altitudes adds to the difficulty in assessing the relative importance of competing forcings discussed in the previous paragraph (lines 46–49). (E) is inferable. In the last sentence of the passage, the author refers to "conventional explanations," which can be characterized as "earlier theories." Since the new evidence calls into question those earlier theories, it is reasonable to infer that a discrepancy existed between earlier explanations and recent scientific evidence. In fact, the third paragraph as a whole explains that discrepency.

QUESTION TYPE #4: RECOGNIZING THE FUNCTION OF SPECIFIC INFORMATION

Some questions are designed to determine whether, in immersing yourself in the details, you lose sight of the author's reason for including the details. To avoid falling into this trap, be sure to interact with the passage at all times, asking yourself what role or function specific information plays in the context in which it is mentioned. Here's how to approach these questions:

- Maintain an *active mind set* as you read. When you come across detailed information in the passage, ask yourself what role these details play in the discussion. Is the author trying to support his or her point with specific examples? Is the author observing similarities and differences between two things? As you read, remember that it is more important for you to understand *why* the author mentions details than to remember the details themselves (you can always look them up).

- Some *inference* is required. You will not find an explicit answer to this question in the passage. In other words, the author is not going to come right out and state, "The reason I am mentioning this particular detail is to support my assertion that . . . " Instead, you must infer the author's purpose in mentioning the detail.

- As with "inference" questions (Type #3), these questions call for you to make only very "tight" inferences; in other words, the author's purpose will be so strongly suggested in the passage that there really is no other reasonable interpretation.

Look for These Wrong-Answer Ploys

- **The response that is *unsupported*.** This response will infer a purpose that is not supported by the information in the passage, possibly by bringing in extrinsic material (information from outside the passage).

- **The response that *exaggerates or distorts* the author's purpose.** As noted earlier, you must make only narrow, or "tight," inferences when inferring the author's purpose in mentioning details. A wrong answer might distort or exaggerate the author's relatively narrow inference.

- **The response that *confuses the information* in the passage or *does not respond to the question.*** The response will restate a point made elsewhere in the passage. This response will be tempting if you recall reading the statement and are confident that the statement is true. Don't be fooled. By focusing your attention on only the relevant portion of the passage, you can be confident that this response, while it may be an accurate statement, is a wrong answer.

- **The response that *confuses the author's position* with that of another, possibly contradicting the information in the passage.** The author may mention certain details to support his or her argument against a position or theory. Be sure not to confuse the author's argument with opposing views.

Example from Yesterday's Question Set

5. The author discusses the effect of clouds on atmospheric temperature most likely in order to show that

   (A) radiative feedbacks can be more difficult to isolate and predict than radiative forcings *(unsupported)*

   (B) the distinction between radiative feedbacks and radiative forcings is somewhat arbitrary *(unsupported)*

   (C) some radiative feedbacks cannot be determined solely by global climate model simulations *(confuses passage information)*

   (D) the climatic impact of some radiative feedbacks is uncertain *(correct response)*

   (E) the NASA-sponsored study is inconclusive as to the effect of ozone on cloud formation and dissipation *(confuses passage information)*

(D) is the best response. Response (D) restates the author's point in the first sentence of the second paragraph. Immediately thereafter, the author discusses clouds as an example of this point: it is difficult to predict the impact of greenhouse gases on clouds and thus on temperature. (A) is *unsupported* by the passage. In the second paragraph, the author discusses two particular examples of radiative changes—one involving radiative forcings (lines 30–32) and the other involving radiative feedbacks (lines 32–34). The author's purpose in discussing these two phenomena is to illustrate the author's previous point that "the interplay between forcings and feedbacks can be quite complex" (lines 19–20). However, the author makes no attempt to compare the relative complexity or uncertainty of these two effects. (B) is unsupported by the passage. In the first paragraph, the author attempts to distinguish between forcings and feedbacks but does not assert or infer that the distinction is somewhat arbitrary. (C) *confuses the information* in the passage and is somewhat nonsensical. It is forcings (not feedbacks) that are specified in (not determined by) global climate model simulations (lines 11–13). Moreover, (C) is wholly unsupported by the information in the second paragraph; nowhere does the author discuss or mention global climate simulations in relation to the effects of clouds on atmospheric temperatures. (E) confuses the information in the second paragraph with the discussion in the third paragraph about the NASA-sponsored study. (E) is also unsupported insofar as the author does not indicate whether the study is conclusive or inconclusive.

QUESTION TYPE #5: EXTRAPOLATING FROM OR APPLYING PASSAGE IDEAS

These questions are not as common as the other types, but nevertheless appear in question sets from time to time. These questions ask you either to apply passage information to new situations or to speculate as to how the passage would continue. The approach here is similar to that of handling "inference questions" (Type #3).

Common Wrong Answer Ploys

- **The response that is *unsupported* by the ideas referred to in the question.** It may require an unwarranted inference, or it may depart from the topic or be irrelevant to the ideas presented in the passage.

- **The response that *runs contrary* to the ideas referred to in the question.** This answer choice can fool you, since all the right words and phrases might be there. However, the answer turns around the idea presented in the passage, possibly by including or excluding a key word.

- **If the questions ask for a logical continuation of the passage, beware of the response that *covers old ground*.** The author's discussion is unlikely to reverse its "flow" and rehash material already treated in the earlier parts of the passage. However, don't rule out this possibility. For example, the author might continue by examining in more detail one of two key points made in the passage. If this is the case, the final sentences will in all likelihood provide a clue that this is the next area of discussion.

Examples from Yesterday's Question Set

6. Based upon the information in the passage, the author would probably agree that scientists could more accurately predict the extent and direction of the greenhouse effect if they were to

   (A) monitor radiative feedbacks and forcings over a longer time period (*not adequately supported*)

   (B) change the direction of research away from determining amounts of radiative changes (*runs contrary*)

   (C) account for the altitude at which cloud formations appear (*confuses passage information*)

   (D) isolate those ozone changes caused specifically by anthropogenic factors (*unsupported—off the topic*)

   (E) isolate the cooling influence of ozone changes from their warming influence (*correct response*)

(E) is the best response. According to the passage, a given vertical distribution of ozone affects atmospheric temperature in both directions at once (lines 41–45). Accordingly, by isolating the cooling influence of a given distribution of ozone from its warming influence, scientists might better predict whether changes in the vertical distribution of ozone will have a net cooling or a net warming effect. (A) is the second-best response. It seems reasonable from a common-sense viewpoint that our ability to forecast the precise extent of the greenhouse effect improves as more data is acquired over time. However, this assertion is neither stated nor implied by the passage itself; thus, it is *not adequately supported*. (B) *runs contrary* to the information in the passage. Radiative changes include changes in ozone, which are the very cause of the greenhouse effect. Thus, scientists should continue attempts to determine the amounts of such changes. (C) *confuses the information* in the passage. The discussion of altitude relates to forcings, while the discussion of clouds relates to feedbacks. (D) is *unsupported—off the topic*. Although the author does indicate in the first paragraph that forcings arise from both anthropogenic and natural causes (lines 6–8), nowhere in the passage does the author attempt to isolate their effects from each other, nor does the author suggest that doing so would enable scientists to better predict the extent of the greenhouse effect.

THE LSAT'S FAVORITE WRONG-ANSWER PLOYS

Here's a handy checklist of the LSAT wrong-answer ploys, in order of frequency of use on the test. Keep this list in mind. It can help you narrow down the answer choices and find the best response.

- **Distorts the information in the passage:** understates, overstates, or twists the information in the passage or the author's point in presenting that information

- **Mentioned in the passage, but does not respond to the question:** includes information found in the passage but does not respond appropriately to the question posed

- **Speculation or unsupported inference:** calls for some measure of speculation in that the statement is not readily (reliably) inferable from the information in the passage

- **Contrary to the passage or stated backwards:** contradicts passage information or gets information backwards

- **Confuses one opinion or position with another:** incorrectly represents the position or opinion of one person or group as that of another

- **Too narrow (specific):** focuses on particular information in the passage that is too specific or narrowly-focused in terms of the question posed

- **Too broad (general):** embraces information or ideas that are too general or widely-focused in terms of the question posed

- **Not mentioned in the passage:** brings in information not found anywhere in the passage

TIPS FOR RESPONDING TO LSAT READING QUESTIONS

Tip #1: Don't Second-Guess the Test Maker

The directions for the LSAT Reading Comprehension section instruct you to choose the "best" response among the five choices. Isn't this awfully subjective? True, there is an element of subjective judgment involved in Reading Comprehension. However, these questions are reviewed, tested, and revised several times before they appear as scored questions on an actual LSAT. *Do not second-guess the test maker's judgment or command of the conventions of Standard Written English!* If you think there are two or more viable "best" responses, *you* (not the test maker) have either misread or misinterpreted the passage, the question, or the answer choices.

Tip #2: Read Every Answer Choice in Its Entirety

Remember, you are looking for the "best" response. Often, more than one answer choice will be viable. Don't hastily select or eliminate answer choices without reading them all. *LSAT test takers miss more questions for this reason than for any other!*

Tip #3: Don't Over-Analyze Questions or Second-Guess Yourself

If you believe you understood the passage fairly well, but a particular answer choice seems confusing or a bit nonsensical, do not assume that it's your fault. *Many wrong answer choices simply don't make much sense!* If an answer choice strikes you this way, don't examine it further; eliminate it! Similarly, if you've read and considered all five choices, and one response strikes you as the best one, *more often than not, your initial response will be the correct one!*

Tip #4: Don't Overlook the Obvious

Reading Comprehension questions vary greatly in difficulty level, which means that many of the questions are really pretty easy. If a particular response seems obviously correct or incorrect, don't assume that you are missing something.

Tip #5: Cross Reference the Questions

Although each question in a set is distinct, it is possible to "check" your responses to certain questions by examining how you responded to certain other questions. Check to see if you have contradicted yourself in your responses. If so, go back and change your answers. For example, your response to a thesis or "main idea" question should be *consistent* with your response to questions that asks about the author's primary purpose, attitude toward the subject, and position on the issue at hand.

Tip #6: Eliminate Responses that Run Contrary to the Thesis

Regardless of the type of question you are dealing with, keep in mind the overall thesis, main idea, or point that the author is making in the passage as a whole. Any answer choice to any question that runs contrary to or is inconsistent with that thesis can be eliminated. It's surprising how many questions can be answered correctly using only this technique.

Tip #7: Keep in Mind Common Wrong-Answer Ploys to Avoid Falling into the Test Makers' Traps

Be assured: The LSAT will keep trying to bait you with its arsenal of wrong-answer ploys. Learn to recognize these ploys, and keep them in mind as you take tomorrow's mini-test as well as the Reading Comprehension section of the Practice Test later in this book.

Reading Comprehension Lesson 3: Mini-Test and Review

Today you will apply what you learned on Days 8 and 9 to three Reading Comprehension passages. After taking this mini-test under timed conditions, review the explanations that follow. Preceding the explanation for each question, the question type and difficulty level are indicated.

READING COMPREHENSION MINI-TEST

Number of questions: 21
Suggested time: 27 minutes

Directions (as printed in test booklet): Each passage in this section is followed by a group of questions to be answered on the basis of what is stated or implied in the passage. For some of the questions, more than one of the choices could conceivably answer the question. However, you are to choose the best answer; that is, the response that most accurately and completely answers the question, and blacken the appropriate space on your answer sheet.

Questions 1–7 are based on the following passage.

Non-indigenous species of plants and animals arrive by way of two general types of pathways. First, species having origins outside of the United States may enter the country and become
(5) established either as free-living populations or under human cultivation—for example, in agriculture, horticulture, aquaculture, or as pets. Some cultivated species subsequently escape or are released and also become established as
(10) free-living populations. Second, species of either U.S. or foreign origin and already within the United States may spread to new locales. Pathways of both types include intentional as well as unintentional species transfers. Rates of species
(15) movement driven by human transformations of natural environments as well as by human mobility—through commerce, tourism, and travel—dwarf natural rates by comparison. While geographic distributions of species natu-
(20) rally expand or contract over historical time intervals (tens to hundreds of years), species' ranges rarely expand thousands of miles or across physical barriers such as oceans or mountains.

Habitat modification can create conditions
(25) favorable to the establishment of non-indigenous species. Soil disturbed in construction and agriculture is open for colonization by non-indigenous weeds, which in turn may provide habitats for the non-indigenous insects that
(30) evolved with them. For example, the European viper's bugloss, a weed common along roads and railroad tracks, provides a habitat for the Eurasian lace bug. Human-generated changes in fire frequency, grazing intensity, as well as soil
(35) stability and nutrient levels, similarly facilitate

the spread and establishment of non-indigenous plants. When human changes to natural environments span large geographical areas, they effectively create conduits for species movement (40) between previously isolated locales. The rapid spread of the Russian wheat aphid to fifteen states in just two years following its 1986 arrival has been attributed in part to the prevalence of alternative host plants that are available when (45) wheat is not. Many of these are non-indigenous grasses recommended for planting on the forty-million or more acres enrolled in the U.S. Department of Agriculture's Conservation Reserve Program.

(50) A number of factors confound quantitative evaluation of the relative importance of various entry pathways. Time lags often occur between establishment of non-indigenous species and their detection, and tracing the pathway for a (55) long-established species is difficult. Experts estimate that non-indigenous weeds are usually detected only after having been in the country for thirty years or having spread to at least ten thousand acres. In addition, federal port inspection, (60) although a major source of information on non-indigenous species pathways, especially for agricultural pests, provides data only when such species enter via scrutinized routes. Finally, some comparisons between pathways defy quan- (65) titative analysis. For example, which is more "important": the entry pathway of one very harmful species or one by which many but less harmful species enter the country?

1. According to the passage, which of the following is true about the European viper's bugloss?

   (A) It serves as a host plant for the Russian wheat aphid.

   (B) Its natural rate of movement is comparable to that of the Eurasian lace bug.

   (C) It finds certain human pathways to be habitable.

   (D) Its movement across physical barriers such as oceans is unlikely.

   (E) Its entry into the United States went undetected for more than thirty years.

2. Which of the following statements about species movement is best supported by the information in the passage?

   (A) Species movement is affected more by habitat modifications than by human mobility.

   (B) Human-driven factors affect the rate at which species move more than they affect the long-term amount of such movements.

   (C) Natural expansions in the geographic distribution of species account for less species movement than do natural contractions.

   (D) Natural environments created by commerce, tourism, and travel contribute significantly to species movement.

   (E) Movement of a species within a continent depends largely upon the geographic extent of human mobility within the continent.

3. According to the passage, the U.S. Department of Agriculture

   (A) contributed to the spread of the Russian wheat aphid

   (B) provides data about non-indigenous species entering the United States through scrutinized routes

   (C) has assumed the responsibility for preventing entry of non-indigenous species onto federal lands

   (D) has attempted unsuccessfully to isolate the Russian wheat aphid

   (E) favors the planting of non-indigenous grasses for the purpose of protecting certain species of insects

4. It can be inferred from the passage that the movement of non-indigenous species is influenced by all of the following EXCEPT:

   (A) soil nutrient levels

   (B) import restrictions

   (C) popularity of aquaculture

   (D) geographic terrain

   (E) fire frequency

5. Which of the following best expresses the primary purpose of the last paragraph?

(A) To explain why it is difficult to trace the entry pathways for long-established non-indigenous species

(B) To describe the events usually leading to the detection of a non-indigenous species

(C) To discuss the role that time lags and geographic expansion of non-indigenous species play in species detection

(D) To point out the inadequacy of the federal port inspection system in detecting the entry of non-indigenous species

(E) To identify the problems in assessing the relative significance of various entry pathways for non-indigenous species

6. Based upon the information in the passage, whether the entry pathway for a particular non-indigenous species can be determined is LEAST likely to depend upon which of the following?

(A) Whether the species is considered to be a pest

(B) Whether the species gains entry through a scrutinized route

(C) The rate at which the species expands geographically

(D) How long the species has been established

(E) The size of the average member of the species

7. Which of the following is the most appropriate title for the passage?

(A) Determining Entry Pathways for Non-Indigenous Species

(B) The Impact of Human Activity on Species Movement

(C) Non-Indigenous Species: Intentional vs. Unintentional Entry Pathways

(D) Non-Indigenous Plants: Pathways for Entry

(E) Problems in Halting the Spread of Harmful Non-Indigenous Species

Questions 8–13 are based on the following passage.

Among the many other things it is, a portrait is a record of the personal and artistic encounter that produced it. It is possible for artists to produce portraits of individuals who have not sat for
(5) them, but the portrait that emerges normally betrays the restrictions under which the artist has labored. Even when an artist's portrait is simply a copy of someone else's work, as in the many portraits of Queen Elizabeth I produced during
(10) her lifetime, the never-changing features of a monarch who refused to sit for her court painters reflect not only the putative powers of an ever-youthful queen but also the remoteness of those attempting to depict her.
(15)   Portraits are "occasional" not only in the sense that they are closely tied to particular events in the lives of their subjects but also in the sense that there is usually an occasion—however brief, uncomfortable, artificial, or unsatisfactory it may
(20) be—in which the artist and subject directly confront each other. Thus, the encounter a portrait records is most tangibly the sitting itself, which may be brief or extended, collegial or confrontational. Cartier-Bresson has expressed his passion
(25) for portrait photography by characterizing it as "a delicate rape," in sharp contrast to Richard Avedon's conception of a sitting. While Cartier-Bresson reveals himself as an interloper and opportunist, Avedon confesses to a role as diag-
(30) nostician and (by implication) psychic healer—not as someone who necessarily transforms his subjects, but as someone who reveals their essential nature. Both photographers appear to agree, however, that the fundamental dynamic in this
(35) process lies squarely in the hands of the artist.
   A quite-different paradigm has its roots not in confrontation or consultation but in active collaboration between artist and sitter. This very different kind of relationship was formulated
(40) most vividly by William Hazlitt in his essay entitled "On Sitting for One's Picture" (1823). To Hazlitt, the "bond of connection" between painter and sitter is most like the relationship between two lovers "in which their self-love
(45) finds an equal counterpart." Hazlitt fleshes out

his thesis by recounting particular episodes from the career of Sir Joshua Reynolds. According to Hazlitt, Reynold's sitters, accompanied by their friends, were meant to enjoy an atmosphere that

(50) was both comfortable for them and conducive to the enterprise of the portrait painter, who was simultaneously their host and their contractual employee. With artists like Reynolds, who I take to be a paradigmatic case, no fundamental dif-

(55) ference exists between the artist's studio and all those other rooms in which the sitters spin out the days of their lives. The act of entering Reynold's studio—this social and aesthetic en-counter—did not necessarily transform those

(60) who sat for him. Collaboration in portraiture such as Reynold's is based on the sitter's com-fort and security as well as on his or her desire to experiment with something new; and it is in this "creation of another self," as Hazlitt put it,

(65) that the painter's subjects may properly see themselves for the first time.

8. Which of the following best expresses the main idea of the passage?

(A) The success of a portrait depends largely upon the relationship between artist and subject.

(B) Photographers and painters differ in their views regarding their role in portrait photog-raphy.

(C) The social aspect of portraiture sitting plays an important part in the outcome of the sit-ting.

(D) Portraits, more than any other art form, pro-vide insight into the artist's social relation-ships.

(E) The paintings of Reynolds provide a record of his success in achieving a social bond with his subjects.

9. In referring to Queen Elizabeth as "ever-youthful" (line 13), the author implies that

(A) she instructed her court painters to paint her portrait in such a way that she appeared younger than she actually was

(B) all portraits of the queen available for copy-ing were painted when she was young

(C) she died at an early age, and so all portraits of her depicted her as a young woman

(D) her youthful appearance belied her actual age

(E) artists who copied her portraits believed that she was younger than she actually was

10. The author quotes Cartier-Bresson in order to

(A) refute Avedon's conception of a portrait sitting

(B) support the claim that portrait sitting can be a confrontational encounter

(C) provide one perspective of the portraiture encounter

(D) show that a portraiture encounter may be ei-ther brief or extended

(E) distinguish a sitting for a photographic por-trait from a sitting for a painted portrait

11. Which of the following best characterizes the por-traiture experience as viewed by Avedon?

(A) A collaboration

(B) A mutual accommodation

(C) A consultation

(D) An uncomfortable encounter

(E) A confrontation

12. A portrait artist operating under the Reynolds paradigm would probably disagree that

(A) a portraiture sitting often changes the way the sitter views himself or herself

(B) the portraiture encounter provides a means for both artist and subject to display their vanity

(C) a successful portrait depends more upon the artist's initiative than upon the subject

(D) the portrait sitting often heightens the sitter's self-knowledge

(E) the success of a portrait depends largely upon whether the artist and sitter are socially com-patible

13. Of the following, it would be most consistent with the information in the passage to assert that Reynolds

 (A) may have provided a transforming experience for some of his sitters

 (B) worked primarily with experienced portrait subjects

 (C) often painted portraits at his subjects' homes

 (D) was usually alone with his sitters while he painted their portraits

 (E) painted portraits primarily of friends and relatives

Questions 14–21 are based on the following passage.

The origin of the attempt to distinguish early from modern music and to establish the canons of performance practice for each lies in the eigh-teenth century. In the first half of that century,
(5) when Telemann and Bach ran the *collegium musicum* in Leipzig, Germany, they performed their own and other modern music. In the Ger-man universities of the early twentieth century, however, the reconstituted *collegium musicum*
(10) devoted itself to performing music from the cen-turies before the beginning of the "standard rep-ertory," by which was understood music from before the time of Bach and Handel.

Alongside this modern *collegium musicum*,
(15) German musicologists developed the historical subdiscipline known as "performance practice," which included the deciphering of obsolete mu-sical notation and its transcription into modern notation, the study of obsolete instruments, and
(20) the re-establishment of lost oral traditions asso-ciated with those forgotten repertories. The cut-off date for this study was understood to be around 1750, the year of Bach's death, since the music of Bach, Handel, Telemann and their con-
(25) temporaries did call for obsolete instruments and voices and unannotated performing traditions—for instance, the spontaneous realization of vo-cal and instrumental melodic ornamentation. Furthermore, with a few exceptions, late baroque
(30) music had ceased to be performed for nearly a

century, and the orally transmitted performing traditions associated with it were forgotten as a result. In contrast, the notation in the music of Haydn and Mozart from the second half of the
(35) eighteenth century was more complete than in the earlier styles, and the instruments seemed familiar, so no "special" knowledge appeared necessary. Also, the music of Haydn and Mozart, having never ceased to be performed, had main-
(40) tained some kind of oral tradition of performance practice.

Beginning around 1960, however, the early musicians—the performers of early music—began to encroach upon the music of Haydn,
(45) Mozart, and Beethoven. Why? Scholars studying performance practice had discovered that the liv-ing oral traditions associated with the Viennese classics frequently could not be traced back to the eighteenth century and that there were nearly as
(50) many performance mysteries to solve for music after 1750 as in earlier repertories. Furthermore, more and more young singers and instrumental-ists became attracted to early music, and as many of them graduated from student and amateur
(55) status to become fully professional, the technical level of early-music performances took a giant leap forward.

As professional early-music groups, building on these developments, expanded their reperto-
(60) ries to include later music, the angry cries from the mainstream could be heard on five conti-nents. The differences between the two camps extended beyond the already fascinating ques-tion of which instruments to use and how (or
(65) whether) to ornament to the more critical mat-ter of style and delivery. At the heart of their dis-agreement is whether historical knowledge about performing traditions is a prerequisite for proper interpretation of music or whether it merely cre-
(70) ates an obstacle to inspired musical tradition.

14. It can be inferred that the "standard repertory" mentioned in lines 11–12 might have included music

    (A) composed before 1700

    (B) of the early twentieth century

    (C) written by the performance-practice composers

    (D) written before the time of Handel

    (E) that called for the use of obsolete instruments

15. According to the passage, German musicologists of the early twentieth century limited performance practice to pre-1750 works because:

    (A) special knowledge was generally not required to decipher pre-1750 music

    (B) unannotated performing traditions had been maintained for later works

    (C) generally speaking, only music written before 1750 had ceased to be performed

    (D) the annotation for earlier works was generally less complete than for the works of Bach and Handel

    (E) music written prior to 1750 was considered obsolete

16. The author mentions the improved technical level of early-music performances (lines 55–57) in order to

    (A) call into question the fairness of the mainstream's objections to the expansion of performance practice to include later works

    (B) explain why an increasing number of young musicians were being attracted to early music

    (C) refute the mainstream's claim that historical knowledge about performing traditions creates an obstacle to inspired musical tradition

    (D) explain the expansion of performance practice to include later works of music

    (E) support the argument that the Viennese classics were more difficult to perform than earlier works

17. The author refers to modern performance practice as a "subdiscipline" (line 16) probably because it

    (A) was not sanctioned by the mainstream

    (B) required more discipline than performing the standard repertory

    (C) focused on particular aspects of the music being performed at the German universities

    (D) involved deciphering obsolete musical notation

    (E) involved performing the works that were being transcribed at the universities

18. According to the passage, performance practice in the early twentieth century involved all of the following EXCEPT:

    (A) deciphering outdated music notation

    (B) varying the delivery of music to suit the tastes of the particular audience

    (C) determining which musical instrument to use

    (D) reestablishing unannotated performing traditions

    (E) transcribing older music into modern notation

19. Which of the following statements, if true, would best support the author's explanation for the encroachment by the early-musicians upon the music of Mozart, Haydn, and Beethoven?

    (A) The mainstream approved of the manner in which the early-musicians treated the music of Bach and Handel.

    (B) Unannotated performing traditions associated with these composers were distinct from those associated with pre-1750 works.

    (C) Most instrumentalists are attracted to early music because of the opportunities to play obsolete instruments.

    (D) The music of these composers is notated more completely than is the music of Bach and Handel.

    (E) The early-musicians and the mainstream both prefer the same style and delivery of music.

20. Which of the following statements is best supported by the passage?

    (A) The scope of performance practice expanded significantly during the latter half of the twentieth century.

    (B) Twentieth-century musicologists interpret early music differently than did musicologists of the eighteenth century.

    (C) Attempts to distinguish between early and modern music date back to the early eighteenth century.

    (D) The works of Mozart are now considered by the mainstream to be "early music."

    (E) Although the definition of early music has changed over the last century, the canons of performance practice have remained relatively unchanged.

21. Which of the following is the most appropriate title for the passage?

    (A) Performance Practice: The Legacy of the German *Collegium Musicum*

    (B) How Far Should Early Music Extend?

    (C) Unannotated Performing Traditions of the Eighteenth and Twentieth Centuries

    (D) Performance Practice and New Interpretations of the Viennese Classics

    (E) Competing Views Regarding the Necessity of Historical Knowledge for Inspired Musical Tradition

Quick Answer Guide

Reading Comprehension Mini-Test

1. C	7. A	13. A	19. B
2. E	8. C	14. E	20. A
3. A	9. B	15. B	21. B
4. B	10. C	16. D	
5. E	11. C	17. C	
6. E	12. C	18. B	

EXPLANATIONS

1. Explicit detail (moderate). Answer: C.

According to the passage, the bugloss is common "along roads and railroad tracks"—that is, along human pathways.

(A) confuses the information in the passage. The bugloss serves as a host plant for the Eurasian lace bug, not for the Russian wheat aphid.

(B) calls for an unwarranted inference. Although it might be inferred that human-driven movement—i.e., movement associated with road construction—of the bugloss and lace bug are comparable, no such inference can be made about their natural movement.

(D) is too broad—although the bugloss' natural movement across physical barriers such as oceans is probably unlikely (based upon the information in the first paragraph), human-driven movement might very well be likely.

(E) is the second-best response. It is possible that (E) is an accurate statement. The European viper's bugloss is a type of weed, and the passage does indeed indicate that non-indigenous weeds usually go undetected for at least thirty years. However, it is unfair to infer that the European viper's bugloss was in fact one such weed.

2. Interpretation (moderate). Answer: E.

Statement (E) restates the author's point in the first paragraph that rates of species movement driven by human transformation of the natural environment and by human mobility dwarf natural rates by comparison (lines 14–18).

(A) is unsupported by the passage. Although the author compares natural species movement to human-driven movement, no such comparison is made as between human modification of habitats and human mobility.

(B) is unsupported by the passage. The author makes no attempt to compare rate (interpreted either as frequency or speed) of species movement to total amounts of movement (distance).

(C) is unsupported by the passage. The author makes no attempt to compare natural expansions to natural contractions.

(D) is nonsensical. Human mobility (commerce, tourism, and travel) do not create "natural" environments. It is human mobility itself, not the "natural environment" created by it, that contributes significantly to species movement.

3. Interpretation (easier). Answer: A.

According to the information in the second paragraph, the rapid spread of the Russian wheat aphid resulted partly from the availability of alternative host plants (non-indigenous grasses) which were recommended for planting on lands controlled by the U.S. Department of Agriculture. Thus, the Department was partly responsible for the rapid spread of the Russian wheat aphid.

(B) confuses the information in the passage. Federal port inspection (not the U.S. Department of Agriculture) provides data about species entering through scrutinized routes.

(C) is unsupported by the passage. The author neither states nor implies that this is one of the Department's duties.

(D) is unsupported by the information in the passage. The author neither states nor implies that the Department made any attempts to isolate the Russian wheat aphid either before or since the rapid spread of the species.

(E) is the second-best response. (E) is only partly supported by the information in the passage. Although it appears that the Department intentionally planted various non-indigenous grasses, as (E) suggests, the author makes no mention of the reason for this.

4. Explicit detail (moderate). Answer: B.

The only discussion in the passage related to importing is the discussion in the final paragraph about the limitations of federal port inspection in detecting the entry of non-indigenous species. While common sense might suggest that import restrictions would probably affect the movement of non-indigenous plants and animals, the subject of import restrictions is not mentioned in the final paragraph or anywhere else in the passage.

(A) is supported explicitly by the passage. According to the passage, human-generated changes in soil nutrient levels "facilitate the spread and establishment of non-indigenous plants" (lines 35–37).

(C) is the second-best response. Although not supported implicitly by the passage, "aquaculture" is mentioned in line 7 as a form of human cultivation which helps to establish non-indigenous species.

Thus, it can be reasonably inferred that the popularity of this activity would affect the movement of certain non-indigenous species.

(D) is supported explicitly by the passage. According to the passage, physical barriers such as mountains (i.e., natural terrain) limit species movement (lines 21–23).

(E) is supported explicitly by the passage. According to the passage, human-generated changes in fire frequency "facilitate the spread and establishment of non-indigenous plants" (lines 35–37).

5. Interpretation (moderate). Answer: E.

In the first sentence of the final paragraph, the author claims that "[a] number of factors confound quantitative evaluation of the relative importance of various entry pathways." In the remainder of the paragraph, the author identifies three such problems: (1) the difficulty of early detection, (2) the inadequacy of port inspection, and (3) the inherent subjectivity in determining the "importance" of a pathway.

(A) is off-focus. Although the author asserts that it is difficult to trace an entry pathway once a species is well established, the author does not explain why this is so.

(B) is off-focus and is too narrow. Although the author does mention that a species is usually not detected until it spreads to at least ten-thousand acres, the author mentions this single "event" leading to detection as part of the broader point that the unlikelihood of early detection contributes to the problem of quantifying the relative importance of entry pathways.

(C) is off-focus. Although the author mentions these factors, they are not "discussed" in any detail, as (C) suggests. Also, the primary concern of the last paragraph is not with identifying the factors affecting species detection but rather with identifying the problems in quantifying the relative importance of various entry pathways.

(D) is too narrow. The author is concerned with identifying other problems as well as in determining the relative importance of various entry pathways.

6. Explicit detail (easier). Answer: E.

Nowhere in the passage does the author either state or imply that the physical size of a species' members is a factor in whether the entry pathway for the species can be determined.

(A) is the second-best response. Unlike Responses (B), (C), and (D), (A) is not supported explicitly by the passage. However, the author mentions in the final paragraph that federal port inspection is "a major source of information on non-indigenous species pathways, especially for agricultural pests." Accordingly, whether a species is an agricultural pest might have some bearing upon whether or not its entry is detected (by port inspectors).

(B), (C), and (D) are all mentioned explicitly in the final paragraph as factors affecting how precisely the entry pathway(s) of a species can be determined.

7. Primary purpose (challenging). Answer: A.

Although (A) may not provide an ideal title for the passage, it is the best among the five responses in expressing the ideas presented in the passage as a whole: the various types of entry pathways (first paragraph), the effects of habitat modification by humans on the establishment of non-indigenous species (second paragraph), and the problems in determining the relative significance of entry pathways (final paragraph).

(B) is too narrow. Although the title suggested in (B) fairly characterizes the author's concern in the second paragraph, it fails to encompass the author's chief concern with identifying the problems in determining the relative importance of various entry pathways.

(C) is off-focus. Although intentional and unintentional pathways are distinguished (in the first paragraph), the remainder of the passage deals solely with unintentional entry.

(D) is too broad in one sense and too narrow in another sense. The author's specific concern is with unintentional entry pathways (not with both intentional and unintentional pathways); in this sense, then, (D) is too broad. At the same time, the passage is concerned not just with plant species but also with animal species; thus, in this sense, (D) is too narrow.

(E) distorts the passage. Although the final paragraph does identify some of the problems in obtaining information needed to prevent the establishment of non-indigenous species, the author does not focus on (or even suggest) the need to halt the spread of harmful non-indigenous species.

8. Main idea (moderate). Answer: C.

Although it is difficult to articulate a single "main idea" or thesis of this passage, the author seems to be most concerned with emphasizing that a portrait sitting is a social encounter, not just an artistic exercise, and that artists consider their relationship with their sitters to be somehow significant. Thus, (C) is a good statement of the author's primary point.

(A) is the second-best response. Without (C), (A) would be the best response; it embraces the passage as a whole and properly focuses on the author's primary concern with exploring the relationship between artist and sitter. However, the passage does not discuss how or whether this relationship results in a "successful" portrait; thus (A) distorts the information in the passage.

(B) is off-focus and calls for an unwarranted generalization. Admittedly, the author does claim that the Reynolds paradigm (described by Hazlitt as well as by the author in the third paragraph) is "quite different" (line 36) from the two paradigms discussed in the second paragraph, and the latter does indeed involve a painter (Reynolds) while the other two paradigms involve photographers (Cartier-Bresson and Avedon). However, nowhere in the passage does the author generalize from this fact that a portrait artist's approach or view depends upon whether the artist is a painter or a photographer.

(D) distorts the information in the passage and departs from the topic at hand. Although the passage does support the notion that a portrait might reveal something about the relationship between artist and sitter, the author neither states nor implies that a portrait reveals anything about the artist's other relationships. Moreover, nowhere in the passage does the author compare portraiture with other art forms.

(E) is too narrow and refers to information not mentioned in the passage. The passage is not just about Reynolds, but about the portraiture encounter in general. Also, the author does not comment on Reynold's "success" or about how his relationship with his sitters may have contributed to his success.

9. Inference (easier). Answer: B.

According to the passage, the queen refused to sit for her court painters. The author also makes clear that the "many portraits" of her were copies of other portraits. Thus, it can reasonably be inferred that the queen was relatively young when the "master" portrait(s)—i.e., the portrait(s) from which copies were painted—was (were) painted.

(A) runs contrary to the information in the passage, which states that the queen refused to sit for her court painters.

(C) calls for an unwarranted inference. Just because all paintings of the queen depict her as a young person, it does not necessarily follow that she died when she was young.

(D) distorts the author's meaning. Considered in context of the discussion in the first paragraph, it is highly unlikely that the author's description of the queen as "ever youthful" should be taken to mean that the queen did not appear to age.

(E) is nonsensical. Artists copying pictures of the queen would probably depict the queen as she appeared in the "master" portrait, regardless of what age the copying artist believed the queen to be at the time.

10. Purpose of detail (easier). Answer: C.

(C) is the best response. In the passage, the author compares and contrasts three different perspectives of the portraiture encounter: (1) Avedon's view, (2) Cartier-Bresson's view, and (3) Reynold's view as interpreted and reflected by Hazlitt. (C) properly expresses the function that the author's discussion of Cartier-Bresson (including the quote) serves in the author's overall discussion.

(A) distorts the author's purpose as well as the meaning of the information in the passage. Although the author is explicit that Cartier-Bresson's conception is quite different from that of Avedon, the author is not concerned with "refuting" Avedon's conception—the author neither states nor implies that Avedon's conception is wrong or inaccurate

in some way. The author is not arguing for one view over another, but is rather simply presenting different personal perspectives of the portraiture encounter.

(B) confuses the information in the passage. It is Avedon, not Cartier-Bresson, whose conception of the portraiture encounter is characterized as confrontational.

(D) confuses the information in the passage. The author states earlier in the paragraph that a sitting may either be "brief or extended, collegial or confrontational" (lines 23–24). The views of Cartier-Bresson and Avedon, discussed immediately thereafter, differ from each other in that Cartier-Bresson conceives his relationship with his sitters as confrontational, while Avedon views it as collegial. However, the author makes no further mention of the length of the sitting, either when describing the views of Avedon and Cartier-Bresson or in any other part of the passage.

(E) distorts the author's purpose and is unsupported by the passage. Nowhere in the passage does the author, either explicitly or implicitly, seek to distinguish between portrait photography and portrait painting.

11. Interpretation (moderate). Answer: C.

(C) is the best response. In the first sentence of the third paragraph, the author distinguishes a "quite-different paradigm" (i.e., the case of Reynolds) from the conceptions of Cartier-Bresson and Avedon in that the Reynolds paradigm "has its roots not in confrontation or consultation but in active collaboration between artist and sitter" (lines 36–38). It is rather obvious from the quotation in the second paragraph that Cartier-Bresson conceives the encounter as "confrontational"; thus, the author seems to be characterizing an Avedon sitting as a "consultation."

(A) confuses the information in the passage. It is the Reynolds paradigm discussed in the third paragraph, not Avedon's view, that the author characterizes as a "collaboration" (line 60).

(B) is a second-best response. Although the term "mutual accommodation" does not appear in the passage, this term suggests a relationship in which both artist and painter allow for the other's needs or desires. Such a description aligns much closer with

Hazlitt's analogy of two lovers than with Avedon's view of the artist as diagnostician and psychic healer.

(D) is a second-best response. According to the passage, Avedon confesses "uncomfortably" to his role as diagnostician and psychic healer (lines 29–30). It does not necessarily follow, however, that Avedon finds his encounters with his sitters to be uncomfortable; in this sense, (D) distorts the information in the passage.

(E) confuses the information in the passage. It is clear from the quotation in the second paragraph that it is Cartier-Bresson (not Avedon) who conceives the encounter as "confrontational."

12. Interpretation (challenging). Answer: C.

(C) is the best response. The author describes a sitting under the Reynolds paradigm as a "collaboration" (lines 37–38) which is based in part on the sitter's "desire to experiment with something new" (lines 62–63), suggesting that the sitter and artist both play active roles in the process. (C) runs contrary to this suggestion.

(A) and (D) are both supported by the last sentence of the passage, which suggests that the portraiture experience provides the sitter with a new (and more accurate) view of himself or herself.

(B) is the second-best response. (B) is not as explicitly supported by the passage as the other incorrect responses. However, (B) is supported (albeit implicitly) by Hazlitt's analogy between the collaboration of artist and subject and the relationship between two lovers. Hazlitt describes both relationships as a sharing of each person's self-love (i.e., mutual displaying of each person's vanity).

(E) is implicitly supported. Hazlitt, as well as the author, seems to emphasize the importance of putting the sitter at ease socially—the artist is host as well as contractual employee, and collaboration (under the Reynolds paradigm) depends ("is based") upon the sitter's comfort. (E) is thus a reasonable interpretation of the Reynolds paradigm.

13. Inference (moderate). Answer: A.

According to the passage, "[t]he act of entering Reynold's studio" . . . "did not necessarily transform

those who sat for him" (lines 57–60). This statement allows for the possibility that some sitters were transformed in some manner (although the author does not state whether this was the case).

(B) runs contrary to the information in the passage. According to the passage, the collaboration in portraiture such as Reynold's is based in part upon the sitter's desire to experiment with something new (line 68). It is reasonably inferable, therefore, that many of Reynold's sitters were not experienced in this area.

(C) runs contrary to the information in the passage. In mentioning "the act of entering Reynold's studio" (lines 57–58) and that "no fundamental difference exists between the artist's studio and all those other rooms in which the sitters spin out the days of their lives" (lines 54–57), the author strongly suggests that Reynold's portraits were created in his own studio rather than at the homes of his subjects.

(D) is explicitly contradicted by the passage, which states that Reynold's sitters were "accompanied by their friends" (lines 48–49).

(E) is implicitly supported by various information in the third paragraph. Hazlitt and the author both emphasize the important role that establishing a social rapport played in the collaboration of Reynolds and his sitters. If Reynolds had limited his portrait subjects to friends and relatives, establishing a rapport would probably not have been necessary for his sitters' comfort. Also, the passage indicates that Reynold's subjects were accompanied by their friends and suggests that this was necessary to help the subjects feel at ease. However, this probably would not have been necessary were Reynolds already a friend of his subjects.

14. Inference (moderate). Answer: E.

It is reasonably inferable from the first paragraph as a whole that the "standard repertory" mentioned in lines 11–12 refers to the music of Bach and Telemann as well as to other ("modern") music from their time (first half of the eighteenth century). In the second paragraph, the author mentions that the music of Bach, Telemann, and their contemporaries called for obsolete instruments (line 19). Thus, the standard repertory might have included music that called for the use of obsolete instruments, as (E) indicates.

(A) runs contrary to the information in the passage. The "standard repertory" refers to the music of Bach, Telemann, and other composers of the first half of the eighteenth century. Thus, it probably did not include music written prior to 1700.

(B) confuses the information in the passage. As noted above, the "standard repertory" refers to the music of Bach, Telemann, and other composers of the first half of the eighteenth century. Thus, it could not have included music written during the twentieth century.

(C) is nonsensical. "Performance practice" refers not to a group of composers but rather to a subdiscipline formed by German musicologists who deciphered and interpreted early works.

(D) runs contrary to the information in the passage. The passage suggests that Handel was a contemporary of Bach. Thus, the standard repertory included works written during, not before, Handel's time.

15. Explicit detail (moderate). Answer: B.

According to the passage, the German musicologists did not study the music of Mozart and Haydn (post-1750 music) because, among other reasons, their music, "having never ceased to be performed, had maintained some kind of oral tradition of performance practice" (lines 39–41). (B) restates this point.

(A) runs contrary to the information in the passage. The author states that later works were not included in the musicologists' studies because, among other reasons, the notation was more complete and the instruments seemed familiar, "so no 'special' knowledge appeared necessary" (lines 37–38). This statement implies, of course, that special knowledge was required to decipher pre-1750 music.

(C) distorts the information in the passage. Although the unannotated oral traditions may have ceased, the author neither states nor implies that the basic works of pre-1750 composers were no longer being performed.

(D) confuses the information in the passage. The works of Bach and Handel were included in the musicologists' early-music studies. The cutoff date for the study was 1750, the year of Bach's death.

Whether notation of works prior to those of Bach or Handel were less complete than notation of works by Bach or Handel is not the issue.

(E) distorts the information in the passage. The author refers to older musical notation, not the music itself, as obsolete (lines 17–18).

16. Purpose of detail (moderate). Answer: D.

At the beginning of the third paragraph, the author states that, beginning around 1960, early-musicians began to encroach upon the works of Haydn, Mozart and Beethoven. The remainder of the third paragraph is devoted to explaining the reasons for this encroachment. One of the contributing reasons given is that the technical level of early-music performances had improved.

(A) is wholly unsupported by the passage. In the final paragraph, the author does mention that the mainstream objected to the early-musicians' encroachment upon later works. However, the author neither defends the early-musicians nor in any other way suggests that these objections were unfair.

(B) confuses cause and effect. It was because more young musicians were being attracted to early music that the technical level of early-music performances began to improve, not the other way around.

(C) confuses the information in the passage. (C) refers to information included in the final sentence of the passage and is irrelevant to the question posed.

(E) is the second-best response. According to the author, improvements in the technical skills of early musicians somehow contributed to the encroachment by early musicians upon the music of Mozart, Haydn, and Beethoven. However, the author does not spell out the precise causal connection. Although it might be inferred that these works were more difficult to perform than earlier works, the author does not make this point explicitly; thus, (E) exaggerates the author's purpose in mentioning this detail. The author mentions the improved technical level of the performances not so much to make a narrow point about how difficult the music was to perform, but rather to explain the reasons for the encroachment upon this music by the early-musicians.

17. Interpretation (easier). Answer: C.

Performance practice, according to the passage, was developed alongside the modern (early twentieth century) *collegium musicum*, which was part of the German university. While the modern *collegium musicum* performed music from before the time of Bach and Handel, the field of performance practice involved certain aspects (e.g., choice of instruments, deciphering notation) of music from the same time period.

(A) does not respond to the question. In itself, Statement (A) finds some support in the passage. The mainstream's objections to the expansion of early music to include later works (see the last paragraph) might be interpreted as disapproval. Even so, this discussion in the final paragraph of the passage is irrelevant to why performance practice is referred to as a "subdiscipline."

(B) is nonsensical. In the context of the passage, the term "discipline" refers to an area or field of study, and so "subdiscipline" refers to a component or more specific area within a broader field of study. An entirely different meaning of the word "discipline" is suggested by (B).

(D) is the second-best response. The fact that performance practice involves the specific task of deciphering musical notation is indeed relevant to why it is called a "subdiscipline"—it involves a narrow area of concern within a broader field of study. However, performance practice includes other concerns as well (most notably, the re-establishment of unannotated performing traditions). Thus, it is termed a "subdiscipline" not just because it involves deciphering musical notation but, more generally, because all of its concerns are also encompassed by a more broadly-defined field of study or discipline. Thus, (D) is too narrow.

(E) confuses the information in the passage. Musicologists involved in the narrow subdiscipline of performance practice transcribed the works performed by musicians at the universities, not the other way around.

18. Explicit detail (easier). Answer: B.

Although performance practice did indeed involve varying the performance of a work of music from one time to the next (by including spontaneous vocal and instrumental ornamentation), the passage neither states nor implies that how the delivery of music varied from time to time depended upon the particular tastes of the audience. Thus, (B) is unsupported by the passage.

(A) and (E) are explicitly supported in the second paragraph, where the author states that performance practice "included the deciphering of obsolete musical notation and its transcription into modern notation" (lines 17–19).

(C) is the second-best response. (C) is not supported by the information in the passage as explicitly as (A), (D), or (E). The author does not state explicitly that performance practice involved determining which musical instrument to use. However, the passage does indicate that early music often called for the use of obsolete instruments and that one of the issues separating the mainstream and the early-musicians was "the already fascinating question of which instruments to use" (line 63–64). Thus, it is reasonably inferable that performance practice involved determining whether modern instruments or earlier (obsolete) instruments were appropriate for a particular piece of music.

(D) is explicitly supported in the second paragraph. The author asserts that the most important concern of performance practice is the "re-establishment of lost oral traditions" (line 20). The author then describes these lost oral traditions as the use of obsolete instruments and voices and unannotated performing traditions.

19. Application (challenging). Answer: B.

According to the passage, one reason for the encroachment was that some of the oral traditions associated with the Viennese classics (the works of Mozart, Haydn, and Beethoven) could not be traced back to the eighteenth century. (B) supports this point by providing specific evidence that this was indeed the case.

(A) is irrelevant. No information in the passage supports the notion that the mainstream's approval or disapproval of how early-musicians treated other works would have been relevant to the early-musicians' encroachment upon the music of Mozart, Haydn, and Beethoven.

(C) is not responsive to the question. If statement (C) were true, and if the music of Mozart, Haydn, and Beethoven did indeed call for the use of obsolete instruments, then this might help to explain why the early-musicians encroached upon the music of Mozart, Haydn, and Beethoven. However, statement (C) would not support the author's explanation but rather would provide an additional explanation; thus, in this respect, (C) is irrelevant.

(D) would actually undermine (weaken) the author's explanation. Early-musicians are interested in exploring unannotated performance traditions. Music that is fully annotated does not allow for such exploration. Thus, if statement (D) were true, the early-musicians would not be interested in the music of Mozart, Haydn, and Beethoven.

(E) is irrelevant. Even if true, statement (E) would not support the author's explanation but rather provide an additional explanation; thus, (E) is irrelevant.

20. Interpretation (easier). Answer: A.

(A) is the best response. According to the passage, beginning around 1960 (i.e., in the latter half of the century), early-musicians began to expand the scope of performance practice to include works by major composers of a later period. (A) paraphrases this rather explicit point.

(B) is wholly unsupported by the passage. Although the scope of the music explored by twentieth-century musicologists may be greater than that of earlier musicologists, the author neither states nor implies that modern musicologists interpret early music differently than did their predecessors.

(C) distorts and runs contrary to the information in the passage. The first sentence of the passage indicates that the origin of the attempt to distinguish early from modern music lies in the eighteenth century. However, this sentence does not indicate that the attempt itself began during this time period. In fact, the passage makes no mention of any such attempt prior to the early twentieth century.

(D) is unsupported and actually runs contrary to the passage. Nowhere does the author indicate that the mainstream's definition of early music might embrace the music of Mozart. To the contrary, the mainstream would probably oppose this notion, since the mainstream objected to the early-musicians' encroachment upon Mozart's music.

(E) is partially accurate, but it is self-contradictory. The definition of early music has indeed changed during the twentieth century to include later works. It is not clear from the information in the passage exactly what all of the canons (rules) of performance practice are. However, one of the canons relates to the scope of music included within this subdiscipline, and the passage makes clear that this scope has indeed changed during the twentieth century. In this sense, then, the second clause of Statement (E) contradicts the first clause.

21. Primary purpose (moderate). Answer: B.

The author's primary concern in the passage is to trace the scope of works included in performance practice from the early twentieth century to the latter half of the century. The author identifies and explains the reasons for the trend of including later works within the scope of so-called "early music" (second and third paragraphs), then refers (in the final paragraph) to a controversy surrounding this trend. (B) reflects the author's primary concern as well as embracing the controversy.

(A) is too broad. While the author does establish that performance practice originated in the German *collegium musicum*, the author's primary concerns are more specific—to explain why the scope of works included in this discipline has expanded and to identify a controversy concerning this expansion.

(C) is off-focus. The author does describe (in the second paragraph) some of the unannotated performing traditions of concern to early-musicians but does not discuss such traditions in much detail.

(D) is off-focus. While the third paragraph does point out that new discoveries led to new interpretations of the music of Mozart, Haydn, and Beethoven, this is not the author's primary concern. The author does not mention what these new discoveries were, nor does the author describe any new interpretations of these works.

(E) is off-focus. The author mentions the competing views to which (E) refers for the first time in the final sentence of the passage.

Analytical Reasoning Lesson 4: Attribute and Grouping Games

Today you will examine various types of "attribute" games and "grouping" games that appear commonly in the Analytical Reasoning section.

Today's Topics

1. The dual attribute game
2. The random attribute game
3. The matrix game
4. The send-and-receive game
5. The simple grouping game
6. The complex grouping game

THE DUAL ATTRIBUTE GAME

Attribute games involve assigning to each subject in the game *one or more characteristics*. The *dual attribute* game involves assigning two characteristics—or *attributes*—to each of the game's subjects. More complex games incorporate conditional rules.

Example 11-1

A basketball team consists of seven members—J, K, L, M, N, P, and Q. Each team member plays one of three positions—guard, forward, or center. At least two of the players are guards, at least two are forwards, and at least one is a center. Each player is on either the injured list or the active list.

    K, N, and P are guards, and J and L are not guards.

    No forward is on the injured list.

    At least two guards are on the active list.

Assume that the team can play only if at least two guards, two forwards, and one center are on the active list. Which of the following statements, if true, would permit the team to play?

(A) Only M and Q are on the injured list.

(B) Only J and L are on the injured list.

(C) Only K and N are on the injured list.

(D) Only L and M are on the injured list.

(E) Only J and Q are on the injured list.

    The following diagramming approach works well for this game type. Notice that the rules are depicted affirmatively in the grid. For example, the rule that "J and L are not guards" has been inverted (each is either a forward or a center) so that the choice between forward and center can be made by circling the appropriate letter. Also notice how the rule that "no forward is on the injured list" is depicted visually. The picture indicates the rule affirmatively (a forward must be on the active list) with a directional arrow that leads from "F" to "A."

	J	K	L	M	N	P	Q
G,F,C	F/C	G	F/C		G	G	
A,I							

≥ 2 G

≥ 2 F

≥ 1 C

The correct response to the question is (C). You can determine the correct response by inserting the information from each answer choice, in turn, into the diagram. The following diagram for response (C) easily allows for two active guards (P and either M or Q), two active forwards (among J, L, M, and Q), and one active center (among J, L, M, and Q).

	J	K	L	M	N	P	Q
G,F,C	F/C	G	F/C		G	G	
A,I	A	I	A	A	I	A	A

You can also derive the solution more intuitively. In each answer choice, only two of the players are on the injured list. At least one of those two players must be either K, N, or P (the three players that must be guards); otherwise, two of the four remaining players would be on the injured list. Since those four remaining players must include a center and two forwards, it would not be possible to assemble an active playing team that includes two forwards and one center. Thus, you can eliminate all answer choices that fail to include either K, N, or P.

THE RANDOM ATTRIBUTE GAME

For some attribute games, it may not be feasible to construct a single grid or template to accommodate all of the rules. An attribute game involving *more than two attributes* generally calls for a more flexible approach. These games may not appear especially difficult at first glance. Nevertheless, they can be very confusing!

Example 11-2

Four children—W, X, Y, and Z—are the only patients in the children's ward of a particular hospital. Each child has either red or brown hair. Each child is assigned to either a private room of his or her own or a semi-private room which is shared with either one or two other children. No two children are the same age.

> X, a girl, is assigned to a private room.
>
> The youngest child is assigned to a semi-private room.
>
> At least one child is a red-haired boy.
>
> Z is not the oldest child and does not share a room with the oldest child.
>
> W and X both have brown hair.

If each of two red-haired children is assigned to a semi-private room, then each of the following, considered individually, could be true EXCEPT:

(A) W is the youngest child.

(B) Y is the oldest child.

(C) W is the oldest child.

(D) Z is the youngest child.

(E) X is the oldest child.

This game involves no fewer than four attributes for each child: hair color (red or brown), gender (male or female), room assignment (private or semi-private), and roommate (if any). It also includes a sequencing feature—relative ages of the children. With this many variables, don't try to use a grid-type diagram. Instead, *take organized notes*, listing the four children and noting those attributes that can be determined for each child:

```
W  Brown
X  Brown/Girl/Private
       Y
Red Boy <
       Z  Doesn't share w/oldest
```

*Youngest shares

What else can be deduced from the rules? Since W and X both have brown hair, either Y or Z must be a red-haired boy, as indicated in the diagram.

The correct response to the question is (B). W and X both have brown hair. Thus, Y and Z must be the two red-haired children who are assigned to semi-private rooms. Although Y or Z, or both, may share a room with W, Y and Z must share a room with each other; otherwise, one of them would have to share a room with X, which would violate the rule that X is assigned to a private room. Since Z cannot share a room with the oldest child, Y cannot be the oldest child.

THE MATRIX GAME

The *matrix* game requires you to make the same series of *yes-or-no* decisions for each of the game's subjects. The term "matrix" refers to the suggested diagram approach.

Example 11-3

During the high-school summer session, six different subjects—art, biology, calculus, driver education, English, and French—are offered. An academic day includes five class periods, and each subject must be offered exactly three times during the day.

> Only calculus and driver education will be offered during the first period.
>
> French and three other classes will be offered during the second period.
>
> Only biology will be offered during the third period.
>
> More subjects will be offered during the fourth period than during the fifth period.

Two subjects that must be offered during the same three periods are

(A) art and biology

(B) art and French

(C) driver education and calculus

(D) driver education and French

(E) English and calculus

In this matrix game, you must decide which of *six* subjects will be offered during each of *five* periods. Thus, the game potentially involves *thirty* "yes-or-no" decisions, which can all be displayed in a checkerboard or matrix.

In any matrix game, *focus on the totals* for each column and for each row of your matrix; these totals will probably be crucial to handling the game. List information about these totals around the perimeter of the matrix. In Example 11-3, each of the six subjects is offered exactly three times; thus, three check-marks must appear in each column—a total of 18 check-marks in the entire matrix. Display the number of check-marks in each row to the right of the matrix.

Here's the key to this game: Since rows 1, 2, and 3 must include a total of seven check-marks, rows 4 and 5 must include a total of eleven check-marks. (Remember: the matrix must include 18 check-marks altogether.) The only way to include eleven check-marks between rows 4 and 5 is to assign six to one and five to the other. Since the rules specify that more subjects are offered during fourth period than during fifth period, six check-marks must appear in row 4, and five check-marks must appear in row 5. Next, evaluating the number of check-marks in each column, you can determine that art, English, and French must each be offered during second, fourth, and fifth periods; otherwise, each of these three subjects would not be offered exactly three times.

	A	B	C	D	E	F	
1	✗	✗	✔	✔	✗	✗	(2)
2	✔				✔	✔	(4)
3	✗	✔	✗	✗	✗	✗	(1)
4	✔	✔	✔	✔	✔	✔	(6)
5	✔				✔	✔	(5)

(3)(3)(3)(3)(3)(3)

The correct response to the question is (B). The question calls for you to compare columns in order to identify an identical pair. Art and French must both be offered during second, fourth, and fifth periods.

THE SEND-AND-RECEIVE GAME

A *send-and-receive* game involves matching each of the game's subjects to *any number* of other subjects. Think about each subject as potentially sending a *message* to each other subject (and each other subject potentially receiving that message).

Example 11-4

Six firms—Jarco, Kanco, Listco, Mapco, Newco, and Optico—can transmit documents via a computer network, but only according to the following restrictions:

Jarco can transmit documents to three of the other firms, one of which is Kanco.

Kanco cannot transmit documents to any other firm.

Listco cannot receive documents from any other firm, although Listco can transmit documents to three of the other firms.

Mapco can receive documents from three of the other firms.

Newco can transmit documents to two of the other firms, one of which is Kanco.

Optico can transmit documents to four of the other firms.

All transmitted documents are received.

No firm can transmit documents to itself.

If Jarco and Listco can each transmit documents to Newco and Optico, all of the following statements must be true EXCEPT:

(A) Mapco can receive documents from Listco.

(B) Kanco can receive documents from Listco.

(C) Mapco can receive documents from Optico.

(D) Optico can transmit documents to Newco.

(E) Newco can transmit documents to Mapco.

As you read the premise and conditions above, did you visualize a map or flow chart in which the game's subjects are connected to one another by arrows? While a flow chart may be appropriate for some logic games, this approach unduly complicates a send-and-receive game. Let's try a simpler and more efficient approach: For each firm, list those firms to which the firm can transmit documents. There is no need to list separately the firms to which, for example, Jarco can transmit and the firms from which Jarco can receive. A second (reciprocal) diagram is unnecessary and will lead to confusion. Next, indicate to the right of each firm how many and which firms the firm can transmit to.

After filling in the lists as completely as possible based upon the information explicit in the rules, ask yourself what else you can deduce from the rules. Here, given that Listco cannot receive documents from any other firm, since Optico can transmit documents to four other firms, those four others must be Jarco, Kanco, Mapco, and Newco. Since Mapco can receive documents from Optico and two other firms, display two "M"s next to the diagram to indicate that a complete diagram must include two additional "M"s. Since Listco cannot receive documents from any other firm, indicate next to the diagram that no "L"s can be inserted. The final diagram, then, looks like this:

J: K̲_ ⏌

K: ∅

L: _ _ ⏌

M:

N: K̲_⏌

O: J̲ K̲M̲N̲⏌

MM

no "L"

In this diagram, a vertical line (|) at the end of a row signifies that no additional firms may receive documents from that firm.

The correct response to the question is (B). Given the additional information in the question, since Mapco can receive documents from Optico and exactly two other firms, those two firms must be Listco and Newco. Our initial diagram can be partially completed as follows:

J: K̲N̲O̲|

K: Ø

L: N̲O̲M̲|

M: MM

N: K̲M̲| no "L"

O: J̲ K̲M̲N̲|

The diagram makes clear that Statements (A), (C), (D), and (E) must all be true. In contrast, Statement (B) cannot be true—Kanco cannot receive documents from Listco because Listco's transmittal roster is already full.

THE SIMPLE GROUPING GAME

Grouping games involve dividing a game's subjects into *at least three* different groups. Simple (easier) grouping games limit the game's parameters and possibilities in one or more of the following ways:

- the number of subjects allocated to each group is fixed

- the groups are distinct and identifiable

- the subjects are distinct and identifiable

Example 11-5
The town of Smallville includes ten residents—A, B, C, D, E, F, G, H, I, and J. Each resident lives on one of three streets—Maple Street, Pine Street, or Elm Street. Either three or four residents live on each of these three streets.

C, E, and J all live on different streets.

B and I both live on Pine Street.

D, F, and H all live on the same street.

If J lives on the same street as A, how many distinct combinations of residents could live on Maple Street?

(A) 1

(B) 2

(C) 3

(D) 4

(E) 5

If you try to employ one of the diagramming techniques for attribute games to Example 11-5, you will discover that an "attribute" approach simply will not accommodate the rules here. Instead, create three distinct spaces or *groups*, each representing a different street. You can deduce several important pieces of information from the rules. First, since the ten residents must be allocated into groups of either three or four, three residents must live on each of two streets, while four residents live on the remaining street. Second, since D, F, and H all live on the same street, either C, E, or J must also live on that street (because C, E, and J all live on different streets). Thus, that street includes four residents. Accordingly, B, I, and exactly one other resident live on Pine Street, while A, G, and exactly one other resident live on the remaining street.

Maple	Pine	Elm
	[BI_]	

3/3/4

C ≠ E ≠ J

[AG_]

[DFH_]

The correct response to the question is (C). If J and A live on the same street, that street (either Maple or Elm) must include exactly three residents—A, G, and J. Alternatively, Maple Street could include D, F, H, and either C or E. Thus, three distinct combinations of residents could live on Maple Street.

THE COMPLEX GROUPING GAME

Grouping games are not always as simple as the one in Example 11-5. Any of the following features would result in a more challenging grouping game:

- the number of subjects allocated to each group is variable
- the groups are indistinguishable
- the subjects are indistinguishable

More "unknowns" in a grouping game generally make for a more complex and time-consuming game.

Example 11-6

Three jars contain a total of twelve jellybeans. Five jellybeans are pink, three are green, two are yellow, and two are black. Each jar contains at least two jellybeans of different colors.

No two jars contain the same number of jellybeans.

No jar contains both pink and green jellybeans.

No jar contains both yellow and black jellybeans.

One of the three jars could contain any of the following assortments of jellybeans EXCEPT:

(A) two black jellybeans and one pink jellybean

(B) two yellow jellybeans and three green jellybeans

(C) one yellow jellybean and two pink jellybeans

(D) one pink jellybean and one black jellybean

(E) one green jellybean and two yellow jellybeans

Two important pieces of information can be determined from the rules. First, although the precise number of jellybeans in each jar cannot be determined, certain parameters can be established. Each jar must contain at least two jellybeans, and no two jars may contain the same number of jellybeans. Thus, only three possible assortments result (excluding the issue of color):

2 - 3 - 7
2 - 4 - 6
3 - 4 - 5

Second, two and only two different colors may be represented in each jar; otherwise, either pink and green jellybeans or yellow and black jellybeans would be included in the same jar. (Either result would violate a rule.) Because visualization is important in a grouping game, your diagram here should include a roster of jellybeans to the side of three distinct spaces representing the three jars. Indicate grouping parameters below the jars. Keep in mind that the jars are indistinguishable, and so you may arbitrarily establish the left jar, for example, as that which will contain the fewest jellybeans:

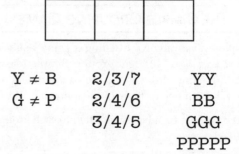

Y ≠ B	2/3/7	YY
G ≠ P	2/4/6	BB
	3/4/5	GGG
		PPPPP

In responding to the question, as you place jellybeans in the jars, simultaneously cross them off the roster. For example, to analyze answer choice (A), try placing two "B"s and one "P" in the first jar. Since each jar may include jellybeans of two and only two different colors, the remaining jellybeans fall logically into their respective groups as follows:

BB	GGG	PPPP
P	Y	Y

Using the same approach for the remaining answer choices, you can quickly deduce that the correct response to the question is (E). Whether one green jellybean and two yellow jellybeans are placed in the first jar or in the middle jar, a rule violation results. Assuming they are placed in the first jar, the middle jar must contain four jellybeans and the remaining jar must contain five. Since pink and black jellybeans cannot be included in the same jar, the last jar must contain all five pink jellybeans, violating the rule that each jar must contain jellybeans of two different colors. Assuming they are placed in the middle jar, the first jar must contain two jellybeans, while the last jar must contain seven. Since pink and black jellybeans cannot be included in the same jar, the first jar must contain both black jellybeans, again violating the rule that each jar must contain jellybeans of two different colors.

Analytical Reasoning Lesson 5: Mini-Test and Review

Today you will apply what you learned on Day 11 to three logic games. After taking this mini-test under timed conditions, review the explanations that follow. Preceding the explanation for each game, the game type and difficulty level are identified.

ANALYTICAL REASONING MINI-TEST

Number of questions: 16
Suggested time: 26 minutes

Directions (as printed in test booklet): Each group of questions in this section is based on a set of conditions. In answering some of the questions, it may be useful to draw a rough diagram. Choose the response that most accurately and completely answers each question and blacken the corresponding space on your answer sheet.

Questions 1–6

On a particular day at a warehouse, each of five workers—Jackson, Klein, Lawry, Manning, and North—performs two different tasks. Each worker performs one task in the morning and one task in the afternoon.

> Three tasks—assembling, boxing, and gluing—are performed in the morning.
>
> Three tasks—gluing, stacking, and loading—are performed in the afternoon.
>
> North and two other workers glue.

> Three of the workers stack.
>
> Jackson does not perform either task that Klein performs.
>
> Lawry does not perform either task that Manning performs.
>
> The five workers listed above are the only workers at the warehouse on that particular day.

1. Which of the following must be false?
   (A) Jackson assembles.
   (B) Klein glues.
   (C) Lawry stacks.
   (D) Manning loads.
   (E) North boxes.

2. If Jackson loads, which of the following must be true?
   (A) Jackson glues.
   (B) Klein stacks.
   (C) Lawry boxes.
   (D) Manning glues.
   (E) North assembles.

3. If Lawry loads, which of the following must be true?

    (A) Either Klein or Manning boxes.
    (B) Either Jackson or Manning glues.
    (C) Either Klein or Lawry glues.
    (D) Either Lawry or Manning boxes.
    (E) Either Jackson or Klein assembles.

4. If Klein is the only worker who assembles, which of the following could be true?

    (A) Manning glues in the morning.
    (B) Jackson loads in the afternoon.
    (C) Lawry glues in the afternoon.
    (D) Klein loads in the afternoon.
    (E) Jackson glues in the morning.

5. If Klein and North perform the same two tasks, all of the following must be true EXCEPT:

    (A) Jackson does not glue.
    (B) Klein does not assemble.
    (C) Lawry does not load.
    (D) Manning does not stack.
    (E) North does not box.

6. If Jackson and Manning perform the same two tasks, one of which is assembling, how many different combinations of task assignments for the five workers are possible on that day?

    (A) 1
    (B) 2
    (C) 3
    (D) 4
    (E) 5

Questions 7–11

Five classic cars—three hardtop models and two convertible models—appear consecutively in a parade. Each car is either a Ford or a Chevy, and each car is either gray, red, or white. Each car is one color only, and each of the three colors is represented at least once among the five cars.

The first and fifth cars to appear are both hardtops.

No Ford is white.

Only one of the hardtops is a Chevy.

7. Which of the following could appear in the parade?

    (A) two white hardtops
    (B) three Ford convertibles
    (C) three gray Chevys
    (D) two Chevy hardtops
    (E) three white Chevys

8. If exactly three of the cars are Chevys, which of the following must be true?

    (A) A convertible immediately follows another convertible.
    (B) A hardtop immediately follows another hardtop.
    (C) A Ford immediately follows another Ford.
    (D) A Chevy immediately follows another Chevy.
    (E) A white car immediately follows another white car.

9. If both convertibles are gray, which of the following must be false?

    (A) All Fords are hardtops.
    (B) All Fords are gray.
    (C) All Chevys are white.
    (D) All gray cars are convertibles.
    (E) All red cars are hardtops.

10. If the first three cars are white, all of the following must be true EXCEPT:

    (A) The first car is a Chevy.

    (B) The fourth car is a Ford.

    (C) The second car is a convertible.

    (D) The fourth car is a hardtop.

    (E) The fourth car is gray.

11. If all Ford hardtops appear consecutively in the parade, which of the following must be true?

    (A) The first car is a Ford.

    (B) The second car is a hardtop.

    (C) The third car is a convertible.

    (D) The fourth car is a Chevy.

    (E) The fifth car is a Ford.

Questions 12–16

Bob has assembled a basket of fruit as a holiday gift for each of his four friends—Susan, Todd, Ursula, and Vadim. A total of fifteen pieces of fruit—five guavas, five mangos, and five kiwis—are distributed among the four baskets according to the following conditions:

> Susan, Todd, and Ursula will each receive exactly two different types of fruit.
>
> Vadim will receive only guavas.
>
> Todd will receive more pieces of fruit than Susan.
>
> Each basket includes at least three pieces of fruit.

12. Which of the following sequence of numbers, representing the number of fruit pieces that Susan, Todd, Ursula, and Vadim receive, respectively, is possible?

    (A) 3, 6, 3, 3

    (B) 3, 3, 5, 4

    (C) 4, 5, 4, 3

    (D) 3, 3, 3, 6

    (E) 3, 4, 3, 4

13. Which of the following statements could be true?

    (A) Todd will receive exactly three pieces of fruit.

    (B) Todd will receive exactly six pieces of fruit.

    (C) Susan will receive exactly five pieces of fruit.

    (D) Vadim will receive exactly six pieces of fruit.

    (E) Ursula will receive exactly six pieces of fruit.

14. If Ursula's basket contains more pieces of fruit than Todd's basket, all of the following must be false EXCEPT:

    (A) Only Vadim will receive guavas.

    (B) Vadim will receive exactly four guavas.

    (C) Todd will receive exactly four kiwis.

    (D) Susan will receive exactly three mangos.

    (E) Ursula will receive exactly two guavas.

15. If Susan's basket contains two guavas and two kiwis, but no other pieces of fruit, which of the following is the number of possible fruit combinations in Todd's basket?

    (A) one

    (B) two

    (C) three

    (D) four

    (E) five

16. If Vadim's basket contains exactly three pieces of fruit, and if Susan's and Ursula's baskets contain identical fruit assortments, which of the following could be true?

    (A) Todd will receive exactly two guavas.

    (B) Susan will receive exactly one kiwi.

    (C) Todd will receive exactly four kiwis.

    (D) Ursula will receive exactly two mangos.

    (E) Todd will receive exactly three mangos.

Quick Answer Guide

Analytical Reasoning Mini-Test

1. E	5. D	9. B	13. B
2. B	6. B	10. E	14. E
3. E	7. E	11. C	15. B
4. A	8. D	12. A	16. D

EXPLANATIONS

Questions 1–6: Dual attribute game (challenging).

This game can be troublesome unless you recognize that additional key facts can be deduced from the rules. Because three workers stack in the afternoon, North must stack; otherwise, either Jackson and Klein would both stack or Lawry and Manning would both stack, resulting in a violation either of the rule that Jackson does not perform either of the two tasks that Klein performs or of the rule that Lawry does not perform either of the two tasks that Manning performs. Accordingly, either Jackson or Klein (but not both) must stack, and either Lawry or Manning (but not both) must stack. As a result, during the afternoon, only one worker may glue (otherwise, no workers would load, which would violate one of the rules), and, in the morning, two workers must glue. One of the two workers who glue in the morning must be North, since the rules specify that North glues, and since we have determined that North must stack in the afternoon. Based upon this additional information, we can construct the following diagram:

$$(J \neq K)(L \neq M)$$
***each worker does 2 different tasks**

Given that each worker must perform two different tasks, that Jackson cannot perform either of the two tasks that Klein performs, and that Lawry cannot perform either of the two tasks that Manning performs, it is helpful to consider Jackson's and Klein's four tasks as a unit, bearing in mind that each task in that unit must be different (and the same for Lawry and Manning).

1. Answer: E.

As noted in the general comments above, N must glue in the morning and stack in the afternoon. Accordingly, N cannot box.

2. Answer: B.

As noted in the general comments above, either J or K must stack in the afternoon. Thus, if J loads (in the afternoon), K must stack (in the afternoon).

3. Answer: E.

Either L or M must stack; thus, if L loads, then M must stack. At least one of the workers must glue in the afternoon; thus, that worker must be either J or K (while the other stacks). Because J and K (in either order) glue and stack in the afternoon, J and K must (in either order) assemble and box in the morning; otherwise, either one would perform the same task in the morning and afternoon or both would perform the same task. As a result, either L or M must glue, while the other either assembles or boxes. Thus, the only statement among the answer choices that must be true is (E).

4. Answer: A.

Among J, L, and M, two workers must box in the morning. Thus, either L or M must glue in the morning (otherwise, L and M would both box), and J must box in the morning. Since either L or M must glue in the morning, neither can glue in the afternoon, and so L and M (in either order) must stack and load in the afternoon. Finally, J and K (in either order) must glue and stack in the afternoon. Since M may either box or glue in the morning, Statement (A) could be true.

5. Answer: D.

N must glue in the morning and stack in the afternoon. Thus, K must also glue in the morning and stack in the afternoon. Since J and K do not perform the same tasks, J must load in the afternoon and either assemble or box in the morning. As a result, L and M must (in either order) glue and stack in the afternoon and (in either order) assemble and box in the morning. Thus, of the five answer choices, only Statement (D) could be false.

6. Answer: B.

Given that J and M perform the same afternoon task, that task must be stacking (see diagram and general comments above), while K and L perform the remaining two afternoon tasks—gluing and loading. Given that J and M both assemble (in the morning), K and L must perform the remaining two morning tasks—boxing and gluing. The same worker cannot glue both in the morning and afternoon, however. Thus, only two possibilities remain: K boxes and glues while L glues and loads, or vice versa.

Questions 7–11: Complex attribute game (moderate).

In this game, each car includes three attributes: top, make, and color. Two conditional rules (the last two rules) and a sequencing feature add to the game's complexity. In order to work through this game efficiently, it is best to construct a diagram in which attributes are matched in roster form without regard to sequence:

The conditional rule that "Only one of the hardtops is a Chevy" has been incorporated into the diagram. The conditional rule that "No Ford is white" has been restated as "All white cars must be Chevys" and expressed symbolically near the diagram.

7. Answer: E.

Two of the three hardtops must be Fords since only one of the hardtops is a Chevy. Fords cannot be white. Thus, no more than one hardtop (the Chevy) can be white, and (A) must be false. (B) violates the statement in the premise that there are two convertibles (not three). (C) is not possible. If three of the cars were gray Chevys, both remaining cars would be Fords; however, no Ford can be white, and so there could be no white car in the parade. This result would violate the statement in the premise that each color must be represented at least once. (D) violates the rule that only one of the hardtops is a Chevy. (E) is possible. One of the two Fords could be red, and the other could be gray.

8. Answer: D.

The two convertibles must both be Chevys. In order to disprove statement (D), the three Chevys would have to be first, third, and fifth. If so, hardtops could not appear both first and fifth. This result would violate one of the rules, and so statement (D) must be true.

9. Answer: B.

Either of the two convertibles could be a Chevy or a Ford. The Chevy hardtop must be white, since each color must be represented at least once. The roster in the diagram above can be filled in as follows:

H	H	H	C	C
Ch	F	F	?	?
w	g/r	g/r	g	g

Either convertible could be a Ford; thus, statement (A) could be true. At least one of the five cars must be red, and that car must be one of the two Fords; thus, statement (B) must be false. Both convertibles could be Fords; thus, statement (C) could be true. The second and third cars could both be red; thus, statement (D) could be true. Only cars 2 and 3 can be red, and these two cars are both hardtops; thus, statement (E) must be true.

10. Answer: E.

If a car is white, it must be a Chevy; thus, the first three cars are all white Chevys. The fourth and fifth cars must be the two Ford hardtops. The first car must be the Chevy hardtop, and the second and third cars must be Chevy convertibles:

(1)	(5)	4	2	3
H	H	H	C	C
Ch	F	F	Ch	Ch
w	g/r	g/r	w	w

Statement (E) is not necessarily true; the fourth car could either be gray or red.

11. Answer: C.

The two Ford hardtops must appear either first and second or fourth and fifth; otherwise, the first and fifth cars could not both be hardtops. If the two Ford hardtops appear first and second, then the Chevy hardtop must appear fifth. On the other hand, if the two Ford hardtops appear fourth and fifth, then the Chevy hardtop must appear first. Two alternative sequences result:

$$1 \quad 2 \quad 3 \quad 4 \quad 5$$
$$H \quad H \quad C \quad C \quad H$$
$$F \quad F \quad ? \quad ? \quad Ch$$

$$H \quad C \quad C \quad H \quad H$$
$$Ch \quad ? \quad ? \quad F \quad F$$

In either sequence, the third car must be a convertible; thus, statement (C) must be true.

Questions 12–16: Complex grouping game (moderate).

The key to working through this grouping game efficiently is to establish at the outset the minimum and maximum number of pieces of fruit that each person may receive. Susan, Ursula, and Vadim must each receive at least three pieces, but Todd must receive at least four pieces (because Todd must receive more pieces than Susan). The maximum number of pieces that any person may receive is six (6 + 3 + 3 + 3 = 15), and only Todd may receive six pieces. (If any other person received six pieces, the total number of pieces would exceed fifteen because Todd must receive at least four pieces.) Ursula and Vadim may each receive as many as five pieces, while Susan may receive only four pieces at maximum. (If Susan received five pieces, Todd would have to receive six, and the total number would exceed fifteen.) We can construct the following initial diagram:

Having established these parameters, questions 12 and 13 are particularly straightforward. Question 16, on the other hand, is especially difficult, requiring a bit more insight than the others.

12. Answer: A.

Todd must receive more pieces that Susan, and the total number must be fifteen. (A) conforms to these conditions. (B) and (D) are not possible because Susan and Todd would receive the same number of pieces; (D) is not possible also because Vadim would receive six pieces, but there are only five guavas available, and the rules stipulate the Vadim receives only guavas. (C) provides for a total of 16 pieces, while (E) provides for a total of only 14 pieces.

13. Answer: B.

As noted in the comments above, Todd can receive six pieces while the other three each receive three pieces. All four other statements, however, must be false, as the comments above make clear.

14. Answer: E.

Ursula may receive no more than five pieces, and Todd may receive no fewer than four pieces (see general comments above). As a result, if Ursula receives more pieces than Todd, then Ursula must receive five pieces, and Todd must receive four pieces. Accordingly, Susan and Vadim must each receive three pieces. Statements (A) and (B) must be false—Vadim will receive three pieces (all guavas), two

guavas remaining for the other three friends. Statements (C) and (D) must be false because each friend (including Todd) must receive at least two different types of fruit. Only Statement (E) is possible.

15. Answer: B.

If Susan receives four pieces, then Todd must receive exactly five pieces while Vadim and Ursula both receive exactly three pieces (see general comments above). Given that Susan receives two guavas and two kiwis, three kiwis and five mangos remain to be allocated between Todd and Ursula. A bit of experimenting reveals that only two allocation schemes are possible—either Todd receives one kiwi and four mangos while Ursula receives two kiwis and one mango, or Todd receives two kiwis and three mangos while Ursula receives one kiwi and two mangos.

16. Answer: D.

Susan and Ursula must each receive exactly three pieces, and Todd must accordingly receive exactly six pieces (see general comments above). Vadim receives three of the five guavas. The remaining two guavas must be allocated one each to Susan and Ursula. Why? The only other choice would be to allocate the two remaining guavas to Todd because Susan and Ursula must receive identical assortments. If this were the case, Todd would also have to receive four pieces of one other type of fruit, either four mangos or four kiwis (each basket must contain exactly two different types of fruit). In this event, however, Susan and Ursula could not receive identical assortments (for example, if Todd were to receive four mangos, either Susan or Ursula would receive the last mango). Thus, the two remaining guavas must be allocated one each to Susan and Ursula. Thus, Susan and Ursula must each receive (in addition to one guava) either two mangos or two kiwis, while Todd receives either one mango and five kiwis or one kiwi and five mangos.

Writing Sample Lesson 1: Planning Your Essay

Today you will familiarize yourself with the LSAT Writing Sample. You will also learn how to take notes, organize the information presented, and formulate persuasive arguments for your essay response.

Today's Topics

1. The Writing Sample at a glance
2. Anatomy of a Writing Sample topic
3. Testing procedures and materials
4. How the Writing Sample is evaluated
5. Taking notes and organizing your thoughts
6. Formulating persuasive arguments

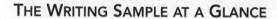

THE WRITING SAMPLE AT A GLANCE

Number questions: 1
Time allowed: 30 minutes
Number of sections: 1 section (not scored)
Appearance relative to other exam sections: last

Basic format:

- two criteria are presented
- two alternatives are described
- test taker argues in favor of one alternative over the other

Ground rules:

- scratch paper is provided
- pens are provided
- there is no "correct" response

This section tests your ability to:

- argue persuasively and cogently
- present your thoughts in an organized, coherent fashion
- use the English language effectively and follow the conventions of Standard Written English

ANATOMY OF A WRITING SAMPLE TOPIC

In the Writing Sample section of the LSAT, you will be asked to choose between two alternatives and defend your choice based on two objectives—or *goals*. Take a look at the sample topic on the next page. Notice that the topic includes three components:

- a *premise,* which establishes a scenario

- two "bulleted" criteria or *goals*

- descriptions of two alternatives or *choices*

The sample topic below is typical; all LSAT Writing Sample topics include these three components. Also keep in mind the following about the Writing Sample format:

- **There is no "right" or "wrong" choice.** Each of the two stated choices will have its merits (strengths) and problems (weaknesses). It is not important to the reader which alternative you choose; what is important to the reader is how effectively you defend your choice.

- **The two choices tend to "polarize" toward different goals.** Invariably, one choice will be stronger in achieving one stated goal, while the other choice will be stronger in achieving the other goal. This feature is quite intentional and is really the heart of the Writing Sample. It's easy enough to argue for either choice based upon the more favorable of the two goals, but it's more challenging to defend your choice in light of the other, less favorable, goal.

- **Exactly two alternatives and exactly two criteria are presented.**

Writing Sample Topic

"Cutters," a contemporary hair-care studio for men and women owned and operated by Jim and Joan Baxter, has been operating from the same downtown location for several years. However, the Baxters must move their studio when their lease terminates next month. They are considering two possible locations. Write an argument for one of the two following choices. Two considerations should influence your decision:

- The Baxters wish to minimize the time and expense involved in starting up business in a new location.

- The Baxters seek maximum potential for business growth and for return on their financial investment.

The Baxters are considering a location on Frye Street where a contemporary-style men's hair salon has recently failed. The Frye Street storefront is only a few blocks away from the Baxters' present location. Although the space would be just large enough to support the Baxters' current operation, they could expand to an adjacent retail space in the same building. While the Baxters' present location is on a busy thoroughfare, Frye Street is a quiet side-street lined with quaint older houses and a few neighborhood stores. Most Frye Street residents are either senior citizens or young couples in their twenties.

The Baxters are also considering a location in the new Fashion Place suburban mall, located about three miles from their present location. The space, which is positioned next to one of the mall's department stores, is large enough for the Baxters' current as well as potential future needs. The monthly rent is approximately twice that of the Frye Street location. Although parking at the mall is ample, no public transportation is available between the mall and the downtown area.

TESTING PROCEDURES AND MATERIALS

After all five multiple-choice sections have been administered, the exam proctor will collect test materials for those sections, then distribute the following materials for the Writing Sample section:

- a sealed two-page test booklet

- an $8\frac{1}{2} \times 11$ sheet of scratch paper (light in color, but not white)

- a black ball-point pen

The essay topic and space for your response are both included on a single page in the sealed test booklet. Attached to the back of the booklet is a yellow sheet on which a carbonless copy of your response is recorded. At the conclusion of the 30-minute Writing Sample section, the proctor will collect your original response but not the carbonless copy. You will remove (tear off) the carbonless copy to take home with you. The LSDAS will send photocopies of your response to each law school to which you direct your LSAT score.

The space available for your essay response will be equivalent to the space provided on page 136. Why isn't more space provided? Because you are being tested on—among other abilities—your ability to consolidate information and to write in a concise, to-the-point manner. Besides, admission-committee members at the law schools would rather read short essays than long ones. (This doesn't necessarily mean that a shorter response is preferable to a longer one—more about that tomorrow.)

The exam proctor will provide each test taker with one sheet of colored *scratch paper* (usually light blue). Why the use of colored, rather than white, scratch paper? Although the testing service trusts you, it does not trust the test taker seated next to you, who may try to bring into the testing room a "cheat sheet" to use during the Writing Sample section. The use of distinctively-colored paper guards against such cheating. The proctor will collect all scratch paper at the conclusion of the Writing Sample section.

No writing implements other than the *black ballpoint pen* provided by the proctor will be permitted during the Writing Sample section. Why a black ballpoint pen? The use of a medium-tip black pen helps to ensure legibility of photocopies and eliminates any possible advantage that might be gained through choice of writing implement. By the way, on the pen will be printed the words "Law School Admission Test," and you can take the pen home with you as a souvenir!

The use of *liquid paper*, or "white-out," is permitted.

HOW THE WRITING SAMPLE IS EVALUATED

What Skills Are Being Tested?

The LSAT Writing Sample is designed to test your ability to support a position and express that position in writing. More specifically, the law schools are interested in:

- your ability to make persuasive and well-reasoned arguments in favor of one position and against another

- your ability to organize your thoughts under pressure of time and to express them in an organized manner

- your command of the language and of the conventions of Standard Written English (vocabulary, usage, grammar, syntax, and so forth)

You are not being tested on your knowledge of "the law" or of any other academic subject. Do NOT write on a topic other than the one specified!

The Writing Sample Evaluation Process

The testing service will not score your Writing Sample but will simply send a photocopy of your essay to each law school to which you direct your LSAT score. Each law school determines its own evaluation guidelines and procedures, as discussed below.

Is every applicant's LSAT essay read at the law school? No. Law schools typically reject applicants out-of-hand who fail to meet some specified minimum GPA/LSAT composite score. In these cases, LSAT Writing Samples are not read. In all other cases, essays will each be read by at least one person at the law school.

Who reads LSAT essays, and how carefully are LSAT essays scrutinized? One or more members of the school's admission committee—comprised mainly of faculty members—may read your essay. If your acceptance at a particular school is highly probable based upon your LSAT score and GPA, then unless you write something extremely inflammatory or careless in your essay, it will not affect your chances of admission. However, the closer you are to being a borderline candidate, the more closely your essay will be scrutinized. For such candidates, the essay may be read by more readers, and it may influence the ultimate admission decision.

Are LSAT essays "scored" or "graded"? The reader might make brief written comments about your essay, as well as annotating your essay by circling or underlining errors in spelling, usage, grammar, and mechanics. The reader will then score your essay according to the guidelines determined by the school. Some form of numerical scoring system is used by nearly all schools. By quantifying Writing Sample evaluations, the school can objectify and streamline the evaluation process. At some schools, essays are scored separately for content, organization, and mechanics; then a composite or total score is computed. Other schools employ a more holistic approach by which a single score is assigned to each essay from the outset.

A Model Scorecard for Self-Evaluation

The sample below provides a scoring system—or "scorecard"—that illustrates how a law school *might* evaluate your essay on a scale of 1 to 5 (5 is best, and 1 is worst). A score of 4 or 5 would help your chances of admission, a score of 3 would not work significantly for you or against you, and a score of 1 or 2 would probably hurt your chances of admission. Use this scorecard to evaluate the essays that you write in response to the topics on Day 15 (Mini-Test) and on Day 29 (Practice Test). (Keep in mind that this scorecard is only a model and that each law school develops its own method and criteria to evaluate essays.)

LSAT Writing Sample Scorecard
5 (outstanding)

An *outstanding* essay includes well-reasoned and highly-persuasive arguments and demonstrates a mastery of the English language and of the elements of effective writing. Specifically, an outstanding essay:

- expressly relates the two choices directly to the two stated criteria

- discusses the merits and weaknesses of both choices vis-á-vis both stated criteria

- incorporates into the analysis all key characteristics of each choice

- acknowledges and effectively rebuts possible opposing viewpoints

- confines the discussion to the stated criteria and choices

- is organized in a manner that clearly conveys the meaning and facilitates the persuasiveness of the arguments

- demonstrates superior facility with English grammar, syntax, and writing mechanics

- demonstrates superior control of the English language in spelling, usage, and diction

4 (strong)

A *strong* essay provides reasonably-persuasive arguments in favor of one choice over the other in a well-organized essay that demonstrates a strong command of the language and the elements of writing. Specifically, a strong essay:

- expressly evaluates important features of both choices in terms of the two stated criteria

- acknowledges and rebuts possible opposing viewpoints

- confines the discussion to the stated criteria and choices

- is clearly organized

- demonstrates good facility with English grammar, syntax, and writing mechanics

- demonstrates good control of the English language in spelling, usage, and diction

- may omit to include key characteristics of one or both choices

- may fail to include a clear introductory or concluding statement

- may include occasional minor flaws in spelling, language usage, or grammar

3 (adequate)

An *adequate* essay demonstrates basic competence in organizing and presenting relevant facts and in formulating reasonably effective arguments. Specifically, an adequate essay:

- weighs the relative merits of each choice by presenting relevant facts

- demonstrates some facility at formulating a cogent argument in favor of one choice over the other

- demonstrates an adequate ability to present an argument within a preconceived organizational format

- indicates adequate control of the language and the conventions of Standard Written English

- may ignore important features of one or both choices

- may fail to expressly relate features of the two choices directly to the stated criteria

- may tend to rely on reiteration of facts and circular arguments

- may include problems in spelling, usage, diction, or other mechanical aspects of writing, although such problems do not interfere significantly with the meaning

2 (limited)

A *limited* essay indicates a basic facility for organizing and presenting facts in support of a choice and demonstrates a basic facility in the use of the English language and the elements of effective writing. Specifically, a limited essay:

- presents relevant facts in support of at least one of the two choices

- demonstrates some ability to organize and present thoughts in a coherent, meaningful manner

- demonstrates basic competence in the use of language and the conventions of Standard Written English

- may lack reasonably-persuasive arguments in favor of one choice over another

- may fail to adequately address one of the two choices or one of the two criteria

- may fail to relate relevant facts to either criterion

- may depart from the stated criteria and discuss irrelevant issues or considerations

- may lack organizational coherence, suggesting inadequate forethought and planning

- may include mechanical errors and problems that interfere somewhat with the meaning

1 (seriously flawed)

A *seriously-flawed* essay indicates significant deficiencies in formulating coherent arguments, organizing thoughts, or communicating through the use of Standard Written English. It might also suggest an inability or unwillingness to follow directions. Specifically, a seriously flawed essay:

- fails to adequately communicate a coherent argument in support of either choice.

- fails to demonstrate original thought, insight, or ability to argue persuasively

- may merely repeat or restate certain facts without any attempt to analyze or evaluate

- may deviate from the stated criteria and/or the stated choices

- may lack organizational structure

- may include significant spelling, grammatical, and syntactical problems that significantly distract the reader and obscure the test taker's intended meaning

TAKING NOTES AND ORGANIZING YOUR THOUGHTS

In approaching the LSAT essay, resist the temptation to start writing your response immediately after reading the topic. Instead, take perhaps 6 to 8 minutes to formulate and organize your arguments, employing the strategies discussed below.

List the Key Features of Each Choice

Use the scratch paper provided to jot down the characteristics of each choice that relate to one or both goals. Try to cover all key features, but don't be too concerned if you omit a few details. A lot of facts are packed into the Writing Sample topic, and you are not expected to address every detail in your response.

Evaluate the Facts as You Take Notes

As you jot down a key characteristic, evaluate it in terms of one or both goals. Ask yourself:

> "Is this characteristic a strength or a weakness in terms of the objectives? Why?"

Jot down a few words that express your idea. Then ask yourself:

> "If I were to choose the other alternative, how would I respond to this strength (or weakness)?"

If an idea occurs to you, quickly jot down a few words that express that idea. By listing and evaluating key features, you are essentially formulating the points of your argument. To help you formulate effective arguments for your essay, a bit later we'll discuss various methods of argumentation.

Consolidate Related Facts

During the exam, the time and space available to express your arguments is severely limited. Try to combine or consolidate features that make essentially the same point or argument. Try to limit yourself to three or four points for each choice. This will allow you to achieve breadth of coverage within the time and space restrictions. In fact, the testing service is gauging your ability to achieve exactly that.

Consider Organizing Notes into "Quadrants"

If you think about it, there are really four distinct issues built into every Writing Sample topic:

- the extent to which the *first alternative* achieves the *first goal*

- the extent to which the *first alternative* achieves the *second goal*

- the extent to which the *second alternative* achieves the *first goal*

- the extent to which the *second alternative* achieves the *second goal*

Consider dividing your notes into four quadrants, one for each of these four issues. Admittedly, the

	FRYE	MALL
Moving Time/Expense	+ hair studio set up already − but renovate (men only)? + rent 1/2 mall rent − expand next door adds $ + keep current customers ? 3 blocks vs. 3 miles	− install new fixtures + will last long time + Frye needs renovation − high rent (may not survive short term)
Growth/Profit Potential	− failed business ? low visibility ? mismanaged + expand next door − may be occupied − expensive	+ dept. store (high traffic) ? will mall succeed? − high rent offsets − more competition in suburbs + larger customer base + large space for growth

quadrant approach is not perfect; it does not accommodate the fact that some characteristics will relate to both goals. Nevertheless, it can be a useful way to organize your thoughts. Try this method as you take the Mini-Test on Day 15. On page 126 there are sample notes for the topic on page 122 using the quadrant approach. A plus (+) indicates a strength and a minus (–) indicates a weakness.

FORMULATING PERSUASIVE ARGUMENTS

Law schools will evaluate your essay for (1) content, (2) organization, and (3) writing mechanics (spelling, grammar, and so forth). Today's lesson will focus solely on the first area; the other two areas are the subjects of tomorrow's lesson.

Discuss Both Alternatives and Both Goals

A highly-effective argument does not ignore an opposing position or an important objective. Even if cogent and well-written, an LSAT essay that discusses only the "winner" or only one of the two goals will not work strongly for you in the admission process.

Acknowledge and Rebut Weaknesses of Your Choice and Strengths of the Other Choice

Your LSAT essay should do more than merely assert a position and reiterate some facts that tend to support that position. An effective participant in a debate will not ignore the weaknesses of his or her position or the merits of the opponent's position. Instead, the participant will acknowledge those weaknesses and merits, then respond to them—or "rebut" them—in a manner that is creative, well-reasoned, and convincing.

Applying this principle to the LSAT essay is easier said than done, of course. Persuasive argumentation, or "rhetoric," is a bit of an art form. Some people have a natural talent in this area, while others need to work at developing their rhetorical skills. If you fall into the latter category, the techniques

discussed below will help you to formulate effective arguments for your LSAT essay.

Engage in Reasonable Conjecture

As you evaluate the facts, you must venture beyond them to speculate as to how those facts might or might not achieve the stated goals. If you are uncomfortable with departing from the facts, get comfortable! Reasonable conjecture is essential to an effective argument. In the Writing Sample topic on page 122, for example, the following points would constitute reasonable speculation that would persuade the reader:

- The prior business at the Frye Street location may have failed due to factors other than lack of traffic.

- Current fixtures at the Frye Street location might not meet the Baxters' needs.

- The Baxters' current customers may be willing to drive to the mall.

- The mall location provides no assurance in itself of success.

Confine Your Arguments to the Stated Goals and Scenario at Hand

A brilliant idea should nevertheless be excluded from your essay if it departs somewhat from the topic or stated goals. Referring to the topic on page 122, the following ideas are probably too tangential and should be omitted:

- There is a trend toward urban redevelopment which may help the Baxters' downtown salon in the future.

- There are other intangible benefits of a quaint, older urban location.

- It wouldn't be fair to the Baxters' long-time faithful clients to move out to the mall.

- The mall location would be more convenient for the Baxters' personal shopping needs.

- The Baxters should also consider the proximity of their salon to their suppliers.

Use Rhetorical Devices for Persuasive Arguments

Hopefully, as you take notes for your essay response ideas will occur to you naturally, without your consciously considering particular rhetorical techniques. If you do get "stuck" for ideas, however, draw upon the following five techniques to get your rhetorical juices flowing.

1. Subordinate one goal to the other. Argue that, while your choice is somewhat weak in terms of one of the two goals, that goal is not as important as the other goal.

Example: The Baxters' primary concern should be with long-term investment return, as additional start-up costs will prove insignificant over time.

2. Explain it away. Argue that an apparent weakness (strength) relies on contingencies that are unlikely or upon factors that don't apply.

Example: Although the prior salon failure on Frye Street might suggest poor growth potential, that failure may have been due to other factors— such as mismanagement or a narrow male-only client base.

3. Turn it around. Argue that an apparent weakness (strength) is actually just the opposite if one looks at it from a different perspective.

Example: The mall space's high-traffic location might seem to provide more long-term profit potential. However, the Baxters may face greater competition in the suburbs from franchise salons.

4. Trivialize it. Argue that a particular weakness (strength), while real, is minor, trivial, or insignificant in comparison to another strength (weakness).

Example: Although the Frye location's low rent would appear to help the Baxters to meet their objectives, any expansion at Frye would come at greater expense, thereby undermining long-term profit goals.

5. Attack the opposing position. Argue that the alternative choice is no stronger, or perhaps even weaker, in achieving a particular goal.

Example: While the initial expense to equip the new space at the mall might be substantial, renovations at Frye Street needed to convert that space from a men-only salon may be just as costly and time-consuming.

Day 14

Writing Sample Lesson 2:
Formatting and Writing Your Essay

Today you will learn how to structure your essay, how to find an effective style and "voice" for it, and how to avoid common mechanical errors.

Today's Topics

1. Piecing together your argument
2. Finding an appropriate and effective writing style
3. Introductions
4. Concluding remarks
5. Tips regarding physical presentation
6. Model responses to yesterday's Writing Sample topic

PIECING TOGETHER YOUR ARGUMENT

How you organize (or fail to organize) your LSAT essay is just as critical as—and arguably more critical than—the essay's content. Your brilliant arguments may be rendered pointless and ineffective if your ideas wander aimlessly so that the reader cannot follow your train of thought. A clear organizational structure suggests to the reader clear thinking and, therefore, sound reasoning.

There are two basic formats for a well-organized LSAT essay. Both formats include a brief introduction and conclusion (more on that later). In reviewing both formats, keep in mind that the "primary" goal is the goal toward which the "winner" polarizes, while the "secondary" goal is the goal toward which the "loser" polarizes.

Format A (Choice-Driven)

First Paragraph:

- one-sentence introduction
- how the "winner" achieves the primary goal
- how the "winner" also achieves the secondary goal

Second Paragraph:

- how the "loser" fails to achieve the secondary goal
- how the "loser" fails to achieve the primary goal

Third Paragraph:

- (one- or two-sentence conclusion)

Format B (Goal-Driven)

First Paragraph:

- one-sentence introduction

- how the "winner" achieves the primary goal

- how the "loser" fails to achieve the primary goal

Second Paragraph:

- how the "winner" achieves the secondary goal

- how the "loser" fails to achieve the secondary goal

Third Paragraph:

- (one- or two-sentence conclusion)

Make sure that your essay conforms to one of these two formats. Do not stray from your chosen format, and do not combine the two formats.

FINDING AN APPROPRIATE AND EFFECTIVE WRITING STYLE

The overall style of the LSAT essay should be relatively formal. Don't try to be conversational, informal, or "cutesy." The tone of your essay should be critical, but not inflammatory or emotional. Do not try to overstate your position by using extreme or harsh language. Do not attempt to elicit a visceral or emotional response from the reader. Appeal instead to the reader's intellect. Think *PBS*, not *MTV*. Follow the guidelines below.

Avoid Gimmicky and Inappropriate Writing Techniques

Do not attempt to grab the reader's attention by using gimmicky devices. In general, it is best to avoid the following techniques:

- dialogue

- rhetorical questions

- slang and colloquial expressions

- quotations

- puns or any other form of humor

Don't Try too Hard to Impress with Your Vocabulary

While your writing style should be somewhat formal, do not try to impress the reader with an erudite vocabulary or with your knowledge of legal terminology. Using obscure, intimidating words or "legalese" may only serve to warn the reader that you are attempting to compensate for a lack of substance. There's nothing wrong with demonstrating in your LSAT essay a broad and educated vocabulary; just don't overdo it.

Develop an "Inventory" of Useful Phrases to Help Your Argument Flow

For many test takers, the most difficult aspect of the LSAT essay is not formulating persuasive ideas but rather finding the best words and phrases to express those ideas. Here is a list of transitional clauses, buzz-words, and rhetorical phrases that you will find useful in piecing together the components of your argument. They can add sophistication and style to your essay and help your ideas to flow.

Use these phrases to acknowledge your choice's weaknesses (or the other choice's merits):

Although it might appear that . . .

Although it would seem that . . .

At first glance, it would seem/appear that . . .

Admittedly, . . .

The chief strength of _____ lies in its . . .

Use these phrases to respond to an apparent weakness (of your choice) or strengths (of the other choice):

However, . . .

Further examination reveals . . .

Upon further inspection, . . .

Closer inspection/scrutiny reveals . . .

Further consideration discloses . . .

A more thorough analysis . . .

In reality, . . .

Actually . . .

When viewed more closely, . . .

When viewed from another perspective, . . .

Further observation shows . . .

Use these words to point out weaknesses of the other choice:

critical/significant/crucial problems

serious drawbacks

problematic

countervailing factors

Use these transition words to connect the components of your argument together:

furthermore

additionally

in addition

also

first, . . . second, . . .

moreover

most important/significantly

finally

Use these words to argue for your choice in terms of one of the goals:

promotes

facilitates

provides a strong impetus

serves to

directly

furthers

accomplishes

attains

achieves

demonstrates

suggests

indicates

Use these words to argue against the other choice in terms of one of the goals:

works against

undermines

thwarts

defeats

runs contrary to

fails to achieve/promote/accomplish

is inconsistent with

would impede

Use these words to subordinate one goal to the other:

ultimate goal/objective/purpose

overriding

primary concern

subordinate

subsumed

Use these phrases for your concluding remarks:

In sum

In the final analysis

. . . interests (objectives/purposes) would be better (more effectively) served (promoted)

Vary Your Sentence Length

You are no doubt aware that you can add interest and sophistication to your writing by varying sentence length and structure. Also consider, however, that short sentences are most effective to *begin* and *end* a train of thought (usually defined by paragraph breaks), especially if your goal is to persuade the reader. Try this technique in your LSAT essay to add some "punch" and sophistication.

Avoid Restating the Facts

Many test takers devote entire sentences and paragraphs to restating, paraphrasing, or reiterating facts. This is a waste of valuable time and space, and it suggests to the reader that the test taker has few ideas of his or her own to convey. Keep in mind that the reader already knows the facts. While there's no way to avoid *referring* to the facts as you make your arguments, get right to the point—preferably in the same sentence.

Be Concise; Avoid Superfluous Words and Phrases

Strive to write in a terse, concise manner, avoiding superfluous words. Here are some commonly-used LSAT essay phrases and their more concise counterparts (in parentheses):

In the event that . . . (If . . .)

Despite the fact that . . . (Although . . .)

. . . in achieving the goal of . . . (. . . to achieve . . .)

An additional consideration is that . . . (Also, . . .)

There are several factors that . . . (Several factors . . .)

Self-references are also superfluous. The reader knows that it is *your* opinions and thoughts that you are expressing in your essay. There's no need to remind the reader of this with phrases such as:

It is my opinion that . . .

I believe that . . .

If I were to choose between . . .

Also avoid meaningless rhetorical phrases. While your objective is to persuade the reader, you are wasting valuable time and space with courtroom clichés such as:

Without a doubt, . . .

It is clear that . . .

No reasonable person would disagree that . . .

The evidence overwhelmingly . . .

Refer to the Two Choices as Briefly as Possible

It is perfectly acceptable to refer to the two choices throughout your essay in some shorthand fashion. In yesterday's Writing Sample topic (page 122), for example, you might simply refer to the Frye Street location as "Frye," while referring to the Fashion Place Mall location as "the mall." There is no need to underline or set off the choices in quotes (unless your task is to choose between two books, plays, or movies).

INTRODUCTIONS

Effective introductory and concluding statements indicate strong organizational skills and help the reader to follow your train of thought. Forget what you've learned about writing introductions for theses, reports, and other papers for college. Those rules don't apply here. You're dealing here with a severely-limited writing space and only 30 minutes. A simple one-sentence introduction that indicates which is the better choice will suffice.

Example: The mall location would better meet the Baxters' objectives.

CONCLUDING REMARKS

Be sure to reserve enough time and space for a brief concluding remark that simply sums up or recapitulates the thrust of your argument. Keep it brief—one or two sentences. Just reiterate the main reasons why your choice is the better one.

Example: In sum, Frye is the better location; it would allow for a fast and inexpensive start-up and an uninterrupted flow of business, in turn ensuring both short-term survival and long-term success.

TIPS REGARDING PHYSICAL PRESENTATION

Your Handwriting Style

Put yourself in the position of the reader, who may be reading a hundred LSAT essays over one weekend during admission season. Yours may be the last essay read! Do the reader a favor and make sure that every word is legible. The reader will not take the time to try to interpret chicken scratches. Your handwriting doesn't have to be pretty—just legible. Hand-printing (instead of writing) is acceptable as well. Avoid using inordinately small or cramped writing just to pack more words into the space provided. Also avoid inordinately large handwriting; otherwise, you may run out of space before you run out of time and ideas.

Scratching Out Words and Phrases (Strike-Throughs)

If you want to delete or alter a few words here and there, go ahead and cross them out. The reader will not look unfavorably upon the occasional strike-through. However, avoid frequent strike-throughs, especially if they involve long phrases or entire sentences. Otherwise, you will quickly run out of writing space, as well as giving the reader the impression that you have trouble organizing your thoughts before writing. If you need to delete lengthy phrases, consider using liquid paper (see below).

Using Liquid Paper (White-Out)

The use of liquid paper, or "white-out," is permitted. Should you use it? For striking the occasional word or short phrase, using white-out is probably not worth your time. However, to strike entire sentences or multiple sentences, consider using white-out, especially if you need the writing space. Remember that the law schools receive a photocopy of your essay, so they can't scratch away your liquid paper to read what you deleted. The reader might detect the use of liquid paper in spots where you've whited out the horizontal guide lines or where your handwriting is a bit rough. However, as long as your writing remains clear and legible, the use of liquid paper will not negatively affect the reader's evaluation.

Writing in the Margins

Photocopies sent to the law schools will include only the writing space itself, not the margins around the perimeter of the writing space. Accordingly, don't use the margins to insert material into your essay; the reader will not even see that material.

Paragraph Breaks and Skipping Lines

By all means, use paragraph breaks to indicate organization and structure. If you use too many, however, you might sacrifice valuable writing space. Consider using two paragraph breaks: one between the two main paragraphs, and one before your conclusion. There is no need to set off your one-sentence introduction as a separate paragraph. Don't skip lines between paragraphs; while doing so might provide the reader with a visual break, it wastes valuable writing space.

MODEL RESPONSES TO YESTERDAY'S WRITING SAMPLE TOPIC

Here are two model responses, one arguing for each of the two choices described in yesterday's Writing Sample topic (page 122). These responses illustrate the organizational and stylistic devices discussed throughout today's lesson. As you read these responses, keep in mind the following:

- They are *models*—intended to exemplify the various suggestions discussed earlier in this lesson and in the yesterday's lesson. Don't expect that you will be able to write essays quite this polished in 30 minutes.

- Although they are models, they aren't perfect. Regardless of how effective an LSAT essay is, there's always *some* room for improvement.

- You could write these responses in the space provided on the LSAT response sheet, although most test takers' responses are a bit briefer.

- They are not all-inclusive. In other words, effective arguments may have occurred to you that are absent in these model responses.

Response #1

(in favor of the Frye Street location)

The Frye Street location is the better choice for the Baxters. The time and cost of renovating the Frye shop would be minimal, since the store is already set up to accommodate a hair studio. Its close proximity would minimize the time and expense of moving as well as providing for uninterrupted business from current clients. A continued stream of business and a low initial rent would ensure short-term survival as well as making it financially feasible to expand to the adjacent space, thereby achieving long-term growth. Although the prior salon failure on Frye Street might suggest poor growth potential, that failure may have been due to other factors—such as mismanagement or a narrow male-only client base.

The mall space's high-traffic location might seem to provide more long-term profit potential. However, the Baxters may face greater competition in the suburbs from franchise salons. More importantly, the Baxters' primary concern should be with short-term survival, since otherwise they cannot achieve their longer-term profit goals. The additional expense of equipping a new retail space, along with a high initial rent, may jeopardize that survival, especially since it may take considerable time to develop a new clientele.

In sum, Frye is the better location; it would allow for a fast and inexpensive start-up and an uninterrupted flow of business, in turn ensuring both short-term survival and long-term success.

Response #2

(in favor of the Fashion Place Mall location)

The mall location would better meet the Baxters' objectives. The strategic high-traffic position next to a department store offers greater opportunity for long-term growth and profit. While the initial expense to equip the new space might be substantial, renovations at Frye Street to convert that space from a men-only salon may be just as costly and time-consuming. Even if not, the Baxters' primary concern should be with long-term investment return, as additional start-up costs will prove insignificant over time.

Admittedly, the relatively close and quiet Frye Street location might help the Baxters retain current customers, thereby offsetting moving expenses. However, failure of the previous hair studio suggests an insufficient demand among nearby elderly residents for a contemporary hair studio. This factor, along with the location's low visibility, is likely to prevent growth. Although low rent would appear to help the Baxters to meet their objectives, any expansion at Frye would come at greater expense, thereby undermining long-term profit goals; the mall location allows for expansion without additional rent.

In the final analysis, the mall is the better choice; while the relative start-up costs are uncertain, the mall location is more certain to achieve the Baxters' overriding objectives of long-term growth and profit.

Day 15

Writing Sample Lesson 3: Mini-Test and Review

Today you will apply what you learned on Days 13 and 14 to a new Writing Sample topic. Limit your time to 30 minutes for this mini-test. Then evaluate your essay, using the scorecard on pages 124–125 as well as comparing your response to the two model responses provided.

WRITING SAMPLE TOPIC

The Riverview city planners are considering various public improvement projects, particularly for the city's largely undeveloped and scenic riverfront. Write an argument in favor of one the following two projects, keeping in mind that the cost of the two projects would be the same. Also keep in mind the following two factors influencing the city's decision:

- The city wants to avoid projects that might undermine its residents' general opinion of the city as a great place to raise children.

- The city wants to stimulate its economy by reviving its waning tourist industry.

One project under consideration, the Riverview Plaza project, would involve converting a large 5-acre vacant parcel of land on the riverfront into an outdoor cultural center. The park-like setting would include a children's petting zoo, picnic facilities, a small botanical garden, and a miniature train ride which would encircle the Plaza. The focal point, however, would be a 1,000-seat amphitheater for showcasing popular performers from the musical and theatrical worlds as well as local talent. The amphitheater could also be used for other community events. The Plaza would also include an old-fashioned ice-cream parlor, a coffee house, and a gift shop. The amphitheater, train ride, and petting zoo would close during the cold-weather winter months, although the remaining facilities would be available year-round.

The other project under consideration is the Riverview Recreation Loop, a four-mile bicycle path around the city. All-weather fitness stations, paddleball and basketball courts, and new playgrounds would be installed at various other points around the Loop. The Loop would pass directly by the local high school and a local elementary school. Special overpasses would be constructed at the more heavily-traveled roadways, although bicyclists would be required to cross traffic at numerous other streets. The Loop would extend along the riverfront, where a new indoor-outdoor skating rink, bearing the name of local resident and former Olympic figure-skating champion, would be constructed. The rink would provide ice skates—as well as bicycles, rollerblades, and pedal-power buggies for the bike path—year-round on an hourly-rental basis.

Use the space below to respond to the Writing Sample topic. Do not write in the margins.

EVALUATE YOUR WRITING SAMPLE

When you have completed your writing sample, evaluate it using the following techniques:

- Score your essay, referring to the scorecard on pages 124–125. Try to be as objective as possible. If you have trouble being objective, ask a friend or teacher to evaluate your essay for you.

- With a yellow highlighter, highlight every sentence in which you accomplished nothing more than restating or paraphrasing the premise, criteria, or characteristics of the choices—that is, in which you merely rearranged and parroted back the facts to the reader. How great a portion of your essay did you highlight? Every sentence in yellow represents wasted space and wasted time—space and time you should use instead to formulate and present original ideas in the form of persuasive arguments.

- With a red pencil, circle (or underline) every grammatical error, awkward sentence, and other mechanical problems. If you're not sure what to circle, ask an English professor to do so. Does your essay look like a sea of red? If so, spend more time working on the mechanics of writing and on your writing style.

READ THESE TWO MODEL RESPONSES

Here are two model responses to today's essay topic. As you read these responses, keep in mind the following four points:

1. These responses are models intended to exemplify the various suggestions discussed in the lessons on Days 13 and 14. Don't expect that you will be able to write essays quite this polished in 30 minutes.

2. Although they are models, they aren't perfect. Regardless of how effective an LSAT essay is, there's always *some* room for improvement. Moreover, there really is no such thing as a perfect LSAT essay.

3. You could write these responses in the space provided on the LSAT response sheet, although most test takers' responses are a bit briefer.

4. The topic is loaded with facts that allow for a great variety of effective arguments. These model responses include only some possible arguments. As a result, don't be concerned if your essay includes arguments that differ somewhat from those presented in the models. Instead, focus on how you performed according to the scorecard on pages 124–125.

Model Response #1

(in favor of the Riverview Plaza)

The Plaza project would be the better choice for the city. The amphitheater, gardens, zoo, and train are all likely to draw tourists while also providing educational opportunities and entertainment to residents and their children. The Plaza's appeal as a tourist attraction might seem to detract from the quality of life for local families. However, due to its location at the riverfront, local residents could easily avoid the area during the height of the tourist season.

The Loop is unlikely to attract a significant number of tourists, who are typically in search of entertainment and relaxation, not vigorous exercise. The Loop offers no activities for tourists that they could not engage in where they live. Admittedly, the various features of the Loop would be attractive to children, thus enhancing the city's reputation as a great place to raise children. However, the bike path itself may actually prove to be a source of worry for parents and danger for children, since it passes through the crowded and "touristy" riverfront and across a number of streets.

In conclusion, the Plaza would be a positive and safer addition to the city for local families, while providing more attractions for tourists. It is, therefore, a better plan than the Loop.

Model Response #2

(in favor of the Recreation Loop)

The city will better meet both of its goals with the Recreation Loop. Its various features would considerably enhance the quality of life for local children. At the same time, the variety and accessibility of its Riverfront features, enhanced by the notoriety associated with the skating rink, is sure to attract tourists year round. Although the cross-traffic at various points around the Loop may seem unsafe for small children, this problem would be partially abated with the planned overpasses and could be further abated with appropriate traffic signals and bicycle-safety education.

Although the Plaza would also attract tourists, especially if well-known performers are featured at the theater, nothing else about the Plaza is particularly unique or more compelling than the Loop. More significantly, the Plaza offers little improvement in the day-to-day quality of life for residents. In fact, in serving mainly as a tourist attraction, it may actually detract from the quality of life for local families.

In sum, while either project is likely to increase tourism, the Loop is the better choice overall considering the welfare of the resident's children.

STILL ROOM FOR IMPROVEMENT?

By now, you should have a fairly clear idea how effectively you respond to the LSAT Writing Sample topic. If you are not satisfied with your performance, take the following remedial steps:

- Review Writing Sample Lessons 1 and 2 (Days 13 and 14).

- Rewrite the essay you wrote today, limiting yourself to fifteen minutes. Unless your essay is either "limited" or "seriously flawed," don't start from scratch. Instead, try to refine and build upon your basic arguments and approach.

- Based upon today's topic, write a new essay in which you argue *for* the choice that you argued against in your first essay. Evaluate that essay as you did the first one. Don't be surprised if you see some marked improvement in your work!

- Recall from Day 14 the two alternative essay formats: (1) choice-driven and (2) goal-driven. Which one did you use in this mini-test? Perhaps the other format would be more natural or comfortable for you. Try it for your rewrite.

Logical Reasoning Lesson 4:
Recognizing Reasoning Errors

Today you will learn how to recognize the various reasoning errors or fallacies that commonly appear in LSAT Logical Reasoning problems.

Todays' Topics

1. Test questions involving reasoning errors

2. Two common statistical fallacies

3. Two common causal fallacies

4. Five common unwarranted assumption fallacies

5. Three common irrelevant appeals fallacies

6. Three common fallacies of refutation

7. Two common conditional reasoning fallacies

8. Two common reasoning errors involving the use of language

TEST QUESTIONS INVOLVING REASONING ERRORS

In LSAT problems involving reasoning errors, the passage contains an argument that employs a questionable argumentative technique or fallacy and your task is to identify the flaw or error in the reasoning. You will not be required to identify the fallacy by its traditional name, instead you will simply be required to select the best description of the reasoning error from the answer choices.

Reasoning error problems make up roughly 8% of the LSAT Logical Reasoning questions, so expect to see at least two problems of this type on each of the two Logical Reasoning sections. Your ability to recognize reasoning errors will also be tested indirectly in some of the parallel reasoning problems on the test.

Reasoning error questions are typically worded as follows:

- Which of the following is the best statement of the flaw in the argument?

- Which one of the following indicates an error in the reasoning leading to the conclusion in the argument?

- Which one of the following questionable argumentative techniques is employed in the passage?

The best way to prepare for this type of question is simply to become familiar with the various types of reasoning errors cataloged below.

TWO COMMON STATISTICAL FALLACIES

The two most common statistical reasoning fallacies are the *fallacy of the biased sample* and the *fallacy of the small or insufficient sample*. Both involve sampling errors. The fallacy of the biased sample is committed whenever the data for a statistical inference are drawn from a sample that is not representative of the population under consideration. Professional statisticians avoid this error through random sampling and other sampling techniques that are designed to eliminate bias in the data used to support their inferences. The fallacy of the small or insufficient sample is committed whenever too small a sample is used to warrant confidence in the conclusion or whenever greater reliability is attributed to the conclusion than is warranted by the sample size. Professional statisticians avoid this error by choosing samples of sufficient size to reduce the margin of error in the conclusion. The fallacy of the insufficient sample is also known as the fallacy of "hasty generalization."

Egregious instances of these two statistical fallacies abound in ordinary discourse. For example, when one condemns all football players on the basis of the inappropriate behavior of a few, or lauds all politicians on the basis of the honesty and integrity of their representative, or vilifies all members of a race on the basis of encounters with only a few individuals, these fallacies are committed. Moreover, in most of the above cases both forms of the fallacy are committed at the same time.

Here's an example of an argument that commits the fallacy of the biased sample:

Example 16-1
> In a recent survey conducted on the Internet, eighty percent of the respondents indicated their strong disapproval of government regulation of the content and access of web-based information. This survey clearly shows that legislation designed to restrict the access or control the content of Internet information will meet with strong opposition from the electorate.

The data for the inference in the above argument are drawn from a sample that is not representative of the entire electorate. Since the survey was conducted on the Internet, not all members of the electorate have an equal chance of being included in the sample. Moreover, persons who use the Internet are more likely to have an opinion on the topic than persons who do not. For these reasons the sample is obviously biased.

Here's an example of an argument that commits the fallacy of the insufficient sample:

Example 16-2
> I met my new boss at work today and she was very unpleasant. Twice when I tried to talk with her she said she was busy and told me not to interrupt her again. Later, when I needed her advice on a customer's problem, she ignored me and walked away. It's obvious that she has a bad attitude and is not going to be easy to work with.

The data for the inference in this argument are insufficient to support the conclusion. Three observations of a person's behavior are not sufficient to support a conclusion about that person's behavior in general. Obviously, the boss could just have been having a bad day or been engrossed in other things.

TWO COMMON CAUSAL FALLACIES

The "After This, Therefore Because of This" Fallacy

By far the most common causal fallacy, and the one most likely to appear on the LSAT, is the *"after this, therefore because of this" fallacy*. This is the fallacy of concluding on insufficient grounds that because some event X *comes after* some other event Y, Y must have *caused* X. Many common bad luck superstitions are examples of this fallacy (e.g., the black cat crossing one's path, walking under ladders, etc.). The error in arguments that commit this fallacy is that their conclusions are causal claims that are not sufficiently substantiated by the evidence. In most instances of this fallacy, the only evidence that is offered to support the causal claim is a positive correlation between two conditions or events; the one that occurs first is identified as the cause, the one that follows is identified as the effect. Typically, the causal connection between the two events is implausible given our general understanding of the world.

Here are two typical examples of the "after this, therefore because of this" fallacy:

Example 16-3
Ten minutes after walking into the auditorium, I began to feel sick to my stomach. There must have been something in the air in that building that caused my nausea.

Example 16-4
The stock market declined shortly after the election of the president, thus indicating the lack of confidence the business community has in the new administration.

In Example 16-3 a causal connection is posited between two events simply on the basis of one occurring before the other. Without further evidence to support it, the causal claim based on the correlation is premature. Example 16-4 is typical of modern news reporting. The only evidence offered in this argument to support the implicit causal claim that the decline in the stock market was caused by the election of the president is the fact that election preceded the decline. While this may have been a causal factor in the decline of the stock market, to argue that it is the cause without additional information and auxiliary hypotheses that make the causal connection plausible is to commit the "after this, therefore because of this" fallacy.

The "Necessary vs. Sufficient" Fallacy

Another common causal fallacy occurs when one confuses a *necessary* condition for the occurrence of some event with a *sufficient* condition for the event's occurrence. One source of this fallacy is a misunderstanding of the meaning of conditional statements. This fallacy is best understood with the help of a few examples.

Example 16-5
The car will start only if the battery isn't dead, so the car will start if the battery isn't dead.

Example 16-6
If you read this book carefully, you'll get a good score on the LSAT. Therefore, you won't get a good score on the LSAT unless you read this book carefully.

In Example 16-5 the confusion of necessary condition with sufficient condition is apparent. While having a "live" battery is certainly necessary for starting the car's engine, it is not sufficient to do this. Many other conditions including a "live" battery must be satisfied to bring this event about. Take special note of the difference between "only if" and "if" in this example. "A only if B" is not equivalent in meaning to "A if B." The former means that B is a necessary condition for A; the latter means that B is a sufficient condition for A. The former is equivalent to "If A, then B"; the latter is equivalent to "If B, then A."

The premise in Example 16-5 states that reading this book carefully is a sufficient condition for getting a good score on the LSAT. The conclusion states that reading this book carefully is a necessary condition for getting a good score on the LSAT. The premise asserts that anyone who reads this book carefully will get a good score; the conclusion asserts that anyone who gets a good score has read this book carefully. Obviously, these are quite different assertions.

FIVE COMMON UNWARRANTED ASSUMPTION FALLACIES

Unwarranted assumptions are assumptions that have no merit or independent justification. The two most common unwarranted assumption fallacies are the *fallacy of composition* and the *division fallacy*.

The Fallacy of Composition

The fallacy of composition is committed when a characteristic of individual members of a group is assumed without warrant to apply to the members of the group collectively. This fallacy is commonly referred to as the "part-whole" fallacy. While it is true that in some cases a property of an individual is transferable to the group of which it is a member, this certainly isn't always the case. The part-whole fallacy mistakenly assumes that this transference always holds.

Here is an example of the fallacy of composition:

Example 16-7
All physical objects are made of atoms. Atoms have no color. This book is a physical object, so it has no color.

In this example, a property that the parts lack is mistakenly assumed to be a property that the whole lacks as well. A little reflection shows that this assumption is false in this case.

The Division Fallacy

The division fallacy is the converse of the composition fallacy. In this case the fallacy is committed when a property of a group is mistakenly assumed to hold true for the individuals that make up the group. This fallacy is commonly referred to as the "whole-part" fallacy. While it is true that in some cases a property of a group is transferable to the individuals in the group, this certainly isn't always the case. The whole-part fallacy mistakenly assumes that this transference always holds.

Here is an example of the division fallacy:

Example 16-8
The LSAT is a challenging exam. Therefore, every problem on the LSAT is a challenging problem.

In this example, a property of the whole exam is assumed to apply to each part of the exam. Clearly, the exam could be challenging even if some of the problems were not challenging.

The False Dichotomy Fallacy

The *false dichotomy fallacy* is also a common unwarranted assumption fallacy. This error is committed when one assumes without warrant that there are only two alternatives and then reasons that since one of the alternatives is false or unacceptable the other must be true or accepted. Of course, in cases where there are in fact only two alternatives, and this fact

is obvious or can be justified, this pattern of reasoning is highly effective and acceptable. Typically, in arguments in which this fallacy occurs no evidence is offered to support the claim that there are only two alternatives available and a little reflection reveals that this claim is not self evident. This fallacy is commonly referred to as the "black-and-white" fallacy.

Here is an example of the false dichotomy fallacy:

Example 16-9
Either we put convicted child molesters in jail for life or we risk having our children become their next victims. We certainly can't risk this, so we had better lock them up for the rest of their lives.

The argument in Example 16-9 assumes that there are only two possible alternatives open to us. No evidence is offered to support this claim and a little reflection reveals that it is not obviously the case. While child molestation is a difficult problem to deal with, it is unlikely that the only solution to the problem is the one mentioned in the argument. It is also unlikely that this is the only way that we can protect our children from becoming the victims of convicted offenders.

The Slippery Slope Fallacy

The *"slippery slope"* fallacy is so named because, like a slippery slope on which you cannot gain a foothold, once you start to slide you continue to slide until you crash to the bottom. Similarly, in this fallacy, it is assumed without justification or proof that once one event occurs a series of events will occur that will end with some undesirable consequence. Since the undesirable consequence is to be avoided, it is reasoned that the initiating event is also to be avoided. Typically, in arguments of this type no evidence is provided that the causal sequence depicted in the argument is the only possible scenario of events. In most cases, a little reflection reveals that the scenario is not even very likely. Without the assumption that each step in the sequence of events is inevitable, the argument is not convincing. This fallacy is also known as the "domino fallacy."

Here's an example of the slippery slope fallacy.

Example 16-10

If pornography is not outlawed once and for all, the spread of pornographic literature will lead to an increase in sex-related crimes such as rape and incest. This in turn will lead to a general moral decay in the society that will cause an increase in crimes of all sorts. Eventually a complete breakdown of law and order will occur, leading ultimately to the total collapse of civilization as we know it. We certainly don't want this to happen, so we had better outlaw pornography before it's too late to do anything about it.

The "All Things are Equal" Fallacy

The *"all things are equal" fallacy* is committed when it is assumed without justification that background conditions have remained the same at different times or at different locations. In most instances this is an unwarranted assumption for the simple reason that things rarely remain the same over extended periods of time, and things rarely remain the same from place to place.

Here's an example of the "all things are equal" fallacy.

Example 16-11

Two years ago when it rained for three days in a row the river jumped its banks and flooded the town. The latest weather forecast predicts that it will rain for at least three days, so it looks as though the town will be flooded again this year too.

The assumption operative in this argument is that nothing has changed in the two years since the last flood. No evidence or justification is offered for this assumption. Moreover, it is just as likely an assumption that things *have* changed and that measures were put in place to avoid a reoccurrence of the flooding.

THREE COMMON IRRELEVANT APPEALS FALLACIES

Irrelevant appeals attempt to persuade others to accept a conclusion by appealing to matters that are not relevant to the truth or correctness of the conclusion. They are considered reasoning errors because they violate the requirement that the reasons offered in support of a claim should provide evidence that the claim is true or correct. In other words, such appeals mistakenly view the goal of argumentation to be simply persuasion, rather than the attainment of the truth.

Appeal to Ignorance

The *appeal to ignorance* is one of the most commonly used ploys to gain acceptance of a claim. The basic form of this fallacy is to argue that a claim is true (or false) solely on the grounds that no one has demonstrated or can demonstrate that the claim is false (or true).

Here's an example of an argument that employs an appeal to ignorance.

Example 16-12

Scientists have not established any causal link between smoking and lung cancer, hence we must simply accept the fact that smoking does not cause lung cancer.

Inability to prove that something is true (or false) cannot, by itself, be taken as evidence that it is false (or true). If this were accepted as a principle of logic, it would follow, for example, that our inability to prove the existence of God would lead immediately to the conclusion that God does not exist and that our inability to prove that UFO's don't exist, would lead immediately to the conclusion that UFO's exist. Likewise, our inability to prove that someone is guilty of a crime, would have to be taken as evidence, on this account, that they were innocent of the crime. This latter example has a ring of truth to it only because our system of law employs the rule that a person is innocent until proven guilty. Inability to prove guilt is not taken as evidence of innocence; rather, it is taken as inability to hold legally blameworthy.

Appeal to Public Opinion

Appealing to public opinion or to what most persons believe is another commonly used ploy to gain acceptance of a claim. Rather than use evidence or reasons that would support the truth of the claim, the author of the argument resorts to consensus prejudices, beliefs, traditions, or customs to gain acceptance of the conclusion. Peer pressure and peer acceptance are relied upon to persuade the unwary, uncritical listener or reader. Typically, no evidence that is relevant to the truth of the claim is offered in the argument. This fallacy is a favorite of politicians and advertisers.

Here's an example of an argument that employs an appeal to public opinion.

Example 16-13

Rick O'Flanagan's newest novel, *Seldom More Often Than Frequently,* has been on the best-seller list for twenty-five weeks in a row. It must be a good book; after all, thirty million readers can't be wrong.

In this example, the only reason given for the claim that the novel is a good book is that it has been read by thirty million people. A little reflection tells us that this, by itself, is not a good reason for this claim. After all, it is also true that thirty million people read tabloids on a regular basis and this is surely not evidence that they are in any sense good.

Appeal to Authority

Another common appeal used to gain acceptance of a claim is the *appeal to authority*. In place of evidence that supports the claim, author's often resort to the testimony or expertise of others to support the claim. This practice is not always suspect. As a matter of fact, we often rely on other persons or sources when accepting claims. We do this, for example, whenever we appeal to scientists, textbooks, doctors, and other experts to support our beliefs. This practice becomes suspect when there is a question about the competence, reliability, qualifications, motives, prejudices, etc., of the persons or sources upon whom we are relying.

The mere fact that an "authority" claims that some claim is or is not true is not, by itself, evidence that it is or is not true. It is a well-known fact among lawyers that, on any topic whatsoever, for every expert there is another expert who can be called to refute any claim made by the other. Similarly, the mere fact that some claim appears in a publication is not, by itself, evidence that the claim is true. After all, some publications, like the wolf in sheep's clothing, try to gain reliability and authoritativeness by mimicking publications that are authoritative and reliable sources of information. Dressing themselves up in the garb of respectable newspapers, tabloids try to fool us into believing that they are also reliable sources of information. Typically, in arguments that employ the appeal to authority to support the conclusion, no evidence is offered to justify our reliance upon the source cited. Once again, this fallacy is a favorite of politicians and advertisers.

Here's an example of an argument that employs an appeal to authority.

Example 16-14

Geena Goodlooks is one of this country's most respected and honored actresses. You can be certain that when she says welfare reform is needed, it has to be true.

In this argument, one has to wonder about the relevance of Geena's testimony to the truth of the claim it supports. No evidence is offered that would justify our reliance upon her testimony on this topic. The fact that she is a "respected and honored" actress hardly qualifies her as an expert on the need for welfare reform.

THREE COMMON FALLACIES OF REFUTATION

Fallacies of refutation are committed in criticizing the arguments of others. Refutation fallacies occur whenever the critic focuses on aspects of the argument that are irrelevant to the reasoning employed in the argument or the truth of the claims that make up the argument. The basic tactic in criticisms that commit fallacies of this type is to scrupulously avoid attacking the argument, and instead attack the author, a side issue, or a deliberately weakened version of the argument. Needless to say, these fallacies are another favorite of politicians.

Attacking the Author

Attacks on the author of the argument take three forms. The attack is focused either on the character, or the motives, or the behavior of the person presenting the argument. The aim of the attack in all three cases is to discredit the conclusion of the person's argument. Assaults of this type are rarely, if ever, relevant to the reasoning employed in the argument or the truth or correctness of the conclusion. They are irrelevant for the simple reason that an arguer's personal character, motives, or behavior are rarely relevant to the correctness of the arguer's reasoning or the truth of the statements employed in the reasoning. Criticisms that employ attacks of these types are commonly known as *"ad hominem* arguments," which means "arguments against the person." It is a safe bet that you will see at least one problem on the LSAT in which this fallacy occurs.

Attacking the author's character. Here's an example of a counter-argument that employs an attack on the *character* of the person advancing the argument.

Example 16-15
When you realize that the man who is trying to convince you that he would be the best president this country has ever seen is in fact a womanizer and an illegal drug user, it's not difficult to draw the conclusion that his arguments are completely unacceptable.

In this example, the presidential candidate's arguments are attacked by pointing out repugnant characteristics of the candidate. No attempt is made to consider or attack the candidate's arguments.

Attacking the author's motives. Here's an example of a counter-argument that employs an attack on the *motives* of the persons advancing the argument.

Example 16-16
The radio and television industry has been lobbying against proposed changes in the laws governing the use of publicly owned transmission frequencies. But just keep this in mind; no matter how good their arguments might be, they stand to lose a great deal if the proposed changes become law.

In Example 16-16 the radio and television industry's arguments are dismissed out of hand on the grounds that they have a vested interest in the outcome. The tactic exhibited in Example 16-16 is commonly called "poisoning the well" because the source of the argument is condemned in order to discredit the argument.

Attacking the author's behavior. Here's an example of a counter-argument that employs an attack on the *behavior* of the person advancing the argument.

Example 16-17
> *Politician:* My esteemed colleague accuses me of misappropriating taxpayer's funds for my own personal use. Well, it might interest you to know that he has the unenviable distinction of having spent more on so-called fact-finding trips to exotic locations all around the world than anyone else in Congress.

The fallacy exhibited in Example 16-17 is commonly called the "you too!" or "two wrongs don't make a right" fallacy. In this example, no attempt is made to attack the colleague's argument, rather the focus of the attack is to accuse the person of similar questionable behavior or wrongdoing.

Attacking a Side-Issue

The "red herring" fallacy. Another fallacious refutation tactic commonly employed is to divert attention away from the argument under consideration and focus instead on a side issue. The popular name for this refutation tactic is *"red herring"* which comes from the fox hunting practice of dragging a cooked herring across the fox's trail to divert the hounds off the scent. The aim of this tactic is simply to obfuscate and avoid the argument rather than offer apt reasons why it should not be accepted.

Here's an example of a counter-argument that employs the red herring fallacy.

Example 16-18
Mandatory life sentences for three-time felons is a bad idea. People who think it's a good idea argue that it will stop violent crime. But, if we really want to stop violent crime, instead of locking people up we should stop portraying violence in movies and on television.

In Example 16-18 the critic shifts attention away from the issue of whether mandatory life sentences should be used to combat violent crime to a related but different issue. Instead of attacking the arguments of the proponents of mandatory life sentences, an alternative solution to the problem is proposed. Obviously, however, merely proposing a different solution to a problem cannot, by itself, be taken as evidence that competing solutions and the arguments that support them are necessarily mistaken or incorrect.

Attacking a Weakened Version of an Argument

The "straw man" fallacy. The *"straw man"* fallacy is committed when a person deliberately misrepresents an opponent's argument in order to make it easier to criticize, or make it so obviously implausible that no criticism is required. Although the misrepresented version is usually only a caricature of the opponent's argument, it is treated by the critic as equivalent to the original. Because the new version is a significantly weakened version of the original argument, the critic seldom has difficulty in defeating it.

Here's an example of a counter-argument that employs the "straw man" fallacy.

Example 16-19

The "right-to-die" bill currently being considered by Congress implies that it's acceptable to take the lives of weak and frail old people who cannot defend themselves. However, anyone who has an ounce of decency knows that this is just plain wrong, so we must make every effort to defeat this legislation.

In Example 16-19, the critic distorts the argument in favor of the legislation by drawing a highly questionable inference from it. The attack then focuses on the purported implication which is quite easily defeated.

Two Common Conditional Reasoning Fallacies

Reasoning that involves conditional sentences can be somewhat tricky. Conditionals are sentences of the form "If A, then B." There are four basic patterns of reasoning involving these statements; two of them are correct forms of reasoning and two of them are fallacious forms of reasoning. The correct forms are illustrated in the following two examples:

Correct Forms of Conditional Reasoning

Example 16-20

If Felix is a cat, then Felix is an animal. Felix is a cat, so Felix is an animal.

Example 16-21

If Felix is a cat, then Felix is an animal. Felix is not a animal, so Felix is not a cat.

A little reflection is all that is required to convince yourself that these two patterns of reasoning are correct.

The basic pattern of Example 16-20 is:

Premise: If A, then B

Premise: A

Conclusion: B

The basic pattern of Example 16-21 is:

Premise: If A, then B

Premise: not B

Conclusion: not A

Every instance of the above two patterns is an argument which is such that if the premises are true, the conclusion must be true. That is, the truth of the premises guarantees the truth of the conclusion.

Fallacious Forms of Conditional Reasoning

The fallacious forms of conditional reasoning are illustrated in the following two examples:

Example 16-22

If Felix is a cat, then Felix is an animal. Felix is an animal, so Felix is a cat.

Example 16-23

If Felix is a cat, then Felix is an animal. Felix is not a cat, so Felix is not an animal.

A little reflection is all that is required to convince yourself that these two patterns of reasoning are fallacious.

The basic pattern of Example 16-22 is:

Premise: If A, then B

Premise: B

Conclusion: A

The basic pattern of Example 16-23 is:

Premise: If A, then B

Premise: not A

Conclusion: Not B

Every instance of the above two patterns is a fallacious argument.

As a general rule, it's a good idea to proceed with caution when dealing with arguments containing conditional statements. The main source of potential confusion is that conditional statements can be expressed in a variety of ways. Whenever possible, restate conditionals and put them into the "If _____, then _____." form before you attempt to evaluate the argument. To appreciate the importance of doing this, consider the following example:

Example 16-24

The treaty will be signed only if both parties agree to end the hostilities. Both parties have indicated agreement to end the hostilities, so the treaty will be signed.

The argument in Example 16-24 is fallacious. This can be seen clearly by restating the argument as follows:

Premise: If the treaty is signed, then both parties agree to end the hostilities.

Premise: Both parties agree to end the hostilities.

Conclusion: The treaty will be signed.

Notice that this restatement reveals that the argument in Example 16-24 has the same basic pattern as the argument in Example 16-22. Notice also that the restatement of the first premise accords with the advice stated earlier in the discussion of Example 16-5.

TWO COMMON REASONING ERRORS INVOLVING THE USE OF LANGUAGE

The Fallacy of Equivocation

The *fallacy of equivocation* occurs when a key word or phrase that has more than one meaning is employed in different meanings throughout the argument. Since the truth of the premises and the conclusion is in part a function of the meanings of the words in the sentences that express them, a shift in meaning of key terms in the argument will enable one to draw conclusions from premises that do not in fact support them.

Here's an example of an argument that commits the fallacy of equivocation.

Example 16-25

Logic is the study of arguments, and since arguments are disagreements, it follows that logic is the study of disagreements.

In Example 16-25 the word "argument" is employed in two different meanings. In the first premise "argument" is used to mean "a discourse in which reasons are offered in support of a claim"; in the second premise "argument" is defined as meaning "a disagreement." If we adopt the second meaning, the first premise is false. If we adopt the first meaning, the second premise is false. Either way, the premises simply fail to provide support for the conclusion.

The Fallacy of Circular Reasoning

There are two basic forms of the *fallacy of circular reasoning* or "arguing in a circle." The first type occurs when one employs a restatement of the premise as the conclusion of the argument; the second type occurs when the truth of the conclusion is presupposed by the premises. Sound reasoning requires that the premises provide independent support for the conclusion. Obviously, the mere restatement of the premises in the conclusion can hardly be regarded as independent evidence that the conclusion is true. Nor can the use of premises that presuppose the truth of the conclusion be regarded as independent evidence that the conclusion is true. In both of these cases, one has merely argued in a circle. The circular reasoning fallacy is commonly referred to as the fallacy of "begging the question."

Here's an example of an argument that commits the first form of the fallacy of circular reasoning.

Example 16-26

Honesty is the best policy for the simple reason that it's best to adopt a practice that will insure that people are treated in a fair, truthful, and trustworthy manner.

In Example 16-26, the conclusion is just a restatement of the premise, since "honesty" means being fair, truthful, and trustworthy.

Here's an example of an argument that commits the second form of the fallacy of circular reasoning.

Example 16-27

My boss told me that I was her favorite employee, so it must be true because there's no way she would lie to her favorite employee.

In Example 16-27, the arguer is trying to prove that he is the boss's favorite employee, but to support the premise that the boss would not lie to her favorite employee, he would have to accept the claim that he was the boss's favorite employee. To do this, however, is to assume the very thing he is trying to prove.

Logical Reasoning Lesson 5: Basic Reasoning Skills

Today you will learn three more of the eight basic logical reasoning skills listed in Day 5.

Today's Topics

1. Identifying principles
2. Identifying the method of arguments
3. Three common rebuttal techniques
4. Recognizing similarities between arguments

IDENTIFYING PRINCIPLES

On Day 5 you learned how to identify the factual assumptions required to make an argument logically correct. Today you will learn how to identify the value assumptions required to make an argument acceptable or convincing to an individual.

Principle questions are typically worded as follows:

- Which one of the following principles, if accepted, would provide the most justification for the conclusion?

- On the basis of their statements, X and Y are committed to disagreeing about the truth of which of the following principles?

Principle questions make up only five to eight percent of the Logical Reasoning problems on the LSAT, so you can expect to see only one or two of these problems on each Logical Reasoning section. There are two basic formats for these problems. In one, an argument is stated in the passage and your task is to ascertain the underlying principle that justifies the author's conclusion. In the other, an argumentative dialogue between two people is presented and your task is to ascertain the underlying principle that they would be committed to agreeing or disagreeing about, given their remarks.

A *principle* is a general rule that justifies a particular action or decision. In most cases, the principle functions as a value assumption in argument. This is especially true of arguments that prescribe a particular course of action or resolution.

Factual Assumptions vs. Value Assumptions

First, let's consider the basic difference between factual assumptions and value assumptions. A factual assumption is an assumption that is operative in an argument that concludes that something is or is not the case. A value assumption is an assumption that is operative in an argument that concludes that some action ought or ought not be performed. Arguments of the latter type are commonly referred to as *prescriptive arguments* because their conclusions prescribe that certain types of conduct or courses of action should or should not be engaged in.

In order to identify value assumptions, it is necessary first to be familiar with some basic values.

Some Commonly Held Values

justice	freedom of speech	creativity
wisdom	individual responsibility	tradition
honesty	equality of opportunity	peace
security	financial independence	cooperation
loyalty	obedience to authority	productivity
courage	equality of condition	tolerance
excellence	freedom from want	harmony
flexibility	autonomy	competition
novelty	generosity	comfort
happiness	profitability	efficiency

Obviously, this list of values is by no means complete, but it serves to give you the basic idea. Chances are you and your friends and family share all or most of the values on the above list. What you may not share, however, are your value *preferences*. When two values conflict, a choice must be made as to which is to be given preference. For example, honesty and loyalty conflict when we have to choose between telling a lie or saving a friend. If we lie, the friend is saved; if we tell the truth, the friend is jeopardized. In cases like this, value preferences will have to be made. Moreover, these preferences will, in many cases, be subconsciously codified and will function as personal rules or principles that will guide our conduct and our decision making. For example, if we choose to tell the truth, and thereby jeopardize the friend the principle that guides us in this decision is that one ought always tell the truth. Persons who lie to save the friend are guided in their decision by a different principle; a principle that reflects a different value preference.

Prescriptive Arguments and Value Assumptions

Recall that prescriptive arguments are arguments in which the conclusion prescribes that certain types of conduct or courses of action should or should not be engaged in. Such arguments will be convincing to an individual only if the individual shares the values and, more importantly, the value preferences of the person presenting the argument. Normally, the values and value preferences of the author are not explicitly stated in the argument; they are simply assumed. For example, consider this argument:

Example 17-1

Every day new evidence is found to support the claim that cigarette smoking is harmful to the health of both the smoker and those in close proximity to the smoker. On the basis of this mounting evidence, the government should prohibit the sale and manufacture of cigarettes.

On the surface, it appears that the premise provides support for the conclusion; that is, it appears to provide a reason why the conclusion ought to be accepted. But notice that it does so only on the assumption that you believe that it is the government's responsibility to take care of people's welfare. If you believe that it is the individual's responsibility to take care of his/her own welfare, you will not find this argument convincing; in fact, from your perspective the premise will not even support the conclusion.

The underlying principle that would have to be shared for the argument in Example 17-1 to be acceptable is that government ought to protect people from harming themselves and others. This principle expresses the author's preference of one value over another; in this case, collective responsibility over individual responsibility. Persons who agree with this principle will find the argument convincing; those who disagree with this principle will find the argument to be unacceptable.

In general, the best way to identify the principle that is operative in an argument is to examine the premises given in support of the conclusion and then determine what value preferences would be required to have those reasons be regarded as more convincing or more desirable than other reasons that might have been offered in support of the conclusion. Alternatively, ask yourself what values are involved in the argument and what preference regarding these values is required to justify the course of action or the decision expressed in the conclusion. Once you have located the value preference, look for an answer choice that reflects this preference.

IDENTIFYING THE METHOD OF ARGUMENTS

In problems that ask you to identify the method of an argument, an argument is stated in the passage and your task is to identify the reasoning technique employed in the argument. You will not be required to identify the technique by name; all that's required is to select the best description of the general reasoning strategy of the argument from the answer choices. Problems of this sort make up about 3% of the LSAT logical reasoning questions, so expect to see one or two of these problems on each Logical Reasoning section.

The method of an argument is simply the way in which the author goes about establishing the conclusion, or in the case of a critical response to an argument, the way in which the author attempts to defeat the conclusion. There are a great number of argumentative techniques that may be used when attempting to establish or defeat conclusions—too many to list all of them here, but familiarity with some of the basic strategies and techniques will prove to be helpful in dealing with these problems.

It is important to note that not all of the methods of establishing or defeating conclusions presented below are necessarily effective or logically correct. The issue in problems of this type is merely to identify the method used by the author, not to determine whether or not it is an effective or logically correct method. Determining the latter is an entirely different matter.

Method questions are worded as follows:

- Which of the following most accurately characterizes the argumentative strategy in the passage?

- The argument proceeds by:

- Which one of the following argumentative techniques is used in the passage?

- The method of the argument is to:

- The argument employs which one of the following reasoning techniques?

Reasoning by Analogy

A common method employed in arguing for a conclusion is to use an *analogy*. Starting with a claim or situation that is familiar and unproblematic, the author argues that the issue in question is very much like the familiar case, and hence that what is true of it is probably true of the case in question. The following example demonstrates this method:

Example 17-2

The mushrooms we saw in the forest yesterday are the same color, size, and shape as those we saw in the grocery store today. Obviously, the mushrooms sold in the grocery store aren't poisonous; hence, it is likely that the ones we saw in the forest aren't poisonous either.

Citing an Authority

Another technique often employed when attempting to establish a claim is to cite an *authority* as the grounds or reason for accepting it. In these cases the authority's or expert's testimony functions as the premise of the argument, and the author's reasoning is that we ought to accept the conclusion simply because some expert or authority claims that it's true. Here's an example:

Example 17-3

Professor Lipscomb, my Physics professor, warned us about the dangers of water and air pollution; that's why I'm supporting the Clean Air and Water initiative.

Statistical Reasoning

Many arguments use *statistics* to establish claims. These arguments normally begin with the recitation of a statistical claim to the effect that some percentage of a certain group have a certain characteristic. It is then indicated that since a given individual is in the group, it follows that the individual is likely (or unlikely) to have the aforementioned characteristic. Here are some examples:

Example 17-4

Two percent of all vegetarians contract colon cancer. Since Sally is a vegetarian it is unlikely she'll get colon cancer.

Example 17-5

Eighty percent of all logic students scored high on the LSAT. Henry is a logic major, so he probably scored high on the LSAT.

Reasoning from Experience

Past *experience* is often taken as a reason for believing that something *is* the case or *will be* the case. Authors who use this type of reasoning typically begin with a statement that delineates some experience they or someone else has had. This stated experience then functions as a premise from which it is argued that some, as yet unexperienced, event or situation will occur. Here's a well-worn example:

Example 17-6

We have observed the sun rising countless times in the past; hence, we can be assured that the sun will rise tomorrow.

A variation of the above method is to argue that some general claim is true on the basis of the observation of a number of instances of the claim. Arguments that employ this kind of reasoning typically begin with premises that document the observed instances; the conclusion typically asserts that what is true of the observed instances is true of all or most instances. Here is an example:

Example 17-7

"Don't worry! All of the lettuce we checked in the shipment was in excellent condition, so you can be assured that all of the lettuce is OK."

Causal Reasoning

Causal conclusions (i.e., conclusions that assert a causal relation between two events) are typically established either by *eliminative reasoning,* or by noting a *significant correlation* between events.

Eliminative Reasoning. Arguments that employ eliminative reasoning usually proceed by isolating a common feature of the events under discussion by a process of elimination. The common feature is then deemed to be the cause. The premises of such arguments usually describe testing procedures aimed at determining which, if any, of a set of properties are causally related to the event in question. Through experiment or observation an attempt is made to eliminate each of these features as a causal candidate. The one that resists these attempts is concluded to be the cause of the event under consideration. Here is an example:

Example 17-8

Six customers of a fast-food restaurant developed food poisoning shortly after eating lunch there. An investigation revealed that they had all drunk different beverages and not all had eaten salads or soups, or french fries. However, they had all eaten chicken sandwiches prepared with different breads. The health department concluded that the cause of the food poisoning was poorly cooked chicken.

Causal reasoning based on a significant correlation. Arguments that assert a causal relation on the basis of a significant correlation between two circumstances typically begin with premises which document the correlation. The correlation is deemed significant if it is such that the suspected cause is not only present whenever the event occurs, but also absent whenever the event fails to occur. Once this is established, it is concluded that the relation between the two events is causal. Here is an example:

Example 17-9

Every time my car hits a pothole in the road the engine misfires, but it never misfires when the road is smooth. Hence, hitting potholes is the cause of the misfiring.

Disjunctive Reasoning

Another common method used to establish a conclusion is to show that it is the only acceptable *alternative* by ruling out all of the other possibilities. Here is an example:

Example 17-10

If Sean went to the beach, he either drove his own car or went with a friend. But Sean's car is in the garage; so he must have gone with a friend because he was seen at the beach early this morning.

Conditional Reasoning

Conditional arguments usually proceed by first stating a conditional statement, and then by asserting or denying the antecedent (i.e., the "if" clause) or the consequent (i.e., the "then" clause) of the conditional statement. Here are some examples:

Example 17-11
> Pigs can't fly. If they could, they would, but they don't, so they can't.

Example 17-12
> If it looks like a duck, walks like a duck, and quacks like a duck, then it's a duck. It looks, walks, and quacks like a duck, so obviously it's a duck.

Example 17-13
> Sam is a basketball player if he's over 6 feet tall. But Sam is only 5' 9", so he's not a basketball player.

THREE COMMON REBUTTAL TECHNIQUES

Discredit the Arguer

Among the most common methods employed to defeat or rebut an argument is to challenge the *motives* or the *integrity* of the person who is presenting the argument. The basic ploy here is to attempt to discredit the argument by discrediting the arguer. Here are some examples:

Example 17-14
> The medical industry has argued vigorously that health-care reform is unnecessary, but we have to keep in mind that the medical industry stands to lose the most if new health care legislation is passed.

Example 17-15
> Professor Martini has presented some strong arguments in favor of the theory of evolution, but none of them are acceptable because it is a well known fact that Martini is an atheist.

Redirect the Argument

Another common method used to defeat an argument is to direct attention away from the main point of the argument to a different, though perhaps related, point, and then attack or defend it rather than the main issue. Here is an example:

Example 17-16
> Mandatory life sentences for three-time felons is a bad idea. People who think it's a good idea argue that it will stop violent crime. But if we really want to stop violent crime, instead of locking people up we should stop portraying violent crimes on television and in movies, because that's where these criminals get their ideas in the first place.

Reduce a Premise to Absurdity

Author's often attempt to defeat an argument by showing that one of its major premises is false or absurd. A common way in which this is done is by first assuming that the premise is in fact true, and then by showing that this assumption leads to an obviously false or absurd claim. By showing that the premise leads to this result, it is thereby shown to be itself false or absurd and hence the argument that employs it as a major premise is defeated. Here's an example of this technique:

Example 17-17
> The evidence that condom use is an effective means to stop the spread of AIDS is hardly conclusive. But assume for the sake of argument that it is. By promoting condom use we encourage young people to think that it's OK to be promiscuous, to have sex with prostitutes, to engage in homosexual activities, in short, to engage in the very activities that spread AIDS. So, rather than limiting the activities that spread this disease, we promote them by promoting condom use.

RECOGNIZING SIMILARITIES BETWEEN ARGUMENTS

Parallel reasoning problems all begin with the same basic set-up. An argument is presented in the passage and in each of the answer choices. The task, however, can differ from problem to problem. In some cases you will be asked to find the argument that parallels the *structure* or *pattern of reasoning* of the argument in the passage, in other cases you will be asked to find the argument that employs the same *method of reasoning*, and in others you will be asked to find the argument that contains the same *reasoning error* as the argument in the passage. Problems of this type make up about 12% of the LSAT logical reasoning questions, so expect to see as many as three of these problems on each Logical Reasoning section.

Questions that ask you to find the argument that has the same *structure or pattern of reasoning* as the argument in the passage are typically worded as follows:

- The argumentative structure of which one of the following most closely parallels that of the argument in the passage?

- The pattern of reasoning displayed in the argument in the passage is most closely paralleled in which of the following arguments?

- Which of the following arguments contains a flawed pattern of reasoning parallel to that contained in the argument above?

- Which of the following, in its logical features, most closely parallels the reasoning in the passage?

Questions that ask you to find the argument that employs the same *method of reasoning* as the argument in the passage are typically worded as follows:

- Which of the following most closely parallels the reasoning in the argument presented in the passage?

- In which of the following is the method of reasoning most parallel to that in the argument above?

Questions that ask you to find the argument that contains the same *reasoning error* as the argument in the passage are typically worded as follows:

- Which one of the following arguments contains a flaw that is most similar to the one in the argument above?

- The faulty reasoning in which one of the following is most parallel to that in the argument above?

Each of these question types requires a slightly different approach, as discussed below.

How to Handle Parallel Structure Problems

Recognizing argument structure. To get a basic idea of what is meant by logical "structure" or "pattern of reasoning" consider the following pair of arguments.

Example 17-18
> All men are mortal. Socrates is a man. Hence, Socrates is mortal.

Example 17-19
> Every dog has a master. Fido is a dog. Therefore, Fido has a master.

While it is evident that the arguments in these examples are about different topics, and hence are quite dissimilar in their content, they are alike in the way in which the information about the topics is presented. Each begins with a general statement claiming that all individuals in a certain class have a certain characteristic, followed by a particular statement that claims that a certain individual belongs to the class mentioned previously, and concluding that the individual has the characteristic mentioned previously. Because of these similarities, the "pattern" or "structure" of these two arguments is the same.

The basic structure or pattern of Example 17-18 and Example 17-19 can be represented as follows:

Premise: All A are B.
Premise: C is an A
Conclusion: C is a B

It is important to note that the content of the argument (i.e., what the argument is about) is irrelevant when trying to determine the structure of the argument; it is not *what* is said in the argument that's important , but rather *the way* in which it is said. The *order* of the premises and conclusion (e.g., which is stated first or second) is also irrelevant when trying to determine the similarity of the structure of arguments. For example, consider the following pair of arguments that have the same structure but whose premises and conclusion are presented in different orders:

Example 17-20

People who are happy are content; hence, since Mary is happy she must be content.

Example 17-21

John must be tall because he is a basketball player and all basketball players are tall.

The similarity in structure of these two arguments becomes readily apparent when we restate them and reorganize them as follows:

Here's the structure of Example 17-20.

Premise: <All> people who are happy are content.
Premise: Mary is happy.
Conclusion: Mary is content.

Here's the structure of Example 17-21.

Premise: All basketball players are tall.
Premise: John is a basketball player.
Conclusion: John is tall.

Determining the pattern or structure of an argument is relatively easy to do so long as you focus on the way in which the argument is expressed rather than on what is expressed in the argument. To put this another way, focus your attention on the syntax of the sentences that comprise the argument, rather than on what the sentences mean.

Here's an example of a pair of arguments that have the same flawed *pattern* of reasoning:

Example 17-22

If the propeller of an airplane breaks while the airplane is in flight, then the airplane will surely crash. The flight recorder clearly indicates that the propeller of John's airplane did not break in flight. Hence, we can be assured that John's plane did not crash.

Example 17-23

If legislation is passed that completely prohibits pornography, then freedom of artistic expression will be greatly restricted. The legislature has indicated that it will not pass legislation that completely prohibits pornography. Hence, freedom of artistic expression will not be severely restricted.

The flawed pattern that Example 17-22 and Example 17-23 share is:

Premise: If A, then B.
Premise: not A
Conclusion: not B

Here's an example of a parallel structure problem as it would appear on the LSAT.

Example 17-24

Either the safe wasn't locked or it was opened by the burglar. But it wasn't opened by the burglar unless he knew the combination. So either it was unlocked or the burglar knew the combination.

The pattern of reasoning displayed in the argument in the passage is most closely paralleled in which of the following arguments?

(A) Either the Slugs will win the Fruit Bowl or the Snails will. The Snails won't win unless they beat the Slugs. Hence, if the Slugs win the Fruit Bowl, the Snails didn't beat them.

(B) God is either unwilling to prevent evil or unable to do so. But he is not unable unless he is not omnipotent. Hence, he is either unwilling or he is not omnipotent.

(C) Either gun control laws are passed or the number of crimes involving hand guns will continue to rise. But gun control laws won't be passed unless the NRA supports them. Hence, if the NRA supports them, gun control laws will be passed.

(D) Professor Lascola is either a realist or an empiricist. But he is not an empiricist if he believes that some concepts are innate. So, if he believes that some ideas are innate, he is not a realist.

(E) Either smoking is harmful or the Surgeon General is incorrect in his warnings about smoking cigarettes. But studies have shown conclusively that smoking is harmful, hence the Surgeon General is correct in his warnings.

Procedure for dealing with parallel *structure* problems. Here's the procedure for dealing with parallel reasoning problems that ask you to find an argument that has the *same structure or pattern of reasoning* as the argument in the passage.

First, get clear about the structure of the argument in the passage. To do this, underline words such as "all," "some," "no" (and their synonyms), and words and phrases such as "and," "or," "if, then," "if and only if" (and their synonyms). Applying this advice to the passage in Example 17-24 the result is as follows:

Either the safe wasn't locked or it was opened by the burglar. But it wasn't opened by the burglar unless he knew the combination. So either it wasn't locked or the burglar knew the combination.

So far, the structure looks like this:

Premise: Either _____ or _____.

Premise: _____ unless _____.

Conclusion: Either _____ or _____.

Second, think about the sentences that fill the blanks. Notice that the first blank of the first premise and the first blank of the conclusion get filled by the same sentence. Notice also that the second blank of the second premise and the second blank of the conclusion also get filled by the same sentence. Notice further that the second blank of the first premise and the first blank of the second premise are not exactly the same sentence. The first blank of the second premise gets filled by the negation of the sentence that fills the second blank of the first premise. Filling in the blanks, the structure looks like this:

Premise: Either A or B.

Premise: not B unless C.

Conclusion: Either A or C.

Third, with this structure in mind look at each of the answer choices to find the one with exactly the same pattern.

(A) doesn't have the same structure as the argument in the passage. The structure of (A) is:

Premise: Either A or B.

Premise: Not B unless C.

Conclusion: If A, then not C.

(B) has the same structure as the argument in the passage. You can convince yourself that this is the case simply by replacing the letters in the above schema by the independent clauses of (B).

(C) does not have the same structure as the argument in the passage. The structure of (C) is:

Premise: Either A or B.

Premise: Not A unless C.

Conclusion: If C, then not A.

(D) does not have the same structure as the argument in the passage. The structure of (D) is:

Premise: Either A or B.

Premise: If C, then not B.

Conclusion: If C, then not A.

(E) does not have the same structure as the argument in the passage. The structure of (E) is:

Premise: Either A or not B.

Premise: A.

Conclusion: B.

How to Handle Parallel Method of Reasoning Problems

Questions that ask you to find the argument that employs the *same method of reasoning* as the argument in the passage should be approached in a different way than those that ask for the argument that has the same structure or pattern of reasoning.

Here's an example of this type of question as it would appear on the LSAT.

Example 17-25

The economy is like a garden in that it experiences periods of growth and periods of latency. In order to thrive, gardens require human intervention by way of cultivation and fertilization, hence for the economy to thrive, human intervention by way of government regulation and monetary stimulus is required.

In which of the following is the method of reasoning most parallel to that in the argument above?

(A) It's true that domestic dogs are similar in many ways to wild wolves, but if dogs were immediately related to wolves, they could not be domesticated, because, to date, no one has ever successfully domesticated a wild wolf.

(B) Provided that the teeth of the dinosaur stegosaurus are like the teeth of the modern herbivores such as the horse and the cow, they are probably ancient ancestors of these animals. However, no evidence can be found that clearly supports this hypothesis. Hence, it is unlikely that modern herbivores descended from stegosaurs.

(C) Measurements taken from fossil remains of tyranosaurus rex are indicative of the entire species only if we can be assured that they are representative. But since we cannot be certain of this, we cannot conclude that all of these animals stood over twenty feet tall.

(D) Computers and machines are extremely complex artifacts just as plants and animals are extremely complex organisms. Machines and computers are made by intelligent beings, hence plants and animals probably have an intelligent maker as well.

(E) It's a well-known law that any two objects that are similar to a third object are similar to one another. Hence, since George's and Cosmo's cars are similar Elaine's, they must be similar to one another.

Procedure for dealing with same *method* problems. Here's the procedure for dealing with parallel reasoning problems that ask you to find an argument that employs the same method of reasoning as the argument in the passage.

First, get clear about the method employed in the argument in the passage. In Example 17-25 the method employed is analogical reasoning. In this argument the economy is likened to a garden and it is argued that because gardens require human intervention in order to thrive, it follows that the economy also requires human intervention in order to thrive.

Next, look for an answer choice that employs analogical reasoning to reach the conclusion. In the above example, the best response is (D). In (D) complex artifacts are likened to complex organisms and it is argued that because complex artifacts have an intelligent maker, it follows that complex organisms also have an intelligent maker.

How to Handle Parallel Reasoning Error Problems

Questions that ask you to find the argument that contains the *same reasoning error or flaw* as the argument in the passage should be approached in the same way as those that ask for the argument that employs the same method of reasoning.

Here's an example of this type of question as it would appear on the LSAT.

Example 17-26

If abortion on demand were to become legal there would be a great increase in abortions. And once abortion became commonplace there would be a weakening of respect for human life in general. Once the respect for human life was weakened we would see an increase in euthanasia of all kinds: the elderly, the mentally handicapped, and the physically disabled. Before long we would get rid of anyone who is unpopular or unproductive. In short, it would threaten our civilization. Therefore, we should oppose any move to broaden the grounds of legal abortion.

The faulty reasoning in which one of the following is most parallel to that in the argument above?

(A) The portrayal of violence on television and in the movies is the main cause of violence in our nation. Hence to get rid of violence in our nation we must censor television shows and movies.

(B) Mandatory life sentences for three-time felons is a bad idea. People who think it's a good idea think that it will stop violent crime. But if we really want to stop violent crime, instead of locking people up we should eliminate the root cause of violent crime by ceasing to glamorize violence in movies and on television.

(C) It has been well established that smoking marijuana leads to heroin use and that heroin use leads to drug addiction. Drug addiction, in turn, leads to crime to support the drug habit. The epidemic of drug related crime is threatening the very core of our existence as a nation. Hence, to stop it, we must not legalize marijuana use.

(D) Parents are wrong to criticize their children for coming home late, smoking, watching too much television, and getting poor grades. After all, they do all of these things and they're not all that smart themselves.

(E) Failure to comply with the directions contained in this chain letter will result in bad consequences. Jane Dugal received this letter and passed it on in the required seventy-two hour period. A week later she won six million dollars in the lottery. Sam Dorfman received it but did not comply with the directions. Within a week after receiving it he was trampled to death by a renegade elephant at the circus.

Procedure for dealing with same *reasoning error* problems. Here's the procedure for dealing with parallel reasoning problems that ask you to find an argument that contains the same reasoning error.

First, to identify the reasoning error in the argument in the passage. The argument in the passage in Example 17-26 commits the "slippery slope" fallacy. In this argument various events are purported to occur as a result of legalizing abortion. The terminus of this sequence of events is a catastrophic event that must be avoided, thus, it is argued, the initiating event should also to be avoided.

Next, look for an answer choice that commits the "slippery slope" fallacy. In the above example, the best response is (C). In (C) marijuana use is linked to heroin use, heroin use is linked to drug addiction, drug addiction is linked to crime which in turn is linked to the downfall of the nation. Since the downfall of the nation is to be avoided, it is argued that marijuana use should be legally curtailed.

Day 18

Logical Reasoning Lesson 6:
Mini-Test and Review

Today you will apply what you learned on Days 16 and 17 to a series of Logical Reasoning passages. After taking this mini-test under timed conditions, review the explanations that follow.

LOGICAL REASONING MINI-TEST

Number of questions: 13
Suggested time: 18 minutes

Directions (as printed in test booklet): The questions in this section are based on the reasoning contained in brief statements or passages. For some questions, more than one of the choices could conceivably answer the question. However, you are to choose the best answer; that is, the response that most accurately and completely answers the question. You should not make assumptions that are by commonsense standards implausible, superfluous, or incompatible with the passage.

1. To allow the press to keep their sources confidential is very advantageous to our country, because it is highly conducive to the interests of our nation that private individuals should have the privilege of providing information to the press without being identified.

   The faulty reasoning in which one of the following is most parallel to that in the argument above?

(A) Freedom of the press is a fundamental feature of all democratic societies. Therefore, if a society has a free press, it is democratic.

(B) The primary reason for widespread unemployment in this nation is that large numbers of people across this great country of ours are out of work.

(C) In democratic societies the press has an inviolable obligation to publish any news that is in the public interest to have published. Thus, in democratic societies the press has a duty to publish news on any topic that the public shows interest in.

(D) Free tuition for out-of-state students would be advantageous to students who otherwise could not attend this university. That's why free tuition ought to be implemented for these students.

(E) Free speech is very advantageous to this country because allowing people to speak their minds without restraint provides a nonviolent means to dissipate their pent up anger and frustration that results from governmental policies and decisions with which they do not agree.

2. Last month video production giant MovieCo announced that it was declaring bankruptcy due to insolvency. Today, another major video production studio—Vidfilms—filed for bankruptcy citing rising production costs as the primary reason for its failure. These facts clearly show that the video production business is in serious trouble and would make a poor investment for the future.

The reasoning in the above argument is most vulnerable to criticism on which of the following grounds?

(A) The argument employs circular reasoning in which the conclusion is merely a restatement of the information stated in the premises.

(B) The argument reaches a general conclusion on the basis of a small number of specific instances.

(C) The argument explains one event as being caused by another event simply because one preceded the other.

(D) The argument depends upon the assumption that there are only two possible alternatives, and having eliminated one, concludes that the other must be the case.

(E) The argument involves an equivocation, in that the word "bankruptcy" is allowed to shift its meaning in the course of the argument.

3. Tax laws are fair only if people don't earn different amounts of money or don't pay the same amount in taxes. The reasons for this are clear. If people earn different amounts of money but everyone pays the same amount in taxes, then those who earn more wind up keeping more, and those who earn less keep less. But if this is the case, tax laws are clearly unfair.

Which of the following, in its logical features, most closely parallels the reasoning used in the passage?

(A) If a person has talent but doesn't develop it, it is a waste. On the other hand, if one has talent and does develop it, it is a wonderful gift. Hence, talent is a wonderful gift only if it is not a waste.

(B) If Oona doesn't go to pre-school, she will either stay at home or remain in day care. But, if she doesn't go to pre-school, she will not learn to get along with other children. So, if she stays at home or remains in day care, she won't learn to get along with other children.

(C) Combustion will not occur if oxygen is not present. But if it doesn't occur, oxygen might nevertheless be present. Hence, the presence of oxygen is necessary but not sufficient for the occurrence of combustion.

(D) If a person is depressed, they often lose the will to live, but if one loses the will to live, then life isn't worth living. Hence, life is worth living only if one is not depressed.

(E) If the energy industry is deregulated but energy related businesses do not profit from it, regulations will be reinstated by Congress. But this will occur only if it can be demonstrated that energy related businesses are likely to fail in the near future. Hence, either the energy industry is deregulated or it can be demonstrated that energy related businesses are likely to fail in the near future.

4. Anti-disarmament spokesperson: If you accept the views of those who support disarmament, then you believe that it's all right to expose our spouses and children to the threat of nuclear attack just to save a few dollars on national defense. Personally, I don't think that risking my family for a few measly dollars is worth it. That's why I cannot accept their views.

Which of the following questionable argumentative techniques does the spokesperson employ in the above argument?

(A) misrepresenting an argument for the purpose of making it easier to attack

(B) drawing attention away from the real issue of an argument and focusing attention on a side issue

(C) attacking the character of the person advancing the argument rather than attacking the argument itself

(D) criticizing an argument by pointing out an inconsistency between what a person says and what he does

(E) attacking the motives of the person advancing the argument rather than attacking the argument itself

5. The divorce rate of couples who live together before they get married is twice as high as that of couples who do not live together before marriage. Thus it is evident that living together before getting married damages a couple's chance for a successful marriage.

The argument proceeds by:

(A) reaching a causal conclusion on the basis of a correlation between two circumstances

(B) generalizing about all couples on the basis of evidence about only those who later divorce

(C) neglecting evidence about couples who are happily married

(D) isolating a common feature through a process of elimination and concluding that this feature is causally related to the event under investigation

(E) reaching a general conclusion on the basis of an unrepresentative sample

6. *Emily:* The best reason I can think of for not using drugs is that drug use is illegal, and one ought to obey the law.

David: How can you, of all people, think that's a good reason when you rarely drive within the legal speed limit!

Which of the following questionable argumentative techniques does David employ in his response to Emily?

(A) rejecting the conclusion of an argument on the basis of a claim about the motives of the person advancing the argument

(B) attacking the person's character rather than her argument

(C) criticizing an argument by pointing out an inconsistency between what a person says and the way in which she behaves

(D) misrepresenting an argument for the purpose of making it easier to attack

(E) drawing attention away from the real issue of the argument to a side issue and attacking it

7. If abortion on demand were to become legal there would be a great increase in abortions. And once abortion became commonplace there would be a weakening of respect for human life in general. Once the respect for human life was weakened we would see an increase in euthanasia of all kinds: the elderly, the mentally handicapped, and the physically disabled. Before long we would get rid of anyone who is unpopular or unproductive. In short, it would threaten our civilization. Therefore, we should oppose any move to broaden the grounds of legal abortion.

Which one of the following questionable argumentative techniques is employed in the argument above?

(A) offering a solution to a problem that is based upon an oversimplified analysis of the cause of the problem

(B) reasoning, without appropriate evidence, that a particular action or event will cause a series of events leading ultimately to an obviously undesirable consequence

(C) reasoning that just because one event precedes another it must be the cause of it

(D) diverting attention away from the argument under discussion to a different or related point and arguing against it

(E) misrepresenting an argument and stating it in a way which makes it easy to ridicule or refute

8. The FatGo diet plan is simple and easy: just drink a can of delicious fruit-flavored FatGo in place of your meals each day. Everyone who has tried it has lost weight, and losses of 10 pounds in the first week are not uncommon. Start drinking FatGo today, and next week you'll be the thin person you've always wanted to be.

The faulty reasoning in which one of the following is most parallel to that in the argument above?

(A) My car was working perfectly until I let you drive it on Saturday. Now it won't even start. You must have done something to it that caused this problem.

(B) Studies reveal that people who do not smoke cigars or cigarettes are involved in far fewer serious automobile accidents than those who do. Thus, if you're involved in a serious accident, it's probably because you smoke.

(C) My former husband was a drunk and a wife beater. From that experience I've learned that all men are no good.

(D) Unregulated commercial interactions will confer on this nation the advantages that result when there is an unrestricted flow of products between countries. That's why free trade will be good for this country.

(E) The main cause of illegal drug use in America is unemployment. Thus, to get rid of the drug problem, we have to develop public works programs so that we can provide jobs for everyone.

9. *Sarah:* Possessing marijuana is not a serious offense because unlike offenses, such as armed robbery, rape and murder, in which other people's basic rights are violated, marijuana possession hurts no one. That's why I think it's unjust to send people to prison just because they have it in their possession.

Todd: I agree that possessing marijuana does not pose a threat to others, but I still think that sending people to prison for possessing marijuana is a good idea because it sets an example and lets others know that illegal drug use simply won't be tolerated.

On the basis of their statements, Sarah and Todd are committed to disagreeing about the truth of which of the following principles?

(A) The punishment should always fit the crime.

(B) Victimless crimes should not punished to the same degree as crimes in which victims are involved.

(C) People should be imprisoned only for crimes in which others are harmed.

(D) People should never be imprisoned just in order to set an example to others.

(E) Marijuana should be legalized.

10. When patients undergoing surgery receive positive reinforcement from their doctors, they invariably have fewer complications and, as a general rule, when patients have fewer complications their recovery time is greatly reduced. Thus, to reduce a patient's recovery time, it is necessary for doctors to provide positive reinforcement to their patients.

The reasoning in the above argument is most vulnerable to criticism on which of the following grounds?

(A) It assumes that receiving positive reinforcement from their doctors will necessarily result in fewer complications.

(B) It assumes that reducing a patient's recovery time is a desirable goal.

(C) It reaches a general conclusion on the basis of insufficient evidence.

(D) It concludes that positive reinforcement by doctors is required to reduce a patient's recovery time, whereas the premises support only the conclusion that it is sufficient.

(E) It fails to consider other means of reducing a patient's recovery time.

11. If legislation completely prohibiting pornography is passed, freedom of artistic expression will be greatly restricted. The legislature has indicated that it will not pass legislation completely prohibiting pornography. Hence, it is likely that freedom of artistic expression will not be severely restricted.

The reasoning in the argument is flawed because:

(A) It fails to recognize the possibility of other factors that might restrict freedom of artistic expression.

(B) The issue of whether pornography is a form of artistic expression has yet to be resolved.

(C) It bases the conclusion on legislation the legislature may pass, rather than on what they have passed.

(D) It assumes that freedom of artistic expression should not be restricted.

(E) It assumes that pornography is an expression of artistic freedom.

12. Scientists cannot afford to mistreat research animals. To be a good research subject, the animal must be adequately fed and housed and kept free of any disease other than the one that may be under investigation. Poor care and treatment will reduce the reliability of the results of the study, and this is something researchers must take every precaution to prevent.

Which one of the following principles, if accepted, would best explain the position taken in the above argument?

(A) Scientists should not mistreat research animals.

(B) Only disease-free animals should be employed as research animals.

(C) Scientists should not deliberately infect research animals with diseases.

(D) Researchers should do everything necessary to ensure the reliability of their results.

(E) Only researchers who love animals should be allowed to use them in scientific experiments.

13. Based on measurements taken from fossil remains of ancient tyrannosaurs, we can reasonably conclude that all of these Upper Cretaceous dinosaurs stood over twenty feet tall.

The method of the above argument is to:

(A) reach a conclusion about a particular member of a class on the basis of evidence about all members of the class

(B) regard a claim that is merely probable as though it were certain

(C) reach a general conclusion on the basis of observed instances

(D) assert a general claim on the basis of insufficient evidence

(E) attempt to establish a general statement whose truth can never be verified

Quick Answer Guide

Logical Reasoning Mini-Test

1. B	5. A	9. C	13. C
2. B	6. C	10. D	
3. D	7. B	11. A	
4. A	8. A	12. D	

EXPLANATIONS

1. Parallel reasoning (moderate). Answer: B.

The argument in the passage can be represented as follows:

Premise: It is highly conducive to the interests of society that private individuals should have the privilege of providing information to the press without being identified.

Conclusion: To allow the press to keep their sources confidential is very advantageous to the country.

An examination of the reasoning in the argument above reveals that it is circular; that is, the conclusion is just a restatement of the premise. What this argument boils down to is simply that it is good for the country to allow the press to keep their sources confidential because doing this is good for the country.

 (B) is the best response. The argument in response (B) can be represented as follows:

Premise: Large numbers of people across this great country of ours are out of work.

Conclusion: There is widespread unemployment in America.

The reasoning in this argument is circular. An examination of the conclusion reveals that it is just a restatement of the premise.

 (A) is an incorrect response. The argument in response (A) can be represented as follows:

Premise: Freedom of the press is a fundamental feature of all democratic societies.

Conclusion: If a society has a free press, it is democratic.

The reasoning in this argument is not circular. The conclusion of this argument is not a restatement of the premise. The premise is equivalent in meaning to the claim that all democratic societies have a free press, i.e., if a society is democratic, then it has a free press. This is not what is stated by the conclusion.

 (C) is an incorrect response. The argument in response (C) can be represented as follows:

Premise: In democratic societies the press has an inviolable obligation to publish any news that is in the public interest to have published.

Conclusion: In democratic societies the press has a duty to publish news on any topic that the public shows interest in.

The reasoning in this argument is not circular because the conclusion is not a restatement of the premise. While the premise and the conclusion may initially appear to have the same meaning, a closer examination reveals that in the premise the phrase "in the public interest" means "that which is relevant to the public's well being," whereas in the conclusion what the "public shows interest in" means "that which they find fascinating."

(D) is an incorrect response. The argument in response (D) can be represented as follows:

Premise: Free tuition for out-of-state students would be advantageous to students who otherwise could not attend this university.

Conclusion: That's why free tuition ought to be implemented for these students.

The reasoning in the above argument is not circular because the conclusion is not a restatement of the premise.

(E) is an incorrect response. The argument in response (E) can be represented as follows:

Premise: Allowing people to speak their minds without restraint provides a non-violent means to dissipate their pent up anger and frustration that results from governmental policies and decisions with which they do not agree.

Conclusion: Free speech is very advantageous to this country.

The reasoning in the above argument is not circular because the conclusion is not a restatement of the premise.

2. Reasoning error (easier). Answer: B.

The conclusion of the argument in the passage is based on two specific examples of failed video production businesses. Since no indication is given in the passage that these two cases are representative of the condition of other video production companies or of the industry at large, the conclusion based upon them that all such businesses are in trouble is highly suspect.

(A) misdescribes the reasoning in the argument. The conclusion of the argument is "the video production business is in serious trouble and would make a poor investment for the future." This sentence is not a restatement of the premises of the argument.

(C) misdescribes the reasoning in the argument. Admittedly, the facts stated in the premises "precede" the conclusion in the sense that they appear at the beginning of the argument and the conclusion appears after them, but this is irrelevant to the reasoning.

(D) misdescribes the reasoning in the argument. No alternatives are mentioned in the passage.

(E) While the word "bankruptcy" appears in both premises, its meaning in both occurrences is the same.

3. Parallel reasoning (challenging). Answer: D.

The argument in the passage can be represented as follows:

Premise: If people earn different amounts of money but everyone pays the same amount in taxes, then those who earn more wind up keeping more and those who earn less keep less.

Premise: If those who earn more wind up keeping more and those who earn less keep less, tax laws are clearly unjust.

Conclusion: Tax laws are just only if people don't earn different amounts of money or don't pay the same amount in taxes.

The logical pattern of this argument can be diagrammed as follows:

Premise: If P, then Q

Premise: If Q, then not R

Conclusion: R only if P

(D) is the best response. The argument in response (D) can be represented as follows:

Premise: If a person is depressed, they often lose the will to live.

Premise: If one loses the will to live, then life isn't worth living.

Conclusion: Life is worth living only if one is not depressed.

A comparison of this argument with the argument above reveals that they share exactly the same logical pattern.

(A) is an incorrect response. The argument in response (A) can be represented as follows:

Premise: If a person has talent but doesn't develop it, it is a waste.

Premise: If a person has talent and does develop it, it is a wonderful gift.

Conclusion: Talent is a wonderful gift only if it is not a waste.

Unlike the argument in the passage outlined above, the "if" clause of the second premise of this argument is not the same as the "then" clause of the first premise.

(B) is an incorrect response. The argument in response (B) can be represented as follows:

Premise: If Oona doesn't go to pre-school, she will either stay at home or remain in day care.

Premise: If Oona doesn't go to pre-school, she will not learn to get along with other children.

Conclusion: If Oona stays at home or remains in day care, she won't learn to get along with other children.

Unlike the argument in the passage outlined above, the "if" clause of the first premise of this argument is the same as the "if" clause of the second premise.

(C) is an incorrect response. The argument in response (C) can be represented as follows:

Premise: If oxygen is not present, combustion will not occur.

Premise: If combustion does not occur, oxygen might nevertheless be present.

Conclusion: The presence of oxygen is necessary but not sufficient for the occurrence of combustion.

The main difference between this argument and the argument in the passage outlined above is to be found in the conclusions of these arguments.

(E) is an incorrect response. The argument in response (E) can be represented as follows:

Premise: If the energy industry is deregulated but energy related businesses do not profit from it, regulations will be reinstated by Congress.

Premise: Regulations will be reinstated by Congress only if it can be demonstrated that energy related businesses are likely to fail in the near future.

Conclusion: Either the energy industry is deregulated or it can be demonstrated that energy related businesses are likely to fail in the near future.

The main difference between this argument and the argument in the passage outlined above is to be found in the conclusions of these arguments.

4. Method (moderate). Answer: A.

The spokesperson presents a distorted account of the views of those who support disarmament and then easily refutes it. The spokesperson's characterization of the pro-disarmament argument leads one to believe that the only reason they offer in support of their view is a savings on national defense, and furthermore, that they think this is more important than the potential risk to the lives of their loved ones. This characterization of the pro-disarmament argument is easy to refute, but it is highly doubtful that this is an accurate portrayal of the argument.

(B) The issue in the argument in the passage is whether disarmament ought to be pursued as a national goal. The spokesperson's argument is focused directly on this issue, and not on a side issue.

(C) and (E) The spokesperson does not directly attack the character or motives of persons who advocate disarmament, but admittedly, their characters and motives are denigrated by the suggestion that they care more about saving a few dollars on national defense than they do about protecting their families.

(D) misdescribes the spokesperson's argument.

5. Method (moderate). Answer: A.

The method employed in the argument in the passage is to reach a causal conclusion on the basis of a correlation between two events. In this case, living together before marriage is correlated with a higher divorce rate. The conclusion drawn from this correlation is that living together before marriage increases the likelihood that the marriage will be unsuccessful.

(A) is the best response.

(B) and (C) are off focus. The task in this problem is to identify the method of the argument in the passage, not to find fault with the argument.

(D) misdescribes the passage. In the passage there is no comparison of features possessed by couples who live together before marriage with features possessed by couples who do not, nor is one identified as the common feature by a process of elimination.

(E) is off focus. The task in this problem is to identify the method of the argument in the passage, not to find fault with the argument. In any case, the representativeness of the sample on which the conclusion is based cannot be ascertained given the information stated in the passage.

6. Method (moderate). Answer: C.

Emily's argument against using drugs is based on the premise that one ought to obey the law. David rejects this premise, not by challenging its truth, but by claiming that Emily often behaves in ways that are inconsistent with it.

(A) and (B) misdescribe David's response. Neither Emily's motives for advancing the argument nor her character are brought into question by David.

(D) misdescribes the passage. David does not restate or misrepresent Emily's argument in the passage.

(E) The point of David's remark is not to draw attention away from the issue of Emily's argument, but rather to draw attention to an apparent inconsistency between Emily's pronouncement regarding obeying the law and her actions.

7. Reasoning error (moderate). Answer: B.

The argument in the passage proceeds by citing a chain of events that are thought likely to occur if the abortion on demand were to become legal. The chain ends with an event that is clearly undesirable, leading to the conclusion that to avoid the undesirable outcome of the series we should not allow the initiating event to occur.

(A) No analysis of the problem under discussion, oversimplified or otherwise, is mentioned in the passage.

(C), (D), and (E) do not provide correct descriptions of the argument in the passage.

8. Parallel reasoning (moderate). Answer: A.

The argument in the passage is an example of "after this, therefore because of this" reasoning; that is, regarding an event that preceded another as being the cause of it. Basically, the argument in the passage is that since the weight loss followed the ingestion of FatGo in place of meals, FatGo is the cause of the weight loss. The reasoning in this argument is faulty because it completely overlooks other possible causes for the weight loss.

(A) is the best response. The reasoning in response (A) is that since the problem with the car followed the person's use of the car, the person's use of the car is the cause of the problem. The reasoning in (A) is similar to the reasoning in the passage.

(B) is an incorrect response. The reasoning in response (B) confuses a correlation between two events with a causal relation between those events. While the occurrence of a correlation between events indicates the possibility that they are causally related, it is also possible that the correlation is just a coincidence. In any case, the reasoning in (B) is not similar to the reasoning in the passage.

(C) is an incorrect response. Response (C) is an example of reasoning to a general conclusion on the basis of insufficient evidence. The fact that one man behaves in a certain way is not sufficient grounds for the conclusion that all men behave in that way. In any case, the reasoning in (C) is not similar to the reasoning in the passage.

(D) is an incorrect response. Response (D) is an example of circular reasoning. The premise and the conclusion of the argument in (D) express the same thing. The reasoning in (D) is not similar to the reasoning in the passage.

(E) is an incorrect response. The premise of the argument in (E) states an oversimplified account of the cause of the problem. The conclusion states a solution to the problem that addresses the cause identified in the premise. The reasoning in (E) is not similar to the reasoning in the passage.

9. Principle (challenging). Answer: C.

Sarah's main reason for not wanting to imprison persons who possess marijuana is that possession of marijuana is not an act that harms others. This indicates that Sarah subscribes to the principle that only crimes in which others are harmed should be punished with imprisonment. Todd's response indicates that he agrees that possessing marijuana does not harm others, but he maintains that persons who possess it should be imprisoned anyway. This indicates that he does not subscribe to the principle that only crimes in which others are harmed should be punished with imprisonment.

(A) There is no indication in the passage that Todd and Sarah would necessarily disagree about the truth of this principle. In fact, it is because Sarah believes that the punishment does not fit the crime in the case of marijuana possession, that she is opposed to sending persons to prison for doing this. Given the information in the passage, Todd's stance on this principle cannot be ascertained.

(B) There is no indication in the passage that Todd and Sarah would necessarily disagree about the truth of this principle.

(D) Todd obviously does not subscribe to this principle because he is quite willing to send persons who possess marijuana to jail in order to set an example to others that illegal drug use will not be tolerated. Sarah's stance on this principle, however, cannot be determined given the information in the passage.

(E) There is no indication in the passage that Todd and Sarah would necessarily disagree about the truth of this principle. Todd's opposition to marijuana possession appears to be based solely on the fact that it is an illegal drug. It is consistent with this opposition that he subscribes to the view that marijuana should be legalized. Sarah's stance on this principle, however, cannot be determined given the information in the passage.

10. Reasoning error (moderate). Answer: D.

The conclusion that can be correctly inferred from the premises of the argument is that when patients undergoing surgery receive positive reinforcement from their doctors, their recovery time is greatly reduced. This means that to reduce a patient's recovery time it is sufficient for the doctor to give the patient positive reinforcement; it does not mean that it is necessary to do this.

(A) and (B) are off focus. Pointing out that an argument involves an assumption does not, by itself, show a weakness in an argument. To function as a criticism of an argument, in addition to pointing out that it involves a particular assumption, it would have to be shown that the assumption was questionable or false.

(C) misdescribes the argument in the passage. No evidence, in the sense of sample cases, is offered in the argument.

(E) is off focus. It is consistent with the conclusion of the argument that other ways of reducing a patient's recovery time might yet exist. In other words, the conclusion does not state that positive reinforcement by doctors is the only way to reduce the patient's recovery time.

11. Reasoning error (moderate). Answer: A.

The argument in the passage considers only one factor that might lead to the restriction of freedom of artistic expression. Concluding that freedom of artistic expression will not be severely restricted because this factor can be eliminated is warranted only if it can be shown that there are no other factors that might have this effect.

(B) brings in information not mentioned in the passage.

(C) The conclusion is stated in such a way as to take into account the fact that the legislature has not yet passed the legislation.

(D) and (E) do not point out flaws in the reasoning of the argument. The fact that an argument makes an assumption, even a false one, is not a reasoning flaw.

12. Principle (moderate). Answer: D.

The only reason offered in the passage for not mistreating research animals is that to do so will reduce the reliability of the results of the study. Furthermore, it is maintained in the passage that this is "something researchers must take every precaution to prevent." The underlying assumption in this argument is that researchers must take every precaution to ensure the reliability of the results of their studies.

(A) would not help to explain the position taken in the passage. The only reason offered in the passage for not mistreating research animals is that to do so will reduce the reliability of the results of the study. Mistreatment that would not jeopardize the results of the study is not discussed in the passage, but, conceivably, if mistreatment would ensure the reliability of the results, it would be allowed.

(B) is inconsistent with the passage. The passage states that research animals should be "kept free of any disease other than the one that may be under investigation." This implies that the research animals need not be disease-free.

(C) would not help to explain the position taken in the passage. If the deliberate infection of research animals would ensure the reliability of the results of the study, it would not be prohibited.

(E) would not help to explain the position taken in the passage. Whether researchers love the animals involved in their research is irrelevant to the position taken in the passage.

13. Method (easier). Answer: C.

The method employed in the argument in the passage is to reach a general conclusion on the basis of observed instances. In this case, observation of fossil remains of an animal is the basis for a conclusion about all animals of the type observed.

(C) is the best response.

(A) The method described in (A) is the opposite of the method employed in the passage.

(B) misdescribes the passage. The phrase "we can reasonably conclude" indicates that the claim expressed in the conclusion is regarded as being probable, not certain.

(D) There is no indication in the passage of the extent of the fossil evidence. Whether or not this evidence is insufficient cannot be determined given the information in the passage.

(E) is off focus. The task in this problem is to identify the method of the argument in the passage, not to find fault with the argument.

Day 19

Analytical Reasoning Lesson 6:
Selection, Spatial, and Tree Games

Today you will examine and learn to handle additional types of logic games that appear commonly on the Analytical Reasoning section.

Today's Topics

1. The simple selection game
2. The complex selection game
3. Spatial games
4. The logic tree game
5. The family tree game

THE SIMPLE SELECTION GAME

Selection games involve dividing subjects into *exactly two* groups. The term "selection" is used here because your task is to select particular subjects from a *roster* or *pool*, while the remaining subjects remain deselected. Two groups result: those subjects that are selected, and those subjects that are not selected. In other words, for each subject you must make a yes-or-no decision—for example, is the subject:

- included or excluded?
- going or staying?
- on or off?

A *simple* (relatively easy) selection game is one that involves a *fixed number* of selected subjects.

Example 19-1
A particular two-story apartment building includes ten units. Apartments A, B, C, D, and E are located on the second floor. Apartments F, G, H, I, and J are located on the first floor. Each apartment is either vacant or occupied.

Six of the apartments are occupied.

Apartments B and C are not both occupied.

Either Apartment D or I, or both, are vacant.

Apartments G and H are either both vacant or both occupied.

Either Apartment E or Apartment J, but not both, is vacant.

If there are more vacant apartments on the first floor than on the second floor, all of the following must be true EXCEPT:

(A) Apartment F is vacant.

(B) Apartment I is vacant.

(C) Apartment B is vacant.

(D) Apartment D is occupied.

(E) Apartment E is occupied.

171

As in any logic game, ask yourself what you can deduce from the rules. Since a total of six apartments must be occupied, four must be vacant. Either E or J is vacant, either D or I must be vacant, and either B or C must be vacant. Thus, G and H cannot both be vacant; otherwise, at least five apartments would be vacant. Accordingly, G and H must both be occupied. The best diagramming approach to a game such as this involves the use of a simple roster, along with a shorthand restatement of the rules. Circle both G and H in the diagram:

(6 OCCUPIED)

```
                    * D̸/I (OR BOTH) VACANT
A  B  C  D  E       * J ≠ E
F  Ⓖ  Ⓗ  I  J       * B̸/C (OR BOTH) VACANT
```

Then, as you respond to the questions, indicate that an apartment is occupied by circling it on your roster, and indicate that an apartment is vacant by crossing it out on your roster.

The correct response to the question is (C). A total of four apartments must be vacant (because six are occupied). Since G and H are both occupied, the other three apartments on the first floor must be vacant, while only one apartment on the second floor is vacant. Since B and C cannot be occupied, either B or C must be the one second-floor apartment that is vacant. Accordingly, A, D, and E must all be occupied:

```
Ⓐ  B  C  Ⓓ  Ⓔ     (4)
F̸  Ⓖ  Ⓗ  I̸  J̸     (2)
```

THE COMPLEX SELECTION GAME

A *complex* (relatively difficult) selection game involves an *unfixed number* of selected subjects. Selection games can be further complicated by the inclusion of conditional statements, which you can easily misinterpret if you're not careful.

Example 19-2

Nine people—P, Q, R, S, T, U, V, W, and X—all wish to go on a particular fishing trip.

> Either V or S must go, but V and S cannot both go.
>
> Among P, T, and X, exactly two must go.
>
> If either T or U goes, both T and U must go.
>
> X will not go unless R goes.
>
> If P or Q (but not both) goes, then V or W (but not both) must go.

1. If fewer people go on the trip than do not go, how many different distinct groups can be assembled to go on the trip?

   (A) 1
   (B) 2
   (C) 3
   (D) 4
   (E) 5

As in Example 19-1, the best diagramming approach here is to use a simple roster, along with a shorthand restatement of the rules. Arrange the subjects in your roster to reflect particular rules. Rephrase conditional statements that are expressed in a confusing manner, being very careful to interpret the statements correctly. For example, the rule that X cannot go unless R goes can properly be restated as "If X goes, then R must go" and expressed in shorthand form.

```
(1) V  S            (TU)
(2) P  T  X         X→R
    Q  R  U  W      P/Q (BNB)→V/W(BNB)
```

As you respond to the questions, select subjects by circling them on your roster, and eliminate subjects by crossing them out on your roster.

The correct response to the question is (B). In order to satisfy the condition in the question stem, no more than four people can go. According to the rules, among P, T, and X, exactly two must go. Assume first that P and T (but not X) go. Since T goes, U must go. According to the rules, either S or V must go. In this case, it must be V that goes, because P is going without Q. (One of the rules requires either V or W to go in this situation.) So one possible combination of four is: P, T, U, V. Next, assume instead that P and X (but not T) go. Since X goes, R must go. Again, V (not S) must also go. So a second possible combination of four is: P, X, R, V. Finally, assume instead that T and X (but not P) go. Since X goes, R must go. Since T goes, U must go. However, the rules require either S or V to go as well, which renders this scenario impossible, given that only four people go. So we're left with two possible combinations (of four) altogether.

SPATIAL GAMES

The Line-and-Node Game

Line-and-node games involve *spatial connections* between the subjects of the game. Your task is to determine how to get from one subject (or node) to the other subjects following the connecting lines. Some lines may be two-way streets, while others may be one-way streets. Also, some subjects might be impossible to reach from certain other subjects. The rules tend to be permissive in nature rather than mandatory; that is, the rules speak in terms of where you *can* go from any given point of departure, rather than compelling you to go. Do not be intimidated by a line-and-node game just because the game looks lengthy. These games tend to be relatively easy.

Example 19-3

A commuter-subway schedule for a particular city lists all of the routes among seven stations—A, B, C, D, E, F, and G. Subways must stop as they pass through every station. In examining the schedule, a commuter has made the following observations:

He may ride from A directly to B and D only.

He may ride from B directly to only one station.

He may ride from C directly to E and F only.

He may ride from D directly to C only.

He may ride from E directly to only one station.

He may ride from F directly to A, C, and G only; he may ride to F directly from C only.

He may ride from G directly to A only.

He may ride from C to D by stopping at one other station first.

He may ride from B to E by stopping at two other stations first.

If the commuter departs from F and makes five stops, which of the following is a complete and accurate list of the stations which might be the fifth stop?

(A) C, D, E, F, G

(B) A, B, D, E, G

(C) A, B, C, E, F, G

(D) B, C, D, E, F, G

(E) A, B, C, D, E, F, G

Example 19-3 may look very much like the send-and-receive games explored on Day 11. However, the recommended approach to send-and-receive games is awkward to use here, where you must trace a route from subject to subject. Instead, construct *a line-and-node* or *flowchart*. It is not important how the stations are arranged. The key is to connect them in a way that accurately reflects the rules of the game. All of the rules, with the exception of the last two rules (involving interim stops), can be charted as follows:

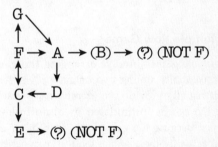

Next, consider the two rules involving interim stops in light of this flowchart. First, if a commuter can ride from B to E by stopping at two other stations during the interim, a route must run directly from B to D. The commuter cannot ride from B through G and D to E because from G he may ride to A only. A commuter cannot ride from B through F and C to E because the only direct route to F is from C. A commuter cannot ride from B through A and D to E because he may ride from D to C only. Second, if a commuter can ride from C to D by stopping at one other station during the interim, a route must run directly from E to D because E is the only station to which the commuter can ride directly from C:

The correct response to the question is (E). From F, the commuter might end at any of the seven stations after five stops. The commuter may ride back and forth between F and C as often as necessary to end at the desired fifth stop:

$$F \rightarrow C \rightarrow F \rightarrow C \rightarrow F \rightarrow A$$
$$F \rightarrow C \rightarrow F \rightarrow G \rightarrow A \rightarrow B$$
$$F \rightarrow G \rightarrow A \rightarrow B \rightarrow D \rightarrow C$$
$$F \rightarrow C \rightarrow F \rightarrow G \rightarrow A \rightarrow D$$
$$F \rightarrow C \rightarrow E \rightarrow D \rightarrow C \rightarrow E$$
$$F \rightarrow G \rightarrow A \rightarrow D \rightarrow C \rightarrow F$$
$$F \rightarrow C \rightarrow F \rightarrow C \rightarrow F \rightarrow G$$

The Multiple Row Game

Multiple row games involve arranging the game's subjects spatially among two or more rows. A diagram is usually provided to identify rows and columns. Do not be intimidated by a multiple-row game just because the game looks lengthy or complex. In actuality, these games tend to be easier-than-average.

Example 19-4

A high-school debating team is traveling by airplane to compete in the national debating championships. The team consists of six students—K, L, M, N, O, and P. The team is accompanied on the trip by two teachers—X and Y. Each student and each teacher has been assigned a seat in either row 1 or row 2 of the airplane. Three executives have also each been assigned a seat in row 1 or row 2. Each row includes six seats, three on each side of the aisle:

SEAT:	A	B	C		D	E	F
row 1	_	_	_	‖	_	_	_
row 2	_	_	_	‖	_	_	_

L and M must sit next to each other, and M must occupy a window seat.

N and O must sit next to each other, and N must occupy an aisle seat.

P and K must sit next to each other, and P must occupy a window seat.

Passengers seated across the aisle from each other are not considered to be seated "next to" each other.

A passenger is seated directly ahead or behind another passenger only if the two passengers share the same seat letter but in adjacent rows.

If X and Y both occupy window seats, and if N is seated directly in front of one of the three executives, any of the following could be true EXCEPT:

(A) O is seated next to an executive.

(B) Y is seated next to an executive.

(C) L and P occupy seats on different sides of the aisle.

(D) O is seated directly in front of K.

(E) M and O occupy seats on the same side of the aisle.

Before responding to the question, it is helpful to realize that two pairs of students (a "pair" includes two students that must sit next to each other) must sit on one side of the aisle while the third pair sits on the other side. The diagrams below indicate two of several acceptable arrangements (notice in the diagrams that P and M are each occupying window seats, while N is occupying an aisle seat, all conforming to the rules of the game):

One possible arrangement:

```
[ P K ] _ | | [ N O ] _
[ M L ] _ | |  _ _  _
```

Another possible arrangement:

```
[M L] _ | | _  _ _
   _ [O N] | | _ [K P]
```

The question is really rather easy to analyze in light of the foregoing scheme. The question stem stipulates that X and Y both occupy window seats. According to the original conditions, P and M also each occupy window seats. Two basic alternatives emerge: either X and Y sit on the same side of the aisle (with [PK] and [ML] all on the other side) or X and Y sit on different sides of the aisle (with [PK] and [ML] on different sides). For example:

One possible arrangement:

```
[ P K ] _ | | [ N O ] X
[ M L ] _ | |  E _  Y
```

Another possible arrangement:

```
[M L] _ | | [N O] Y
  X _ _  | | E [K P]
```

In considering the diagrams immediately above, bear in mind that these do not represent the only possible positions for X and Y. For instance, the positions of X and Y could be reversed. Similarly, [PK] and [ML] could be reversed. Finally, the horizontal "mirror image" of each diagram would also be valid. In any event, however, [NO] must sit in row 1, and O must sit next to either X or Y. Why? Because the

question stem stipulates that N sits directly in front of one of the executives. Thus, N must sit in row 1 as indicated in the diagrams above.

The correct response to the question is (A). O must sit between N and one of the two teachers and therefore cannot sit next to an executive.

The Circle Game

Circle games almost invariably involve people seated around a round table; and the seats are always equally-spaced. Circle games can be quite confusing because there is no definite starting place (or ending place) for the sequence. For example, in a circle of eight seats, a person seated two seats away from another person would also be seated six seats away from that person. If you are not ready with a systematic approach, this type of game can be quite confounding. The key to cutting through the confusion is in the diagram approach.

Example 19-5

Four people—A, B, C, and D—are to be seated at a round table. There are six chairs equidistantly spaced around the table.

A must sit two seats from B.

C must sit next to either A or B, or both.

If D sits next to A, which of the following must be true?

(A) A sits directly across from an empty chair.

(B) D sits directly across from an empty chair.

(C) D sits two seats from an empty chair.

(D) A sits next to an empty chair.

(E) C sits next to an empty chair.

Based on the rules alone, you can eliminate C from the only position which is next to neither A nor B, and the resulting diagram may look something like this:

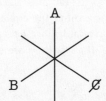

Notice that, in the diagram above, only one of the two possible positions of B (relative to A) is accounted for. A second (alternative) diagram is not necessary, since the rules are not concerned with direction (left or right). Alternative diagrams would simply be mirror images of each other, and either diagram would be sufficient to analyze the question. In answering the question, however, accounting for both possible positions of D (either to the left or to the right of A) does suggest two distinct variations (which are not mirror images) of the basic diagram. The position of one of the empty chairs can now be determined (an empty chair is represented by an "X"). Notice that a total of four possible arrangements result—only the positions of C and the second empty chair remain undetermined:

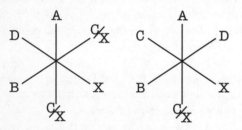

By referring to this diagram, it is clear that the correct response to the question is answer choice (C); in either diagram, D must sit two seats from an empty chair.

Keep in mind that Example 19-5 is a relatively simple game. A circle game may involve a greater number of seats and subjects. A circle game may incorporate some other issue—for example, whether each subject is male or female. Nevertheless, Example 19-5 illustrates a number of features that are unique to circle games. The following suggestions should help you avoid common mistakes and handle this game type efficiently.

Draw spokes, not circles. The game may involve anywhere from 5 to 10 (and most likely either 6 or 8) different positions around the circle, usually seats around a table. Invariably, the seats are equidistant around the table; that is, they are spaced evenly.

Represent the seats as ends of intersecting spokes rather than points around the perimeter of a circle. Spokes are easier to draw, and they make clear whether two subjects are seated directly across from one another (a common issue in circle games).

Circle sequences are "unfixed." In all circle games appearing on past exams, the various positions around the circle have not been numbered or otherwise specifically identified. Unless the seats are distinguishable (and they probably won't be), you may arbitrarily choose any position (such as the top of the circle) as a starting point in building your diagram.

Mirror images. Often, the rules suggest two basic alternate diagrams, which are simply mirror images of each other. You can safely disregard one of the diagrams when answering the questions. Example 19-5 illustrates this point—the initial diagram omitted to account for the possibility that B sits two seats to the left of A. Accounting for this possibility results in two mirror image diagrams, either of which suffices to analyze the question.

Look for a key axis. A rule that stipulates that two particular subjects are positioned directly across from each other suggest an axis, and all of the remaining subjects must be grouped or separated on either side of that axis. Approach the game from this viewpoint.

Left/right orientation. It is unlikely that any rule or question will involve direction (left or right), since direction is ambiguous without knowing whether a person is facing toward or away from the center of the circle.

THE LOGIC TREE GAME

The rules of a *logic tree* game can be characterized as the building blocks of logic trees. Your primary task is to construct the tree through repeated application of a *formula* or alternative formulas. Because these games deal with abstract relationships and conditional statements, they tend to be difficult.

Example 19-6

Gremlins are always either white, orange, or brown in color.

Any mating involving an orange gremlin produces only brown gremlins.

Any mating involving a white gremlin produces only white gremlins.

No mating between two brown gremlins ever produces a brown gremlin.

Any of the following could be among the four grandparents of a brown gremlin EXCEPT:

(A) exactly four brown gremlins

(B) exactly three brown gremlins

(C) exactly two orange gremlins

(D) exactly one orange gremlin

(E) exactly three orange gremlins

Example 19-6 is typical of a logic tree game in that several alternative formulas result from the rules. For example, a brown gremlin can result only from the mating of either two orange gremlins or one orange and one brown gremlin. That is, there are two alternative formulas for producing a brown gremlin. An orange gremlin can result only from the mating of two brown gremlins (because an orange parent produces only brown offspring and a white parent always produces white offspring). That is, there is only one formula for producing an orange gremlin. As long as an orange gremlin does not participate in a mating, the mating might produce a white gremlin. Thus, there are three alternative formulas for producing a white gremlin. Listing each and every different formula may, however, result in confusion. Instead, indicate general formulas as follows:

$$O \rightarrow B$$

$$W \rightarrow W$$

$$(BB) \rightarrow \frac{O}{W}$$

The arrows in this diagram are significant in that they suggest a rule of condition (an if/then statement), and so the contrapositive rule of logic is likely

to come into play (see "Formal Logic—Everything You Need to Know for Logic Games" in Day 2).

The correct response to the question is (E). Neither parent of a brown gremlin can be white (a white gremlin produces only white gremlins). Both parents of a brown gremlin cannot be brown. Thus, two possibilities exist with respect to the parents of a brown gremlin—one must be orange while the other is either brown or orange:

$$(O\ O) \rightarrow B$$

$$(O\ B) \rightarrow B$$

Orange offspring can be produced only by two brown parents. Thus, in the first scenario, all four grandparents must be brown. Brown offspring can be produced only from either two orange parents or one orange parent and one brown parent (the identical formula as that in the diagram immediately above). Adding this information to the diagram above:

$$(1) \quad \begin{matrix} (B\ B) \rightarrow \\ (B\ B) \rightarrow \end{matrix} \begin{pmatrix} O \\ O \end{pmatrix} \rightarrow B$$

$$(2) \quad \begin{matrix} (B\ B) \rightarrow \\ (O\ \frac{B}{O}) \rightarrow \end{matrix} \begin{pmatrix} O \\ B \end{pmatrix} \rightarrow B$$

At most, then, two of the grandparents can be orange. Thus, answer choice (E) is the correct response. Notice that analyzing the question required repeated application of one or more formulas. Remember that these formulas are the blocks with which you must construct a logic tree for a question.

THE FAMILY TREE GAME

Family tree games, as the term suggests, involve familial relationships among the subjects. The terms "paternal" and "maternal" are occasionally used in family-tree games. "Paternal" refers to a father's side of the family; for example, your paternal grandmother is your father's mother. "Maternal" refers to a mother's side of the family; for example, your maternal grandfather is your mother's father. Remote relationships, such as "second" cousins and cousins "once removed," are not included.

Family tree games always call for you to establish the relationships among various family members, but they may also require you to identify the gender (sex) of one or more family members. Example 19-6 involves both issues.

Example 19-7

Six people—A, B, C, D, E, and F—are related to X—a woman—as X's husband, sister, son, daughter, mother, and aunt, although not necessarily in that order.

C and D are either both male or both female.

Either A or B, or both, are male.

Either E or F, or both, are female.

If B is F's daughter, which of the following statements could be true?

(A) A is X's sister.

(B) F is C's aunt.

(C) E is D's nephew.

(D) E is A's granddaughter.

(E) B is D's niece.

A variety of alternative symbols and techniques can be used to construct a family-tree diagram. You may prefer to use your own symbols instead of those used below. There are several different ways to distinguish between males and females in a family-tree diagram. One way is to indicate a male with a square and a female with a circle. Another helpful idea for indicating gender is to consistently place a husband to one side—for example, to the left—of his wife.

In the question at hand, two of X's six relatives are male and four are female. Since C is of the same sex as D, both must be female; otherwise, neither A nor B could be male. The gender combinations are

displayed below. Roster #1 assumes that A and B are both male, while roster #2 assumes that either A or B, but not both, is male:

(1) $\boxed{A}$ $\boxed{B}$ $\textcircled{C}$ $\textcircled{D}$ $\textcircled{E}$ $\textcircled{F}$

(2) $A \neq B$ $\textcircled{C}$ $\textcircled{D}$ $E \neq F$

In order to visualize the various family relationships, you should also construct a family tree around X. Although X's aunt could be either X's father's sister or mother's sister, this distinction does not come into play in the game, and so in the diagram below X's aunt is indicated as X's mother's sister:

The correct response to the question is (E). Given that B is F's daughter, B and F must either be X's daughter and husband, respectively, or X's sister and mother, respectively. Statement (E) could be true—F would be X's mother, D would be F's sister, and B would be X's sister. Statement (A) must be false—if A is X's sister, A and B would both be female, which is impossible. Statement (B) must be false—none of the six relatives could be F's niece. Statement (C) must be false—E and D would have to be X's son and sister, respectively. Accordingly, F and B would have to be X's husband and daughter, respectively; however, E and F cannot both be male. Statement (D) must be false—E and A would have to be X's daughter and mother, respectively; if so, B could not be F's daughter.

Analytical Reasoning Lesson 7: Mini-Test and Review

Today you will apply what you learned on Day 19 to three logic games. After taking this mini-test under timed conditions, review the explanations that follow. Preceding the explanation for each game, the game type and difficulty level are identified.

ANALYTICAL REASONING MINI-TEST

Number of questions: 18
Suggested time: 26 minutes

Directions (as printed in test booklet): Each group of questions in this section is based on a set of conditions. In answering some of the questions, it may be useful to draw a rough diagram. Choose the response that most accurately and completely answers each question and blacken the corresponding space on your answer sheet.

Questions 1–7

From among eight volunteers—A, B, C, D, E, F, G, and H—a park ranger must select at least four for a search party. The park ranger's selections are bound by the following restrictions:

If A is selected, B must be selected.

If either C or D is selected, both C and D must be selected.

If E is selected, D cannot be selected.

Either E or G must be selected, but E and G cannot both be selected.

H and B cannot both be selected if G is selected.

1. Which of the following could be a complete and accurate list of the search-party members?
   (A) H, G, A, F
   (B) H, D, C, F
   (C) B, D, G, F, H
   (D) E, A, B, F, H
   (E) G, C, D, B, H

2. If G is NOT selected, all of the following must be true EXCEPT:
   (A) B will be selected.
   (B) A will be selected.
   (C) E will be selected.
   (D) C will not be selected.
   (E) D will not be selected.

3. If the search party includes G and exactly four other volunteers, which of the following volunteers must be one of those four?
   (A) B
   (B) C
   (C) F
   (D) A
   (E) H

4. If the search party includes the maximum number of volunteers, which of the following is a complete and accurate list of the volunteers NOT included in the search party?

(A) E

(B) G

(C) E, A

(D) E, H

(E) G, C, D

5. If A and H are both selected, with respect to how many volunteers can it be determined whether or not the volunteer is selected?

(A) 4

(B) 5

(C) 6

(D) 7

(E) 8

6. If the search party includes A and exactly three other volunteers, how many distinct combinations of search-party members are possible?

(A) 1

(B) 2

(C) 3

(D) 4

(E) 5

7. G must be selected for the search party if:

(A) A is not selected

(B) B is not selected

(C) C is not selected

(D) F is not selected

(E) H is not selected

Questions 8–12

Bob is planning a backpacking trip in Pine National Park. The park contains seven camps—A, B, C, D, E, F, and G. Bob must begin and end his trip as well as spend each interim night only among these seven camps. His trip is subject to the following restrictions:

From Camp A, campers may hike directly to Camp B only.

From Camp B, campers may hike directly to Camps A and D only.

From Camp C, campers may hike directly to Camps B and F only.

From Camp D, campers must not hike to any other camp.

From Camp E, campers may hike directly to Camp C only.

From Camp F, campers may hike directly to Camps A and C only.

From Camp G, campers may hike directly to Camps E and F only.

Except where a round trip between two camps is possible, the elevation of each camp is higher than that of the next camp visited.

8. If Bob plans to visit all seven camps without visiting the same camp twice, which of the following routes can he follow, from first to last camp visited?

(A) E, G, F, C, A, B, D

(B) G, E, C, F, A, B, D

(C) F, G, E, C, D, B, A

(D) G, F, E, C, A, B, D

(E) G, E, C, B, D, F, A

9. If Bob plans to begin and end his trip at the same camp, spending one interim night in the park, how many distinct routes may he follow?

(A) 2

(B) 3

(C) 4

(D) 5

(E) 6

10. Any of the following could be true EXCEPT:

(A) Camp C is higher in elevation than Camp A.

(B) Camp E is lower is elevation than Camp D.

(C) Camp C is higher in elevation than Camp F.

(D) Camp E is neither higher nor lower in elevation than Camp A.

(E) Camp F is neither higher nor lower in elevation than Camp D.

11. If Bob visits at least two camps in addition to the camp at which he begins his trip, with respect to how many different departure points is it certain that Bob will descend from each camp to the next?

    (A) 0
    (B) 1
    (C) 2
    (D) 3
    (E) 4

12. Assume that Bob visits a total of three different camps, including the camp at which he begins his trip. If he makes exactly two interim overnight stops between the beginning and the end of his trip, he could begin his trip at any of the following camps EXCEPT:

    (A) Camp A
    (B) Camp B
    (C) Camp C
    (D) Camp E
    (E) Camp G

Questions 13–18

Around a circular table are seated four married couples—Bob and Connie, Dan and Ellen, Gary and Holly, and Jack and Karen. All eight people are equally spaced around the table.

> No husband sits next to his wife.
>
> Bob is seated next to Karen.
>
> Dan and Ellen sit directly across from each other.
>
> Connie is seated next to Holly.

13. With respect to which of the following pairs of people can the two people be seated next to each other?

    (A) Connie and Karen
    (B) Holly and Bob
    (C) Gary and Jack
    (D) Ellen and Holly
    (E) Karen and Jack

14. If Gary sits directly across from Jack, which of the following must be true?

    (A) Gary sits next to either Dan or Ellen.
    (B) One person separates Jack from Ellen.
    (C) Bob sits next to either Dan or Ellen.
    (D) Ellen sits next to either Holly or Connie.
    (E) Two people separate Connie from Gary.

15. If Holly is separated from Karen by only one other person, which of the following is a complete and accurate list of the people who may sit directly across from Karen?

    (A) Gary, Jack
    (B) Jack, Ellen
    (C) Connie, Gary
    (D) Bob, Connie
    (E) Jack, Connie

16. If Connie sits directly across from Bob and next to Ellen, which of the following people must sit next to Gary?

    (A) Dan
    (B) Karen
    (C) Jack
    (D) Bob
    (E) Connie

17. If Jack sits next to Ellen, and if Gary sits next to Dan, then Bob may sit next to any of the following people EXCEPT:

    (A) Ellen
    (B) Gary
    (C) Jack
    (D) Karen
    (E) Dan

18. If Jack sits directly across from Holly, how many different seating arrangements for the eight people are possible?

    (A) 1
    (B) 2
    (C) 3
    (D) 4
    (E) 5

Quick Answer Guide

Analytical Reasoning Mini-Test

1. D	6. C	11. A	16. B
2. B	7. B	12. A	17. E
3. B	8. B	13. D	18. D
4. D	9. C	14. A	
5. D	10. B	15. A	

EXPLANATIONS

Questions 1–7: Complex selection game (moderate).

Two alternative rosters can be used as a basic diagram. In the diagram below, the left-hand diagram assumes that E, but not G, is selected, while the right-hand diagram assumes that G, but not E, is selected. According to the rules, if E is selected, D cannot be selected, and C and D must both be selected if either is selected. Thus, we can cross out (deselect) C and D in the left-hand diagram.

$$
\begin{array}{cc}
\text{A B } \cancel{C}\ \cancel{D} & \text{A B C D} \\
\text{\textcircled{E} F } \cancel{G}\ \text{H} & \cancel{E}\ \text{F \textcircled{G} H}
\end{array}
$$

$$
\text{A} \rightarrow \text{B}
$$
$$
\text{[C D]}
$$
$$
\text{G} \rightarrow \cancel{\text{\textcircled{H}}}\ \cancel{\text{\textcircled{B}}}
$$

The rules are represented in symbolic form below the two alternative rosters. As you respond to the questions, circle volunteers on the roster as you determine that they must be selected, and cross out those volunteers that you determine cannot be

selected. This approach is appropriate for all of the questions except for Question 1.

1. Answer: D.

The most efficient way to approach this question is to consider one rule at a time, scanning the answer choices to eliminate violators. For example, consider the rule that H and B cannot both be selected if G is selected. A quick glance at the answer choices reveals that (C) and (E) both violate this rule. Answer choice (A) violates the rule that if A is selected, B must also be selected. Answer choice (B) violates the rule that either G or E must be selected.

2. Answer: B.

If G is not selected, then E must be selected, Accordingly, we need to consider only the left-hand diagram, in which G, C, and D are all de-selected. At least three volunteers among A, B, F, and H must be selected. One of those three must be B; otherwise, A, but not B, would be selected, which would violate the rule: "If A is selected, then B must be selected." Thus, all answer choices except (B) must be true.

3. Answer: B.

Only the right-hand diagram, in which G is selected, applies here. According to the questions, exactly four other volunteers must be selected. If neither C nor D were selected, then A, B, F, and H would all be selected; this result, however, would violate the rule: "H and B cannot both be selected if G is selected." Thus, C and D must both be selected. (Remember that if either C or D is selected, both must be selected.)

4. Answer: D.

A bit of intuition helps determine the maximum number of search-party members. Intuitively, it would seem that the largest possible search party would include C and D, since either both or neither must be selected. Proceeding from this assumption, G, but not E, will be selected. Of the remaining four volunteers, the most that can be selected together is three—A, B and F may all be selected together. H cannot be selected under this scenario since B and G are both selected.

5. Answer: D.

Since A is selected, B must also be selected. Since G cannot be selected if B and H are both selected, G cannot be selected. Accordingly, E must be selected (only the left-hand diagram applies), and neither C nor D may be selected. F is the only volunteer with respect to whom it is uncertain whether the volunteer is selected.

6. Answer: C.

Consider first the left-hand diagram (E, but not G, is selected). Since A is selected, B must also be selected. Either of the two remaining volunteers—F and H—could be included in the four-member search party. Thus, two possible combinations result: A, B, E, and F or A, B, E, and H. Next, considering the right-hand diagram. Again, since A is selected, B must also be selected. B and H cannot both be selected. The only remaining volunteer is F, resulting in only one possible combination: A, B, F, and G. The total number of possible combinations, considering both diagrams, is three.

7. Answer: B.

If B is not selected, A cannot be selected. Considering the left-hand diagram, only three volunteers—E, F, and H—would be available. Thus, only the right-hand diagram, in which G is selected, can be considered.

Questions 8–12: Line-and-node game (easier).

The most difficult aspect of this game is understanding the premise and constructing a proper diagram. Once this is done, analyzing the questions is not a difficult task. The rules suggest a line-and-node or flowchart approach; as you construct a diagram, you must bear in mind that unless Bob can make a round trip between two camps, he will descend in elevation from one camp to the next. For example, since Bob may hike directly from G to E but cannot hike directly from E to G, G must be higher in elevation than E. Continuing this analysis, E must be higher in elevation than C, since Bob can hike from E to C but not from C to E. Since Bob can hike from C to F as well as from F to C, it cannot be determined which camp (if either) is higher in elevation. Using this approach, a flow chart may be constructed as follows (a horizontal relationship indicates that relative elevation cannot be determined):

As you interpret this diagram, it is crucial to bear in mind that the elevations of F and A vis-a-vis E, C, B, and D cannot be determined. For example, it is possible that both F and A are actually lower in elevation than D.

8. Answer: B.

If Bob visits all seven camps, he must begin at Camp G and end at Camp D. To avoid visiting any camp more than once, only one route is available to Bob: G to E to C to F to A to B to D.

9. Answer: C.

In order for Bob to begin and end at the same camp, he must begin as well as end his trip at Camp A, B, C, or F. Four distinct routes are possible:

A to B and back to A

B to A and back to B

C to F and back to C

F to C and back to F

10. Answer: B.

Bob must descend in elevation from one camp to the next (except between camps where a round trip is possible); thus, Camp E must be higher in elevation than Camp D. Any of the other four statements could be true.

11. Answer: A.

Regardless of which camp Bob departs from, he might either move laterally or ascend in either direction across the dotted paths in the diagram. The only exception is Camp D; but the question stipulates that Bob must visit at least two camps, so he cannot depart from Camp D.

12. Answer: A.

In order to meet the conditions of the question, the route must include either F and C or A and B, and Bob must make a round trip between those two camps on either the first and second day of the trip or on the second and third day of the trip. Camp B is a possible departure point—B to A to B to D. Camp C is a possible departure point—for example, C to F to C to B. Camp E is a possible departure point—E to C to F to C. Camp F is a possible departure point—for example, F to A to B to A. However, if Camp A is Bob's departure point, he either makes two interim overnight stops but visits only two camps (A and B) or he visits three camps (A, B and D) but makes only one interim overnight stop (at Camp B).

Questions 13–18: Circle game (challenging).

In this circle game, alternative diagrams may be needed to help you work through some of the questions. The key to organizing this game is to recognize that Dan and Ellen create an axis (the vertical axis in the diagram below), and that Connie and Holly must both sit on the same side of this axis, while Bob and Karen must both sit on the other side. Both pairs cannot sit on the same side of the axis because there are only three positions on each side. Accordingly, Gary and Jack must sit on different sides of the axis. The resulting core diagram might appear as follows (the positions in the diagram are numbered here solely for the purpose of facilitating the explanations that follow):

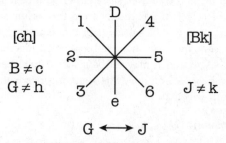

Since the game does not concern direction (left or right), it is not necessary to consider the mirror image of this diagram (however, see Question 6).

13. Answer: D.

Referring to the diagram above, Connie and Karen must sit on different sides of the axis. Holly and Bob must be similarly separated, as must Gary and Jack. Holly and Gary are married to each other and thus cannot sit next to each other. Therefore, all answer choices but (D) can be eliminated.

14. Answer: A.

Gary and Jack must sit in either positions 3 and 4 or 1 and 6 in order to avoid separating Connie from Holly or Bob from Karen. In either case, Gary must sit next to either Dan or Ellen. (B) must be false, since Jack cannot sit in positions 2 or 5. (C) is not necessarily true—Bob may sit in position 5, as well as in positions 4 or 6. (D) is not necessarily true—Holly and Connie may sit in positions 1 and 2 (in either order).

(E) is not necessarily true—Gary could sit in position 6, with Connie in position 3.

15. Answer: A.

Holly and Karen must sit either in positions 1 and 4, respectively, or in positions 3 and 6, respectively. In either event, Connie and Bob must sit in positions 2 and 5, respectively. Thus, either Gary or Jack may sit across from Karen.

16. Answer: B.

In the diagram above, Connie must sit in position 3, and Bob must accordingly sit in position 4. Since Connie must sit next to Holly and Bob must sit next to Karen, Holly and Karen must sit in positions 2 and 5, respectively. Jack cannot sit next to Karen (Jack's wife), and so Jack must sit in position 1, while Gary must sit in position 6. Thus, Gary sits next to Ellen and Karen.

17. Answer: E.

Construct two alternative diagrams to position Jack on either side of Ellen. Given that Gary sits next to Dan, Gary must sit directly across from Jack in order to avoid separating Connie from Holly and Karen from Bob:

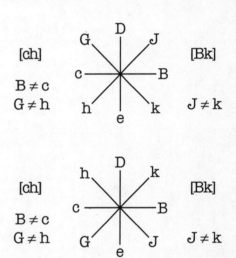

In the first diagram, Bob may sit in either position 5 or 6, next to either Gary and Karen or Ellen and Karen. In the second diagram, Bob must sit in position 5 and immediately between Jack and Karen (otherwise, Jack and Karen, who are spouses, would sit next to each other). In either case, Bob cannot sit in either of the two positions (1 or 4) next to Dan.

18. Answer: D.

In the initial diagram on page 184, Holly and Jack cannot sit in positions 2 and 5, respectively, since Bob and Karen would thereby be separated. Thus, Holly and Jack must sit either in positions 1 and 6, respectively, or 3 and 4, respectively. In either event, only one arrangement is possible, since Holly cannot sit next to Gary and Jack cannot sit next to Karen:

The mirror images of each of the two diagrams must also be considered as distinct arrangements. Thus, a total of four possible seating arrangements result.

Practice Test Section 1:
Logical Reasoning

Today you will take a full-length Logical Reasoning section under actual test conditions. Allow yourself exactly 35 minutes to complete the 25 questions in this section.

Directions *(as printed in test booklet): The questions in this section are based on the reasoning contained in brief statements or passages. For some questions, more than one of the choices could conceivably answer the question. However, you are to choose the best answer; that is, the response that most accurately and completely answers the question. You should not make assumptions that are by commonsense standards implausible, superfluous, or incompatible with the passage.*

---

1. Softec, a small computer software company, has introduced more new software products than any of its competitors during the past year. This is undoubtedly the reason that it enjoyed greater financial success than its competitors during this period.

   Which of the following, if true, would provide the most support for the conclusion above?

   (A) The software products introduced by Softec were favorably reviewed by most major computer magazines.

   (B) None of Softec's competitors introduced new software products during this period.

   (C) Softec and its competitors are equally well-managed companies with insignificant differences in their marketing strategies.

   (D) Software innovations and applications are now the major driving force of the computer revolution.

   (E) Softec is one of the leading innovators in the fastest growing segment of the computer software market.

2. A recipe for cooking potatoes states that potatoes should be cooked in boiling water for twenty minutes to be properly prepared . This holds only for potatoes that have been diced into one-inch cubes—smaller cubes would require proportionately less cooking time and larger ones proportionately more. It is important that potatoes not be overcooked, since this greatly diminishes their food value. Undercooking also should be avoided because undercooked potatoes cannot be properly digested.

   If the above statements are true, which of the following conclusions is most strongly supported?

   (A) Whole potatoes, when properly cooked, cannot be properly digested.

   (B) Potatoes that are diced into one-half-inch cubes and cooked in boiling water for twenty minutes will likely have little food value.

   (C) Potatoes that are properly digestible must be cooked in boiling water for at least twenty minutes.

(D) Boiling in water is the only method of cooking potatoes that will ensure high food value and proper digestibility.

(E) To be prepared properly, potatoes must be boiled in water for at least twenty minutes.

3. Many rare or endangered plant species are sources of drugs and chemicals that have proven to be useful in medicine and in agriculture. It is likely, therefore, that many plants that are now extinct would have served as the source of useful drugs and chemicals as well. Thus, if we want to ensure that drugs and chemicals from plants are available in the future, we must make every effort to preserve these precious natural resources.

Which of the following is an assumption on which the above argument depends?

(A) Only rare or endangered plant species have proven to be useful as sources of drugs and chemicals.

(B) Extinct plant species would have provided useful drugs and chemicals.

(C) Efforts are not now being made to preserve plant species.

(D) Using plants as a source of drugs and chemicals will not threaten their survival.

(E) All plant species are sources of useful drugs and chemicals.

4. Lying is morally justified only if it is done to save a person's life. But most people lie not because a life is in danger but only to avoid the unpleasant consequences of telling the truth. Thus, most lies that are told are morally unjustified.

In which of the following is the pattern of reasoning most parallel to that in the argument above?

(A) Capital punishment is justified if it deters people from taking another's life. But it has been demonstrated conclusively that capital punishment is not an effective deterrent. Thus, capital punishment is not justified.

(B) Capital punishment is justified only if we are certain that the convicted offender is actually guilty of the crime. But there are many cases in which persons who are not guilty are convicted of capital offenses. Therefore, in many cases capital punishment is unjustified.

(C) Capital punishment is morally wrong only if it does not promote the greatest good for the greatest number of people. But sacred religious texts do not condemn capital punishment as being morally wrong. Thus, capital punishment promotes the greatest good for the greatest number of people.

(D) If the defendant in a murder trial is determined to be guilty beyond a reasonable doubt, the maximum penalty allowed under the law can be imposed. But most defendants in murder trials are not determined to be guilty beyond a reasonable doubt. Therefore, the maximum penalty is seldom imposed.

(E) Corporal punishment for persons who commit violent crimes is justified if and only if the punishment will alter the persons' behavior in the future. But most persons who commit violent crimes are corporally punished not in order to alter their future behavior, but only to exact revenge. Therefore, most instances of corporal punishment are unjustified.

5. Blood pressure varies over a 24-hour period, with a low point occurring when resting in a reclining position. Memory recall varies with blood pressure such that whenever blood pressure is lowered, recall time is lengthened. This correlation suggests that low blood pressure is the cause of slow recall and, consequently, that recall time should shorten when blood pressure is raised. However, tests show that recall time does not shorten when blood pressure is raised.

If the statements above are true, they provide the most support for which one of the following?

(A) Persons with neither high nor low blood pressure have normal memory recall time.

(B) Low blood pressure is not the cause of increase in memory recall time.

(C) There is no relation between blood pressure and memory recall time.

(D) Persons with high blood pressure will have fast memory recall.

(E) High blood pressure causes a decrease in memory recall time.

6. New genetic testing procedures have been developed that can detect the presence or absence of dirolin in foods. Dirolin is the toxin that causes food poisoning in humans. While rarely fatal if identified and treated in its early stages, food poisoning causes severe intestinal illness and vomiting. It is for this reason that the Department of Public Health and Safety should require that all processed foods be subjected to the new testing procedures.

Which one of the following, if true, would require the author to reconsider the conclusion?

(A) A recent Disease Control Agency report states that reported cases of food poisoning have declined steadily over the past decade.

(B) Death as a result of food poisoning is extremely rare in modern first-world countries.

(C) Current processing procedures employed in preparing foodstuffs are extremely effective in preventing and detecting dirolin contamination.

(D) The bacillus that produces dirolin can be easily treated with modern antibiotics.

(E) Improper preserving and processing procedures are responsible for the presence of dirolin in prepared foods.

7. In a recent medical experiment, twenty volunteers who were not immune to yellow fever lived for an extended period of time in a mosquito-proof environment with patients who had advanced cases of yellow fever. During this period the volunteers were in constant contact with these patients, yet none of the volunteers developed the disease. This experiment was repeated in a non-mosquito-proof environment, and several of the volunteers were bitten by mosquitoes. In this instance, the ones bitten all developed yellow fever. That mosquito bites, and not contact with persons who have this disease, is the cause of yellow fever can be confidently concluded on the basis of these two experiments.

The argument above employs which one of the following methods of argumentation?

(A) establishing a causal conclusion through a process of elimination of all but one of the candidate causes

(B) establishing a causal conclusion on the basis of the identification of an event that precedes the effect

(C) establishing a causal conclusion on the basis of an analogy between two different environments

(D) establishing a causal conclusion on the basis of a significant correlation between two circumstances

(E) employing the expert testimony of the experimenters as grounds for the conclusion

8. The overall demand for used computers has risen dramatically in the past few years. Most of this increase is due to the explosion of entertainment software products aimed at young first-time computer users. As is to be expected, this demand has exerted an upward pressure on prices of used computers. As a result, we can expect that an increasing number of computer owners will be selling their old computers in order to buy the latest models.

Which of the following, if true, would most help to support the conclusion in the argument above?

(A) Computer technology is progressing so rapidly that computers purchased a year ago are now virtually obsolete.

(B) Exciting new software is being developed that can only run on the latest computer models.

(C) Most computer users do not know how to upgrade their old computers to accommodate the latest software products.

(D) It is less expensive to buy a new computer than to buy the components and build one yourself.

(E) The primary reason computer owners have not bought new computers or used computers that are newer models is that their old computers have little or no resale value.

9. Experiments with dogs to determine whether the Heimlich maneuver could be used effectively to resuscitate drowning victims are cruel and needless. Cruel, because the dog's windpipe is often broken by the maneuver; needless, because a dog's respiratory system is not comparable to that of humans. For these reasons, these experiments are not condoned by state or federal medical review boards.

Which of the following is an assumption on which the argument depends?

(A) State and federal medical review boards do not condone experiments on dogs.

(B) State and federal medical review boards do not condone experiments on animals that are not comparable to humans or that suffer harm as a result of the experiment.

(C) State and federal medical review boards do not condone experiments involving drowning.

(D) State and federal medical review boards do not condone experiments that are cruel and needless.

(E) State and federal medical review boards do not condone experiments involving the Heimlich maneuver.

10. Unless a settlement can be reached, the truce will be violated by one of the parties to the dispute. But a settlement can be reached only if the border issues can be resolved, and the border issues can be resolved only if both parties are willing to give up the territory they captured during the hostilities.

If the statements above are true, but both parties are not willing to give up the territory they captured during the hostilities, then each of the following must also be true EXCEPT:

(A) A settlement can't be reached and the truce will be violated by one of the parties to the dispute.

(B) The border issues cannot be resolved.

(C) The truce will not be violated by either of the parties to the dispute.

(D) A settlement cannot be reached.

(E) The border issues cannot be resolved, nor can a settlement be reached.

11. Residential water use has been severely restricted in response to the current drought in our state. However, current reservoir levels are at the same height as during the drought that occurred here eight years ago. Because residential water use was not restricted then, it should not be restricted now.

Which of the following, if true, would most seriously undermine the author's contention?

(A) No new reservoirs have been constructed in the state since the last drought.

(B) The population of the state has grown at a steady rate of over two million people a year since the last drought.

(C) Residential water use makes up over fifty percent of the total water use.

(D) The restrictions on residential water use are projected to last for only two months during the summer.

(E) Since the last drought, water-conserving devices are required by law to be installed in all new residential construction.

12. Whenever inflation increases, the stock market declines; and whenever interest rates decrease, the stock market advances. However, since interest rates have not decreased nor has inflation increased, the stock market will neither decline nor advance.

Which one of the following arguments contains a flaw that is most similar to the one in the argument above?

(A) Whenever it rains, the streets get wet. But, casual observation confirms that the streets aren't wet, so it can be confidently concluded that it hasn't rained.

(B) Whenever the president vetoes a bill, Congress attempts to override it; and whenever they attempt to override it, they run into serious opposition from the president's supporters, so Congress rarely succeeds in overriding a presidential veto.

(C) When students receive individual tutoring, they invariably get good grades, and, as a general rule, when students get good grades, their self-esteem is greatly enhanced. Thus, to enhance a student's self-esteem, it is necessary to provide individual tutoring.

(D) When children study logic at an early age, they never have trouble learning mathematics; so, if they have trouble learning mathematics, it's probably because they didn't study logic early on.

(E) Lawyers lose their cases whenever they go to trial without proper preparation. Good lawyers never go to trial without proper preparation, which is why they never lose their cases.

13. *Drug manufacturer:* The drugs we now produce for the treatment of heart disease meet all current federal government standards but have significant detrimental side effects. Since recent medical research has discovered new drugs that are as effective as the ones we now produce but cause fewer side effects, we should begin phasing out our current products and take the necessary steps to begin manufacturing these new drugs.

Which one of the following principles, if true, would most help to justify the drug manufacturer's conclusion?

(A) Drug manufacturers should produce all new drugs that medical research discovers.

(B) Drug manufacturers should strive to produce drugs that treat illnesses with the fewest possible side effects.

(C) Drug manufacturers should make sure that their products are up to date with current medical research.

(D) Drug manufacturers should make sure that their products meet federal government standards.

(E) Drug manufacturers should be informed of current medical research.

14. Recent clinical tests clearly demonstrate that Psor-Be-Gone is an effective treatment to reduce the recurrence of psoriasis. Of 23 patients who previously had severe recurrent cases of psoriasis (a bacterial infection of the skin), only two had a recurrence after regular treatment with Psor-Be-Gone. This is a recurrence rate of less than ten percent. In contrast, in a double-blind experiment 15 control subjects who were treated with a placebo in place of Psor-Be-Gone had a recurrence rate of eighty percent.

Which of the following, if true, would provide the most support for the conclusion in the above argument?

(A) Numerous independent studies have shown the active ingredient in Psor-Be-Gone to be an effective anti-bacterial agent for a wide spectrum of skin disorders.

(B) Most of the ingredients in Psor-Be-Gone are completely inert.

(C) None of the patients treated with Psor-Be-Gone had any adverse skin reactions.

(D) Psor-Be-Gone has been scientifically proven to be an effective treatment for numerous common skin diseases.

(E) The placebo used in the control group experiment did not contain the active ingredient found in Psor-Be-Gone.

15. It is the sacrosanct duty of the press to publish any news that is in the public interest to have published. There can be no doubt that the public has demonstrated considerable interest in the Adamson murder case, especially since the details of the private lives of the people involved have been displayed in the tabloid magazines and television talk shows every day. Thus, the press has an obligation to publish the details of the private lives of all of the people involved in this case.

A reasoning error in the argument is that:

(A) The reasons given in support of the conclusion presuppose the truth of that conclusion.

(B) The argument employs a key term or phrase in two different meanings.

(C) The argument assumes that just because the press has a duty to publish something, it should publish it.

(D) It bases the conclusion on the unwarranted assumption that whatever is in the public interest to have published ought to be published.

(E) It incorrectly assumes that just because the public is interested in some topic, they are also interested in the private lives of the people involved.

16. Excessive alcohol consumption has been conclusively demonstrated not only to be a serious health hazard to the individual who overindulges, but also a significant safety hazard to those in close proximity to that individual. Therefore the government should ban all forms of public communication that promote or favorably depict excessive alcohol consumption.

Which one of the following principles, if established, would most strongly support the above argument?

(A) People should not be allowed to do things that harm themselves or pose safety risks to others.

(B) Beer, wine, and liquor advertisers should not be allowed to promote excessive consumption of their products.

(C) Depictions of drunkenness ought not to be tolerated in movies or on television.

(D) The various forms of public communication should be used only to promote and depict healthful and safe activities.

(E) Products that pose serious health and safety risks should be banned.

17. In the context of illegal drug trafficking, deterrence is a particularly unconvincing rationale for the death penalty. The main reason is that drug trafficking is extremely lucrative and may well be worth the gamble. This is true especially for the economically disenfranchised members of our society. Also, given the extremely high level of violence associated with illegal drug trafficking, the criminal justice system's penalties are unlikely to be a more effective deterrent than the violence to

which one exposes himself or herself upon entering the trade.

The conclusion of the above argument is best expressed by which of the following?

(A) Drug trafficking is extremely lucrative and is worth the gamble, even if the price of being caught and convicted is the death penalty.

(B) The death penalty will not deter drug trafficking.

(C) The death penalty should be imposed on drug traffickers.

(D) The violence of the drug scene is not an effective deterrent to stop drug traffickers from entering the trade.

(E) Most drug traffickers are economically disenfranchised members of our society.

18. The use of computers has increased so much over the past ten years that now they are found in most homes and workplaces. Yet, relative to the number of computer users, the number of people who understand how computers work has dramatically decreased over this same period. This trend must be reversed in the future if computer users are to rely upon the accuracy of the information computers provide.

Which of the following, if true, would most seriously undermine the author's contention?

(A) Computer technology is advancing faster than most people can keep up with.

(B) Knowledge of how a computer works is necessary for knowing whether the information provided by the computer is accurate.

(C) The accuracy of the information computers provide can be independently verified without knowing how computers work.

(D) Most computer scientists don't understand fully how computers work, so they couldn't teach others how they work.

(E) It is not necessary to know how a computer works to know how to use one.

19. The medical licensing board of this state maintains that only medical schools that are accredited by the board should be permitted to train doctors. The primary reason given for this policy is that doctors who are trained at non-accredited institutions may lack the training necessary to become competent practitioners. But since the licensing board is composed entirely of doctors and they obviously have a financial interest in limiting the supply of new doctors, their reasoning cannot be taken seriously.

    Which one of the following argumentative techniques is used in the passage?

    (A) The licensing board's argument is undermined by pointing out that one of the statements used to support the conclusion is false.

    (B) The licensing board's argument is discredited by questioning the motives of the board in advancing it.

    (C) The licensing board's argument is discredited by showing that the board is not a reliable authority on the topic of the argument.

    (D) The licensing board's argument is discredited by pointing out that other institutions besides those accredited by the board can train competent doctors.

    (E) The licensing board's argument is challenged on the grounds that the major premise on which the board bases its conclusion is highly questionable.

20. Physicians should make every effort to identify the organism that is causing an infectious disease, for then they can use specific drugs instead of wide-spectrum antibiotics against that organism. This is desirable because specific drugs have fewer unwanted side effects and their use is less likely to produce multiple drug resistance.

    What is the main point of the above argument?

    (A) Physicians don't always know the specific cause of an infectious illness.

    (B) Using wide-spectrum antibiotics is a good idea when the exact cause of an infectious disease is not known.

    (C) Whenever possible, physicians should use drugs that have few unwanted side effects.

    (D) Every effort should be made to identify the specific cause of an infectious disease before treating it.

    (E) Multiple drug resistance should be avoided at all costs.

21. Every philosopher of science of the twentieth century who was either a realist or an empiricist was influenced by a group of philosophers known collectively as the logical positivists. The philosophical writings of this group deal primarily with the methodology of science and the question as to whether our belief that scientific theories are true can be justified. Their arguments on the latter topic are so compelling that no one who is influenced by them holds that scientific theories can be proven to be true.

    If the statements above are true, which one of the following conclusions must be true on the basis of them?

    (A) No twentieth-century philosophers of science who are realists maintain that scientific theories can be proven to be true.

    (B) Every twentieth-century philosopher of science who believes that scientific theories cannot be proven to be true was influenced by the logical positivists.

    (C) The logical positivists were the only twentieth-century philosophers to influence philosophers of science who believe that scientific theories cannot be proven to be true.

    (D) Every philosopher of science in the twentieth century who was influenced by the logical positivists believes that scientific theories are false.

    (E) Every twentieth-century philosopher of science who was not influenced by the logical positivists believes that scientific theories can be proven to be true.

22. Recent reports from waste management companies indicate that disposable plastic containers make up an increasingly large percentage of the waste they collect. As a result, landfills and incineration sites now deal almost exclusively with the disposal of plastics, whereas glass and metal containers previously made up the bulk of their refuse. It is evident from this radical change in disposal patterns that the use of plastic containers has virtually replaced the use of glass and metal containers.

Which of the following, if true, would most seriously call into question the conclusion above?

(A) Metal and glass containers are more expensive to manufacture than plastic containers.

(B) An increasing proportion of metal and glass containers is now being recycled.

(C) Plastic containers can be used over and over again before being discarded.

(D) Plastic containers decompose faster than metal and glass containers.

(E) Environmentalists have been unsuccessful in their attempts to decrease the production of plastic containers.

23. According to modern science, everything in the universe is composed of atoms that are exceedingly small. So small, in fact, that they cannot be seen even with the most powerful microscopes because they do not provide sufficient stimulus for the optic nerve, even when magnified. But, if it is true that everything in the universe is composed of invisible atoms, surely it follows that everything in the universe is invisible. The patent absurdity of this, however, is clearly evidenced by the fact that tables, chairs, and everyday objects are visible. So it follows that modern science must be mistaken in claiming that everything is composed of atoms.

Which of the following best describes a flaw in the author's reasoning?

(A) The author's reasoning depends upon the mistaken belief that just because something occurred prior to something else it must be the cause of it.

(B) The author's reasoning depends upon the mistaken belief that what is true of the parts is necessarily true of the whole.

(C) The author uses the word "invisible" in two different senses.

(D) The author's reasoning depends upon the mistaken belief that the origin of a view is relevant to its truth or falsity.

(E) The author's reasoning depends upon the mistaken belief that whatever cannot be proven to be true must be false.

24. Contrary to popular belief, there are cases in which wearing a seat belt can actually endanger one's life rather than protect it. In one recent accident, for example, a car hit a tree and, except for a small space on the floor, was completely crushed. Luckily, the driver was not wearing a seat belt and was thrown to the floor on impact. Had he been wearing a seat belt he would surely have been killed. Cases like this lead me to conclude that we should not be required by law to wear seat belts.

Which of the following is an assumption on which the above argument depends?

(A) Laws should not require an individual to engage in an act that may endanger his or her life.

(B) Most people believe that the mandatory seat-belt law saves lives.

(C) Obeying the mandatory seat-belt law will not necessarily protect the wearer in automobile accidents.

(D) The mandatory seat-belt law should not be obeyed.

(E) Obeying the seat-belt law isn't always a good idea.

25. Unequal pay for men and women is a completely indefensible practice and one that must be stopped immediately. After all, can anyone seriously doubt that women have as much right to self-esteem as men? Surely this fact alone is reason enough to justify their right to earn as much money as men.

Which of the following is an assumption on which the above argument depends?

(A) A person who has less money than another has less self-esteem.

(B) People who do not have jobs lack self-esteem.

(C) Women and men who perform similar jobs should earn similar salaries.

(D) Equal pay for equal work is a constitution-ally guaranteed right of all workers.

(E) High self-esteem is as important to women as it is to men.

Quick Answer Guide

Practice Test Section 1: Logical Reasoning

1. C	8. E	15. B	22. B
2. B	9. D	16. D	23. B
3. D	10. C	17. B	24. A
4. B	11. B	18. C	25. A
5. B	12. E	19. B	
6. C	13. B	20. D	
7. A	14. A	21. A	

Review of Practice Test Section 1: Logical Reasoning

Today you will evaluate and review the Logical Reasoning practice section that you took yesterday. For each question, the question type and the difficulty level are identified.

1. Assessing the effect of additional information (moderate). Answer: C.

The task in this problem is to find an answer that strengthens the argument; that is, one that offers support for the major assumption of the argument or that provides additional evidence for the conclusion. The major assumption of the argument is that there are no reasons other than the one stated (viz., the introduction of more new software products than its competitors) that account for Softec's greater financial success than its competitors. Response (C) supports this assumption by eliminating other relevant reasons that could account for Softec's greater success. The fact that Softec and its competitors do not differ in other respects that have direct bearing on their financial success provides support for the contention that the reason for Softec's superior financial success was its software products.

(A) It is consistent with response (A) that Softec's competitors software products were also favorably reviewed. For this reason response (A) does not provide additional support for the conclusion.

(B) is consistent with the stated premise of the argument. It does not provide additional evidence for the conclusion.

(D) Since Softec and its competitors are in the same industry, the fact stated in response (D) would not account for Softec's greater financial success.

(E) It is consistent with this claim that some of Softec's competitors are also leading innovators. This claim does not provide additional evidence for the conclusion.

2. Inference (easier). Answer: B.

From the information stated in the passage, it can be inferred that one-half-inch cubes would require proportionately less cooking time than the twenty minutes required for one-inch cubes. Cooking them for twenty minutes would consequently result in severe overcooking, and this in turn would result in a significant lessening of their food value.

(A) is unsupported by the passage and contradicts information stated in the passage viz., "undercooked potatoes cannot be properly digested."

(C) is unsupported by the passage. The passage clearly states that only potatoes that are diced into one-inch cubes will be properly prepared by being cooked in boiling water for twenty minutes; potatoes that are smaller than this would require proportionately less time to be properly digested.

(D) is unsupported by the passage. Other cooking methods are not discussed in the passage.

(E) is unsupported by the passage and is too broad. This applies only to potatoes that are diced into one-inch cubes or larger. Smaller cubes would require less than twenty minutes to be properly prepared.

3. Assumption (challenging). Answer: D.

The denial of the claim asserted in response (D) is incompatible with the argument; that is, if using plants as a source of drugs and chemicals threatened their survival, then efforts to preserve them would be thwarted. This indicates that the assumption operative in the argument is that using plants for these purposes will not threaten their survival.

(A) misstates information stated in a premise of the argument. (B) is a paraphrase of a premise of the argument. (C) brings in information not mentioned in the passage. (E) overstates information mentioned in one of the premises.

4. Parallel reasoning (challenging). Answer: B.

The argument in the passage can be restated as follows:

Premise: Lies are morally justified *only if* they are told to save a person's life.

Premise: *Most* lies are *not* told to save a person's life.

Conclusion: *Most* lies are morally *un*justified.

(B) is the best response. The argument in response (B) can be restated as follows:

Premise: Capital punishment is justified *only if* the convicted offender is guilty.

Premise: *Many* convicted offenders are not guilty.

Conclusion: *Many* instances of capital punishment are *un*justified.

A comparison of this argument with the passage argument outlined above reveals a close similarity between the premises and conclusions of these arguments. In each, the first premise is constructed by connecting two independent clauses with the phrase "only if"; the second premise states the denial of the clause following "only if;" the conclusion states the denial of the clause preceding "only if."

(A) is an incorrect response. The argument in response (A) can be restated as follows:

Premise: Capital punishment is justified *if* it deters people from taking another's life.

Premise: Capital punishment does *not* effectively deter people from taking another's life.

Conclusion: Capital punishment is *un*justified.

Contrary to initial appearances, the first premise of this argument is not comparable to the first premise of the passage argument outlined above. A simple example will demonstrate the difference. Compare the following two statements:

1. Combustion will occur *only if* oxygen is present.
2. Combustion will occur *if* oxygen is present. These two statements have different meanings— the first states that the presence of oxygen is a necessary condition for combustion, the second states that it is a sufficient condition. The first is true; the second is false.

(C) is an incorrect response. While the first premise of the argument in response (C) is comparable to the first premise of the passage argument, the second premise and the conclusion of these arguments are not comparable.

(D) is an incorrect response. The argument in response (D) can be restated as follows:

Premise: *If* the defendant in a murder trial is determined to be guilty beyond a reasonable doubt, *then* the maximum penalty allowed under the law can be imposed.

Premise: *Most* defendants in murder trials are *not* determined to be guilty beyond a reasonable doubt.

Conclusion: The maximum penalty is seldom imposed.

This argument does not have the same structure as the argument in the passage.

(E) is an incorrect response. The argument in response (E) can be restated as follows:

> **Premise:** Corporal punishment for persons who commit violent crimes is justified *if and only if* the punishment will alter the persons' behavior in the future.

> **Premise:** *Most* persons who commit violent crimes are corporally punished *not* in order to alter their future behavior *but* only to exact revenge.

> **Conclusion:** *Most* instances of corporal punishment are *un*justified.

This argument does not have the same structure as the argument in the passage. The first and second premises of this argument are not comparable to the first and second premises of the argument in the passage.

5. Inference (moderate). Answer: B.

The information in the passage can be restated as follows:

> **Premise:** If low blood pressure is the cause of slow recall, then recall time should shorten when blood pressure is raised.

> **Premise:** Tests show that recall time does not shorten when blood pressure is raised.

The conclusion that can be inferred from these premises is that low blood pressure is not the cause of slow recall. Response (B) is a paraphrase of this claim.

(A) is unsupported by the passage. The relationship between high and low blood pressure and "normal" recall time is not discussed in the passage.

(C) is inconsistent with information in the passage. The second sentence states that "memory recall varies with blood pressure such that whenever blood pressure is lowered, recall time is lengthened." It is this invariant relation between memory recall and blood pressure that suggests the hypothesis that the two are causally related.

(D) is unsupported by the passage. The relationship between high blood pressure and memory recall time is not discussed in the passage.

(E) is unsupported by the passage. The effect of high blood pressure on memory recall time is not discussed in the passage.

6. Assessing the effect of additional information (easier). Answer: C.

The task in this problem is to find an answer that weakens the argument; that is, one that undermines the major assumption of the argument, attacks a stated premise, or suggests an alternative conclusion that could be inferred from the premises. The major assumption in the argument is that current dirolin contamination detection methods are inadequate, ineffective, or completely lacking. Response (C) effectively undermines this assumption.

(A), (B), (D), and (E) bring in information that neither undermines the major assumption of the argument, attacks a stated premise, nor suggests an alternative conclusion that could be inferred from the premises.

7. Method (moderate). Answer: A.

The only causes of yellow fever that are discussed in the passage are mosquito bites and contact with persons who have the disease. Experiments are devised to decide between them, and on the basis of the outcome of the experiments, contact with persons who have the disease is eliminated as the cause.

(B) is an incorrect response. No event that precedes the onset of yellow fever is identified in the passage.

(C) is an incorrect response. The two environments mentioned in the passage are not analogous.

(D) is an incorrect response. No correlation between two circumstances is mentioned in the passage.

(E) is an incorrect response. No expert testimony of the experimenters is cited in the passage.

8. Assessing the effect of additional information (moderate). Answer: E.

The task in this problem is to find an answer that strengthens the argument; that is, one that offers support for the major assumption of the argument or that provides additional evidence for the conclusion. The primary reason given in the argument for expecting an increasing number of computer owners to sell their old computers is that increased demand for used computers has exerted an upward pressure on prices of used computers. This suggests that the reason computer owners had not sold their old computers previously is that their old computers did not have sufficient resale value to enable them to purchase newer models. Response (E) explicitly states this reason and thus provides additional evidence for the conclusion.

(A), (B), and (C) bring in information not mentioned in the passage. Admittedly, each of these responses provide a reason why computer owners might sell their old computers and buy newer models. However, none of these responses provide a reason for the expected increase in the number of computer owners who will do this. Consequently, none of these responses provide additional evidence for the conclusion.

(D) does not provide additional evidence for the conclusion, nor does it provide support for the major assumption of the argument.

9. Assumption (easier). Answer: D.

In the passage, evidence is presented to support the premise that experiments with dogs to determine the effectiveness of the Heimlich maneuver in resuscitating drowning victims are cruel and needless. From this premise, it is concluded that the experiments are not condoned by state and federal medical review boards. The logical gap in the argument that must be filled is the connection between experiments that are cruel and needless and experiments that are not condoned by state and federal review boards. Response (D) states the required connection.

(A) does not fill a logical gap in the argument. The fact that the experiments are performed on dogs rather than some other animal is irrelevant to the logic of the argument.

(B) is too broad. The assumption required to fill the gap in the argument must link experiments that are cruel *and* needless to those that are not condoned. Response (B) links experiments that are cruel *or* needless to experiments that are not condoned.

(C) does not fill a logical gap in the argument. The fact that the experiments are concerned with drowning victims rather than some other topic is irrelevant to the logic of the argument.

(E) does not fill a logical gap in the argument. The fact that the experiments involve the Heimlich maneuver is irrelevant to the logic of the argument.

10. Inference (moderate). Answer: C.

The information in the passage and the question stem can be restated as follows:

> **Premise 1:** Either a settlement can be reached or the truce will be violated by one of the parties in the dispute.
>
> **Premise 2:** If a settlement is reached, the border issues can be resolved.
>
> **Premise 3:** If the border issues can be resolved, then both parties are willing to give up the territory they captured during the hostilities.
>
> **Premise 4:** Both parties are not willing to give up the territory they captured during the hostilities.

(C) is the best response. From premise 4 and premise 3 it follows necessarily that the border issues cannot be resolved. From this claim and premise 2 it follows necessarily that a settlement cannot be reached, and from this claim and premise 1 it follows necessarily that the truce will be violated by one of the parties to the dispute. This latter claim contradicts response (C); consequently (C) cannot be true given the information in the passage.

(A) states a conjunction of two claims that must be true given the information in the passage. From premise 4 and premise 3 it follows necessarily that the border issues cannot be resolved. From this claim and premise 2 it follows necessarily that *a settlement cannot be reached*, and from this claim and premise 1 it follows necessarily that *the truce will be violated by one of the parties to the dispute*. Since both of the underlined sentences follow necessarily from the premises, the conjunction of these claims must be true given that the premises are true.

(B) must be true given the information in the passage. From premise 4 and premise 3 it follows necessarily that the border issues cannot be resolved.

(D) must be true given the information in the passage. From premise 4 and premise 3 it follows necessarily that the border issues cannot be resolved. From this claim and premise 2 it follows necessarily that a settlement cannot be reached.

(E) states a conjunction of two claims that must be true given the information in the passage. From premise 4 and premise 3 it follows necessarily that *the border issues cannot be resolved*. From this claim and premise 2 it follows necessarily that *a settlement cannot be reached*. Since both of the underlined sentences follow necessarily from the premises, the conjunction of these claims must be true given that the premises are true.

11. Assessing the effect of additional information (easier). Answer: B.

The major assumption of the argument in the passage is that there are no relevant differences between the conditions present during the previous drought and the current drought that would necessitate the water use restrictions imposed in response to the current drought. Response (B) undermines this assumption and, as a result, undermines the author's contention. The fact that there is a significant increase in the number of water users points to a relevant difference between the two situations that accounts for the difference in the restrictions.

(A), (C), (D), and (E) are incorrect responses. The task in this problem is to find an answer choice that weakens the argument; that is, one that undermines the major assumption of the argument, attacks a stated premise, or that suggests an alternative conclusion that could be inferred from the premises. The responses listed above do none of these.

12. Parallel reasoning (challenging). Answer: E.

The argument in the passage is composed of two sub-arguments, both containing the same flaw. The basic pattern of both of these sub-arguments is:

Premise: Whenever A, B

Premise: Not A

Conclusion: Not B

The flaw in this pattern of reasoning is apparent in the following example:

Premise: Whenever it rains, the streets get wet.

Premise: It's not raining.

Conclusion: The streets aren't wet.

The conclusion does not follow from the premises for the simple reason that the streets might have gotten wet in some other way, e.g., a broken fire hydrant. The argument in the passage can be represented as follows:

1. **Premise:** Whenever inflation increases, the stock market declines.

   Premise: Inflation has not increased.

   Conclusion: The stock market will not decline.

2. **Premise:** Whenever interest rates decrease, the stock market advances.

   Premise: Interest rates have not decreased.

   Conclusion: The stock market will not advance.

(E) is the best response. The argument in response (E) can be restated as follows:

Premise: *Whenever* lawyers go to trial without proper preparation, they lose their cases.

Premise: Good lawyers do *not* go to trial without proper preparation.

Conclusion: Good lawyers do *not* lose their cases.

A comparison of the pattern of this argument with the pattern above reveals the same flaw in reasoning.

(A) does not contain a reasoning error or flaw that is similar to the one in the argument in the passage. The pattern of reasoning in response (A) can be represented as follows:

Premise: Whenever it rains, the streets get wet.

Premise: The streets are not wet.

Conclusion: It has not rained.

This pattern is not similar to the argument in the passage.

(B) does not contain a reasoning error or flaw that is similar to the one in the argument in the passage. The pattern of reasoning in response (B) can be represented as follows:

Premise: Whenever the president vetoes a bill, Congress attempts to override it.

Premise: Whenever Congress attempts to override it, they run into serious opposition from the president's supporters.

Conclusion: Congress rarely succeeds in overriding a presidential veto.

This pattern is not similar to the argument in the passage.

(C) does not contain a reasoning error or flaw that is similar to the one in the argument in the passage. The pattern of reasoning in response (C) can be represented as follows:

Premise: Whenever students receive individual tutoring, they invariably get good grades.

Premise: Whenever students get good grades, their self-esteem is greatly enhanced.

Conclusion: To enhance a student's self-esteem, it is necessary to provide individual tutoring.

This pattern is not similar to the argument in the passage.

(D) does not contain a reasoning error or flaw that is similar to the one in the argument in the passage. The pattern of reasoning in response (D) can be represented as follows:

Premise: If children study logic at an early age, they never have trouble learning mathematics.

Conclusion: If children have trouble learning mathematics, they probably did not study logic at an early age.

This pattern is not similar to the argument in the passage.

13. Principle (easier). Answer: B.

The main reason given by the drug manufacturer for phasing out current drug products and manufacturing the new ones is that the new ones produce fewer side effects. The argument is basically as follows:

Premise: The new drugs cause fewer side effects than our current drugs.

Conclusion: We should produce these new drugs.

The underlying assumption of this argument is that we should produce drugs that cause the fewest side effects. This assumption is an instance of the general principle stated in response (B).

(A) and (C) are too broad. The drug manufacturer's rationale for producing the new drugs is not the fact that they are new or that they are up to date with current medical research but rather the fact that they cause fewer side effects.

(D) and (E) raise peripheral issues that are not germane to the argument. Being informed of current medical research or making sure that products meet federal standards would not help to justify the drug manufacturer's decision to produce the new drugs.

14. Assessing the effect of additional information (moderate). Answer: A.

The task in this problem is to find an answer that strengthens the argument; that is, one that offers support for the major assumption of the argument or that provides additional evidence for the conclusion. Response (A) provides additional evidence for the conclusion. The fact that the active ingredient in Psor-Be-Gone has been demonstrated to be an effective wide-spectrum anti-bacterial agent in independent tests adds credence to the claim that it is an effective treatment of the specific bacterium that causes psoriasis.

(B) Since "inert" means "having no active properties," the fact that most of the ingredients in Psor-Be-Gone are inert would not provide additional evidence for the claim that it is an effective treatment to reduce the recurrence of psoriasis.

(C) Brings in information not mentioned in the passage. The nature of the reactions to treatment with Psor-Be-Gone are not discussed in the passage.

(D) Without knowing more about the causes of the skin diseases for which Psor-Be-Gone has been scientifically proven to be an effective treatment, this fact alone does not provide additional evidence for the claim that it is an effective treatment to reduce the recurrence of psoriasis.

(E) In order to qualify as a placebo, the medicine used in the control group experiment could not contain the active ingredient found in Psor-Be-Gone. The fact that it did not is assumed in the argument.

15. Reasoning error (challenging). Answer: B.

The argument employs the key phrase "public interest" in two different ways. In the first sentence of the passage, the term is used to describe news that is "in the public interest," i.e., news that has some relevance to the public's well being. In the second sentence the term is used to refer to news that the "public has . . . interest in," i.e., news that they find fascinating. The shift in the use of this phrase is apparent in the following simplified restatement of the argument:

> **Premise:** The press has a duty to publish news that is *in the public interest*.
>
> **Premise:** There is public interest in the private lives of persons involved in the Adamson murder case.
>
> **Conclusion:** The press has a duty to publish news of the private lives of persons involved in the Adamson murder case.

(A) is an incorrect response. The reasons given in support of the conclusion are the following:

> **Premise:** The press has a duty to publish news that is in the public interest.
>
> **Premise:** There is public interest in the private lives of persons involved in the Adamson murder case.

These reasons do not presuppose that the press has a duty to publish news of the private lives of persons involved in the Adamson murder case.

(C) does not describe a reasoning error nor does it state an assumption of the argument.

(D) is not an assumption of the argument; it is a restatement of the first sentence and functions as a premise in the argument.

(E) The argument does not depend on this assumption.

16. Principle (moderate). Answer: D.

The main reason given for advocating a ban of forms of public communication that promote or favorably depict alcohol consumption is that this activity is unhealthy and unsafe. The underlying assumption in this argument is that the promotion or favorable depiction of unsafe or unhealthy activities is not an appropriate function of these forms. Response (A) provides support for this assumption by specifying that the forms of public communication should be used only to promote and depict healthy and safe activities.

(A), (B), (C), and (D) are incorrect responses. The task in this problem is to find an answer that strengthens the argument; that is, one that offers support for the major assumption of the argument or that provides additional evidence for the conclusion. The responses listed above perform neither of these functions.

17. Conclusion (easier). Answer: B.

The conclusion of the argument is stated in the first sentence of the passage. In the remainder of the passage reasons are offered in support of this sentence. The phrase "the main reason is that" signals that the second sentence states a premise. This premise is elucidated further in the third sentence. The word "also" at the beginning of the third sentence indicates an additional premise. Of the answer choices, (B) comes closest to asserting what is asserted in the first sentence, viz., "deterrence is a particularly unconvincing rationale for the death penalty."

(A) is a restatement of a premise of the argument.

(C) is off-focus. The issue in the argument is not whether the death penalty should be imposed on drug traffickers, but rather whether it would provide an effective deterrence to drug trafficking.

(D) is a plausible implication of the last sentence in the passage. This sentence expresses a premise of the argument—not the conclusion.

(E) misinterprets information in the passage. The passage states that economically disenfranchised members of our society may regard drug trafficking as worthy of the gamble. It is neither stated nor implied in the passage that most drug traffickers are economically disenfranchised members of our society.

18. Assessing the effect of additional information (moderate). Answer: C.

The task in this problem is to find an answer that weakens the argument; that is, one that undermines the major assumption of the argument, attacks a stated premise, or that suggests an alternative conclusion that could be inferred from the premises. The major assumption in the argument is that it is necessary to know how computers work in order to rely upon the accuracy of the information computers provide. Response (C) directly contradicts this assumption, thereby seriously undermining the author's conclusion.

(A) supports the premise that "the number of people who understand how computers work has dramatically decreased."

(B) supports the major assumption of the argument, thereby strengthening, not weakening, the author's contention.

(D) brings in information not relevant to the argument.

(E) is off the topic. The relationship between knowing how a computer works and knowing how to use a computer is not discussed in the passage.

19. Method (easier). Answer: B.

The medical licensing board's argument is criticized on the grounds that the board's membership is composed of doctors who have a vested interest in limiting the supply of new doctors, and that it is this self-serving motive that is the real reason for their position.

(A) is an incorrect response. The primary reason offered in support of the medical licensing board's conclusion is "that doctors who are trained at non-accredited institutions may lack the training necessary to become competent practitioners." The truth of this claim is not challenged in the passage.

(C) is off-focus. The medical licensing board's expertise on the topic is not questioned in the passage.

(D) is off-focus. No reference to the capability of other institutions to train competent doctors appears in the passage.

(E) The major premise on which the board bases its conclusion is "that doctors who are trained at non-accredited institutions may lack the training necessary to become competent practitioners." This premise is not attacked or criticized in the passage.

20. Conclusion (easier). Answer: D.

The final conclusion of the argument is stated in the first clause of the first sentence; the phrase "for then," that prefaces the second clause of this sentence, signals the major premise of the argument. The final sentence states a reason in support of the major premise. Untangled, the argument looks like this:

Premise: Specific drugs have fewer unwanted side effects and their use is less likely to produce multiple drug resistance.

Intermediate Conclusion: It is desirable to use specific drugs against organisms that cause infectious diseases instead of wide-spectrum antibiotics.

Final Conclusion: Physicians should make every effort to identify the organism that is causing an infectious disease.

(A) is unsupported by the passage. It is neither stated nor implied in the passage that physicians don't always know the specific cause of an infectious illness.

(B) is unsupported by the passage. It is neither stated nor implied in the passage that the use of wide-spectrum antibiotics is a good idea when the exact cause of an infectious disease is not known.

(C) is supported by the passage, but it is an assumption of the argument, not the main point of the argument.

(E) is unsupported by the passage. It is neither stated nor implied in the passage that multiple drug resistance is to be avoided.

21. Inference (moderate). Answer: A.

The following information is stated in the passage:

(1) Every philosopher of science of the twentieth century who was either a realist or an empiricist was influenced by the logical positivists.

(2) No one who was influenced by the logical positivists maintains that scientific theories can be proven to be true.

From the information stated in (1) it necessarily follows that every philosopher of science of the twentieth century who was a realist was influenced by the logical positivists. Moreover, given this and the information stated in (2), it necessarily follows that no twentieth century philosophers of science who are realists maintain that scientific theories can be proven to be true.

(B) does not necessarily follow from the information stated in the passage. The supposition that there is some twentieth-century philosopher of science who maintains that scientific theories cannot be proven to be true but was not influenced by the logical positivists is consistent with the information stated in the passage.

(C) is unsupported by the passage. The passage states that no one who was influenced by the logical positivists maintains that scientific theories can be proven to be true. From this it does not follow that the logical positivists were the only philosophers to have this influence.

(D) is unsupported by the passage. The passage states that no one who was influenced by the logical positivists maintains that scientific theories can be proven to be true. From this it cannot be concluded that persons influenced by the logical positivists maintain that scientific theories are false; that is, the inability to prove that a theory is true does not logically imply that the theory is false.

(E) is unsupported by the passage. The passage states that no one who was influenced by the logical positivists maintains that scientific theories can be proven to be true. This claim is equivalent to the claim that everyone who was influenced by the logical positivists maintains that scientific theories cannot be proven to be true; it is not equivalent to, nor does it logically imply, the claim that everyone who was not influenced by the logical positivists maintains that scientific theories can be proven to be true.

22. Assessing the effect of additional information (easier). Answer: B.

The task in this problem is to find an answer that weakens the argument; that is, one that undermines the major assumption of the argument, attacks a stated premise, or that suggests an alternative conclusion that could be inferred from the premises. The major assumption in the argument is that glass and metal containers are not being disposed of in some way other than the way mentioned in the passage. Response (B) undermines this assumption, thereby calling into question the conclusion of the argument.

(A) brings in information not mentioned in the passage. The relative costs of manufacturing metal, glass, and plastic are not addressed in the passage, nor does this information undermine the major assumption of the argument, attack a stated premise, or suggest an alternative conclusion that could be inferred from the premises.

(C) brings in information not mentioned in the passage. The fact that plastic containers are reusable is not an issue in the argument, nor does this information undermine the major assumption of the argument, attack a stated premise, or suggest an alternative conclusion that could be inferred from the premises.

(D) brings in information not mentioned in the passage. The fact that plastic containers decompose faster than metal and glass containers is not an issue in the argument, nor does this information undermine the major assumption of the argument, attack a stated premise, or suggest an alternative conclusion that could be inferred from the premises.

(E) brings in information not mentioned in the passage. The fact that environmentalists have not succeeded in their attempts to decrease the production of plastic containers is not an issue in the argument, nor does this information undermine the major assumption of the argument, attack a stated premise, or suggest an alternative conclusion that could be inferred from the premises.

23. Reasoning error (moderate). Answer: B.

By arguing that "if it is true that everything in the universe is composed of invisible atoms, surely it follows that everything in the universe is invisible." The author relies upon the mistaken assumption that the whole must have the same properties as its parts, or more generally, that what is true of the parts is necessarily true of the whole.

(A) is an incorrect response. No antecedent event is cited as the cause of some other event in the passage.

(C) Admittedly, the word "invisible" appears a number of times in the passage; however, its meaning remains the same in all occurrences, viz., that which cannot be seen with the eye.

(D) While modern science is cited in the passage as the origin of the view that everything in the universe is composed of atoms, this fact is not taken as a reason for rejecting the view.

(E) The argument does not rely upon this belief. No attempt is made in the passage to show that the claim that everything in the universe is composed of atoms cannot be proven to be true.

24. Assumption (moderate). Answer: A.

The argument in the passage is essentially that we should not be required by law to wear seat belts because wearing them may endanger our lives. The argument can be represented as follows:

> **Premise:** Wearing seat belts can endanger our lives.
>
> **Conclusion:** We should not be required by law to wear seat belts.

The logical gap in this argument that must be filled is the link between acts that we are required by law to do and activities that may endanger us. Response (A) expresses the necessary link.

(B) is implied by the passage. In the first sentence it is stated that "contrary to popular belief, there are cases in which a seat belt can actually endanger one's life rather than protect it." This implies that most people believe that wearing a seat belt will save their life.

(C) is implied by the passage. In the first sentence it is stated that "contrary to popular belief, there are cases in which a seat belt can actually endanger one's life rather than protect it." This implies that wearing a seat belt will not necessarily protect the wearer in automobile accidents.

(D) is off-focus. The issue in the argument is not whether the seat belt law should be obeyed, but rather whether it should be a law in the first place.

(E) is a colloquial paraphrase of the first sentence of the passage.

25. Assumption (moderate). Answer: A.

The argument in the passage is essentially that women have the right to earn as much money as men because they have as much right to self-esteem as men. The argument can be represented as follows:

> **Premise:** Women have as much right to self-esteem as men.
>
> **Conclusion:** Women have the right to earn as much money as men.

The logical gap in this argument that must be filled is the link between a person's self-esteem and the amount of money they earn. The suggestion is that a person's self-esteem is determined by the amount of money they have—the more money they have, the more self-esteem; the less money they have, the less self-esteem. Of the answer choices, response (A) best expresses this assumption.

(B) is off-focus. The argument is concerned only with unequal pay for men and women. This implies that they have jobs.

(C) is a paraphrase of the first sentence of the passage. In the first sentence it is stated that "unequal pay for men and women is a completely indefensible practice." (C) is just another way of saying this.

(D) brings in information not mentioned in the passage. The constitutionality of unequal pay for women and men is not discussed in the passage.

(E) is off-focus. The relative importance of self-esteem to men and women is not addressed in the argument. Response (E) does not express an assumption of the argument, but rather another plausible reason why women and men should receive equal pay.

Day 23

Practice Test Section 2: Reading Comprehension

Today you will take a full-length Reading Comprehension section under actual test conditions. Allow yourself 35 minutes to complete the 28 questions in this section.

Directions *(as printed in test booklet): Each passage in this section is followed by a group of questions to be answered on the basis of what is* stated *or* implied *in the passage. For some of the questions, more than one of the choices could conceivably answer the question. However, you are to choose the* best *answer; that is, the response that most accurately and completely answers the question.*

Questions 1–6 are based on the following passage.

Late Victorian and modern ideas of culture are indebted to Matthew Arnold, who, largely through his *Culture and Anarchy* (1869), placed the word at the center of debates about the goals
(5) of intellectual life and humanistic society. Arnold defined culture as "the pursuit of perfection by getting to know the best which has been thought and said." Through this knowledge, Arnold hoped, we can turn "a fresh and free thought
(10) upon our stock notions and habits." Although Arnold helped to define the purposes of the liberal arts curriculum in the century following the publication of *Culture*, three concrete forms of dissent from his views have had considerable
(15) impact of their own.

The first protests Arnold's fearful designation of "anarchy" as culture's enemy, viewing this dichotomy simply as another version of the struggle between a privileged power structure
(20) and radical challenges to its authority. Arnold certainly tried to define the arch—the legitimizing order of value—against the an-arch of existentialist democracy, yet he himself was plagued in his soul by the blind arrogances of the reac-
(25) tionary powers in his world. The writer who regarded the contemporary condition with such apprehension in *Culture* is the poet who wrote "Dover Beach," not an ideologue rounding up all the usual modern suspects.

(30) Another form of opposition saw Arnold's culture as a perverse perpetuation of classical and literary learning, outlook, and privileges in a world where science had become the new arch and from which any substantively new order of
(35) thinking must develop. At the center of the "two cultures" debate were the goals of the formal educational curriculum, the principal vehicle through which Arnoldian culture operates. However, Arnold himself had viewed culture as en-
(40) acting its life in a much more broadly conceived set of institutions.

Today, however, Arnoldian culture is sustained by multiculturalism, a movement aimed largely at gaining recognition for voices and
(45) visions that Arnoldian culture has implicitly suppressed. In educational practice, multiculturalists are interested in deflating the imperious authority that "high culture" exercises over curriculum while bringing into play the principle
(50) that we must learn what is representative, for we have overemphasized what is exceptional. The multiculturalists' conflict with Arnoldian culture has clear affinities with the radical critique; yet multiculturalism affirms Arnold by returning us
(55) more specifically to a tension inherent in the idea of culture rather than to the culture-anarchy dichotomy.

The social critics, defenders of science, and multiculturalists insist that Arnold's culture is
(60) simply a device for ordering us about. Instead, it is designed to register the gathering of ideological clouds on the horizon. There is no utopian motive in Arnold's celebration of perfection. Perfection mattered to Arnold as the only back-
(65) ground against which we could form a just image of our actual circumstances, just as we can conceive finer sunsets and unheard melodies. This capacity which all humans possess, Arnold made the foundation and authority of culture.

1. The author of the passage is primarily concerned with
   (A) arguing against those who have opposed Arnold's ideas
   (B) describing Arnold's conception of culture
   (C) explaining why Arnold considered the pursuit of perfection to be the essence of culture
   (D) tracing Arnold's influence on the liberal arts educational curriculum
   (E) examining the different views of culture that have emerged since the mid-eighteenth century

2. Based upon the author's interpretation of Arnoldian culture, with which of the following statements would Arnold most likely disagree?
   (A) The capacity to conceive perfection is the foundation of culture.
   (B) Culture operates in a wide array of social institutions.
   (C) Existential democracy is culture's enemy.
   (D) The educational curriculum should de-emphasize what is representative.
   (E) The anarchy-culture dichotomy embraces the struggle against the privileged power structure.

3. It can be inferred from the passage that the two-cultures debate
   (A) emerged as a reaction to the multiculturalist movement
   (B) developed after 1869
   (C) influenced Arnold's thinking about culture
   (D) was carried on by American as well as European scientists
   (E) led to a schizophrenic educational system

4. All of the following statements about multiculturalists are supported by the passage EXCEPT:
   (A) They affirm Arnold's thesis through their opposition to his culture.
   (B) They protest Arnold's designation of anarchy as culture's enemy.
   (C) They seek to suppress the voices and visions of Arnold's allies.
   (D) They oppose the pursuit of perfection in schools of higher education.
   (E) They consider Arnold's culture to be imperious and arrogant.

5. In criticizing Arnold's dissenters, the author employs all of the following methods EXCEPT:

(A) pointing out the paradoxical nature of an argument against Arnoldian culture

(B) presenting evidence that conflicts with a claim made by Arnold's dissenters

(C) asserting that a claim made by the dissenters is an oversimplification

(D) drawing an analogy between one of the dissenters' claims and another insupportable theory

(E) suggesting that the focus of one of the dissenters' arguments is too narrow

6. It can be inferred from the information given that Arnoldian culture is perpetuated today by

(A) the two-cultures debate

(B) postmodernists

(C) imperious elitists

(D) existentialists

(E) social critics

Questions 7–13 are based on the following passage.

Tuberculosis has two general stages relevant to its transmission and infectivity: tuberculosis infection (sometimes also called latent tuberculosis) and active tuberculosis. Active
(5) tuberculosis manifests itself in a variety of ways, depending in part on the primary site of infection in the body. Pulmonary tuberculosis is the most common form of the disease, leading to cavity formation and progressive destruction of
(10) lung tissue. Pathologic and inflammatory processes associated with pulmonary tuberculosis produce weakness, fever, chest pain, cough, and when a small blood vessel is eroded, bloody sputum. Although only pulmonary and laryngeal
(15) tuberculosis are contagious through the airborne route, another active form—extrapulmonary tuberculosis—can affect other sites in the body. Dissemination begins in the lungs, which are the initial site of the infection, and travels through
(20) the body or through lymphatics to regional lymph nodes, resulting in the formation of small miliary (seed-like) lesions or life-threatening meningitis.

The cellular immune system is believed to
(25) play a central role in the development of tuberculosis. While some of the relevant immunologic processes have been identified, fundamental questions remain concerning the interplay and regulation of immunologic forces that both in-
(30) hibit and actually contribute to the disease process itself. Airborne particles containing tubercle bacilli that are inhaled and that reach the lower parts of the lung are initially engulfed by macrophages—a type of scavenger cell—in the
(35) alveoli (terminal air sacs in the lung). If the bacilli are not destroyed by the alveolar macrophages, the bacilli multiply, killing the cell and attracting nonactivated macrophages from the bloodstream. In these new macrophages, the
(40) bacilli multiply logarithmically. Antigenic substances present within or secreted by tubercle bacilli stimulate T-lymphocytes (CD4 cells) to produce chemical substances (lymphokynes), which activate these new macrophages, enabling
(45) them to destroy or inhibit the bacilli. This process of cell-mediated immunity (CMI) forms one part of the body's immune response to tuberculosis.

A related immune process—delayed-type
(50) hypersensitivity (DTH)—is an inflammatory response that destroys bacilli-laden unactivated macrophages. An overabundance of DTH is blamed for most of the tissue damage characteristic of pulmonary tuberculosis. Death of tissues
(55) leads to caseating granulomas and liquefaction of solid caseous waste, producing cavities in the tissue. Within the liquefied caseum, tubercle bacilli multiply outside of the cells, reaching tremendous numbers. Host resistance may be
(60) overwhelmed, and the bacilli may develop resistance to antimicrobial drugs. Liquefaction and cavity formation allow the disease to become contagious because the bacilli spread via airways to other parts of the body and to the outside air.

7. In the passage, the author's primary concern is to

(A) examine the different stages in the development of tuberculosis in the body

(B) describe the role of the body's immune system in the development of tuberculosis

(C) distinguish between contagious and non-contagious forms of tuberculosis

(D) describe the physiological effects of various forms of tuberculosis

(E) discuss the interplay between two types of immune responses to tuberculosis

8. Among the following, it is most reasonably inferable from the information in the passage that extrapulmonary tuberculosis

(A) is contagious through the airborne route

(B) usually begins in the lymph nodes

(C) is less common than pulmonary tuberculosis

(D) is more likely than pulmonary tuberculosis to result in death

(E) is disseminated by way of activated macrophages

9. Among the following, which would the author probably agree contributes LEAST to the development or spread of tuberculosis?

(A) liquefaction of caseous waste

(B) tubercle bacilli

(C) T-lymphocytes

(D) caseating granulomas

(E) unactivated macrophages

10. According to the passage, lymphokynes

(A) are produced by tubercle bacilli

(B) produce T-lymphocytes

(C) attract macrophages from the bloodstream

(D) aid in the destruction of bacilli

(E) destroy unactivated macrophages

11. The passage provides information for answering all of the following questions EXCEPT:

(A) How do tubercle bacilli escape from the body to the outside air?

(B) In what ways does the body's immune system actually contribute to the development of tuberculosis?

(C) How do various forms of tuberculosis manifest themselves in the body?

(D) What is the mechanism by which the body produces macrophages?

(E) How does the body's immune system respond to the presence of tubercle bacilli?

12. Which of the following best expresses the main idea of the passage?

(A) The immune system both inhibits and contributes to the development of tuberculosis.

(B) Research suggests that airborne tubercle bacilli are primarily responsible for the development of contagious tuberculosis.

(C) The interplay and regulation of various immunological forces affecting tuberculosis remain largely uncertain.

(D) The immune system plays a more significant role in the development of contagious tuberculosis than in that of non-contagious tuberculosis.

(E) Immune-system responses play a more integral part in disease processes than previously believed.

13. Among the following, the passage would most likely continue by

(A) identifying treatments which may reverse the harmful effects of immune-system responses on the development of tuberculosis

(B) defining latent tuberculosis and describing its manifestations

(C) describing the process by which extra-pulmonary tuberculosis spreads through the body

(D) raising questions about the interplay of immunological processes pertaining to the development of tuberculosis

(E) examining the physiological factors that determine susceptibility to contagious tuberculosis

Questions 14–20 are based on the following passage.

There are two cornerstones of economic reform in the formerly-Communist states: liberalization of prices (including exchange rates) and privatization. Radical economists call for imme-
(5) diate liberalization, with the only remaining wage regulation in the state sector, accompanied by a restrictive fiscal and monetary policy to harness inflation. Conservative economists, however, favor gradual market deregulation in view
(10) of the dangers of inflation, unemployment, and economic instability. The "gradualists" would have the government prepare enterprises for market shocks, for example, by breaking monopolies before prices and foreign trade are
(15) liberalized or by limiting production of heavy-industry products such as coal and steel. If the gradualists have their way, however, economic reform could dissolve in the hands of bureaucrats incapable of facing the problems that a real tran-
(20) sition to a market economy brings.

Privatization can also be approached either gradually or rapidly. Under the gradual approach, a state bureau would decide if and when an enterprise is prepared for privatization and
(25) which form is most suitable for it. Slow privatization, some experts claim, is the only way to establish true private ownership, because only those who have to pay for property rights with their own money will show an interest in the
(30) enterprise and will be engaged in its management. Although this argument is not without merit, gradual privatization would nevertheless only prolong the core problems of inefficiency and misallocation of both labor and capital.
(35) Under one approach to rapid privatization, enterprise shares would be distributed among employees who would become the enterprise's owners. This socialist-reform approach discriminates in favor of workers employed by modern,
(40) efficient enterprises; it also places workers' property at great risk by requiring investment in one specific enterprise rather than diversifying investments.

The better approach to rapid privatization
(45) involves distribution of enterprise shares, free of charge, among all the people by means of vouchers—a kind of investment money. Some critics charge that voucher holders would not be interested in how their enterprises are managed, as
(50) may be true of small corporate shareholders in capitalist countries who pay little attention to their investments until the corporation's profits fail to meet expectations, at which time these shareholders rush to sell their securities. While
(55) the resulting fall in stock prices can cause serious problems for a corporation, it is this very pressure that drives private firms toward efficiency and profitability. Others who oppose voucher privatization predict that most people
(60) will sell their vouchers to foreign capitalists. These skeptics ignore the capacity of individuals to compare the future flow of income secured by a voucher to the benefits of immediate consumption. Even if an individual should decide to
(65) sell, the aim of voucher privatization is not to secure equality of property but rather equality of opportunity.

14. Which of the following does the author associate with gradual market deregulation?

(A) A restrictive monetary policy

(B) A policy requiring monopolistic enterprises to split into two or more enterprises

(C) Government subsidization of steel producers

(D) State agencies' determining when enterprises should be privatized

(E) A fall in stock prices

15. With respect to which of the following pairs of terms does the author implicitly equate the two terms with each other?

(A) Voucher privatization and gradual privatization

(B) Socialist-reform privatization and investment-money privatization

(C) Price liberalization and market deregulation

(D) Gradual privatization and gradual liberalization

(E) Rapid privatization and voucher privatization

16. Which of the following is LEAST accurate in characterizing the author's method of argumentation in discussing the significance of falling stock prices (lines 54–58)?

    (A) Describing a paradox that supports the author's position

    (B) Asserting that one drawback of an approach is outweighed by countervailing considerations

    (C) Rebutting an opposing position by suggesting an alternative explanation

    (D) Discrediting an opposing argument by questioning its relevance

    (E) Characterizing an argument against a course of action instead as an argument in its favor

17. Which of the following is NOT mentioned in the passage as a possible adverse consequence of rapid privatization?

    (A) Instability in stock prices

    (B) Loss of ownership in domestic private enterprises to foreign concerns

    (C) Financial devastation for employees of private enterprises

    (D) Inequitable distribution of wealth among employees of various enterprises

    (E) Undue prolongation of inefficiency and misallocation

18. In responding to those "skeptics" who claim that people will sell their vouchers to foreign capitalists (lines 61–64), the author implies that

    (A) foreign capitalists will not be willing to pay a fair price for the vouchers

    (B) the future flow of income is likely in many cases to exceed the present exchange value of a voucher

    (C) foreign investment in a nation's enterprises may adversely affect currency exchange rates

    (D) although the skeptics are correct, their point is irrelevant in evaluating the merits of voucher privatization

    (E) foreign capitalists are less interested in the success of voucher privatization than in making a profit

19. Which of the following would the author probably agree is the LEAST desirable outcome of economic reform in formerly-Communist countries?

    (A) Effective allocation of labor

    (B) Equitable distribution of property among citizens

    (C) Financial security of citizens

    (D) Equal opportunity for financial success among citizens

    (E) Financial security of private enterprises

20. Which of the following best expresses the main idea of the passage?

    (A) The two most important principles of post-Communist economic reform are liberalization of prices and privatization.

    (B) Voucher privatization is the best approach to economic reform in the formerly-Communist nations.

    (C) Economists disagree as to whether deregulation and privatization in formerly-Communist nations should be accomplished rapidly or gradually.

    (D) A gradual approach to post-Communist economic reform is less likely to succeed than is a rapid approach.

    (E) Each proposed method of post-Communist economic reform has both its advantages and drawbacks.

Questions 21–28 are based on the following passage.

Christina Rossetti's potent sensual imagery—the richest since Keats—compelled Edmond Gosse, perhaps the most influential literary critic in late Victorian England, to observe that this
(5) Victorian poetess "does not shrink from strong delineation of the pleasures of life even when denouncing them." In the face of Rossetti's virtual canonization by critics at the end of the nineteenth century, however, Virginia Woolf
(10) ignores her apparent conservatism, instead seeing in her curiosity value and a model of artistic purity and integrity for women writers. In 1930, the centenary of Rossetti's birth, Woolf identified her as "one of Shakespeare's more recent sisters"

(15) whose life had been reclusively Victorian but whose achievement as an artist was enduring.

Woolf remembers Rossetti for her four volumes of explosively original poems loaded with vivid images and dense emotional energy. "A *(20)* Birthday," for instance, is no typical Victorian poem and is certainly unlike predictable works of the era's best known women poets. Rossetti's most famous poem, "Goblin Market," bridges the space between simplistic fairy tale and complex *(25)* adult allegory—at once Christian, psychological, and pro-feminist. Like many of Rossetti's works, it is extraordinarily original and unorthodox in form. Its subject matter is radical and therefore risky for a Victorian poetess because it implies *(30)* castigation of an economic (and even marital) marketplace dominated by men, whose motives are, at best, suspect. Its Christian allusions are obvious but grounded in opulent images whose lushness borders on the erotic. From Rossetti's *(35)* work emerge not only emotional force, artistic polish, frequently-ironic playfulness, and intellectual vigor but also an intriguing, enigmatic quality. "Winter: My Secret," for example, combines these traits along with a very high (and un- *(40)* Victorian) level of poetic self-consciousness.

"How does one reconcile the aesthetic sensuality of Rossetti's poetry with her repressed, ascetic lifestyle?" Woolf wondered. That Rossetti did indeed withhold a "secret" both from those *(45)* intimate with her and from posterity is Lona Packer's thesis in her 1963 biography of Rossetti. Packer's claim that Rossetti's was a secret of the heart has since been disproved through the discovery of hundreds of letters by Rossetti, which *(50)* reinforce the conventional image of her as pious, scrupulously abstinent, and semi-reclusive. Yet the passions expressed in her love poems do expose the "secret" at the heart of both Rossetti's life and art: a willingness to forego worldly plea- *(55)* sures in favor of an aestheticized Christian version of transcendent fulfillment in heaven. Her sonnet "The World," therefore, becomes pivotal in understanding Rossetti's literary project as a whole—her rhymes for children, fairy tale nar- *(60)* ratives, love poems, bleak verses of spiritual

desolation, and devotional commentaries. The world, for Rossetti, is a fallen place. Her work is pervasively designed to force upon readers this inescapable Christian truth. The beauty of her *(65)* poetry must be seen therefore as an artistic strategy, a means toward a moral end.

21. Based upon the information in the passage, Virginia Woolf would most likely agree that Rossetti's work

(A) exposes a secret about Rossetti's life

(B) describes yet at the same time denounces life's pleasures

(C) has an enigmatic quality

(D) affirms that Rossetti was pious and reclusive

(E) serves as a model of artistic integrity

22. All of the following are mentioned in the passage as qualities that emerge from Rossetti's work EXCEPT:

(A) lush imagery

(B) ironic playfulness

(C) stark realism

(D) unorthodox form

(E) intellectual vigor

23. The author implies that Rossetti's style was similar to that of

(A) Keats

(B) Shakespeare

(C) Gosse

(D) Woolf

(E) Packer

24. Which of the following statements is most reasonably inferable from the passage?

    (A) "Winter: My Secret" is Rossetti's best-known poem.

    (B) Rossetti was not among the best-known poets during her era.

    (C) The accounts of Rossetti's life contained in Packer's biography of Rossetti differ from those included in Woolf's biography of Rossetti.

    (D) Rossetti's display of poetic self-consciousness drew criticism from her contemporaries.

    (E) "Goblin Market" was published later than "A Birthday."

25. The passage mentions all of the following types of works by Rossetti EXCEPT:

    (A) the love poem

    (B) the sonnet

    (C) the one-stanza canzone

    (D) the children's rhyme

    (E) the devotional commentary

26. The author discusses Packer's thesis and its flaws in order to

    (A) contrast the sensuality of Rossetti's poetry with the relative starkness of her devotional commentary

    (B) reveal the secret to which Rossetti alludes in "Winter: My Secret"

    (C) call into question the authenticity of recently discovered letters written by Rossetti

    (D) compare Woolf's understanding of Rossetti with a recent, more enlightened view

    (E) provide a foundation for the author's own theory about Rossetti's life and work

27. The author implies that Rossetti's "The World"

    (A) combines several genres of poetry in a single work

    (B) was Rossetti's last major work

    (C) is the most helpful expression of Rossetti's motives

    (D) was Rossetti's longest work

    (E) reflects Rossetti's shift away from her earlier feminist viewpoint

28. Which of the following best expresses the main idea of the passage?

    (A) Newly-discovered evidence suggests that Rossetti's works were misinterpreted by earlier critics and scholars.

    (B) Rossetti can be compared to Shakespeare both in her private life and in the enduring quality of her work.

    (C) Victorian poetry can be properly interpreted only by considering the personal life of the particular poet.

    (D) The apparent inconsistency between Rossetti's personal life and literary work are explained by Rossetti's poems themselves.

    (E) Rossetti's artistic integrity served as a model for later women poets.

Quick Answer Guide

Practice Test Section 2: Reading Comprehension

1. A	8. C	15. C	22. C
2. E	9. C	16. C	23. A
3. B	10. D	17. E	24. B
4. B	11. D	18. B	25. C
5. D	12. A	19. E	26. E
6. C	13. D	20. D	27. C
7. B	14. B	21. E	28. D

Review of Practice Test Section 2: Reading Comprehension

Today you will evaluate and review the Reading Comprehension practice section that you took yesterday. For each question, the question type and difficulty level are identified.

1. Primary purpose (moderate). Answer: A.

The author's threshold purpose, articulated in the final sentence of the first paragraph, is to identify the significant forms of dissent to Arnoldian culture. But the author proceeds to do more than merely identify and describe these forms of dissent; the author is also critical of the dissenters, for example, because they have misunderstood Arnold. Response (A) embraces both the author's threshold and ultimate concerns.

(B) is off-focus. Although the author does define and describe throughout the passage Arnold's conception of culture, the author is more concerned with how others have reacted to and been influenced by his ideas.

(C) is off the topic. Although the author does claim that Arnold considered the pursuit of perfection to be the essence of culture, the author offers little explanation as to why Arnold believed as he did.

(D) is off-focus. The passage includes no detail about specific ways that Arnold's ideas molded or otherwise influenced the liberal arts curriculum.

(E) is too broad. The passage concerns only Arnold's views and the views of those who opposed Arnoldian culture.

2. Interpretation (challenging). Answer: E.

Admittedly, the author views "this dichotomy simply as another version of the old struggle between a privileged power structure and radical challenges to its authority" (lines 17–20). However, the author continues by suggesting strongly that the resemblance between Arnold's anarchy-culture dichotomy and the struggle against established authority is only an apparent one: in light of Arnold's "Dover Beach" and in light of the fact that Arnold was himself plagued by the "blind arrogances of the reactionary powers in the world" (lines 24–25), the interpretation of Arnold's dichotomy as "simply one more version of the old struggle . . . " misunderstands Arnold.

(A) is consistent with Arnold's views as described in the final sentence of the passage. The "capacity" to which the author refers in the final sentence is the ability of humans to conceive the ideal (perfection is the ideal) for the purpose of forming "a just image of our actual circumstances" (lines 65–66).

(B) is consistent with Arnold's views as described in the third paragraph. The author states that "Arnold himself had viewed culture as enacting its life in a much more broadly conceived set of institutions" than just the educational system (lines 39–41).

(C) is consistent with Arnold's views as described in the second paragraph: the author states that Arnold designated "anarchy" as culture's enemy (line 17) and that he sought to define arch "against . . . the an-arch of existentialist democracy" (lines 22–23). Considering these two statements together, it can be inferred that Arnold viewed existential democracy as an enemy of culture.

(D) is consistent with Arnold's views. The author emphasizes throughout the passage Arnold's argument for the pursuit of perfection (i.e., culture); thus, Arnold would probably agree that we should study the "exceptional" (see line 51) rather than the "representative." Also, response (D) is inconsistent with the multiculturists' viewpoint as described in the third paragraph: "we must learn what is representative, for we have overemphasized what is exceptional" (lines 50–52). By implication, Arnold would probably agree with statement (D).

3. Inference (easier). Answer: B.

Arnold's *Culture* was published in 1869. The three forms of opposition to Arnold's ideas as presented in this work, therefore, must have emerged later than 1869.

(A) distorts the information in the passage. The author identifies the two-cultures debate and the multiculturalist movement as two distinct forms of dissent (opposition to Arnoldian culture). However, the author neither states nor implies that either form resulted in the emergence of or had any influence upon the other.

(C) confuses the information in the passage. It was Arnold's earlier ideas that sparked the two-cultures debate, not the other way around.

(D) brings in information not mentioned in the passage. Nowhere in the passage does the author identify or refer specifically to American or European scientists.

(E) calls for an unwarranted inference. While opposing forces in the debate did have their own opposing ideas about what an educational curriculum should include, the author neither states nor implies that the debate resulted in a schizophrenic system.

4. Interpretation (moderate). Answer: B.

Response (B) confuses the information in the passage. It is the radical critique discussed in the second paragraph, not the multiculturists, that can be seen as protesting Arnold's "fearful designation of 'anarchy' as culture's enemy" (lines 16–17).

(A) is consistent with the author's view of multiculturalism as expressed in the fourth paragraph: the multiculturalists' conflict with Arnold is inherent in ("returns us to") the (Arnold's) idea of culture. Thus, this conflict actually supports (affirms) Arnold's notion of culture.

(C) is consistent with the author's description of the multiculturist agenda. According to the author, the multiculturists "are interested in deflating the imperious authority that 'high culture' exercises over curriculum" (lines 47–49). Response (C) restates this idea.

(D) is consistent with the author's description of the multiculturist agenda. According to the author, the multiculturists are interested in "bringing into play the principle that we must learn what is representative, for we have overemphasized what is exceptional" (lines 49–51). Response (D) restates this idea.

(E) is consistent with the author's description of the multiculturist agenda. According to the author, the multiculturists "are interested in deflating the imperious authority that 'high culture' exercises over curriculum" (lines 47–49). Considered in the context of the author's broader discussion, the multiculturists are clearly referring here to Arnold and his allies.

5. Interpretation (challenging). Answer: D.

The only analogy in the passage is found in the final paragraph, in which the author compares striving for perfection (i.e., culture) to conceiving "finer sunsets and unheard melodies" (line 67). Although the author uses this analogy to help the reader understand the author's final argument against Arnold's dissenters, this analogy is not in the nature of "an unsupportable theory" which the author compares to a claim made by Arnold's dissenters, as response (D) suggests.

(A) The method suggested in (A) is used by the author in the fourth paragraph to criticize multiculturalists, whose conflict with Arnold (according to the author) only serves to affirm Arnold's notion of culture.

(B) In the second paragraph, the author employs the method suggested in (B) to criticize those who protested Arnold's culture-anarchy dichotomy. The author counters such protests by asserting that the protesters misinterpret Arnold. The author bases this assertion on two pieces of evidence: (1) Arnold's "Dover Beach," and (2) the fact that Arnold was "plagued in his soul by the blind arrogances" of reactionary powers.

(C) In the final paragraph, the author employs the method suggested in (C) to criticize all three schools of dissent. According to the author, the social critics, defenders of science, and multiculturists "insist that Arnold's culture is simply a device for ordering us about" (lines 59–60). The author then suggests that this criticism is too simple in that Arnold's culture is about much more than merely suggesting what humans should do.

(E) The method suggested in (E) is used by the author in the third paragraph to criticize the "defenders of science." The author suggests that the defenders of science, by placing the formal educational curriculum at the center of the two-cultures debate, miss Arnold's much-broader view as to the social institutions in which culture enacts its life (lines 39–41).

6. Inference (moderate). Answer: C.

In the first paragraph, the author states that Arnold helped to define the purposes of the liberal arts curriculum in the century following the publication of his *Culture*. In the fourth paragraph, the author claims that today's multiculturist movement, which opposes Arnoldian culture, is interested in deflating the "imperious authority that 'high culture' exercises over curriculum" (lines 47–49). It is reasonably inferable, then, that these imperious elitists are modern-day allies of Arnold who have perpetuated his ideas about culture through their authority over today's educational curriculum.

(A) runs contrary to the information in the passage. The first sentence of the fourth paragraph ("Today, however, Arnoldian culture is sustained by multiculturalism") implies that the two forms of dissent discussed earlier—the protest against Arnold's

culture-anarchy dichotomy and the two-cultures debate—cannot be credited with sustaining Arnoldian culture today. Moreover, the author neither states nor implies that the two-cultures debate continues to this day.

(B) brings in information not mentioned in the passage. Nowhere in the passage does the author mention or allude to "the postmodernists."

(D) confuses the information in the passage. The only mention of existentialism is in the first paragraph, where the author describes Arnold's view of existential democracy. The author neither states nor implies that existentialists are in any way responsible for sustaining Arnoldian culture today.

(E) runs contrary to the information in the passage. The first sentence of the fourth paragraph ("Today, however, Arnoldian culture is sustained by multiculturalism") implies that the two groups of dissenters discussed earlier—the social critics who protested Arnold's culture-anarchy dichotomy and the defenders of science—cannot be credited with sustaining Arnoldian culture today.

7. Primary purpose (moderate). Answer: B.

While the first paragraph is introductory in nature (terms are defined and classified), the author's main concern in the remainder of the passage is to describe how different immune responses (two are described: CMI and DTH) both inhibit and contribute to the development of tuberculosis.

(A) is off-focus. In the first sentence of the passage, the author identifies the two stages of tuberculosis—tuberculosis infection (latent tuberculosis) and active tuberculosis. However, there is no further discussion or mention of latent tuberculosis. The remainder of the passage deals with the various forms of active tuberculosis and with its development.

(C) is off-focus. Although in the first paragraph the author does distinguish between contagious and non-contagious tuberculosis, the passage includes no further discussion of the differences between these two types.

(D) is off-focus. Although some of the physiological effects of pulmonary and extrapulmonary tuberculosis are listed in the first paragraph, there is no further discussion of symptoms or manifestations.

(E) is the second-best response. Admittedly, the author does indicate, in the first sentence of the final paragraph, that DTH and CMI are "related," suggesting that there is indeed some interplay between these two types of immune responses. However, the author's broader concern is to describe how each of these two responses both inhibits and contributes to the development of tuberculosis. The precise manner in which the two types of responses are related to each other is not discussed in any detail; thus, (E) is off-focus.

8. Inference (moderate). Answer: C.

Pulmonary tuberculosis is "the most common form of the disease" (lines 7–8). Since extrapulmonary tuberculosis is mentioned as "another form" of tuberculosis, it must be less common than pulmonary tuberculosis.

(A) contradicts the passage. "Only pulmonary and laryngeal tuberculosis are contagious through the airborne route" (lines 14–16). Thus, extrapulmonary tuberculosis (another form) cannot also be contagious in this manner.

(B) contradicts the passage; the lung is the initial site of the infection (lines 18–19).

(D) is the second-best response. Response (D) is supported by the passage insofar as the author mentions that extrapulmonary tuberculosis can result in "life-threatening meningitis," while not mentioning any life-threatening results of pulmonary tuberculosis. However, just because no mention is made of the possible threat to life posed by pulmonary tuberculosis, it does not necessary follow that this form does not result in death. No information is provided to enable the reader to compare the rates of death resulting from the two forms. The author neither states nor implies that one form is more likely to result in death than the other. Thus, (D) requires an unwarranted inference.

(E) confuses the information in the passage. Macrophages do not "disseminate" tuberculosis, as response (E) suggests. Rather, they play a role in the body's immune response, engulfing tubercle bacilli that reach the lungs (lines 32–35).

9. Interpretation (easier). Answer: C.

T-lymphocytes, a type of cell, produce a chemical substance that activates macrophages, enabling the macrophages to destroy or inhibit bacilli. The spread and multiplication of bacilli seems to be the primary developmental process involved. Thus, it appears that T-lymphocytes inhibit rather than contribute to the development of the disease.

(A) is explicitly contradicted by the passage. According to the passage, liquefaction of caseous waste is one of two factors that allow the disease to become contagious (lines 61–64). Thus, liquefaction clearly contributes to the spread of tuberculosis.

(B) is implicitly contradicted by the passage. The spread and multiplication of tubercle bacilli seem to be the primary developmental processes. Other aspects of the disease process mentioned in the passage are reactions to the invasion into the lungs and subsequent multiplication of bacilli.

(D) is implicitly contradicted by the passage. Caseating granulomas (along with liquefaction of solid caseous waste) contribute to the production of tissue cavities (lines 54–56), which in turn allows bacilli to spread via airways to other parts of the body and to the outside air (lines 61–64). Thus, caseating granulomas clearly contribute to the spread of tuberculosis.

(E) is implicitly contradicted. According to the passage, the body produces an inflammatory response (DTH) which destroys bacilli-laden unactivated macrophages. This response, however, results in tissue damage, leading to liquefaction and cavity formation which in turn allow the disease to become contagious. Thus, unactivated macrophages contribute indirectly to the spread of the disease.

10. Explicit detail (easier). Answer: D.

According to the passage, lymphokynes activate macrophages, enabling them to destroy or inhibit bacilli.

(A) confuses the information. T-lymphocytes, not bacilli, produce lymphokynes.

(B) confuses the information in the passage. T-lymphocytes produce lymphokynes, not the other way around.

(C) confuses the information in the passage. According to the passage, it is the presence of tubercle bacilli (not lymphokynes) in the lung that attracts macrophages from the bloodstream.

(E) confuses the information in the passage. It is DTH, not lymphokynes, that destroys unactivated macrophages.

11. Explicit detail (easier). Answer: D.

Although the passage indicates that macrophages are attracted from the bloodstream, no information is provided concerning how the body actually produces macrophages.

(A) is answered explicitly by the last sentence of the passage.

(B) is answered implicitly in the passage. The body's immune system responds to the presence of bacilli in the lung by sending macrophages to the lung to engulf and destroy the invading bacilli. However, the passage notes that this response sometimes results in (1) the logarithmic multiplication of bacilli (second paragraph) or (2) a related immune-system response (DTH) which leads to tissue damage and the spread of bacilli to other parts of the body (third paragraph).

(C) is answered (partly) in the first paragraph, which mentions some symptoms of both pulmonary (lines 10–14) and extrapulmonary tuberculosis (lines 21–23).

(E) is answered explicitly and extensively in the passage. In fact, the second and third paragraphs are devoted entirely to answering this question.

12. Main idea (moderate). Answer: A.

While the first paragraph is introductory in nature (terms are defined and classified), the author devotes the remainder of the passage to describing how different immune responses (two are described—CMI and DTH) both inhibit and contribute to the development of tuberculosis.

(B) may be supported by the passage, but it is off-focus. The author implies that contagious tuberculosis is contracted by inhaling airborne bacilli (see, for example, the last sentence of the passage). However, this is not the passage's focus; nowhere in the passage does the author assert that research shows airborne bacilli, not some other phenomenon, to be primarily responsible for the contraction of tuberculosis.

(C) is supported by the passage, but it is off-focus. Admittedly, in the second paragraph the author states that "fundamental questions remain concerning the interplay and regulation of immunologic forces that both inhibit and actually contribute to the disease process." However, the author does not continue by raising any such questions. Instead, the discussion focuses more narrowly on the interplay of such forces. Thus, since (C) does not relate to the author's primary concern in the passage, it is not the main idea.

(D) is unsupported by the passage. The author neither states nor implies that the role of immune-system responses depends upon whether the tuberculosis is contagious or non-contagious.

(E) is too broad and is unsupported by the passage. The passage is concerned not about the disease process in general but rather about tuberculosis specifically; in this sense, (E) is too broad. Also, nowhere in the passage does the author discuss or mention any prior theories or explanations regarding the role of the immune system in the development of tuberculosis.

13. Extrapolation (challenging). Answer: D.

The author mentions in lines 26–31 that while some immune responses relevant to tuberculosis have been identified, questions remain about immunological forces affecting tuberculosis. The author then devotes the remainder of the passage to discussing two immune-system processes that have been identified: CMI and DTH. However, the author never does identify or discuss the remaining "fundamental questions" mentioned earlier. Thus, it is reasonable that the author would continue by discussing these questions.

(A) is wholly unsupported by the passage. Nowhere in the passage does the author either express or imply a concern with identifying any treatment for tuberculosis.

(B) is inconsistent with the focus of the passage. Latent tuberculosis refers to the infection stage (rather than the active stage) of the disease. The author mentions latent tuberculosis (lines 3–4) only to help define active tuberculosis, which is the author's more narrow concern. No information in the passage suggests that the author might return to discuss latent tuberculosis.

(C) runs contrary to the passage. Admittedly, in the first paragraph the author does distinguish extrapulmonary tuberculosis from other forms— i.e., the pulmonary and laryngeal forms. This distinction is based upon the primary site of the infection (lines 4–7). However, response (C) suggests that the distinction lies in the immune-system response rather than the location of the infection. Moreover, nowhere in the second or third paragraphs (where the discussion of immune-system response occurs) does the author suggest that the responses discussed therein are different from those relating to extrapulmonary tuberculosis.

(E) is unsupported by the passage. The author neither expresses nor suggests a concern with how certain physiological traits affect susceptibility to tuberculosis.

14. Explicit detail (easier). Answer: B.

One of the possible features of gradual deregulation mentioned in the first paragraph is the breaking of monopolies by the government. (B) simply restates this possible feature.

(A) confuses two different areas of discussion in the passage. The passage associates a restrictive monetary policy with immediate rather than gradual deregulation.

(C) contradicts the passage. The author associates government limitation of steel production with gradual deregulation (lines 11–16). Government subsidization would, to the contrary, result in increased steel production.

(D) confuses two different areas of discussion in the passage. It is gradual privatization, not gradual deregulation, with which the author associates the feature mentioned in (D) (lines 22–25).

(E) confuses two different areas of discussion. The author associates falling stock prices (line 55) with voucher privatization, not with gradual deregulation.

15. Interpretation (easier). Answer: C.

In the second sentence, the author indicates that one of the key features of immediate (price) liberalization is the elimination of wage regulation; thereby, the author equates, at least to an extent, price liberalization and wage regulation. Moreover, in the next sentence, the author contrasts "gradual market deregulation" with "immediate liberalization," further suggesting the interchangeability of the terms "market deregulation" and "price liberalization."

(A) is contradicted by the passage. Voucher privatization is one of two types of rapid, not gradual, privatization.

(B) is contradicted by the passage. The third paragraph makes clear that voucher privatization and socialist-reform privatization are two separate and distinct approaches to rapid privatization. Since the passage indicates that a voucher is "a kind of investment money" (line 47), the two terms in (B) are not interchangeable.

(D) confuses two unrelated terms mentioned in the passage. Privatization and liberalization are two separate and distinct concepts. Liberalization is discussed in the first paragraph, while privatization is examined in the remaining paragraphs.

(E) is the second-best response. Although voucher privatization is discussed as an approach to rapid privatization, it is only one of two approaches; the other approach is socialist-reform privatization. Accordingly, it is unfair to equate the two terms listed in (E).

16. Interpretation (challenging). Answer: C.

Although the author does respond to what might be one undesired result of voucher privatization— falling stock prices—as well as explain the cause of falling stock prices, the author does not offer an "alternative" explanation for this phenomenon, as suggested by (C). Moreover, the author's purpose in discussing falling stock prices is not to explain their cause but rather to acknowledge that what appears to be an undesirable consequence of voucher privatization may actually help to bring about a desirable result (see (B) and (E)).

(A) The author acknowledges falling stock prices as one potential drawback of voucher privatization in that it might cause serious problems for an enterprise. However, the author asserts that it is the fear of this very consequence that will drive enterprises to efficiency and profitability. This phenomenon can be characterized, then, as a paradox, since what appears to be negative is actually positive when viewed differently. The author uses this paradox to undermine the critics' argument, thereby supporting the author's pro-voucher position.

(B) is one way of characterizing the author's line of reasoning. The author does indeed acknowledge falling stock prices as one potential drawback of voucher privatization. Then, in the same sentence, the author goes on to assert that the fear of falling stock prices will drive enterprises to efficiency and profitability. This rebuttal, then, can be characterized as the author's attempt to introduce a countervailing (competing) consideration that is of overriding concern.

(D) is a good characterization of this discussion. The author does not disagree that voucher holders will have little interest in the management of their enterprises. The author does imply, however, that this fact is beside the point since it is the enterprises' fear of a sell-off that will drive the enterprise to efficiency and profitability, not the extent of voucher-holder involvement in management.

(E) is perhaps the best characterization among the responses of the author's line of reasoning. The author indeed acknowledges falling stock prices as one potential drawback of (argument against) voucher privatization in that it might cause serious problems for an enterprise. However, in the same sentence, the author suggests that, paradoxically, it is the fear of this very consequence that will drive enterprises to efficiency and profitability. This rebuttal, then, can be viewed as the author's attempt to recharacterize a negative feature as a positive one.

17. Explicit detail (moderate). Answer: E.

The author foresees prolonged inefficiency and misallocation as a consequence of gradual, not rapid, privatization (lines 31–34).

(A) and (B) are each explicitly mentioned in the last paragraph as possible consequences of voucher privatization (one of the two approaches to rapid privatization), at least according to critics of this approach.

(C) refers to the danger under the socialist-reform approach (one of two approaches respecting rapid privatization) that employees will expose themselves to undue risk if they are invested only in their employer-company (at least according to the author, who would agree with critics of rapid privatization on this point).

(D) refers to the discrimination in favor of those who happen to be employed by modern or efficient enterprises that may result under the socialist-reform approach (one of the two approaches to rapid privatization), at least according to the author, who would agree with critics of rapid privatization on this point. The shares of these employees, the criticism goes, will be more valuable than the shares of those who work for older or less-efficient firms.

18. Inference (moderate). Answer: B.

The author responds to the skeptics' claim by pointing out that people are likely to weigh the future flow of income from a voucher against the benefits of selling their vouchers now and using the proceeds for consumption. Were people not likely (at least in many cases) to hold their vouchers after weighing these two alternatives, the author would not have made this argument. Thus, the author is implying that indeed in many cases the future flow of income from a voucher will exceed the present value of the voucher.

(D) is the second-best response. Admittedly, the final sentence of the last paragraph does suggest that the author views the skeptics' argument as irrelevant; in this sense, (D) has some merit. However, in the preceding sentence, the author seems to disagree with the skeptics as to whether people will sell their vouchers to foreigners. Thus, the author does not acknowledge that the skeptics are correct.

(A), (C), and (E) are unsupported by the author's response to the skeptics' claim.

19. Extrapolation (moderate). Answer: E.

(E) is the best response. The author's willingness to place a private enterprise at risk for the broader purpose of achieving a free-market system is suggested by at least two areas of discussion in the passage. In the first paragraph, the author tacitly disagrees with the gradualists who favor bracing enterprises for the shock of deregulation to help them survive the transition. In the fourth paragraph, while advocating voucher privatization, the author admits that this approach may very well result in the instability of stock prices; yet the author seems to view the insecurity caused by market pressures as "good" for private enterprises in that it will drive them to efficiency—a sort of sink-or-swim approach.

(A) is explicitly supported. The author identifies misallocation of labor as a core problem that must be addressed if economic reform is to succeed (lines 33–34).

(B) is supported implicitly by the passage. The author argues against the socialist-reform approach to privatization on the basis that distribution of enterprise shares under this approach would discriminate against employees of less profitable enterprises—i.e., that this distribution system would be inequitable (unfair). Note that the term "equitable" means "fair," not necessarily "equal."

(C) is the second-best response. Response (C) is implicitly supported. One of the author's arguments against the socialist-reform approach is that employees of less profitable companies would be placed at undue financial risk. Accordingly, the author seems to value, at least to some extent, the financial security of employees (citizens). Although (C) is a less likely "objective" of economic reform than (A) or (D), the objective identified in response (E) is clearly less "desirable" from the author's viewpoint than the objective referred to in response (C).

(D) is explicitly supported by the passage. The author states in lines 65–67 that the aim of voucher privatization (which the author advocates) is to secure equality of opportunity. The "opportunity" to which the author refers here is the freedom to determine what use of one's vouchers will be most advantageous financially.

20. Main idea (moderate). Answer: D.

(D) is the best response. Response (D) encompasses the author's treatment of both liberalization and privatization by referring more generally to "economic reform," as well as referring to both the rapid and gradual approaches to each of these two aspects of economic reform. Just as crucial, response (D) includes the author's position in the issue: The author favors rapid reform to gradual reform.

(A) is too narrow in its scope. It restates the point in the first sentence of the passage which is intended to merely provide a framework for the discussion that follows.

(B) is too narrow in its scope. Voucher privatization may be the best approach to privatization, at least according to the author. However, response (B) fails to encompass the second "cornerstone" of economic reform: liberalization (deregulation), which is the concern of the first two paragraphs.

(C) is the second-best response. Response (C) encompasses all approaches to economic reform discussed in the passage. However, it omits the author's position on the issue and therefore is not a viable best response.

(E) is too broad in that it incorporates ideas outside of the passage. The passage does not indicate "advantages" of either rapid or gradual deregulation and does not cite any "advantages" of the socialist-reform approach to privatization. (E) is also too narrow in the sense that it fails to reflect the author's position on the issues.

21. Explicit detail (easier). Answer: E.

In lines 11–12, the author states that Woolf saw in Rossetti "a model of artistic purity and integrity for women writers."

(A) and (C) confuse the opinions of Woolf with those of the author. The author does indeed discuss, in the third and fourth paragraphs, how some of Rossetti's works revealed a secret about her life and art. Also, in lines 37–38 the author does claim that from Rossetti's work emerges (among other qualities) "an enigmatic quality." However, these are the author's opinions, not those of Woolf.

(B) confuses the opinion of Woolf with that of Edmond Gosse. It was Gosse, not Woolf, who commented that Rossetti "'does not shrink from a strong delineation of the pleasures in life even when denouncing them'" (lines 5–7).

(D) confuses the information in the passage. In the third paragraph, the author discusses how Rossetti's recently discovered letters confirm that she was pious, scrupulously abstinent, and semi-reclusive. These are not Woolf's impressions of Rossetti's work but rather the author's analysis of Rossetti's personal letters.

22. Explicit detail (easier). Answer: C.

In describing Rossetti's work, the author never uses the words "stark" or "realism," nor does the author describe her work in any way that might be expressed by either of these terms.

(A), (B), and (E) are all mentioned explicitly in the second paragraph (lines 35–38) as qualities that emerge from Rossetti's work.

(D) is the second-best response. The author refers to the form of Rossetti's works in reference specifically to "Goblin Market," claiming that in its unorthodox form "Goblin Market" is like many of Rossetti's works. In this way, the author identifies "unorthodox form" as one quality that emerges from Rossetti's work.

23. Inference (easier). Answer: A.

(A) is the best response. The author claims that Rossetti's potent sensual imagery was "the richest since Keats" (line 2). Thus, it can be inferred that Rossetti's style was similar to that of Keats in that both writers used potent sensual imagery.

(B) is the second-best response. (B) distorts the comparison in the passage between Rossetti and Shakespeare. It was Woolf who compared Rossetti to Shakespeare; also, the similarities Woolf noted between the two writers regarded their personal lives and the enduring quality of their works, not their writing styles.

(C), (D), and (E) are all discussed in the passage as critics of Rossetti. Their writing styles are wholly irrelevant to and are not discussed at all in the passage.

24. Inference (moderate). Answer: B.

In the first sentence of the second paragraph, the author states that "'A Birthday' is no typical Victorian poem and is certainly unlike predictable works of the era's best-known women poets." It is reasonably inferable that Rossetti was not among the era's best-known women poets, at least during her time.

(A) is contradicted by the passage. The author states that "Goblin Market" is Rossetti's most famous poem (line 23).

(B) confuses the information in the passage. Woolf reviewed but did not write a biography of Rossetti.

(D) distorts the information in the passage. The author does indicate that in "Winter: My Secret," Rossetti displayed a high level of poetic self-

consciousness (lines 38–40). However, the author neither states nor implies that Rossetti drew criticism during her lifetime as a result. To the contrary, the fact that she was virtually canonized by critics at the end of the nineteenth century (lines 7–9) suggests her work was the object of very little negative criticism from her contemporaries.

(E) distorts the information in the passage. Although the author discusses "Goblin Market" after "My Birthday," the author neither states nor implies which work was written earlier.

25. Explicit detail (easier). Answer: C.

(C) is the best response. The passage makes no mention of this literary form.

(A), (B), (D), and (E) are all mentioned explicitly in the last paragraph as different types of works by Rossetti.

26. Function of detail (challenging). Answer: E.

The author's threshold purpose in discussing Packer's biography is to affirm that Rossetti's style of writing was not a reflection of her personal lifestyle. Having dismissed the theory that Rossetti was keeping secrets about her life, the author goes on (in the final paragraph) to offer a better explanation for the apparent contradiction between Rossetti's lifestyle and the emotional, sensual style of her poetry.

(A) distorts the information in the passage. First, the passage does not indicate that Rossetti's devotional commentary was in the form of prose rather than poetry. Second, nowhere in the passage does the author compare or contrast Rossetti's devotional commentary with her other works.

(B) distorts and actually runs contrary to the author's purpose. The author discusses Packer's biography to affirm that Rossetti's style of writing was not a reflection of her personal lifestyle—in other words, that she was not keeping secrets about her life. In this sense, response (B) actually runs contrary to the author's purpose.

(C) distorts the information in the third paragraph. The author does not raise the issue of whether these letters were actually written by Rossetti. In fact, insofar as the author mentions these letters to disprove Packer's thesis, the author seems to affirm that the letters are indeed authentic.

(D) distorts and actually runs contrary to the information in the passage. The author compares Woolf's view only with that of Gosse, who actually preceded Woolf; in this sense, then, response (D) distorts the information in the passage. Second, Packer's thesis does not reflect a more enlightened view; to the contrary, the author points out that Packer's thesis has been disproved.

27. Inference (moderate). Answer: C.

In the final paragraph, the author states that "'The World'" is "pivotal in understanding Rossetti's literary project as a whole." Based upon the remainder of the final paragraph, the author seems to understand Rossetti's "literary project as a whole" as an attempt to convey an inescapable Christian truth to her readers (see lines 62–64). It is reasonably inferable, then, that "The World" provides significant insight into Rossetti's motives.

(A) is contradicted by the passage. The author identifies "The World" as a sonnet (one type of poetry), never suggesting that it might incorporate other types of poetry as well.

(B) calls for speculation. Although "The World" is the last of Rossetti's works discussed in the passage, it does not necessarily follow that it was Rossetti's last major work.

(D) calls for speculation. The author neither states nor implies that "The World" is Rossetti's longest work; indeed, nowhere in the passage does the author mention the length of any of Rossetti's works.

(E) distorts the information in the passage. The author suggests that "The World" is pivotal in understanding Rossetti's general literary agenda— to convey an inescapable Christian truth to her readers. However, the author neither states nor implies that Rossetti's motives in writing "The World" or her viewpoint at the time she wrote it departed from earlier motives or viewpoints.

28. Main idea (moderate). Answer: D.

The author's primary concern in the first two paragraphs is to point out that Rossetti's work conflicts with her apparently conservative personal life. The author's own impressions of Rossetti's work are corroborated by those of Woolf and Gosse. The third paragraph begins by asking how to reconcile this apparent conflict. (The newly discovered letters discussed in the third paragraph only reinforce the inconsistency between her personal life and literary work.) In the last paragraph, the author attempts to explain the inconsistency by examining Rossetti's love poems (particularly, her sonnet "The World").

(A) is the second-best response. The newly-discovered personal letters disprove Packer's thesis that Rossetti may have had personal affairs of the heart that she kept secret. Thus, Packer (and possibly Woolf) may have misinterpreted Rossetti's works by assuming that Rossetti wrote from personal experience. However, the author does not make this point explicit in the passage. Moreover, this point is far too narrow. It ignores the author's own explanation (in the final paragraph) for the apparent inconsistency between Rossetti's personal life and her work.

(B) is off-focus. Admittedly, in the first paragraph the author does point out that Woolf compared Rossetti to Shakespeare in both of these respects. However, the author makes no further attempt to explain or describe these similarities. Moreover, the point made in response (B) is Woolf's point, not the author's.

(C) distorts the author's argument and is too broad. First, in the last paragraph the author seems to claim that, through a proper reading of Rossetti's love poems, one can understand the ironic, enigmatic, contradictory nature of her work (in turn explaining the inconsistency between Rossetti's personal life and work). In this sense, response (C) distorts and actually runs contrary to the author's argument. Second, the passage concerns only Rossetti, not Victorian poetry or poetry in general, as (C) suggests; in this sense, then, (C) is too broad.

(E) is off-focus. While the author does point out in the first paragraph that Woolf viewed Rossetti's work as a model for women writers, this is Woolf's point, not the author's. Moreover, the author does not elaborate on this point—there is no further discussion of particular women writers who might have seen Rossetti as a model for their own work.

Day 25

Practice Test Section 3: Analytical Reasoning

Today you will take a full-length Analytical Reasoning section under actual test conditions. Allow yourself exactly 35 minutes to complete the 24 questions in this section.

Directions (as printed in test booklet): Each group of questions in this section is based on a set of conditions. In answering some of the questions, it may be useful to draw a rough diagram. Choose the response that most accurately and completely answers each question.

Questions 1–7

Of nine members on a baseball team, four bat right-handed, three bat left-handed, and two are switch hitters. Each of the nine players bats once and only once in the batting order.

Exactly two left-handed batters bat consecutively.

The switch hitters do not bat consecutively.

No two right-handed batters bat consecutively.

A right-handed batter bats fourth.

1. All of the following are possible batting assignments in order from first to third EXCEPT:

    (A) right-handed batter, switch hitter, left-handed batter

    (B) right-handed batter, left-handed batter, switch hitter

    (C) switch hitter, left-handed batter, right-handed batter

    (D) switch hitter, right-handed batter, left-handed batter

    (E) left-handed batter, right-handed batter, switch hitter

2. Which of the following is an acceptable batting order for the fifth, sixth, and seventh positions, in that order?

    (A) right-handed batter, left-handed batter, left-handed batter

    (B) left-handed batter, switch hitter, switch hitter

    (C) switch hitter, right-handed batter, left-handed batter

    (D) left-handed batter, right-handed batter, right-handed batter

    (E) switch hitter, left-handed batter, left-handed batter

227

3. If a right-handed batter bats second, it must be true that

   (A) a right-handed batter bats ninth
   (B) a left-handed batter bats fifth
   (C) a switch hitter bats seventh
   (D) a right-handed batter bats sixth
   (E) a left-handed batter bats eighth

4. If left-handed batters bat second and eighth, all of the following must be true EXCEPT:

   (A) A right-handed batter bats first.
   (B) A switch hitter bats fifth.
   (C) A right-handed batter bats sixth.
   (D) A switch hitter bats seventh.
   (E) A right-handed batter bats ninth.

5. Assume that left-handed batters bat both fifth and sixth. Considering only whether a batter is right-handed, left-handed, or is a switch hitter, what is the total number of possible batting orders?

   (A) 2
   (B) 3
   (C) 4
   (D) 5
   (E) 6

6. If all left-handed batters bat after all switch hitters, all of the following must be false EXCEPT:

   (A) A left-handed batter bats seventh.
   (B) A switch hitter bats second.
   (C) A left-handed batter bats ninth.
   (D) A right-handed batter bats eighth.
   (E) A switch hitter bats fifth.

7. If both switch hitters bat after all left-handed batters, which of the following must be true?

   (A) A switch hitter bats seventh.
   (B) A left-handed batter bats fifth.
   (C) A left-handed batter bats first.
   (D) A switch hitter bats sixth.
   (E) A right-handed batter bats eighth.

Questions 8–12

Eight voters—Perez, Quinn, Raffi, Sperry, Trager, Utley, Villar, and Wieser—are voting in two elections. Each voter must vote for either Able or Berman, and each voter must vote for either Cargis or Dorsey. The election results are as follows:

   Berman received exactly four votes.

   Raffi, Sperry, and Trager voted for Able.

   Villar did not vote for the identical two candidates as either Wieser or Utley.

   Wieser did not vote for the identical two candidates as Utley.

8. The elections must have resulted in

   (A) a tie between Able and Berman
   (B) a tie between Cargis and Dorsey
   (C) Berman defeating Able
   (D) Cargis defeating Dorsey
   (E) Dorsey defeating Cargis

9. With respect to which of the following pairs of voters is it possible that the two voters voted for the same two candidates?

   (A) Raffi and Sperry
   (B) Trager and Perez
   (C) Villar and Trager
   (D) Utley and Quinn
   (E) Wieser and Perez

10. What is the greatest number of voters who could have voted for Cargis?

   (A) 4
   (B) 5
   (C) 6
   (D) 7
   (E) 8

11. If Perez and Quinn voted for different candidates in the election between Cargis and Dorsey, then it CANNOT be true that:

    (A) exactly two voters voted for both Berman and Cargis

    (B) exactly three voters voted for both Berman and Dorsey

    (C) exactly four voters voted for both Able and Dorsey

    (D) exactly one voter voted for both Able and Cargis

    (E) exactly three voters voted for both Able and Dorsey

12. If Villar and six other voters voted for Dorsey, which of the following is a complete and accurate list of those voters whose choices with respect to both elections can be determined?

    (A) Villar, Perez, Quinn

    (B) Raffi, Sperry, Trager

    (C) Villar, Wieser, Utley

    (D) Raffi, Sperry, Trager, Utley, Villar

    (E) Raffi, Sperry, Trager, Perez, Quinn

Questions 13–18

In a series of chemistry experiments, each experiment involves combining the contents of two different beakers. A beaker may contain one of three chemical compounds—X, Y, or Z—in either a gaseous or liquid medium. Two beakers containing the same chemical compound must never be combined, and gaseous Z must never be combined with liquid Y. The results of the series of experiments are as follows:

Each experiment produces exactly one chemical compound—X, Y, or Z—in exactly one medium—gas or liquid.

Combining X and Y produces Z.

Combining X and Z produces X.

Combining Y and Z produces Y.

A gas may result only by combining a liquid and a gas.

Combining a gas and a liquid produces a liquid if and only if X is used.

13. An experiment in which gaseous Y and liquid Z are combined produces:

    (A) liquid X

    (B) liquid Y

    (C) liquid Z

    (D) gaseous X

    (E) gaseous Y

14. Liquid X will be produced by combining:

    (A) gaseous X and liquid Y

    (B) liquid X and gaseous Z

    (C) liquid Y and liquid Z

    (D) gaseous Z and gaseous Y

    (E) gaseous Y and liquid Z

15. How many different results are possible from a single experiment?

    (A) 2

    (B) 3

    (C) 4

    (D) 5

    (E) 6

16. If each chemical compound is used exactly four times in six simultaneous experiments, which of the following statements must be true?

    (A) Exactly one of the experiments produced Z.

    (B) Exactly two of the experiments produced X.

    (C) Exactly three of the experiments produced Y.

    (D) Exactly two of the experiments produced a gas.

    (E) Exactly two of the experiments produced a liquid.

17. Two and only two possible different experiments will produce which of the following?

    (A) liquid X

    (B) liquid Y

    (C) liquid Z

    (D) gaseous X

    (E) gaseous Y

18. If the results of two simultaneous experiments are combined in a third experiment to produce a gas, any of the following might have been used in at least one of the three experiments EXCEPT:

    (A) gaseous X

    (B) gaseous Y

    (C) gaseous Z

    (D) liquid X

    (E) liquid Y

Questions 19–24

Six commuters—C, D, E, F, G and H—participate in a van pool together. The seating capacity of the van is eight; two of the seats are empty. The seats are arranged in three rows as follows:

(front of van)

row 1:	1	2
row 2:	3	4	5
row 3:	6	7	8

Seat 1 is the driver's seat. Seats 4 and 7 are the only two seats that are considered "middle" seats. Two commuters can converse with each other only if they are sitting either immediately next to each other or diagonally from each other. However, the driver cannot converse with any other commuter. A commuter is seated "diagonally" from another commuter if the commuter is in an adjacent row and one seat to the left or right from the other commuter. The commuters' seating arrangement is subject to the following conditions:

> Either E, F, or G always drives the van.
>
> Neither C nor D will sit in a middle seat.
>
> G will not sit in row 3.
>
> H and D must sit next to each other.

19. Which of the following is an acceptable seating arrangement, in order, for seats 1, 2, 3, and 4?

    (A) G, D, empty seat, empty seat

    (B) F, C, E, H

    (C) G, empty seat, F, C

    (D) E, F, C, empty seat

    (E) C, G, F, E

20. Among the following pairs of commuters, with respect to which pair is it always true that the two commuters CANNOT converse with each other?

    (A) G and H

    (B) F and C

    (C) C and D

    (D) E and F

    (E) D and E

21. If seat 6 and seat 8 are empty, which of the following must be true?

    (A) H occupies seat 4.

    (B) G occupies seat 1.

    (C) F occupies seat 2.

    (D) E occupies seat 7.

    (E) D occupies seat 3.

22. The fewest number of commuters that can converse is

    (A) 0

    (B) 1

    (C) 2

    (D) 3

    (E) 4

23. If D converses with G during a commute, which of the following must be true?

    (A) E is driving the van.

    (B) Seat 3 is empty.

    (C) H occupies seat 7.

    (D) D occupies seat 5.

    (E) Seat 2 is empty.

24. If H can converse with exactly two other commuters, with respect to which of the following seats is it NOT possible to determine whether the seat is occupied?

    (A) seat 1

    (B) seat 2

    (C) seat 4

    (D) seat 6

    (E) seat 7

Quick Answer Guide

Practice Test Section 3: Analytical Reasoning

1.	C	7.	B	13.	E	19.	D
2.	C	8.	A	14.	B	20.	C
3.	A	9.	B	15.	C	21.	A
4.	D	10.	D	16.	B	22.	D
5.	D	11.	B	17.	B	23.	C
6.	A	12.	E	18.	C	24.	D

Review of Practice Test Section 3: Analytical Reasoning

Today you will evaluate and review the Analytical Reasoning section that you took yesterday. For each question set, the game type and difficulty level are identified.

Questions 1–7: Simple linear sequence game (easier).

One viable approach to this game is to jot down the possible sequences, considering together that a right-handed batter bats fourth and that no right-handed batters bat consecutively. First consider a right-handed batter batting first (sequences 1–3 below), then consider a right-handed batter batting second (sequences 4–6 below). Also consider that unless a sequence contains at least two adjacent empty slots, it can be eliminated, since two left-handed batters bat consecutively. (Eliminate sequence 4 below.) Finally, insert those two left-handed batters wherever you can. The result is five alternative scenarios:

1. R L L R _ R _ R _
2. R _ _ R _ R _ _ R
3. R _ _ R _ _ R _ R
X4. _ R _ R _ R _ R _
5. _ R _ R _ R L L R
6. _ R _ R L L R _ R

Another (and probably more efficient) approach is to simply construct one initial diagram which indicates that a right-handed batter must bat fourth, while indicating the other rules near that diagram:

$$\underset{1\ \ 2\ \ 3\ \ 4\ \ 5\ \ 6\ \ 7\ \ 8\ \ 9}{\_\ \_\ \_\ \overset{\textcircled{R}}{\_}\ \_\ \_\ \_\ \_\ \_}$$

R R R R	[L L] ≠ L
L L L	S ≠ S
S S	R ≠ R

1. Answer: C.

The quickest way to locate the correct answer here is to consider, one at a time, each restriction regarding the first three batters. Then scan the answer choices for violations. If you consider that a right-handed batter cannot bat third, a quick glance down the list of third batters reveals the correct answer immediately—only in answer choice (C) does a right-handed batter bat third.

233

2. Answer: C.

Narrow down the choices by considering the conditions one at a time and scanning the answer choices for violations. Considering that a right-handed batter bats fourth and that right-handed batters cannot bat consecutively, (A) can be eliminated. Considering that the two switch hitters cannot bat consecutively, (B) can be eliminated. (D) and (E) each require that two or more right-handed batters bat consecutively. (C) is the only choice that does not violate any rule.

3. Answer: A.

Given that a right-handed batter bats second, then the remaining two right-handed batters must bat either sixth and ninth or seventh and ninth. (In either case, a right-handed batter must bat ninth.) Otherwise, either no two left-handed batters would bat consecutively or two right-handed batters would bat consecutively. Either result would violate a rule.

4. Answer: D.

Given that left-handed batters bat second and eighth, a bit of experimenting reveals that only two viable sequences result:

R L L Ⓡ S R S L L
R L S Ⓡ S R L L R
1 2 3 4 5 6 7 8 9

Thus, either a switch hitter or a left-handed batter can bat seventh.

5. Answer: D.

Given that left-handed batters bat fifth and sixth, two initial possibilities result:

R _ Ⓡ L L R _ R
_R _ Ⓡ L L R _ R
1 2 3 4 5 6 7 8 9

The first diagram above presents two possible sequences—a switch hitter batting eighth while a left-handed batter and the other switch hitter bat second and third, in either order. The second

diagram presents three possible sequences—a left-handed batter batting first, third, or eighth, with the two switch hitters occupying the remaining two positions.

6. Answer: A.

A bit of intuition and experimenting reveals that the first left-handed batter in the order must bat fifth, and no later, resulting in two possible sequences:

S R S Ⓡ L R L L R
S R S Ⓡ L L R L R
1 2 3 4 5 6 7 8 9

The foregoing sequences make clear that statement (A) could be true, while each of the other four statements must be false.

7. Answer: B.

Given that both switch hitters bat after all left-handed batters, a bit of experimenting reveals that a switch hitter can bat sixth at the earliest. Two possible sequences result:

R L L Ⓡ L S R S R
R L L Ⓡ L R S R S
1 2 3 4 5 6 7 8 9

In either case, a left-handed batter must bat fifth.

Questions 8–12: Complex grouping game (moderate).

In this game, your task is to allocate eight subjects (the voters) among four different groups (who they voted for):

- the group who voted for Able and Cargis

- the group who voted for Able and Dorsey

- the group who voted for Berman and Cargis

- the group who voted for Berman and Dorsey

According to the rules, Berman receives exactly four votes. As a result, Able must also receive exactly four votes (from Raffi, Sperry, Trager and one other voter). Considering together the last two conditions, Utley, Villar, and Wieser must all be included in different groups. Accordingly, one of those three voted for Able, while the other two, along with Perez and Quinn, voted for Berman. The rules can now be incorporated into a group-oriented diagram as follows:

$$\text{(R S T)}\begin{cases}\text{[A C]}\\\text{[A D]}\end{cases}$$

$$\text{(P Q \_)}\begin{cases}\text{[B C]}\\\text{[B D]}\end{cases}$$

$$\text{U} \neq \text{V} \neq \text{W}$$

In the following explanations, voters and candidates are identified by the first letter of their last name, as in the diagram above.

8. Answer: A.

Because A received exactly four votes, B must also have received exactly four votes.

9. Answer: B.

R, S, T, and one other voter voted for A. That other voter must be either U, V, or W. Therefore, T and P could not both have voted for A.

10. Answer: D.

V, U, and W must all be included in different groups. Thus, at least one voter among these three must have voted for D rather than for C.

11. Answer: B.

P and Q both voted for B (see general comments above). If one voted for C while the other voted for D, then P and Q must each be joined by exactly one other voter (among V, U and W) in their respective groups (see diagram above). Otherwise, among V, U, and W, two would be in the same group together, resulting in a rule violation.

12. Answer: E.

According to the question, seven of the eight voters voted for D. As a result, exactly one voter voted for C. Accordingly, either the [AC] group includes one voter while the [BC] group includes no voters, or

vice-versa. However, if that one voter is assigned to the [AC] group rather than the [BC] group, V, W, and U cannot all be separated into different groups. Thus, one voter must be assigned to the [BC] group while none of the voters are assigned to the [AC] group. Accordingly, R, S, and T must all have voted for A and D, while P and Q must both have voted for Berman and D. (Group assignments for W, U, and V cannot be determined.)

Questions 13–18: Logic tree game (challenging).

In approaching this game, begin by listing the formulas suggested by the rules. In doing so, several important additional facts may be deduced. Considering the last two rules together, if either two liquids or two gases are combined, the result must be a liquid, while if a liquid and a gas are combined, the result is a gas if Y and Z are used or a liquid if either X and Y or X and Z are used. Since a gas may be produced only if Y and Z are combined, any experiment combining X and Y or X and Z must produce a liquid. This additional information is necessary to analyze the questions.

13. Answer: E.

Combining Y and Z produces Y. Combining a liquid and a gas produces a gas if X is not used. Thus, the experiment produces gaseous Y.

14. Answer: B.

According to the rules, combining X and Z in any form produces liquid X.

15. Answer: C.

Without restriction, a total of six different results would be possible—X, Y, or Z each in either liquid or gaseous form. However, any experiment using X must produce a liquid rather than a gas (see general comments above). Thus, an experiment combining X and Y or X and Z must produce liquid Z and liquid X, respectively. Gaseous Z and gaseous X are impossible results.

16. Answer: B.

A bit of intuition or experimenting reveals that three experiments—combining X with Y, X with Z, and Y with Z—must each be performed twice if each chemical compound is to be used four times in six experiments. Thus, Z, X, and Y must each be produced twice. Accordingly, statement (B) must be true, while statements (A) and (C) must be false. A liquid may result from a minimum of four to a maximum of six of the experiments (see general comments above). Accordingly, statement (D) is not necessarily true, while statement (E) must be false.

17. Answer: B.

In an experiment combining Y and Z, the rules stipulate that gaseous Z must not be combined with liquid Y. Thus, Z and Y are either both liquid, both gas, or Z is liquid while Y is gas. In each of the first two cases, liquid Y results. In the last case, gaseous Y results (because X is not used). Thus, Y may result from only one of two different experiments—combining liquid Y and liquid Z or combining gaseous Y and gaseous Z. Answer choices (A) and (C) are incorrect—liquid X and liquid Z may each result from any one of four different experiments. Answer choice (D) is incorrect because gaseous X is an impossible result (see question 3). Answer choice (E) is incorrect because only one experiment—combining gaseous Y and liquid Z—will produce gaseous Y.

18. Answer: C.

If either X or Z results from an experiment, it must be in liquid form (see general comments above). Thus, since the end result in this experiment is a gas, it must be gaseous Y. Gaseous Y can be produced only by combining gaseous Y and liquid Z. Liquid Z can be produced only by combining X and Y, although X and Y may each be in either gas or liquid form. Thus, the only answer choice that cannot be used in any of the three experiments is gaseous Z.

Questions 19–24: Multiple row game (moderate).

The key to working through this game efficiently is to realize that H must occupy either seat 4 or seat 7. Why? D and H must sit next to each other. They cannot sit in row 1, since neither of them can drive the van. D cannot occupy a middle seat (that is, seat 4 or seat 7). Thus, H must occupy one of the two middle seats. Every question in this game includes this logical link as part of the analysis.

19. Answer: D.

In response (A), D occupies seat 2; this is unacceptable, however, because D must sit immediately next to H (H cannot drive). In response (B), H occupies seat 4. Since D must sit next to H, D must occupy seat 5 (seat 3 is occupied by E). This leaves no seat for G in either row 1 or row 2, violating the rule that "G will not sit in row 3." The arrangement indicated by response (C) would place C in seat 4, which is one of the middle seats, violating the rule that C will not occupy a middle seat. In response (E), C drives the van (the driver occupies seat 1), violating the rule that "either E, F, or G always drives the van."

20. Answer: C.

Since D will not sit in a middle seat, H must sit in one of the two middle seats (either seat 4 or seat 7), with D immediately next to H (in seat 3, 5, 6, or 8). Since C cannot sit in a middle seat, it is impossible for C and D to either sit next to each other or diagonally from each other.

21. Answer: A.

If seat 6 and seat 8 are empty, D and H (who must sit next to each other) must occupy row 2. Since D will not sit in a middle seat, H must occupy seat 4, while D occupies either seat 3 or seat 5.

22. Answer: D.

This question requires a bit of intuition or experimentation. To minimize the number of commuters who can converse, seat 4 must be empty—any commuter occupying seat 4 could converse with commuters in seats 2, 3, 5, 6, and 8. Assuming, then, that seat 4 is empty, H must sit in seat 7 with D in either seat 6 or 8. H can converse with D as well as with the commuter in either seat 3 or seat 5 (or both). Assuming that one of those two seats is empty, H can still converse with two other commuters (who in turn can converse with H). Therefore, at a minimum, three commuters (H, D, and one other under this "minimum conversation" scenario) can converse.

23. Answer: C.

Where is G sitting? G is not driving, since the rules prohibit the driver from conversing with another commuter. The rules also prohibit G from sitting in row 3. Thus, G must sit in seat 2, 3, 4, or 5. However, if G were to occupy seat 2 and converse with D, D would be in seat 4, which violates the rule that D cannot occupy a middle seat. Accordingly, G must sit in row 2. D, then, must sit in row 3, in either seat 6 or 8. In either case, H sits next to D in seat 7.

24. Answer: D.

H must occupy either seat 4 or seat 7 (see general comments above). If H were to occupy seat 4, then D would occupy either seat 3 or seat 5, and of course H could converse with D. However, H could not be limited to conversing with only one additional commuter. Thus, H must occupy seat 7 (and D must occupy either seat 6 or seat 8). Given that H occupies seat 7, the only way to limit H to conversing with only two others is to position the two empty seats among seats 3, 5, and 6. Accordingly, seats 1, 2, and 4 must be occupied (of course, seat 1 must be occupied in any event).

Practice Test Section 4:
Logical Reasoning

Today you will take a full-length Logical Reasoning section under actual test conditions. Allow yourself exactly 35 minutes to complete the 25 questions in this section.

Directions *(as printed in test booklet): The questions in this section are based on the reasoning contained in brief statements or passages. For some questions, more than one of the choices could conceivably answer the question. However, you are to choose the* best *answer; that is, the response that most accurately and completely answers the question. You should not make assumptions that are by commonsense standards implausible, superfluous, or incompatible with the passage.*

---

1. The nutrient value of animal products is indisputable. Complete protein—the kind with sufficient quantities of the eight amino acids—is found only in animal products. The human body cannot manufacture these eight amino acids, so they must be supplied through proper diet.

   Which of the following is the main point of the argument above?

   (A) Animal products are the main source of the eight amino acids that make up complete protein.

   (B) A proper diet must contain the eight amino acids.

   (C) Animal products must be included in a proper diet.

   (D) Amino acids cannot be manufactured by the human body.

   (E) Animal products are nutritious sources of food.

2. The earth-moon system, the satellites of Jupiter, and the moons of Saturn are all examples of planetary systems in which a satellite moves in the gravitational field of a much more massive body. In every one of these systems the satellite moves in an elliptical orbit.

   If the statements above are true, they provide the most support for which one of the following?

   (A) The more massive a body the more gravitational pull it exerts on another body.

   (B) Only elliptical orbits can account for the various phases of the moon as seen from earth.

   (C) Non-elliptical orbits violate the laws of celestial mechanics.

   (D) The moons of the planet Uranus move in elliptical orbits.

   (E) All celestial bodies move in elliptical orbits.

3. The mean price of new cars in Heavenly Hills is $38,563; in Cargo the mean price is only $23,769. Therefore, if you are in the market for a new car, you are likely to get a better deal on it in Cargo.

Which of the following best describes the flaw in the author's reasoning?

(A) The author's conclusion is based on a comparison that does not necessarily involve comparable things.

(B) The author assumes that the number of cars sold in Heavenly Hills is the same as the number sold in Cargo.

(C) The author has confused the mean average price with the median average price.

(D) The author assumes that new cars in Cargo are less expensive than new cars in Heavenly Hills.

(E) The author assumes that new car dealers in Cargo are more willing than Heavenly Hills dealers to make good deals on new cars.

4. Due to the fact that mean water temperatures in the oceans of the world have not changed significantly over the past century it is evident that the expected rise in global air temperatures as a result of ozone depletion has not yet begun.

Which of the following, if true, most substantially weakens the above argument?

(A) Ocean surface water temperatures fluctuate by as much as 20 degrees yearly.

(B) Air to water heat transfer is such that a rise of 10 degrees in air temperature will cause a rise of 1 degree of water temperature over a 24 hour period.

(C) Global ocean water temperatures are controlled mainly by polar ice.

(D) Global air temperatures have not varied significantly over the past decade.

(E) The rate of ozone depletion has been shown to be significantly less than as was first reported by scientists.

5. Flagrant violations of human rights were cited by the Astonian government as the official reason for ceasing to provide military support to the embattled country of Cretia. But, at the same time, military support continues to be provided to countries with far worse human-rights records than Cretia. Hence, despite the official explanation for this change in policy, this reversal cannot be accounted for solely by the Astonian government's commitment to human rights.

Which of the following, if true, would most strengthen the conclusion in the above argument?

(A) Cretia's neighboring countries recently entered into a non-aggression pact with one another.

(B) Astonia recently entered into long-range trade agreements with Cretia's neighboring countries.

(C) The newly elected head of the Cretian government is an avowed anti-Astonian.

(D) Cretia has a longer record of human-rights abuse than other countries to which military support is provided by Astonia.

(E) The Astonian government's decision to provide military support to a country is made mainly on the basis of the country's capability of defending itself from outside aggression.

6. It is commonly held in discussions of capital punishment that there is no evidence that the death penalty deters. This is simply untrue. We have an enormous amount of both informal and formal evidence—from everyday experience and from such "experiments" as increasing the fees for parking violations—that, as a general rule, the greater the punishment, the fewer people will behave in the punished way. Thus, it is perfectly reasonable to expect that the death penalty would have a more dissuasive effect than would life imprisonment.

Which of the following must be assumed for the above argument to be logically correct?

(A) Everyday experience shows that the death penalty deters.

(B) Life imprisonment does not act as a deterrent to murder.

(C) The death penalty is a greater punishment than life imprisonment.

(D) Potential murderers consciously weigh the alternatives beforehand and decide that the crime is worth life in prison, but not death.

(E) The more severe the punishment, the more it acts as a deterrent.

7. Since solid-state components of electronic devices are easily damaged by ionizing radiation, they would be useless in a nuclear war because they would not function properly. The crucial lesson to be drawn from this is that vital electronic equipment should not use solid-state components, but rather should use vacuum tubes or fiber optics.

Which of the following best expresses the main point of the passage?

(A) Electronic devices equipped with solid-state components will not function properly in a nuclear war.

(B) Vacuum tubes and fiber optics are better components for electronic devices than solid-state components.

(C) Electronic equipment should not be equipped with solid-state components.

(D) Vital electronic equipment should be equipped with vacuum tubes and fiber optics.

(E) Solid-state components of electronic devices are easily damaged by ionizing radiation.

8. Historians universally agree that all democracies in the past have eventually perished as a result of disputes between competing groups of special interests, coupled with gross inefficiency, waste and corruption in government, and a decline in the moral values of the society at large. Everyday the news reports confirm that all of these maladies are currently present in the United States of America.

Given that the statements above are true, which of the following conclusions is most strongly supported?

(A) Communism is a better form of government than democracy.

(B) Non-democratic societies do not suffer from the same problems as democratic societies.

(C) If the experience of past democracies is a reliable indicator, democracy in the United States is in decline.

(D) News reports generally focus only on negative news.

(E) In the future, the United States will be a dictatorship.

9. Card games requiring more than one player, such as poker and bridge, employ strategies aimed at outwitting the opponent; however, card games that are played alone, such as games of solitaire, do not. Hence, strategies that aim at outwitting an opponent are not an essential feature of all card games.

Which of the following most closely parallels the reasoning in the above passage?

(A) Games of chance, such as roulette and craps, employ odds that are detrimental to the player, but favorable to the house. Since these are the only kinds of games that are found in gambling casinos, having odds that favor the house is an essential feature of all games played in gambling casinos.

(B) Most aircraft have wings, but others, such as helicopters, do not. Hence, having wings is not an essential property of all aircraft.

(C) Chez Bon's most celebrated features are its great food and extensive wine list. But, since these are features of many other fine restaurants as well, they are not the only features which define the essence of this outstanding restaurant.

(D) It has been reliably reported that deer occasionally eat meat, but if deer were not primarily vegetarians they would have much different shaped teeth than they do. Hence, being a vegetarian is an essential feature of being a deer.

(E) All cats are meat eaters and being a meat eater is the defining characteristic of being a carnivore. Hence, being carnivorous is essential to being a cat.

10. The average annual salary for executives at World-Wide Travel last year was $55,000, while the average salary for travel consultants was $47,000. The average annual salary for all employees was $38,000.

If the above information is correct, which one of the following conclusions can be properly inferred from it?

(A) There were fewer executives than travel consultants at World-Wide Travel last year.

(B) No travel consultants earned more than an executive last year.

(C) There was at least one employee who earned less than the average for a travel consultant.

(D) Some travel consultants earn more than the lowest paid executives.

(E) All executives earn more than travel consultants.

Questions 11 and 12 are based on the following passage.

An auto mechanic who is too thorough in checking a car is likely to subject the customer to unnecessary expense. On the other hand, one who is not thorough enough is likely to miss some problem that could cause a serious accident. Therefore, it's a good idea not to have your car checked until a recognizable problem develops.

11. Which one of the following, if true, casts the most doubt on the argument?

(A) Mechanical problems that can cause serious accidents are easily detectable by a mechanic even before they become recognizable to the customer.

(B) Due to the high cost of skilled labor, some auto garages limit the amount of time spent on auto checkups.

(C) Drivers who are not trained mechanics generally have difficulty in recognizing that their car has a problem.

(D) Many mechanics spend neither too little nor too much time when checking a car.

(E) Most people cannot afford to have their cars checked for problems regularly.

12. Which one of the following, if true, provides the most support for the above argument?

(A) The more complete the mechanical checkup, the more likely a problem, if present, will be discovered.

(B) Some people have enough mechanical knowledge to recognize a problem with their car.

(C) Not all tests performed by mechanics are time consuming and expensive.

(D) Most mechanical problems that are potentially dangerous or expensive to repair cannot be detected by routine checkups no matter how thorough they are.

(E) Many auto mechanics lie to customers about the mechanical condition of their cars.

13. A study of six patients who all suffer from a rare form of cancer revealed that though they all live in different locations in the county and have quite different medical histories, diet, and personal habits—two smoke cigarettes and three drink alcoholic beverages—they are all employed at a company that manufactures herbicides and pesticides. From this study it can be concluded that exposure to the chemicals produced by the company is the probable cause of the disease.

The argument proceeds by:

(A) reaching a general conclusion on the basis of insufficient evidence

(B) isolating a common feature through a process of elimination and concluding that this feature is causally related to the event under investigation

(C) reaching a general conclusion on the basis of the experiences of the six patients

(D) providing information that allows the application of a general claim to a specific case

(E) indirectly showing that exposure to the chemicals produced by the company is the likely cause by demonstrating that none of the other alternatives is the cause

14. The College Board recently decided to recenter the scores on standardized college admission tests to reflect the composition of the test takers. The College Board explained the recentering—lowering the definition of what is average—on grounds that students who take college admissions tests today—30% from minority groups and 53% women—cannot be expected to achieve the same test scores as the original reference group of 1941, which was predominantly white and 82% male.

Which of the following is an assumption on which the College Board's decision depends?

(A) Women and minorities have a lower level of general intelligence than white males.

(B) Admission tests are a lot more difficult today than they were in 1941.

(C) The original reference group of 1941 was not representative of the test takers during that period.

(D) The definition of "average" has changed since 1941.

(E) Fewer people went to college in 1941 than do so today.

15. Seventeenth-century scientists argued that a void must exist in nature on the grounds that if there were no void, that is if all space were filled with matter, movement would be impossible. Movement would be impossible, they reasoned, because a body could not move unless it displaced another body. But to do this would require that the space occupied by the other body is empty, which it clearly is not because the other occupies it, thus movement is impossible.

Which of the following, if true, provides the most support for the scientists' conclusion?

(A) Instantaneous spatial displacement of one body by another is possible.

(B) Instantaneous spatial displacement of one body by another is impossible.

(C) Sequential spatial displacement entails that to move one body all other bodies would have to be moved.

(D) Sequential spatial displacement of one body by another is possible.

(E) Sequential spatial displacement of one body by another is impossible.

16. Given that the stated goal of environmentalists is to reduce the amount of carbon dioxide in the atmosphere while at the same time preserving existing plant life on earth, there are two very good reasons for harvesting living trees from old-growth forests. First, doing so would reduce the amount of carbon dioxide in the atmosphere for the simple reason that when old trees die they decompose, thereby releasing their stored carbon dioxide. Second, it would make room for more young trees which absorb carbon dioxide thereby further reducing the amount of carbon dioxide in the atmosphere.

Which one of the following, if true, most seriously weakens the above argument?

(A) Levels of carbon dioxide in the atmosphere have remained relatively constant over the past 100 years.

(B) Reduction in the amount of carbon dioxide in the atmosphere is necessary to reduce the "greenhouse effect."

(C) The amount of carbon dioxide released into the atmosphere through the decomposition of old trees is insignificantly small when compared to the amount released by agricultural waste.

(D) Old-growth forests are the habitat of many species which will not survive if these forests are destroyed.

(E) A reduction in the amount of carbon dioxide in the atmosphere is detrimental to plant life.

17. Analytic propositions provide no information about any matter of fact. This applies to all analytic propositions. In other words, they are entirely devoid of information about the world. It is for this reason that no empirical evidence can refute them.

    Which of the following must be assumed for the above argument's conclusion to be properly drawn?

    (A) The truth or falsity of analytic propositions cannot be determined by empirical evidence.

    (B) Analytic propositions are neither true nor false.

    (C) Analytic propositions are completely uninformative.

    (D) Empirical evidence can only refute propositions that provide information about matters of fact.

    (E) Propositions that are entirely devoid of information about the world are false.

18. Gasoline additives are designed to clean the electronic sensors in the ignition systems of modern automobiles. Because of the prevalent use of these additives in gasoline over the past decade, car manufacturers have been able to design engines that meet the stringent federally mandated emission standards. Unfortunately, current additives contain ingredients that threaten the ozone and will be illegal to use in the near future. Despite the fact that there is no likelihood that current emission standards will be changed, car manufacturers are confident that they will continue to be able to produce engines that meet them.

    If the above statements are true, which of the following is the most strongly supported inference?

    (A) New additives will be developed that do not contain ozone threatening ingredients.

    (B) Gasoline-powered internal combustion engines will be replaced by hydrogen-powered engines.

    (C) The electronic sensors in the ignition system will be eliminated.

    (D) Smaller engines will be developed that are more fuel efficient.

    (E) Gasoline powered engines will be outlawed in the near future.

19. Persons who do not control their cholesterol levels are more likely to have heart disease than those who do. However, even among those who do not control their cholesterol levels, the majority do not have heart disease. Therefore, to avoid heart disease, there is no need to adopt a diet that is low in cholesterol rather than one that is high in cholesterol.

    The pattern of flawed reasoning displayed in the above argument most closely resembles the reasoning in which one of the following?

    (A) People who swim every day are more likely to develop ear infections than those who jog. However, daily joggers are more likely to develop foot problems than swimmers. Hence, people who want to avoid foot problems and ear infections shouldn't jog or swim on a daily basis.

    (B) There is no need to abstain from smoking in order to decrease the likelihood of contracting lung disease because even though smokers are more likely to die of lung disease than non-smokers, most smokers do not die of lung disease.

    (C) Overweight people are more likely to die at a young age than persons who are physically fit. However, a surprisingly large number of young physically fit people die in sports-related accidents each year. Hence, to avoid an early death, it is probably best to be neither overweight nor physically fit.

    (D) Crimes of passion are more likely to be committed by young people than old people. Yet many old people are capable of extremely strong emotional outbursts. Hence, middle-aged people are less likely to commit crimes of passion than either young people or old people.

(E) Persons who exercise daily are more likely to live longer than persons who do not exercise. But "daily exercise" means at least 20 minutes of strenuous aerobic exercise, not just walking around the block or bicycling to the store. For this reason, unless your willing to really work up a sweat every day, there is little reason to exercise daily.

20. Parents cannot be with their teenage children every minute of the day and, even if they could, they would not always be able to stop them from doing things that might cause harm to other people or other people's property. That's why they should not be blamed or punished for crimes that their teenage children commit.

Which of the following general principles, if established, would most help to justify the conclusion in the argument above?

(A) All activities that teenage children engage in should be supervised by adults.

(B) Teenage children should be treated as adults in the criminal justice system.

(C) People should be held accountable for only those actions over which they have control.

(D) Parents should supervise the activities of their teenage children as much as possible.

(E) Parents have the responsibility to teach their teenage children the difference between right and wrong.

21. Persons who advocate capital punishment typically do so on the grounds that it is a more effective deterrent than life imprisonment. So far this has not been conclusively established, but assuming for the moment that it is true, the question remains as to whether the goal of deterrence justifies the state-sanctioned murder of people who are under lock and key and are no longer a threat to anyone. Clearly, this is not something that any civilized society can condone, so it is simply erroneous to claim that this provides a valid reason for this barbaric form of punishment.

The method of the argument is to:

(A) discredit the argument in favor of capital punishment by showing that one of its premises is unacceptable because it leads to an unacceptable claim

(B) discredit the argument in favor of capital punishment by questioning the motives of the persons who advance it

(C) discredit the argument in favor of capital punishment by arguing that the fact that many people agree with the conclusion does not make it true

(D) discredit the argument in favor of capital punishment by showing that the conclusion of the argument is assumed in the premises

(E) discredit the argument in favor of capital punishment by showing that persons who advance the argument are uncivilized

22. *Democratic Senator:* The fact that the Republicans have not articulated one good reason in support of their opposition to cuts in social security payments to the elderly shows that they are obviously in favor of them.

Which of the following best describes the flaw in the senator's reasoning?

(A) arguing that there are only two possible alternatives to choose from, and since one can be eliminated the other must be true

(B) arguing that a claim is true because of the lack of evidence that it is false

(C) arguing that what is true of some members of a group must also be true of all members of the group

(D) inferring a conclusion from unrepresentative or biased data

(E) drawing a general conclusion from too small a sample of cases

23. Captive animals are more interesting research subjects than are wild animals. That's why researchers can learn more from studying captive animals than from studying wild animals.

Which of the following is an assumption upon which the above argument depends?

(A) Researchers study only subjects they are interested in.

(B) In general, the more that can be learned from a research subject, the more interesting it is to study.

(C) In general, the more interesting a research subject, the more that can be learned from studying it.

(D) Researchers learn less from studying subjects they are not interested in.

(E) In general, researchers prefer studying interesting subjects more than non-interesting subjects.

24. *George:* What benefit will taxpayers get from the installation of automated flight centers at privately owned airports? The answer is none, and that's why I am opposed to using taxpayer funds for this purpose.

Henry: I agree that there won't be any direct benefit to taxpayers from these projects, but the fact is that automatic flight centers will greatly increase the amount of traffic these airports can safely accommodate, and they are just too costly for private companies to install without government subsidies.

On the basis of their statements, George and Henry are committed to disagreeing about the truth of which of the following principles?

(A) Taxpayer funds should be used only to fund projects that benefit taxpayers.

(B) Airport safety should always take precedence over other factors when improving airports.

(C) Government subsidies should never be given to privately held companies.

(D) Automated flight centers should be installed at all airports.

(E) Taxpayer funds should only be used to fund those projects to which taxpayers have given their approval.

25. There is no such thing as one single scientific method. Instead, there is a jumble of methods ranging from careful observation and collection of data from which hypotheses are advanced to mere conjecture of the underlying causes. Moreover, no attempts to rationally justify the various methods of science as sources of truth have as yet proven fruitful. For these reasons it can be concluded that science is not preferable to religion or mythology when it comes to finding out the basic truths of the universe.

Which one of the following claims, if true, would most weaken the author's position in the passage?

(A) Science is based on reason, whereas religion and mythology are based on faith.

(B) Unlike religion and mythology, the various methods of science all yield accurate predictions, and yielding accurate predictions is an indicator of truth.

(C) Religion and mythology are based on superstition and ignorance.

(D) There is widespread agreement among scientists about the nature of the universe but little agreement among the practitioners of religion and mythology.

(E) More technological advances have been made in the past two centuries, during which science has reigned, than in the preceding twenty centuries, in which mythology and religion reigned.

Quick Answer Guide

Practice Test Section 4: Logical Reasoning

1. C	8. C	15. B	22. B
2. D	9. B	16. E	23. C
3. A	10. C	17. D	24. A
4. C	11. A	18. A	25. B
5. E	12. D	19. B	
6. C	13. B	20. C	
7. D	14. A	21. A	

Day 28

Review of Practice Test Section 4:
Logical Reasoning

Today you will evaluate and review the Logical Reasoning practice section that you took yesterday. For each question, the question type and difficulty level are identified.

1. Conclusion (moderate). Answer: C.

The main point or final conclusion of this argument is not overtly stated. The intermediate conclusion is stated in the last line—"so they must be supplied through proper diet." The pronoun "they" in this line refers back to the eight amino acids, which, we were told earlier are found in sufficient quantities only in animal products. Since these eight amino acids can only be found in animal products and they are necessary for a proper diet, it can be concluded that animal products must be included in a proper diet. This is the main point of the argument and this is exactly what response (C) asserts.

(A) is simply a restatement of the second sentence of the argument. This sentence functions as a premise—not a conclusion—in the argument.

(B) is an incorrect response. In this question you are asked to find the main point or final conclusion. Response (B) states an intermediate conclusion—not the final conclusion.

(D) is a generalization of one of the premises. In the passage we are told that the "human body cannot manufacture these eight amino acids." Response (D) asserts this claim more broadly.

(E) is a restatement of the first sentence in the passage. Response (E) states neither a premise nor a

conclusion of the argument; it functions merely to introduce the topic.

2. Inference (moderate). Answer: D.

From the information given in the passage we can reasonably assume that Uranus and its moons constitute a planetary system. From this assumption and the claim that in all of the planetary systems mentioned the satellite moves in an elliptical orbit, we can infer that the moons of the planet Uranus move in elliptical orbits. This is exactly what response (D) asserts.

(A) is unsupported by the passage. Response (A) states something that is true according to modern physics, but the premises in the passage do not provide any logical support for this claim.

(B) brings in information not mentioned in the passage. The phases of the moon as seen from earth are not discussed in the passage.

(C) makes too broad a claim. The information in the passage is restricted to laws governing planetary systems.

(E) is too broad. The passage concerns only planetary systems—not all celestial bodies.

3. Reasoning error (moderate). Answer: A.

The passage does not indicate whether the cars sold in Heavenly Hills were the in the same price range (i.e., similar makes and models) as the ones sold in Cargo. The mean price is simply the total dollar amount of the cars sold divided by the number of cars sold. If the cost of each of the individual cars sold in Heavenly Hills was higher than those sold in Cargo, then the mean price would also be higher. For example, it could be that only one car was sold in each place—a high priced luxury car costing $38,563 in Heavenly Hills and a moderate priced compact car costing $23,769 in Cargo. In this case the mean price of cars in Heavenly Hills would be $38,563 and the mean price of cars in Cargo would be $23,769. From this example it can be clearly seen that (A) is the best response because unless the cars are comparable, the author's conclusion that a person is likely to get a better deal in Cargo than in Heavenly Hills does not follow.

(B) Even if the number of cars sold in both places were the same, it would not follow that a person would get a better deal in Cargo than in Heavenly Hills unless the cars were comparable.

(C) The median average price is simply the middle price in a series of prices with an odd number of items, or the price midway between the middle two prices in an even series. Given that the median price of new cars in Heavenly Hills was $38,563 whereas the median price in Cargo is $23,769, nothing could be inferred regarding the general prices of cars in either location. Since this is the case, a confusion of mean average price with median average price would not account for the flaw in the author's reasoning.

(D) The claim that new cars in Cargo are less expensive than new cars in Heavenly Hills is not an assumption in the argument, but rather a loose restatement of the conclusion.

(E) The argument does not rely upon this assumption. At best, it is an inference that could be made from the conclusion of the argument.

4. Assessing effect of additional information (moderate). Answer: C.

The task in this problem is to find an answer that weakens the argument; that is, one that undermines the major assumption of the argument, attacks a stated premise, or that suggests an alternative conclusion that could be inferred from the premises. The major assumption in the argument is that water temperatures in the oceans of the world are controlled by global air temperatures. Response (C) directly contradicts this assumption, and consequently, if true, substantially weakens the argument.

(A) is consistent with the claim that "mean water temperatures in the oceans of the world have not changed significantly over the past century."

(B) While this is an interesting fact about air to water heat transfer, it is irrelevant to the argument. Consequently, its being true would have no effect on the argument one way or another.

(D) is consistent with the implied claim that global air temperatures have not risen over the past century.

(E) Whether the ozone depletion rate is more or less than reported by scientists is irrelevant to the underlying assumption that water temperatures in the oceans of the world are controlled by global air temperatures.

5. Assessing effect of additional information (challenging). Answer: E.

The task in this problem is to find an answer that strengthens the argument; that is, one that offers support for the major assumption of the argument or that provides additional evidence for the conclusion. Of the answer choices, response (E) is the best choice because it does the latter; that is, it provides a convincing rationale for the seemingly inconsistent action on the part of the Astonian government.

(A) is consistent with the claim that Cretia is an "embattled country." While response (A) might provide a reason for Cretia's need for military support, it does not provide a rationale for the seemingly inconsistent action on the part of the Astonian government.

(B) is the second best response. Response (B) provides a plausible reason for the Astonian government's shift in policy, but to accept it as the best response we would have to make superfluous assumptions about how these trade agreements impact Astonia's foreign policy decisions.

(C) is the third best response. While response (C) provides a rationale for Astonia's shift in policy, to accept it as the best response would require making a number of superfluous assumptions about the Astonian government's foreign policy making principles.

(D) conflicts with information provided in the passage regarding Cretia's human-rights record as compared to other countries. Moreover, the fact that Cretia has a worse record than other countries to which military support is provided by Astonia does not provide a convincing rationale for Astonia's change in policy towards Cretia.

6. Assumption (easier). Answer: C.

The argument stated in the passage is basically as follows:

> **Premise:** The greater the punishment, the fewer people will behave in the punished way.
>
> **Conclusion:** The death penalty will have a more dissuasive effect than would life imprisonment.

The assumption required to fill the gap in the above argument is that the death penalty is a greater punishment than life imprisonment. This is exactly what response (C) asserts.

(A) does not fill a logical gap in the argument. It is maintained in the passage that the death penalty deters. Response (A) simply provides additional evidence that this is the case.

(B) does not fill a logical gap in the argument. Whether or not life imprisonment acts as a deterrent to murder is irrelevant to the main point of the argument.

(D) does not fill a logical gap in the argument. Response (B) is consistent with the conclusion and may offer a rationale for the greater dissuasive effect of the death penalty.

(E) is a loose paraphrase of a stated premise of the argument—namely, "the greater the punishment, the fewer people will behave in the punished way."

7. Conclusion (moderate). Answer: D.

The phrase "The crucial lesson to be drawn from this" signals the final conclusion of the argument. (D) expresses a pared down paraphrase of the sentence that immediately follows this phrase.

(A) is a restatement of a premise in the argument.

(B) is too broad. The argument establishes only that vacuum tubes and fiber optics are better components for *vital* electronic devices than solid-state components.

(C) is too broad. The argument establishes only that *vital* electronic equipment should not be equipped with solid-state components.

(D) is a premise in the argument.

8. Inference (easier). Answer: C.

The task in this problem is to find the answer choice that is most likely to be true on the basis of the information stated in the passage. Basically what the stated information boils down to is that the United States suffers from all of the problems that led to the demise of other democracies in the past. Given this, the inference that the United States will likewise perish as a result of these problems is highly probable. Of the answer choices, (C) come closest to asserting this claim. It should be noted that while answer choice (C) requires that we assume that the United States of America is a democracy, this assumption is *not*, by commonsense standards, an implausible, superfluous, or incompatible assumption.

(A) No mention of communism appears in the passage. To infer the claim asserted in response (A) would require a number of superfluous assumptions.

(B) No comparisons between non-democratic societies and democratic societies are warranted given the information stated in the passage. To infer the claim asserted in response (B) would require numerous superfluous assumptions.

(D) The degree of likelihood that the claim asserted in response (D) is true is indeterminable given the information stated in the passage.

(E) The degree of likelihood that the claim asserted in response (E) is true is indeterminable given the information stated in the passage.

9. Parallel reasoning (moderate). Answer: B.

The reasoning in the passage runs basically as follows: X is not an essential feature of Y because it is not present in all Y's. Schematically, the argument looks like this:

Premise: Some Y's are X's.

Premise: Some Y's are not X's.

Conclusion: X is not an essential feature of all Y's.

The answer choice that most closely parallels this structure will be the best choice.

(B) is the best response. A close examination of the argument in answer choice (B) reveals exactly the same structure as the argument in the passage as is demonstrated below:

Premise: Some aircraft have wings.

Premise: Some aircraft do not have wings.

Conclusion: Having wings is not an essential feature of all aircraft.

(A) is an incorrect response. The argument in answer choice (A) can be represented as follows:

Premise: All games played in gambling casinos have odds that are favorable to the house.

Conclusion: Having odds that are favorable to the house is an essential feature of all games played in gambling casinos.

The general structure of this argument is:

Premise: All Y's are X's.

Conclusion: X is an essential feature of all Y's.

This structure is not similar to the structure of the argument in the passage.

(C) is an incorrect response. The argument in answer choice (C) can be represented as follows:

Premise: Chez Bon has features A and B.

Premise: Many other restaurants have features A and B.

Conclusion: A and B are not the only features that define the essence of Chez Bon.

The structure of this argument is clearly not comparable to the structure of the argument in the passage.

(D) is an incorrect response. The argument in answer choice (D) can be represented as follows:

Premise: Deer must be vegetarians because of the shape of their teeth.

Conclusion: Being a vegetarian is an essential feature of being a deer.

The structure of this argument is clearly not comparable to the structure of the argument in the passage.

(E) is an incorrect response. The argument in answer choice (E) can be represented as follows:

Premise: All cats are meat eaters.

Premise: Being a meat eater is the defining characteristic of being a carnivore.

Conclusion: Being carnivorous is essential to being a cat.

The structure of this argument is clearly not comparable to the structure of the argument in the passage.

10. Inference (moderate). Answer: C.

The task in this problem is to find the answer choice that must be true or that is most likely to be true given the information stated in the passage. If executives and travel consultants were the only employees, the combined average for all employees would be $51,000. Since the passage states that combined average for all employees was $38,000, it can be inferred that there must have been other employees besides executives and travel consultants. Furthermore, it can be inferred that the average salary of these other employees was $12,000 ($55,000 + $47,000 + X / 3 = $38,000). Moreover, while the number of other employees is indeterminable, since their average salary was $12,000 it can be inferred that at least one of them must have earned less than $47,000, so it follows that at least one employee must have earned less than the average for a travel consultant. This is exactly what answer choice (C) states.

(A) is an incorrect response. Contrary to this claim it is consistent with the information stated in the passage that there were more executives than travel consultants. This can be demonstrated with a simple example. Suppose there were three executives each earning $55,000. The average for executives in this case would be $55,000 as stated in the passage. Suppose further that there were only two travel consultants each earning $47,000. Again the average is as stated in the passage. In this hypothetical example the number of travel consultants is less than the number of executives.

(B) is an incorrect response. Contrary to this claim it is consistent with the information stated in the passage that some travel consultants earned more than some executives. For example, suppose there were only two executives at World-Wide Travel last year; one earned $85,000 and the other earned $25,000. In this case the average for executives is $55,000 as stated in the passage. Suppose further that there were only two travel consultants; one earned $60,000 and the other earned $34,000. Again the average salary for travel consultants is as stated in the passage. In this hypothetical example, a travel consultant earns more than an executive, clearly demonstrating that (B) cannot be inferred from the stated information.

(D) is an incorrect response. Contrary to this claim it is consistent with the information stated in the passage that no travel consultants earn more than the lowest paid executive.

(E) is an incorrect response. Contrary to this claim it is consistent with the information stated in the passage that some executives do not earn as much as some travel consultants.

11. Assessing effect of additional information (moderate). Answer: A.

The task in this problem is to find an answer that weakens the argument; that is, one that undermines the major assumption of the argument, attacks a stated premise, or that suggests an alternative conclusion that could be inferred from the premises. Response (A) attacks one of the stated premises of the argument (viz., a mechanic "who is not thorough enough is likely to miss some problem that could cause a serious accident.") Since (A) contradicts one of the premises of the argument, accepting (A) as true effectively undermines or weakens the argument.

(B), (C), (D), and (E) are incorrect responses. None of them asserts a claim that undermines an assumption of the argument, attacks a stated premise, or provides an alternative conclusion that

could be inferred from the premises. Consequently, none of these answer choices weakens the argument.

12. Assessing effect of additional information (moderate). Answer: D.

The task in this problem is to find an answer that strengthens the argument; that is, one that offers support for the major assumption of the argument or that provides additional evidence for the conclusion. Response (D) offers additional evidence for the conclusion. The claim that the thoroughness of routine checkups is inconsequential in detecting dangerous or costly mechanical problems provides an additional reason for waiting to have your car checked until a recognizable problem develops.

(A) does not provide additional evidence for the conclusion nor does it offer support for the major assumption of the argument. Moreover, it is potentially inconsistent with the first premise which implies that unnecessary expense is to be avoided.

(B) is the second-best response. Response (B) offers an additional reason why *some* people should wait to have their car checked until a recognizable problem develops. In the stated argument, however, the conclusion applies to *all* people, so (B) has minimal evidential value for the conclusion.

(C) does not provide additional evidence for the conclusion nor does it offer support for the major assumption of the argument. In fact, (C) provides a reason for not waiting until a recognizable problem develops to have your car checked.

(E) does not provide additional evidence for the conclusion nor does it offer support for the major assumption of the argument. Even if we accept the claim that many mechanics lie to their customers about the mechanical condition of their cars, it does not follow that they all do this. It is only this latter claim that could provide additional evidence for the conclusion.

13. Method (moderate). Answer: B.

The argument in the passage presents a textbook example of eliminative causal reasoning—reasoning in which a common causal factor is discovered through a process of elimination of possible factors. This is exactly the method described in answer choice (B).

(A) is an incorrect response. The conclusion of the argument in the passage applies only to the six patients in the study—it is not a sweeping generalization about all persons who suffer from the rare form of cancer mentioned. Given that this is the case, the evidence cited in the passage is sufficient to support it.

(C) is an incorrect response. No specific experiences shared by the six patients are cited in the passage as grounds for the conclusion. The conclusion is reached by finding a factor that all six patients share.

(D) is an incorrect response. No general claim is offered as a premise in the argument.

(E) is an incorrect response. No attempt is made in the passage to demonstrate or prove that other factors are not causally related to the disease. Alternative factors such as diet, personal habits, etc., are eliminated simply because they are not shared by all of the patients who suffer from the disease.

14. Assumption (challenging). Answer: A.

There are, admittedly, a number of possible assumptions that could be operative in the College Board's decision, but, of the answer choices listed, (A) is the best choice. No premise is stated in the passage that explains why students who take college admissions tests today "cannot be expected to achieve the same scores as the original reference group of 1941." This is the gap in the argument that must be filled. Since the only difference between the two groups of test-takers that is cited in the passage is their composition, it is reasonable to assume that there is some difference between the two groups that somehow accounts for the expected difference in achievement. (A) maintains that this difference is a difference in intelligence, thereby providing an explanation of why today's students cannot be expected to achieve the same scores as the 1941 reference group.

(B) does not fill the gap in the College Board's argument. The reasons offered in support of their decision focused only on facts about changes in the composition of the test takers. It would be superfluous to assume that the content of the tests had changed in ways which made them more difficult today than in 1941.

(C) does not fill the gap in the College Board's argument. The reasons offered in support of their

decision focused only on facts about changes in the composition of the test takers. It would be superfluous to assume that the makeup of the reference group was not representative of the 1941 test takers.

(D) is not an assumption in the argument because it does not provide an explanation of why today's test takers cannot be expected to achieve the same scores as the 1941 reference group.

(E) may provide an explanation of the change in the composition of test takers since 1941, but it would not explain why today's test takers cannot be expected to achieve the same test scores as the 1941 reference group.

15. Assessing the effect of additional information (challenging). Answer: B.

The task in this problem is to find an answer that strengthens the argument; that is, one that offers support for the major assumption of the argument or that provides additional evidence for the conclusion. The major assumption of the scientists' argument is that no two bodies can occupy the same space at the same time. Response (B) provides support for the major assumption by ruling out the possibility of instantaneous spatial displacement of one body by another.

(A) is inconsistent with the major assumption. If instantaneous spatial displacement of one body by another is possible, then one body would be able to occupy the space of another at the same time.

(C), (D), and (E) do not provide support for the major assumption, nor do they provide additional evidence for the conclusion.

16. Assessing the effect of additional information (moderate). Answer: E.

The task in this problem is to find the answer that weakens the argument; that is, one that undermines the major assumption of the argument, attacks a stated premise, or that suggests an alternative conclusion that could be inferred from the premises. The major assumption of the argument is that the two elements of the stated goal of environmentalists are compatible with one another; that is, that preserving existing plant life and at the same time reducing the amount of carbon dioxide in the atmosphere are not conflicting aims. Response (E) directly contradicts this assumption, and as a result weakens the argument.

(A) is off-focus. The fact that the levels of carbon dioxide in the atmosphere have remained constant over the past 100 years is consistent with the stated premises of the argument. Furthermore, response (A) does not undermine the major assumption of the argument, nor does it suggest an alternative conclusion that could be inferred from the premises.

(B) states a possible rationale for the environmentalists' concern to reduce the amount of carbon dioxide in the atmosphere, however, it does not provide information that would undermine the argument's major assumption, attack a stated premise, or provide an alternative conclusion that could be inferred from the premises.

(C) and (D) raise peripheral issues that are not addressed in the argument. Neither of these responses undermines the argument's major assumption, attacks a stated premise, or suggests an alternative conclusion that could be inferred from the premises.

17. Assumption (easier). Answer: D.

The argument in the passage can be restated as follows:

> **Premise:** Analytic propositions do not provide information about any matter of fact.
>
> **Conclusion:** Empirical evidence cannot refute analytic propositions.

In this restatement it is fairly obvious that the assumption that is required for the conclusion to be properly drawn is one that will link empirical evidence with propositions that provide information about matters of fact. Response (D) provides this link, thus closing the gap in the stated argument. This closure is clearly demonstrated in the following reconstruction of the argument.

> **Premise:** Analytic propositions do not provide information about any matter of fact.
>
> **Assumption:** Empirical evidence can only refute propositions that provide information about matters of fact.

> **Conclusion:** Empirical evidence cannot refute analytic propositions.

(A) is implied by the conclusion of the argument. Response (A) does not state an assumption of the argument.

(B) brings in information that is irrelevant to the stated argument.

(C) is a generalization of one of the stated premises. Response (C) does not state an assumption of the argument.

(E) is irrelevant to the stated argument.

18. Inference (moderate). Answer: A.

The task in this problem is to find the answer choice that is most likely to be true given the information stated in the passage. The passage states that gasoline additives have enabled car manufacturers to design engines that meet the emission standards in the past. From this information it is reasonable to infer that this is the direction most likely to be taken in the future; that is, it is highly likely that new additives will be developed that do not contain ozone threatening ingredients.

(B), (C), (D), and (E) are unsupported by the passage. There is no information in the passage that suggests that any of these responses is likely to be true.

19. Parallel reasoning (moderate). Answer: B.

The argument in the passage can be restated as follows:

> **Premise:** Persons who do not control their cholesterol levels are more likely to have heart disease than persons who do.
>
> **Premise:** Most persons who do not control their cholesterol levels do not have heart disease.
>
> **Conclusion:** There is no need to control one's cholesterol level in order to avoid heart disease.

(B) is the best response. The argument in response (B) can be restated as follows:

Premise: Smokers are more likely to die of lung disease than non-smokers.

Premise: Most smokers do not die of lung disease.

Conclusion: There is no need to abstain from smoking in order to decrease the likelihood of contracting lung disease.

A comparison of this argument with the argument in the passage outlined above reveals a striking similarity in the structure of the premises and the conclusions of these arguments.

(A) is an incorrect response. The argument in response (A) can be represented as follows:

Premise: People who swim every day are more likely to develop ear infections than those who jog.

Premise: Daily joggers are more likely to develop foot problems than swimmers.

Conclusion: People who want to avoid foot problems and ear infections shouldn't jog or swim on a daily basis.

A comparison of this argument with the argument in the passage outlined above reveals significant differences in the premises and the conclusions of these arguments.

(C) is an incorrect response. The argument in response (C) can be represented as follows:

Premise: Overweight people are more likely to die at a young age than persons who are physically fit.

Premise: Many young physically fit people die in sports-related accidents each year.

Conclusion: It is probably best to be neither overweight nor physically fit in order to avoid an early death.

A comparison of this argument with the argument in the passage outlined above reveals significant differences in the premises and the conclusions of these arguments.

(D) is an incorrect response. The argument in response (D) can be represented as follows:

Premise: Crimes of passion are more likely to be committed by young people than old people.

Premise: Many old people are capable of extremely strong emotional outbursts.

Conclusion: Middle-aged people are less likely to commit crimes of passion than either young people or old people.

A comparison of this argument with the argument in the passage outlined above reveals a significant difference in the second premise and in the conclusion of these arguments.

(E) is an incorrect response. The argument in response (E) can be represented as follows:

Premise: Persons who exercise daily are more likely to live longer than persons who do not exercise.

Premise: "Daily exercise" means at least 20 minutes of strenuous aerobic exercise.

Conclusion: Unless you are willing to do 20 minutes of strenuous exercise, there is little reason to exercise daily.

A comparison of this argument with the argument in the passage outlined above reveals a significant difference in the second premise and in the conclusion of these arguments.

20. Principle (easier). Answer: C.

The argument in the passage basically maintains that parents should not be held accountable for crimes their teenage children commit because they don't always have complete control over their actions. This argument can be represented as follows:

Premise: Parents don't always have complete control over the actions of their teenage children.

Conclusion: Parents should not be held accountable for crimes their teenage children commit.

The major assumption in this argument is that parents should be held accountable for only those actions performed by their teenage children over which the parents have control. This assumption is an instance of the general principle stated in (C).

(A) would not help to justify the conclusion. The premise of the argument concedes that adult supervision is not sufficient to preclude the possibility of criminal action on the part of teenagers.

(B) would not help to justify the conclusion. The treatment of teenage children by the criminal justice system is irrelevant to the issue of whether or not parents should be held accountable for their children's actions.

(D) would not help to justify the conclusion. The premise of the argument concedes that even if parents supervise their teenage children, they might not be able to stop them from doing things that might cause harm to other people or their property.

(E) would not help to justify the conclusion.

21. Method (moderate). Answer: A.

In the passage the argument in favor of capital punishment is challenged on the grounds that its major premise leads to the unacceptable claim that murdering people "who are under lock and key and are no longer a threat to anyone" is justified. On this basis the major premise is rejected as unacceptable. Response (A) best describes the method employed in this passage.

(B), (C), (D) and (E) incorrectly describe the method of the argument in the passage. In each of these responses, issues that are irrelevant to the argument in the passage are addressed.

22. Reasoning error (easier). Answer: B.

In the argument in the passage, the Republicans' failure to articulate good reasons in support of their opposition to cuts in social security is taken as evidence that they are in favor of cuts in social security. Of the answer choices, response (B) best describes this reasoning error.

(A) incorrectly describes the argument in the passage. No alternatives are mentioned in the passage.

(C) is an incorrect response. The argument in the passage does not conclude that *all* Republicans favor cuts in social security on the grounds that *some* do; it concludes this on the grounds that Republicans have failed to present evidence of their opposition to cuts in social security.

(D) and (E) incorrectly describe the argument in the passage. There are no cases or data presented in the passage.

23. Assumption (moderate). Answer: C.

The gap in the argument that needs to be filled is the relationship between interesting research subjects and subjects from which more can be learned. Response (C) expresses this relationship and, as the following restatement of the argument clearly shows, fills the gap in the argument in the passage.

Premise: Captive animals are more interesting research subjects than are wild animals.

Assumption: The more interesting a research subject, the more that can be learned from studying it.

Conclusion: Researchers can learn more from studying captive animals than from studying wild animals.

In choice (A), the denial of this claim is consistent with the information stated in the passage; consequently, it cannot be an assumption of the argument.

(B) states the required relationship in reverse. To satisfy yourself that this statement of the relation does not fill the gap in the argument, try it in the above restatement of the argument in the passage.

In choice (D), the denial of this claim is consistent with the information stated in the passage; consequently, it cannot be an assumption of the argument.

In choice (E), the denial of this claim is consistent with the information stated in the passage; consequently, it cannot be an assumption of the argument.

24. Principle (moderate). Answer: A.

George's opposition to the installation of automated flight centers at privately owned airports is based on the claim that, in this instance, taxpayers' funds will be used to do something from which they derive no benefit. The underlying principle George is appealing to is that taxpayers' funds should be used only to fund projects that benefit taxpayers. Henry responds that the fact that taxpayers won't benefit from the installation of the centers is not a compelling reason for not using taxpayers' funds to install them. This response to George's argument clearly indicates that Henry is not committed to the view that taxpayers' funds should be used only to fund projects that benefit taxpayers.

(B) is an incorrect response. George and Henry could agree that as far as "other factors" are concerned, as a general rule airport safety should always take precedence when improving airports. George is committed to opposing only those improvements that are made with taxpayers' funds from which they derive no benefit.

(C) is an incorrect response. Henry clearly indicates his willingness to give government subsidies to privately held companies. George could conceivably be willing to do this as well so long as some benefit is realized by the taxpayer.

(D) is an incorrect response. George and Henry could conceivably agree that all airports should have automated flight centers, but disagree about how these centers should be funded.

(E) introduces issues that are not addressed in the passage.

25. Assessing the effect of additional information (moderate). Answer: B.

The task in this problem is to find an answer that weakens the argument—that is, one that undermines the major assumption of the argument, attacks a stated premise, or that suggests an alternative conclusion that could be inferred from the premises. The major assumption of the argument is that there are no additional reasons for preferring science over religion and mythology as a source of truth. Response (B) undermines this assumption by pointing out that science differs from religion and mythology in that its methods yield accurate predictions and that this is a reliable indicator of truth.

(A), (C), (D), and (E) are incorrect responses. None of these responses asserts a claim that undermines an assumption of the argument, attacks a stated premise, or provides an alternative conclusion that could be inferred from the premises. Consequently, none of these answer choices weakens the argument.

Practice Test: Writing Sample

Today you will respond to a Writing Sample topic under timed conditions. Allow yourself exactly 30 minutes to complete your essay. Evaluate your essay using the scorecard on pages 124–125 and the two model responses provided.

WRITING SAMPLE TOPIC

Adams Elementary, a private school for first-grade through fifth-grade, received a large donation, and different plans are being considered for the use of the funds. Write an argument in favor of one of the following two proposals, keeping in mind two guidelines:

- Adams Elementary School wants to improve its students' scores on standardized math, reading, and social-studies achievement tests.

- Adams Elementary School wants to preserve its reputation for innovation and for encouraging students' parents to become actively involved in their children's education.

One plan is to adopt a one-year program called "Back to Basics," developed and provided by Educare, a regional educational consulting firm. "Back to Basics" has been approved by the state's bureau of education and adopted by several regional elementary schools. The program emphasizes fundamental math and reading skills through the use of Educare's unique lesson plans, books, and other materials. The program is designed to implement the latest academic theories about how children learn.

An integral feature of the program is its emphasis on hands-on learning and on group activities. As part of the program, Educare conducts monthly weekend workshops for the teachers to help them use the materials effectively in the classroom and to discuss and evaluate current motivational and instructional theories. Educare also arranges for periodic trips to local libraries and to the local Children's Science Museum.

The alternative plan is to establish a computer laboratory at the school. The laboratory would replace one of the existing classrooms, and the displaced class would be assimilated by one or more of the other classes. Currently, each classroom at Adams has one computer. The laboratory would increase the number of computers at the school by two-hundred percent. Funding is sufficient to provide state-of-the-art Internet access for two years and to acquire a basic educational-software library. Adams hopes to make the laboratory available to students, teachers, and their families during evenings and weekends. Funds are available to hire a computer consultant to monitor and troubleshoot the computer system part-time during school hours. While some of the teachers at Adams are interested in computers, insufficient funds are available to pay a teacher separately for providing computer instruction.

Use the space below to respond to the Writing Sample topic. Do not write in the margins.

EVALUATE YOUR WRITING SAMPLE

Evaluate the writing sample you just completed, using the following techniques:

- Score your essay, referring to the scorecard on pages 124–125. Try to be as objective as possible. If you have trouble being objective, ask a friend or teacher to evaluate your essay for you.

- With a yellow highlighter, highlight every sentence in which you accomplished nothing more than restating or paraphrasing the premise, criteria, or characteristics of the choices—that is, in which you merely rearranged and parroted back the facts to the reader. How great a portion of your essay did you highlight? Every sentence in yellow represents wasted space and wasted time that you should use instead to formulate and present original and persuasive arguments.

- With a red pencil, circle or underline every grammatical error, awkward sentence, and other mechanical problem. If you're not sure what to circle, ask an English professor to do so. Do you look at a sea of red as you gaze at the annotated essay? If so, spend more time working on the mechanics of writing and on your writing style.

MODEL RESPONSES TO TODAY'S WRITING SAMPLE TOPIC

Here are two model responses, one arguing for each of the two choices described in today's Writing Sample topic. As you read these responses, keep in mind the following:

1. They are *models*. Don't expect that you will be able to write essays quite this polished in 30 minutes.

2. Although they are models, they aren't perfect. Regardless of how effective an LSAT essay is, there's always *some* room for improvement.

3. You could write these responses in the space provided on the LSAT response sheet.

4. They are not all-inclusive. In other words, effective arguments may have occurred to you that are absent in these model responses.

Model Response #1

(in favor of Back to Basics)

Adams should adopt the "Back to Basics" program. Its emphasis on basic math and reading skills would seem the most direct and effective way possible to improve achievement scores in those areas; and the program's approval by the state, along with its adoption by other schools, provides some assurance that the program will be effective. The alternative plan would be less effective in achieving this goal, since available time for each student in the lab would probably be quite limited, especially considering the problem of inadequate staffing. Finally, while computers may help to motivate some students, Educare's program also appears to provide fun, interactive learning experiences.

"Back to Basics" would also better preserve Adams' reputation—the use of new teaching theories and techniques would ensure its continued reputation for innovation, while the field-trip component of the program would allow for parent participation. While the computer-lab program might seem more innovative, without sufficient funding for upgrades and support, Adams could easily fall behind as technology advances.

In sum, "Back to Basics" is more likely to achieve the schools goals; test scores are more certain to improve, while the innovative and experiential nature of the program is sure to preserve the school's reputation.

Model Response #2

(in favor of the computer lab)

The computer lab is the better choice. Interactive software and Internet access not only is innovative but also will motivate students to develop the basic skills and knowledge needed for higher standardized test scores. Although regular classrooms would be more crowded, it might be possible to move computers from the classrooms to the lab to free up space. Doing so would also eliminate the distracting tendencies of computers from the classroom, allowing students to better focus on fundamentals. The problem of insufficient funds for computer instruction can be solved by soliciting parent volunteers, thus preserving Adams' reputation for parent involvement.

While "Back to Basics" appears consistent with Adams' reputation for innovation, it doesn't allow for much parent involvement, since parents are not likely to be familiar with the materials and methods. Although parents could become involved in field trips, such involvement may be too infrequent to be meaningful. Although "Back to Basics" may improve reading and math test scores, it fails to embrace social science. Furthermore, the weekend workshops may take their toll on the teachers who may quickly lose motivation and enthusiasm.

Thus, both the innovative and well-rounded education afforded by a computer lab, along with its attractiveness for parents and teachers, render this proposal the better choice for Adams.

STILL ROOM FOR IMPROVEMENT?

By now, you should have a fairly clear idea how effectively you respond to an LSAT Writing Sample topic. If you are not satisfied with your performance, take the following remedial steps:

- Review Writing Sample Lessons 1 and 2 (Days 13 and 14).

- Rewrite the essay you wrote today, limiting yourself to fifteen minutes. Unless your essay is either "limited" or "seriously flawed," don't start from scratch. Instead, try to refine and build upon your basic arguments and approach.

- Based upon today's topic, write a new essay in which you argue *for* the choice that you argued against in your first essay. Evaluate that essay as you did the first one.

Day 30

Countdown to the LSAT

Your first task today is to evaluate your practice-test performance. This lesson also provides a procedural checklist for the weeks leading up to your LSAT, for exam day, and for the weeks that follow your test.

Today's Topics

1. Evaluating your practice-test performance
2. LSAT checklists

EVALUATING YOUR PRACTICE-TEST PERFORMANCE

If you have not already done so, tally up your raw score for all four multiple-choice sections of the Practice Test, referring to the answer keys on pages 196, 215, 231, and 247. Then evaluate that score using the score conversion table on page 4.

LSAT CHECKLISTS

The procedures, deadlines, and regulations discussed in this section are intended only to highlight some of the key steps in the process of getting ready for the LSAT. For the final word on everything related to the LSAT, be sure to consult the *LSAT/LSDAS Registration and Information Book*.

8 Weeks Prior to the Exam

Obtain the Registration Book. Use the form included in the book to register for the LSAT. Read the book from cover to cover. Most procedural questions about the LSAT and about the LSDAS are answered in the book.

Decide where you want to take the LSAT. A complete list of all available LSAT test sites is included in the Registration Book. On the LSAT registration form, you will be asked to specify your first two test-site choices. Most test takers prefer to take the exam at the nearest available location. However, if you are in college and away from your home, you may prefer to go home for an extended weekend and take the LSAT there, away from the distractions associated with the collegiate living environment. Another consideration is the testing accommodations themselves. Some testing rooms are equipped with long tables, others with standard classroom desks, while others are equipped with theater-style fold-away desktops. If possible, avoid a test site equipped with fold-away desktops.

Register early for the LSAT. Make sure that you register for the LSAT on or before the regular postmark registration deadline—4 to 5 weeks prior to the exam date. (Precise dates are specified in the Registration Book.) Late registration is permitted up to a certain date with payment of an additional late-registration fee. (Deadlines and fees are specified in the Registration Book.) Telephone registration with payment by credit card is permitted only for late registration. Walk-in (exam-day) registration is not permitted. Register as early as possible to ensure a seat at your first- or second-choice test site. Early registration is particularly crucial for the October exam, which is by far the most popular of the four exams offered during the year.

4 Weeks Prior to the Exam

Make a final determination about where you wish to take the LSAT. After registering for the LSAT and paying the registration fee, you can request a change of test site for an additional fee up until about 3 *weeks* prior to the exam.

2 Weeks Prior to the Exam

Look over your LSAT admission ticket. If you mailed your registration form by the postmark deadline but have not yet received your LSAT admission ticket in the mail, contact the testing service to be sure that your registration is being processed. When you receive your LSAT admission ticket, look it over to make sure that you are properly identified and have been assigned to an appropriate test site.

2 Days Before the Exam

Get a good night's sleep tonight. Most people can get by without a lot of sleep for one day. Insufficient sleep is more likely to catch up with you on the second day.

The Day Before the Exam

Take the day off. Clear your mind and engage in relaxing activities. Don't think about or talk about the LSAT. Having already worked through this book, no amount of last-minute preparation for the LSAT will be of any real benefit.

Arrange for backup transportation to the test site. In case your first means of transportation is unexpectedly unavailable on exam day, make sure you have a "Plan B." Remember: automobiles do break down unexpectedly from time to time.

Go for a drive to the test site. Find the building and room where the test will be administered. If the building and room is open, go in and check out the

facilities so that you know what to expect the next day. Check the size and style of the desks and chairs, check to see if there is a clock and whether there are vending machines, water fountains, and rest rooms nearby. You will be under enough stress the next morning without worrying about finding your way around a strange place.

Set out everything you need for tomorrow. Have all of the following items ready to go before you retire for the night:

Required:

- one current form of photo identification that includes your signature

- your LSAT admission ticket

- two or three #2 pencils with good erasers

Recommended:

- directions to the test site

- a silent timing device

- a highlighter pen

- liquid paper

- a comfortable sweater, sweatshirt, or light jacket

- a pencil sharpener

- snack foods (fruit, nuts, granola bars, etc.)

Set two alarms to wake you up on exam day. In case of a electrical-power outage, one alarm should be battery operated. Also, ask a friend to give you a wake up call to ensure that you don't hit your alarm's snooze button and go back to sleep.

The Day of the Exam

Eat a good breakfast. No lunch break is provided during the exam. Be sure to eat enough to keep you going for at least five hours.

Leave early for the test site. The LSAT admission ticket will indicate when you should arrive at the test site. Make sure you depart early enough to arrive by that time.

Take along the morning newspaper. Plan on delays and idle time before (and possibly during) the LSAT.

Keep your mind off the test by taking along some reading material to pass the time.

Don't forget your admission ticket, photo identification, etc. Review the list of items that you (should have) set out the day before to take with you to the test site. WARNING: Don't inadvertently leave any of these items in your car at the test site. (Any LSAT supervisor will tell you that last-minute dashes back to the car for forgotten items are very common.)

If you are ill on exam day. If illness or some other emergency prevents you from taking the exam, you do not need to contact the testing service or anyone at the test site to cancel. Your absence at the test site will not be reported *per se*, although cancellations are reported on your score report. Rest assured: the fact that you canceled the test or canceled your score will not adversely affect your chances of admission to law school.

Checking in. To be admitted to the test site you must present your admission ticket and one form of *photo* identification that includes *your signature*. An acceptable form of identification might include a driver's license, student identification card, or passport. The supervisor will check the examinee roster for your name.

Prepare to be thumbprinted! Sure, the testing service trusts *you*; but it does *not* trust the suspicious character seated next to you. Every test taker is thumbprinted when checking in to help ensure that no registrant has sent someone else to take the test for them. After completion of all multiple-choice sections, testing staff-members will check photo identification once again (to ensure that the individuals who checked in are the same individuals who actually took the complete exam).

Seating arrangements. The exam supervisor will separate test takers with empty desks or chairs to reduce the likelihood of cheating. You are not permitted to choose your own seat. Nevertheless, if your chair squeaks, or if you are seated near a drafty, poorly lit, or uncomfortable area, ask to move. Supervisors are instructed to honor all reasonable requests to relocate.

Bringing personal belongings into the testing room. Your personal belongings are permitted in the testing room but must be stowed under your desk or table at all times during the exam.

Beverages and food. Beverages are not permitted in the testing room. You are permitted to bring snacks into the testing room, but you must stow your snacks beneath your desk and cannot eat in the test room. If either during or between exam sections you wish to eat snacks that you brought, you must take your snacks outside the room and eat there.

Instructions and more instructions. Once you are settled in your seat, expect to spend at least 20 minutes filling in circles on your bubble-sheet to provide information about you and about the test you are taking. The supervisor will then review the testing procedures as well as the rules for examinee conduct. As with any standardized test, the exam supervisor will recite all instructions from a pre-written script.

All test booklets are not the same. On the cover of your test booklet will appear a large bold letter—either "A," "B," or "C"—that indicates which *version* of the LSAT you will be taking. Although the four scored sections will be identical for all test takers, the test sections are ordered differently in different versions. Also, the trial section will vary among different versions. The primary purpose of administering different test versions is to prevent cheating.

Starting and stopping each section. The supervisor will keep time during each section and announce when you may start and stop each section. During each exam section, you are not permitted to work ahead or go back to other sections.

Recording your answers. You must record all your answers with a #2 pencil on a separate answer sheet provided by the supervisor. Answers recorded in the test booklet will not be scored. Be sure to blacken in an answer for every question, since there is no penalty for incorrect reposes.

Timing devices. Silent timing devices are permitted. It is recommended that you take a watch with you to the exam, since there is no guarantee that there will be a functioning clock in the testing room.

Supervisor announcements concerning remaining time. The supervisor will issue *one* verbal 5-minutes-remaining warning during each exam section. The purpose of this warning is to allow you to adjust your pace so that you can finish the section and fill in all of the bubbles on your answer sheet.

Breaks between exam sections. A 10–15 minute break is provided after the *third* test section (1 hour, 45 minutes into the exam). At the completion of the multiple-choice portion of the LSAT, the testing staff will collect test booklets and distribute Writing Sample materials, so a break of sorts occurs at this point as well. Otherwise, there will be no break between test sections.

Leaving the room during the exam. You may leave the room at any time during the exam, although you must first obtain the supervisor's permission. If you do leave the room, you will not be permitted to make up that time. Be forewarned: A member of the testing staff might accompany you to and from the rest room!

Unexpected delays and problems. A variety of unexpected problems can interfere somewhat with the administration of the LSAT. Unexpected noise from the outside, windy or unusually cold or hot weather, and power failures are the most common uncontrollable problems. Some problems can be solved by relocating to another room in the building or to another building altogether. If any environmental problem occurs that might distract you, by all means bring the matter to the supervisor's attention.

Canceling your test at the test site. At any time during the test or immediately afterwards, you can cancel your test simply by completing a specified portion of the answer sheet. If you cancel your test in this manner, no score will be tabulated. Cancellations are irreversible; accordingly, think twice before hastily canceling your test while still at the test site. Instead, reflect for a day or two on your performance; the testing service allows you to cancel your score within 5 days after the test. As noted earlier, your score report will indicate cancellations, although canceled scores will not be included in the report. (Also remember that cancellations will not adversely affect your chances of admission.)

Take home some souvenirs of the LSAT. The supervisor will of course collect all test booklets after the exam. Remember, however, that a carbonless copy of your writing sample and the black pen provided for the Writing Sample section are yours to take home with you!

During the Week After the Exam

Requesting a refund if you do not take the exam. If you do not actually take the exam for which you register, a *partial* refund is allowed if requested in writing anytime before the exam or within *1 week* following the exam.

Applying your registration fee to a later LSAT. If you decide to postpone taking the LSAT, for an additional fee the service will apply a portion of your registration fee to a subsequent exam, but only upon written request up until *1 week* after the original exam date.

Canceling your test score. If you wish to cancel your score for the exam that you just took, the testing service must receive proper written notification of cancellation within 5 working days after the exam.

5 Weeks after the LSAT

Your LSAT score report. An LSAT score report is mailed to you 4 to 6 weeks after the exam. The report will include:

- a 5" by 8" copy of the entire exam (see the "NOTE" below, however), except for the Writing Sample Topic, a copy of which you took home with you on exam day

- your raw score, your scaled score, and a conversion table to determine your percentile ranking

- your response to each question and the correct response to each question

Thus, you will have all the information to assess your strengths and weaknesses on the exam. This should help you determine whether you should retake the test and, if so, what areas you should focus on in preparing for the test again.

NOTE: If you take the exam in December, you will not receive a copy of the exam. December exams are not disclosed.

NOTES

NOTES

NOTES

NOTES

NOTES

NOTES